NEW YORK STATE

GHOSTS

Volume One

Also by David J. Pitkin

Ghosts of the Northeast

Haunted Saratoga County

Spiritual Numerology: Caring for Number One

AURORA PUBLICATIONS
E-MAIL ADDRESS:

pitkinaurora@aol.com

NEW YORK STATE

STATE

GHOSTS

David J. Pitkin

Aurora Publications
Chestertown, NY

Aurora Publications
P.O. Box 690
Chestertown, NY 12817

Publication Data

Pitkin, David J.   1939-
New York State Ghosts
Includes Index
ISBN 978-0-9663925-5-5
1. Ghosts. 2. New York State
Library of Congress Control Number: 2006904143

Table of Contents

Introduction

My first ghost event came in 1968, when I, as a non-believer in ghosts, was barely able to assimilate the experience. Integrating all that happened that day and, more important, what that all *meant*, took many more years. Throughout the period from 1968-1998, I listened to tales of others' experiences, went on investigative jaunts—some with fascinating phenomena, did great amounts of reading in parapsychology, attended lectures, and sought answers that would square with my spiritual principles. In 1998, I wrote my first book, a compilation of ghost stories from the Saratoga County area, a volume that was well-received, encouraging me to continue sharing my discoveries with others.

In the early 1970s, I had a dream in which I was emerging from a large, old stone school building. As I passed through the archway into the outdoors, a voice boomed down at me, "Those who wish to teach must also be willing to learn!" I awoke awed at the implications. Of course, I was teaching junior high school at the time and wondered if the message applied only to my profession. Apparently not.

After that first book, I found many people hungering for first-person stories of experience with the world beyond ours. I became a story teller and continued to write books. But wherever I spoke, there were dozens of people with sophisticated questions. "*How* do they (ghosts) do that?" "*Why* do they do that?" and so forth. More philosophical work for me to do, and I've made an effort to find answers.

At first, I had little understanding of those issues. All I wanted to do in my first book was to simply share some neat stories with others. However, reader interest began to push me to more profound levels of searching, speculation and education. Not much of it has been easy, although those on the other side keep me supplied with plenty of fresh contacts and stories. Learning something new and changing old parameters of thought and behavior are difficult, and some of my new-found wisdom has been purchased in sorrow. That is why so few are willing to undertake that quest into the unknown regions. New behaviors often can only come from new thinking, and often that is painful. But for me, I *have to* know.

As I began this book of strictly New York State stories, I became aware that my spiritual instructors have always been there, providing just the right level of experience for my level of understanding. As one of my guides told me, "David, you haven't been the easiest subject to work with. You find it hard to shut up and just *listen*!" Recently, they told me that I *am* becoming more tractable, for which I give thanks.

My previous books have concentrated on both history and mystery and were quite upbeat, mainly because of the positive ghost-person relationships that I discovered and described. In fact, one on-line reviewer of *Ghosts of the Northeast* blasted me for being "too Christian." To be honest about it, no priest, minister or nun of any Christian denomination has become a public backer of my writings. Here and there I have found a nun, a priest or two, a rabbi and a minister who have confided their personal beliefs and experiences, but not to share widely. Generally, my quest to experience and write is spurred by the powerful interest that I find in young adults who have either stumbled into the world of spirit by accident or who have lived with phenomena all their lives. The common denominator for most of them has been a lack of orthodox religious training or support.

It's my guess that you, reader, have never attended a mainline house of worship where the pastor announced that, "Today, I'm going to talk about your potential for meeting those of your loved ones who have died." It just isn't done. Understandably, the clergy leaves the dead to bury the dead. Unfortunately, science knows that death doesn't happen as quickly as many suppose; it can be a process taking years before "we" are no more. Many souls, once separated from the body, though retaining their living consciousness, are unable or unwilling to leave the body even after its burial. For that reason, graveyards have long been known for ghost sightings.

Most ghosts are trapped, compulsively attached to some facet of the ended life of their body, and cannot let go of this physical plane of life, and as a result, they have an addictive quality to their roaming. My learning suggests that there are many beings (light people, spirit guides or angels) active *just beyond* our realm, waiting, even anxious, to escort departed souls across the gulf and into what might be called Paradise. Many, for various reasons mentioned in the following stories, are reluctant, even adamant about not severing ties to the limited view of the universe that their consciousness has known. They just won't *look* at those discarnate helpers and admit they've died. They won't *know* and they won't *go*!

Therefore, these beings, some our former friends and enemies, our children and parents or grandparents, our clients, neighbors and loved ones, remain imprisoned by their incapacity and lack of will to go and *know* the greater meaning of Life by its ending. Who, then, will help them? This is a unique challenge for the new century: not just to know or feel the presence of spirits, but to extend compassion to them in a world where many people have difficulty in mustering good will or sensitivity even to the living ones. Ghosts and spirits need to be released. Too many of the living get gratification from keeping them imprisoned in a place where they can no longer thrive.

As a history lover and Social Studies teacher, one of my first loves was Corinth, my birthplace, a mill town on the Hudson River, where old timers still remembered the last Native Americans to dwell in Indian Hollow. Nearby, in the Palisade rock formations, we sought million-year-old plant and animal fossils. As children, we walked old 'Indian trails' on the hillsides and had plenty of family members and community elders who were glad to share tales of ancestors, ghosts and spirits. There were many descendants of immigrants in my childhood and I treasured each group's memories. I am also fortunate to have had wonderful teachers who could excite the imaginations of youngsters, so I can see in retrospect that books such as this one were just waiting in time for me to produce.

I enjoy life in my native state, New York, and have traveled widely within its borders, finding lovely cities, dazzling wilderness landscapes, historic rivers and canals, and countless folktales from the immigrant groups that journeyed here. I have many times played a part in preserving that history. But what I love most are the countless villages, towns, hamlets and small cities with their great local pride, wonderful architecture from days gone by and, oh yes, ghosts. Enjoy New York State's ghosts.

David J. Pitkin
Chestertown, NY
July 4, 2006

CHAPTER 1

HAUNTED
OLD HOUSES

The Dark Man

The Old Farmhouse on Old Route 5

Anne bought one of the oldest houses in Chittenango, NY, in 1999. It was an architectural puzzle, with its earliest part dating from 1797 and the remainder from 1808. Just off Old Route 5, the street parallels the old Iroquois Indian Path by which the Six Nations traded and communicated. "We have five fireplaces in the house, lots of acreage, and a beautiful old orchard in the back. I fell in love with it as soon as I saw it. But some of the more obscure history wasn't long in revealing itself to us," she laughed.

"On the first day, my mom was lifting pots and pans out of boxes in the kitchen. I was on my knees on the floor, taking the utensils from her and storing them in the lower cupboard. I looked at Mom and the man standing behind her, took the pot she held out, turned and placed it in the cupboard, and then it struck me. Who *was* that man? I turned but he was gone. I then ran upstairs to see if my son had been fooling me by dressing up in a big navy coat with brass buttons. He denied any prank, and as I walked back downstairs, I recalled that the figure had long hair tied back, and it seemed as if he knew that I'd spotted him, and *that* was why he dissolved.

"Another day, with all the unpacking still going on, I closed our cats in the kitchen so they wouldn't interfere with our work. Just a minute later, I saw the latch on the old kitchen door lift. It jiggled up and down for a minute, and I went to see who was on the other side, since I knew the cats couldn't make it move. Nobody was there. After several years, I've determined that only that door, near where I first saw the dark man, has such a moving latch.

"Not long afterward, my father was admitted to the hospital and my mother went to visit him. I watched their dog, and as midnight approached, I took him out for his evening walk. As we walked up the road, we both spotted a man some distance ahead of us, walking toward me, and I was a little unnerved. Who else beside me would be out walking so late? Could he be a transient or someone dangerous? Just then, the figure dissolved into thin air about forty feet ahead of me. I couldn't figure out who he was or how he had disappeared so quickly. The dog and I turned and headed for the house fast. All the while we scurried home, it began to dawn on me that I'd seen a *ghost*!"

On another occasion, Anne returned from work to find the several television sets in the house all turned on. She knew for sure that they had all been off when she left home that morning, yet here they were, in a locked house, all playing to nobody. "During our first Christmas season in the house, the volume on our radio got louder and louder, then softer and softer, until we could hardly hear it. From that time onward until 2002, we also noticed the electrical appliances would turn on and then off. However, since that time, they have operated normally. The main problem now is that our doors rattle, but no one ever enters."

One day a friend came to help her fix the dryer in the upstairs bathroom. "I had just said to my friend that my son would be home soon, when we heard the front door slam and heavy footsteps begin climbing the stairs." When she called out to the boy there was no response, and a quick search of the upstairs turned up nobody. "Yes, I often hear steps on the stairs, as if someone invisible has done a hard day's work and is finally headed to bed. But, of course," she smiled, "there is never anybody *real* to see!

"My son had a group of friends stay overnight a few years ago, and they were all sprawled asleep on the floor. One of them suddenly awoke and asked the others who had gotten up and stood over him, as he'd seen a shape hovering above his sleeping bag. All denied it, saying they had been sound asleep. The boys became frightened and all went home early.

"Another time, I awoke to see an orb of light moving from the bathroom into my bedroom. It just couldn't *be*, I decided, and pulled the covers over my head. An hour later, I looked, but whoever or whatever it was, the light had gone and I was alone. Sooner or later I knew I had to get to the bottom of it all, and one of my friends put me in touch with a psychic. When I first spoke to the woman, she told me she didn't want any details about my house before she began her reading. My friend and her dad came over to sit with me that night of the psychic's scheduled visit. We heard her rapping on the front door, and then, a dozen things seemed to happen at once!

"I have a big, twenty-pound Maine Coon cat, and he sleeps on an upstairs bed almost all day, seldom moving. As I opened the front door to let the psychic in, I only had time to note that she had brought a male friend. At that moment, my cat zoomed down the stairs, sprang straight at the stranger, and began to claw him. Only the man's leather jacket saved him from some serious scratches. The cat has never done that before or after, but *something* got into him that night. I later wondered about it all, when the psychic told me her companion often did exorcisms. Now, how did the cat know? And what or who woke it up to come downstairs and attack him? We never figured it out."

After the kitty was put away, the visitors walked through the house seeking sensations. As they passed the kitchen door with the "nervous latch," the woman told Anne that the hair on her arms and head was standing up. Some powerful energy was there in the place where Anne had spied the dark man. Both people told her they sensed two spirits inhabiting the house. One, a man, seemed to originate from the house's earliest days, as he stayed only in the old section of their home. Their description of the entity exactly matched Anne's vision, complete with hair, coat, and buttons!

Upstairs, however, they sensed an older German woman who seemed preoccupied with housekeeping. Both the man and the woman seemed to be friendly spirits, they told her, and they encouraged Anne to speak to them. Nevertheless, a year later when her son returned home from Atlanta, he was pulled off his bed by a strong invisible hand. The poor lad fled the house to stay with friends and wouldn't return. Another individual came to the house and, using a pendulum, explored the building. He related a story very much like that of the psychic and her male companion.

"So every day is a new adventure here," Anne told me. "I have three granddaughters and arranged their framed photos in a certain way in the living room. Every time I looked, however, one of the pictures was turned sideways. I'd straighten it but soon afterward, I would find it turned again. One day recently, I changed the positions of the three pictures, moving one from the middle to the end of the lineup. Nothing has moved since then. I sure do wish I knew what *that* all meant."

It is a nice old house and a portion of its history seems ever-present. Anne notes that from time to time, she smells the apple blossoms from the orchard, even when the trees are not in bloom. "Another interesting thing is that many times, when I come home from work all tired out, there is the smell of fresh-baked apple pie filling the house. Too bad these pastries don't make the transition to the physical world—they smell so good!"

Ghosts (most of them), once people get used to them, usually become just a part of the everyday atmosphere. For the present, as happens with so many other folks living with ghosts, it seems that Anne will continue to co-habit with the past residents of the house until they leave for a more permanent home.

Still at Home

Fred O'Dell's Faxton Street house

Jerry Waskiewicz isn't an easy guy to fool. While in the service, he was a Military Policeman stationed in Germany. Later, he worked as chief photographer for the Defense Nuclear Agency at the Pentagon in Washington, DC. In civilian life, he worked as the civilian chief photographer at Griffiss Air Force Base in Rome, NY, supervising twelve other photographers. Now in his late fifties, Jerry is still analytical and skeptical as he writes and photographs for many newspapers all over northern New York State.

"When I lived in Utica, however, I had some experiences that really pushed the limit on what I could believe," he told me. "As with so many folks who encounter their first ghost, my encounters took place in my own home.

"My wife and I bought the house at 44 Faxton Street, not far off the Parkway, because we liked its Victorian Queen Anne décor. It was, and is still, a huge place, three stories tall, plus a tower. Most of the information we collected listed a number of previous owners, dating from the builder, George Gates, the president of the Continental Can Company in 1886.

"There was a huge double parlor, maybe 20 x 30 feet in size, a beautifully paneled oak dining room, a marvelous intercom system that you had to blow into, such as the Navy used to have, and a great wrap-around porch. We were happy to buy it in November 1983 and show it off to our friends.

"I'll never forget our first night in the house, though. The building was completely empty, no furniture at all, so my wife and I bedded down in sleeping bags in the parlor. As we were drifting off to sleep, suddenly there came a resounding SLAM from up on the third floor. I snuggled a bit deeper into the

4

sleeping bag. My wife sat up, really alarmed, and asked, 'Aren't you going up there?' For a minute I didn't answer. Then, I reminded her that the sellers had said there was a certain *something* in the house, but nothing really troublesome or hurtful, and we would discover it for ourselves. 'Maybe we just *discovered* it. I'll wait until tomorrow, and then go look,' I told her."

The pair made a careful survey of the house the next morning, and, as expected, they found nothing amiss. Thus, they began the furnishing of the old house, acquiring furniture that seemed fitting. They had a lot of friends and wanted to entertain often. And they did.

"We had many parties there, but not ones flowing with booze or drugs. We just enjoyed a good time and wanted to share it with others. At one of these festivities, I stood for a moment at the foot of the ornate stairway, which wound its way upward from platform to platform. That particular evening, I spotted my friend Ed, just descending the stairs. At about the fourth step from the top, he suddenly moved laterally to the other side of the step, as if to let someone go by. He continued down on that side of the stairs until he met me. 'What were you doing up there at the top? What was all that fancy footwork? Were you dancing?' I asked him.

'Naw, somebody coming up the stairs just wanted to get past me, so I moved over to let them go by,' Ed said.

'Now look, Ed, I was watching you all the way down,' I told him, 'and there was *nobody else* on the stairs!'

'*Sure* there was,' he countered, 'I *saw* them.'

'Well, what did the person look like? Man or woman?'

'I didn't pay too much attention. A guy, I guess.'

"I questioned Ed about the person's appearance or dress, but he couldn't give any specific information beyond that it was a *somebody*," Jerry told me. "Now, I thought that was strange, but Ed hadn't been drinking, and I'm the kind of guy that cuts others some slack, so I forgot it for the time being.

"Then, some months afterward, my wife confronted me one day. 'Why do you keep messing with my dried flowers?' she asked. I didn't understand what she was talking about. Yes, we had dried flower arrangements that she had made; she liked decorations and was artistic. We had a long table in the parlor and she had placed a long runner on top, along with dried flowers in baskets. I thought they were pretty, but I seldom went out of my way to inspect them. She then told me that she had found dried flower petals strewn across the floors and table top. We had no pets, and she knew for sure that *she* hadn't disturbed the arrangements that she had so painstakingly created, so it *had* to be me! I'm not sure how I got out of that one, but these little incidents began to accumulate, and I found myself pondering some quite un-military explanations."

Jerry related that he had found some handmade bricks in the house, each one stamped with the initials F.O. He was curious about the company or person who had made them, but it wasn't until a year later that he found old papers that included the name Fred O'Dell, a resident of 44 Faxton Street who had been a men's clothing salesman for Wickes and Greenman in downtown Utica during the early 1930s to 1950s. Same initials, I mused. "We later discovered that Fred had been an inveterate smoker, and then, when I pulled up an old rug upstairs, I found countless cigarette burns on the hardwood floor," he told me. "I covered the area with new wall-to-wall carpet. We considered that the room may have been old Fred's bedroom, and from somewhere we learned that he had been bedridden during the late 1950s or early 1960s.

"Then, that fall in 1985, things really started to get spooky. Originally, we figured, the maid and butler had quarters on the house's third floor, which was common in Victorian houses, and that is where so much of the activity took place. We had a little second floor porch or balcony on the front of the house and it was enjoyable to stand out there in nice weather. Every fall, however, I would close and lock the door for the winter.

"One evening, my wife and I returned home from work. I started up the wood stove, and she went upstairs. Then I heard her scream, 'Somebody broke into the house—the upstairs door is open!' I hot-footed it upstairs and began the walk down the murky hallway that must have been sixty feet long. The closer I got to that room, the colder it got. Wow, maybe we *do* have a ghost in here, I thought. I entered the bedroom and found the outside balcony door fully open. I was astounded because I remembered locking it firmly a few weeks earlier, and the key was still in the inside lock. And it couldn't have blown open because the carpet was so high that we had to really tug that inner door to open it. Another strange thing. To come in from that porch, assuming it was a burglar, one would have to pull the outer screen door outward. And there was two feet of undisturbed snow outside the screen door, and no footprints in the snow!

"We stood and stared at the door. It had to have been opened from inside—and no one was home. It was really hard to sleep that night."

Jerry remembered another phenomenon that intrigued the couple. On one occasion, there were four witnesses—one of them, an Air Force maintenance man. "I liked stained glass and had made my own Tiffany-style swag lamp to hang in the kitchen. My four friends came to visit one fall day, and we stood in the kitchen, chatting. All of a sudden, that lamp began to move, slowly at first, then quite rapidly. At its greatest arc it probably swung six inches to either side. That was quite a heavy lamp with all its glass and lead joints.

"At first we considered there must be a breeze blowing it, as there were several doorways and big windows there. But all the windows were shut, as were the doors. There is no way that a little breeze could be blowing. And it would take a *wind* to move a heavy lamp that much; of course there was no wind and none of us could feel even a slight breeze. One of the guys asked, 'Jerry—*that* your ghost?' I told him that it must be, as there was no other plausible explanation. So I just spoke aloud, 'Fred, stop that. You're scaring my friends!' In just a second, the lamp stopped moving. I never saw it swing again as long as I lived there. In retrospect, I've considered that Fred just wanted to let the group know he was there."

Sometime afterward, Jerry and his wife separated, and the house was put up for sale. Jerry now lives in Boonville, but he has discovered another house with "spirit" up there. "When I moved into the Faxton Street house, the people said we'd discover the *something* that was there. I didn't bother to tell the new owners about Fred," he smiled. "Fred will introduce himself when he's ready."

A House Full

Clara West's House

"My dad, Wilfred Byrne, said that when he was a little boy, he used to walk past an old house on this property and there, near an old pear tree, he would see a woman dressed in black. What puzzled him was that no such old woman lived here at the time," said Clara West. At ninety years of age, she remembered most events of the Twentieth Century in the Town of Chester.

Conrad Marschalk, a "city man," came to Byrnes Road in 1900 and tore down the old house that her father had seen, replacing it with a castle-like Victorian house. "My father had been a caretaker for Mr. Marschalk, who loved the Adirondacks. But in 1914, his wife wanted their boys to have a proper city education, so they sold to my father, and I was born here in 1916. Some of my earliest memories are of hearing odd sounds in the house, so I think whatever invisible person or persons makes them came from the earlier family or house," Clara said.

As a young girl, she often overheard the adults talking about ghosts. As she got older, Clara heard rumors that the owner of the original house had been a hard man. He had agreed to take care of his mother-in-law but reckoned that she didn't need to live in *his* house, so he fixed up an old chicken coop on the property for her. One bitterly cold winter, the man forgot to add firewood to his mother-in-law's stove and the elderly woman was found frozen to death, thereby becoming the prime candidate for one of the West house's ghosts.

"We've never been scared here," she told me in a quiet, matter-of-fact manner, "because there have been *so many* episodes. One night I awoke about 2 a.m. and heard our old clock strike the hour. It occurred to me that nobody had wound it in months, and I stayed awake to hear if it would strike again, but it didn't. I used to hear doors opening and closing throughout the house when nobody else but me was here. My adult sons say they still hear the sounds, but I think *I've* learned to tune them out. On occasion, we have heard someone or something 'run' up the keys on the old piano in the living room, despite the cover being closed." As she escorted me through the house, I noted that not only was the piano lid closed, but there were decorative objects on top of it, making the causation even more mysterious.

She recounted the many times she or other family members heard footsteps on the stairs to the second floor or on the stairs to the attic. Nobody is ever there when a curious person checks. Another mystery is the identity of the unseen presence that bumps Clara when she's doing the dishes. "Sometimes, I just know that someone is in the kitchen with me, and after that there is a gentle nudge, almost as if someone wants to be noticed. But nobody is there when I turn. The ghost is very active at times, and then it is quiet for long intervals."

Betty, Clara's daughter, recalled a day in 2005 when Clara was away. Working in the laundry room, Betty heard a female voice call her name, and it sounded like her mother, but that was clearly impossible. "Frank, my husband, sometimes hears our son, Brian, calling him," Betty told me. "He always calls out, 'What do you want?' but there is never an answer. And sometimes Brian is certain that I am calling him from the front room, though I'm not there.

When our daughter, Emily, was ten, she awoke around midnight to hear a female voice calling from near the window, 'Emily, Emily, come here,' though nobody was visible. The next morning, she told us about the incident, and I told her, 'Emily, don't you ever *go!*' Soon after that incident, I got really angry and walked into Emily's room when she wasn't there. I gave that ghost a lecture—'you've scared *me* for years, but don't you *dare* to scare my children!'" Soon after that incident, Clara is certain she saw a shadow crossing the living room during the day.

Then Betty smiled, remembering another incident when her daughter, Kathleen invited her cousin to sleep over. "They went up to bed and Kathleen flipped back the blanket and sheets on her bed, only to find a row of tacks, points up, underneath. At first, she thought it was somebody's prank, but no one else had been in that room before the girls arrived. And the stories and memories just go on and on," she smiled. "We have a small angel atop our Christmas crèche. One evening, we saw it rise up off its dowel holder and drop to the floor. On another occasion, we found the outside front storm door open a few inches. It is always latched from inside and the inner door locked, too. Who could open it from outside, or from the inside, when *that* door is also locked?" As with so many of the strange incidents in the West house, all normal explanations are checked out first, but many times the ghost gets the blame.

Betty continued, "My daughter-in-law, Kelli, doesn't want to visit here anymore because the first time she visited she heard what she described as 'old-time music' up in the attic, then came the sound of dancing feet." Clara smiled and joined in the discussion, "Yes, that was the night of my eightieth birthday, and maybe the ghost decided to join the celebration." Betty remembered that her older brother, Lester, and his wife had slept in Grandpa's old room once. He told her, "My wife had gone to sleep and I was about to doze off when I heard the sounds in the attic overhead. I immediately became alert and continued to hear footsteps upstairs. They moved toward the closed attic door, but when they reached the wall, the door swung open and all the noises stopped. And nobody was in the doorway."

Another time, Lester brought his van into the driveway near the house one night, hoping to begin repairs on it early the next morning. In the middle of the night, Betty awoke, hearing voices and other noises out near the van. In the morning, she chided her brother for working at night, but Lester strenuously denied having been out of bed.

"My son, Brian, has had so many experiences here," Betty said. "He usually slept in the small room at the top of the stairs. One morning, he told us about awakening during the night to hear Grandpa snoring away in his bed.

The boy knew Grandma was also in bed, as she had a heart condition and didn't get up at night. Nevertheless, he heard footsteps slowly climbing the stairs and stopping outside his door. With all family members accounted for in the boy's mind, he dove under the covers.

"And my daughter Margie had almost the same experience on another night when she slept in that room. She awoke in the middle of the night, hearing noises just outside the bedroom door, and sat up, expecting someone to come in. The hallway was quiet outside, but she was sure she'd heard the sounds. Turning to her little dog, Abby, who always slept with her, Margie asked, 'Abby, did *you* hear that?' The poor dog was shaking and huddled underneath the blanket.

"Brian had something similar happen with him. He awoke in the night to hear someone rapping on the window of his second floor bedroom. When the knocking stopped, the cat jumped down off his bed and went over to investigate the window from which the rapping had come. My other children had experiences of their own," Betty told me. "My brother, Albert, awoke one night to hear a banging and rattling sound coming from Grandpa's bedroom. He got up to investigate and found one of the three windows vibrating, though the other two windows were absolutely still. That seemed to rule out the wind. I, myself, felt my bed unaccountably shaking when I slept in that room, and Brian told me that he had a 'falling dream' when he slept there, and he awoke to find the bed shaking," she told me. "My Uncle Bob slept there when he visited once and heard his bedroom door open in the middle of the night. He opened his eyes fully and saw a dark man at the foot of his bed—a misty figure. Then, almost as if he realized he'd been spotted, the ghost man dissolved into the wall!"

The family's stories just seemed to go on without end. Nevertheless, with few exceptions, the residents now seem to be rather indifferent. Clara grew up with the phenomena and so did Betty. Now, as Betty's children are adults, the mystery seems to have paled. Clara said that in 2002, she and Brian sat in the living room watching a television drama. From the stairs, the pair heard the sound of work boots clumping down the steps. The program was interesting and Clara said to Brian, "Who do you think *that* is?" Brian, without taking his eyes from the interesting program, responded that he sure didn't know, and they continued watching the drama on the screen, unmindful of the "old show" taking place around them.

On another evening, Brian and his grandmother sat engrossed in another television movie. From upstairs came the unmistakable sound of a window being raised and then slamming down. Brian turned to Clara and asked, "You going to go up and see who *that* is?" Clara responded, without missing a minute of the program, "No, I don't believe I will." And so it goes. If families aren't too scared of ghost phenomena, it's easier just to treat the entities as mischievous children and try to ignore them.

Women

In March 2006, fellow researchers and I visited an old brick farmhouse atop a ridge north of Amsterdam, NY. Susan, my longtime investigative sidekick, as well as sensitives Adrienne and Sharon, arrived at the 1784 home built by a Revolutionary War veteran of the Tryon County Militia. Originally, the farm had included more outbuildings and over one hundred acres of farmland overlooking the Mohawk Valley to the south. In retrospect, I'm glad I had the foresight to bring several *women* with me.

Today, the old house owned by Peggy and Richard, is being renovated and turned once more into a true home. Richard had invited me to bring my investigators, but had said nothing else about the place. Nevertheless, a building of that age was sure to contain at least "house memories" of its former inhabitants and, hopefully, active entities with whom we could interact. The husband and wife and two of their three children, Kate and Richard, took a break from sawing and hammering in order to allow us to quietly sense the place.

All interior plaster and lath had been removed, and there was a sense of openness or spaciousness within as we could peer between the wall studs. None of us knew what to expect as we toured the old rooms separately. Each walked, stopped, listened and took notes, which we intended to compare at the end of our investigation. I was the last to enter, walking through what had apparently been a kitchen, though Richard, Sr. initially told us that a short (not original) extension of the house (which might also have been an earlier kitchen) had been removed some years ago.

In my mind's eye, I noted a rather prosperous-looking, smiling, rotund man dressed in early 1800s clothing, standing inside the kitchen, as if to welcome me to his fine home. I got no identification, but I thought the gentleman might have been the builder in his old age or one of his sons. Sue saw a similarly-dressed man inside the front room. The entity was depressed, she sensed, and felt he had been a failure. In our debriefing afterward, Richard Sr. and Peggy mentioned that, indeed, a former owner, faced with financial difficulties, had been forced to deed the property to his brother in order to keep the farm in the builder's family hands. Sue smelled pipe smoke accompanying this sad gentleman.

Then, walking into the living room and examining an old fireplace with its original cooking crane, I saw a shabbily-dressed man quietly playing a fiddle in the corner, and I felt impelled to bounce on my feet to his unheard, lively tune. A moment later, as I approached the old front door, I had the sense that a long-ago black-coated parson (Dutch Reformed Church?) was about to knock and offer comfort to the family whose child (I imagined) had died. "They will cope," I heard.

I next examined a downstairs hallway before heading upstairs. Three steps from the top, I sensed a child calling out plaintively, "Mama." I imagined that children's cribs or beds must have once graced the large upstairs landing, now bright in the Saturday morning sun.

Moving toward the front of the house, I found a large sitting room or parlor, which may also have been a bedroom in former times. A nice old fireplace was built into the front wall. With no particular sensations, I moved about the upstairs, thinking I heard the word, "settling," in a back former bedroom. Then, admiring the simple yet elegant banister, I climbed the steep stairs to the third floor. Two long chambers could be seen beneath the eaves flanking the small upstairs hallway, and I had the sensation that these oblong areas had originally been used to dry tobacco leaf or some other herb from the gardens. A single bedroom occupied most of the center front.

Young Richard stood and watched as I roamed and listened. When I completed my tour of the room and was about to depart, he told me that this would eventually be his room in the restored house, though he was a bit mystified by the atmosphere in the space. "Several times I have come up and wandered through, thinking about how I'll place the furniture, and then, leaving the door ajar, I go downstairs. Yet, on my next trip up, even if it's only a short time later, I find the door closed and latched." We smiled at one another, sure that this was a sign of a presence. I went downstairs to confer with my fellow team members.

Sharon and Sue were already chatting about the strong female presence they felt throughout the house. We verbally retraced our individual entries and shared our experiences in each room. Richard, Sr. and Peggy stood by to offer validation or comments. I was the only one in our group to sense the musician fiddling in the corner, but young Richard remarked that he, also, often felt, heard, or sensed sprightly music in the room, as well as the inclination to dance or hop around. "I find it hard to just stand still in here," he said. It was common to have house parties in the old days. The father informed us that the large front door had been unused by recent former residents, and one family had actually placed a bed against the portal.

Adrienne had already walked around the exterior of the house and mentioned the many small gravestones in the family cemetery in the back field—an indication of many children's deaths over the two hundred plus years of habitation. All of the women in our group mentioned the strong feminine vibrations felt in the upstairs. Adrienne sensed a strong matriarchal energy in the front upstairs room; though none of us could discern whether or not the entity had been a member of the original family. In that large front room with a fireplace, Susan sensed a woman spirit who was very upset about her husband remarrying after her death. Later, we learned that the first owner *did*, in fact, remarry a much younger woman after his first wife died.

Apparently, that second marriage produced other stresses, as Sue sensed a young girl with brown hair, perhaps ten years old, in a second floor bedroom. The child was upset that she now had a step-mother and felt betrayed and hurt to have her mother replaced.

Especially in a rear bedroom, Adrienne sensed an older woman, perhaps a grandmother that had died, likely in great pain.

Our group, which now included owners and their children, stood on that floor and marveled at the one thing we all could agree on: the strength and endurance of the house's previous inhabitants, especially the women. These residents seem to have tasted too many of the misfortunes that accompany all lives. Sometimes they bent, then physically and emotionally straightened themselves again and forged ahead, tending to the farm animals and fields. What strength we perceived! It was helpful to our debriefing that Peggy and Richard,

Sr. had already done so much historical research on the house and grounds, as it allowed them to verify some of our hunches.

Up to the third floor we walked, and again pondered the long eaves spaces. The owner went into the center bedroom and opened small, square doors in the bedroom side wall, openings into the eaves area. We speculated that these may have been used to direct or control air currents into the side spaces, perhaps serving to air condition what must have been a terribly hot area during the summers. Possibly, the air flow may also have helped to dry tobacco leaves or herbs, if indeed those were brought upstairs. We talked about the strong energy that each person had sensed in that center bedroom and young Richard retold his experiences with the door latch.

Could this top room have been used by a servant? To the left, through a small door and underneath the eaves, Susan sensed a serving girl, and she and Adrienne got the word "brogue" at almost the same instant. The invisible girl conveyed to Susan that she had gotten very sick there, and one wonders if her illness killed the girl.

Then, Richard, Sr. showed us that, inside one of those small doors written in pencil or old ink was the inscription "May 23, 1847," and above that, in a large hand, the inscription "Rebe…" with the ending hard to discern. Could it have been "Rebekah" or "Rebecca?" Many times, as noted elsewhere in this book, a signature is enough of an energy connection to its former world for a spirit to hold onto it and manifest on the earth plane long after body death. We wondered if this was one of the stronger spirits in the house, though at the time, we didn't know if there was a woman of that name in the long-term owners' or succeeding families. That fact was confirmed later by Richard, Sr.. Before we descended the stairs, Susan got a bright orb image on her digital camera screen. There were other light spots too, but she felt those were more the result of dust particles moving in the attic light.

Our group explored the barns and then visited the old cemetery out back. Though it is no longer on his land, the present owner told us that he tries to keep the burial ground's brush cut down, a daunting task born of respect for the deceased settlers. The stones were not the marble that is often found in more prosperous Mohawk Valley cemeteries, but more of a hard, grey stone, unadorned by anything other than names or initials. Only a few of the stones were inscribed in fine relief lettering, again reflecting the financial struggle that must have attended the lives of so many on the farm.

There is much work on our group's part remaining to be done before we can say we *know* with any assurance who the remaining spirits might be. Strong women from the past seem likely to still be overseeing the present owners' restoration of the homestead. Or the women spirits may still be doing the chores of their time, unmindful that hundreds of years have passed. Though hard was their lot, it seems to have been happy and rewarding work.

We returned to our car to drive away, and the hammering and sawing resumed inside the old building—a *new* family was working to make this *home*.

Poof!

Herbert is a logical guy with a background in law enforcement. Now retired from that job, he has renewed his interest in preserving local historical sites. A down to earth man, he's another of those who have experienced the dwellers of the other world.

Some years ago, he purchased a 160 year-old house on County Highway 107 near Amsterdam. Long before, it had been a tavern favored by the teamsters who plied the route between Johnstown and Saratoga. Then it became a farm, and finally, after the soil gave out, it was put on the market, and Herbert's love of history drew him to buy it.

"That first night, only my son and I stayed there. We chose one room and bedded down. Neither of us slept very soundly, though we didn't share that fact with one another until some months later. At that time, we revealed to one another that, on that first night, we both sensed that someone else was present or was observing us, though neither of us saw anything. Today we call the room our library, and it's where we installed the computer.

"Some years later, I met a woman who had been born in that house and in that room. I met another who had grown up in the house," he told me, "and I asked her about the prior uses of that room. She told me, 'that was the sick room when I grew up there. If any family member became ill, they were taken to that room.' It wasn't clear if anyone had died there, though. Now, when I work on my computer there, especially at night," he told me, "it's as if I'm under observation again. When that feeling is strongest, I turn quickly and glimpse a small cloud of vapor behind me, though it dissipates rapidly. At other times, as I have a light behind me, I sense the shadow of someone or something moving between the light and myself, though I never see anybody causing that flickering shadow."

Herbert said that in his early years of residence, he began to think of the presence in the downstairs as male and the one upstairs as female. "One night I came in and, walking to the foot of the stairs, looked up and saw what I took to be a misty woman at the top of the stairs. I went up to see if my daughter had gotten out of bed or what might be wrong. The figure vanished, so I looked in my daughter's bedroom and found her sound asleep. Then I checked on my son, but he was asleep, too. So I guessed it was a woman ghost, though I never saw her again.

"Many times, when I'm working upstairs at night, I'll hear footsteps downstairs, but no one is ever there. One night, after working a night shift, I came home to find my wife scared out of her wits, standing with a loaded pistol at the top of the stairs. She told me she had been about to go down and discover who was noisily walking in the dining room. But, having just entered the house and passed through each room, I *knew* no one was there. 'It can make a person a bit nervous when they have to live with a ghost,' she told me with a grin."

Herbert told me that his daughter-in-law had once glimpsed a figure walking into her bedroom at night, but couldn't tell if it was male or female. And his soon-to-be son-in-law, sleeping on the downstairs couch, the next morning asked Herbert why he had come to stare at him during the night. "I told him I hadn't been out of bed upstairs all night," but the boy was steadfast in his claim that a man had walked to the side of the couch and stood, staring at him the previous night. I was the only other man in the house!"

The other phenomenon is the cigar smoke. Herbert told me that several times, when he sat on the couch in the living room, he'd smelled a cigar, but nobody in the family smokes. When he met the former woman owner, she agreed that, in her time, *her* family also smelled the cigar but had found a way to end it. "My mother used to yell at the smoker ghost, 'Take it outside!' And the smell vanished quickly."

In such cases, it is usual to suspect a deceased previous owner, an individual that has not yet broken his or her ties to the house or to tobacco. "I discovered that the previous owner had been killed on a nearby hill back during Prohibition, probably in the early 1930s," Herbert said, and, unless one of the "sick people" had transitioned in the house, this anonymous man gets the nod as the instigator. The entity may, indeed, not accept that he has died and may come home at night, puzzled by "the newcomers."

Two Old Maids?

Dan and Sue are retired teachers, and all they asked for was the chance to restore the wreck of an historic house and then enjoy the peace and quiet of retirement. The first, they have almost completed. The second, not yet. Someone keeps distracting them.

The Schermerhorn House

"This old house was in terrible shape when I came here in 1991," Dan Dayton told me. "Many who looked at the house believed it would be merciful to just tear it down. Though I taught Industrial Arts for years, I knew that to restore it would be a real challenge. I'm not kidding when I tell you there were fifty pails on the attic floor to catch all the roof leaks! This was the Simon Schermerhorn homestead, with seven bedrooms and six fireplaces, a mid-1800s gentleman's home, and it deserved better treatment than it had received over the last fifty years."

The earliest records suggest John I. Schermerhorn as the builder, perhaps as early as the 1820s. We know Simon Schermerhorn (1827-1901), who (probably) built an addition on the home on Schermerhorn Road in 1857, was the eighth generation of the family in the Schenectady area, though how he came to own John's house isn't clear. Simon married Helen Vedder that year, and the couple eventually had eight children. In time, only daughters Alice and Mary remained to maintain the Schermerhorn legacy of public service which their father had initiated, serving as school superintendent and NY State Assemblyman. Alice and Mary, the last of Simon's children, died without marrying, perhaps leading to a neighboring patch of woods' moniker, "Old Maid's Woods." Alice, the last survivor, died in 1954 at age ninety-four.

From historic research done by the present owners, it seems as if the original, front part of the house was built earlier than 1857, probably by Simon's relative, John I. Schermerhorn. Exactly how it came into Simon's ownership hasn't yet been determined. After Alice's death, the house then had several owners, and one buyer and his wife successfully voided their purchase offer after hearing rumors of a Schermerhorn ghost on the premises. As the most recent owners, the Daytons set about modernizing but also restoring the Victorian beauty, which is seen in the cornices, woodwork, and paneled ceilings.

One of the first tasks was to install modern wiring, and Dan and his first wife ran into a difficulty. In the upstairs walls, there were firestops between the studs, but those in the Schermerhorn upstairs walls were not in a normal position. Thus, Dan had difficulty in pushing wires up into the attic space. He told me that

The Schermerhorn Family c. 1880

during a break in the work, his wife had gone into the attic and quietly told the ghost that they weren't attempting to destroy anything but, instead, wanted to make the house nice again. On his next push, Dan said, the wires went easily up past the fire breaks and into the attic. An appreciative and cooperative ghost.

Sue, Dan's present wife, smiled and exclaimed that neither of them were believers in ghosts at first. "We don't believe in this stuff and laugh at it," she said. "Nevertheless, we know that many of the goings-on here are unexplainable in any other way. See this door?" She pointed to an interior kitchen door. "It has a sturdy lock, but very often it is open, after I've just closed and secured it. It opened itself maybe *twenty-five times* last year," she told me. That door leads to the library room. I suggested that a domestic or family member from another time apparently hadn't let go of housekeeping yet or remains drawn to the room by a strong emotional memory.

"We had a back hall light that used to turn itself off and on regularly, so we just accepted it, and nowadays it comes on less frequently unless we turn it on," Sue told me. As I mentioned nighttime in the big old house, Sue smiled, "Let me tell you about an incident from a few years ago, just to show you how blasé we've become. In the middle of the night we both awoke, startled by a sound. Someone with heavy feet was clomping up the stairs and along the hallway. 'Dan, hear that?' I asked. He replied that he, too, had heard it, and I asked him to describe the sound. He told me someone was walking heavily in the hallway—just what I'd heard. But I wasn't afraid of any of it. Then, we went right back to sleep.

"When I came to live here, I had an intuition on many occasions that I shouldn't enter the upstairs room that serves as Dan's office. I can't say that I

18

believed a ghost was in there, but sometimes I'd just stand in the doorway and tell the spirit or spirits what was on my mind—what activities of theirs I found bothersome," she laughed. Then, she told me of the decorative candlesticks in the dining room, three to a candelabra. "Every time I went in, I was certain to find at least one of those candles lying at an angle. I even tried stickum stuff in the candle holder, but they always managed to flop. Finally, in exasperation, I moved the right candelabra to the left and vice versa. The candles have remained upright every day since. Who moved them? Not us! And why did it matter to the ghost?

"We had an upcoming party a few months ago, and I didn't want the ghost to be upset at the sudden influx of strangers and commotion, so I just walked to the dining room doorway and informed her (I think at least one of the ghosts is female) and that was that. The party was a success and came off without a hitch.

"Then, last week, I smelled cigarette smoke in the back hallway, which has happened several times. Neither Dan nor I smoke, and I went to investigate. It wasn't stale smoke, but fresh, as if someone had just passed through the hallway, puffing away. Needless to say, no smoker was in the house, but could Alice or Mary be sneaking a smoke?"

When I asked if anyone had ever died a violent death in the house, Dan raised an eyebrow and said, "Two!" The most notable of these was Maria, the wife of *John* Schermerhorn, before Simon's time. The story isn't clear, but records show that she was shot in the foyer in 1825 by a school teacher (all three of us groaned!) named Van Patten. There are many stories, rumors really, that Van Patten was a rejected suitor for John's daughter, but that is unlikely because little Sarah was only 10 at the time, so the murder motives aren't clear. And that bit of evidence suggests to me that Maria may be one ghost of long standing. Someone told Dan a few years ago that there had been a second violent death on the property, but he has found no substantiation for that at this time. A previous owner of the Schermerhorn House in the 1960s often complained that objects in the house levitated and moved about from time to time, and it sounded to me as if a housekeeper remains at work doing domestic chores, unmindful of her bodily death.

"Old Simon had a slave or two," Dan told me, showing a document whereby Schermerhorn had freed a twenty-five-year-old slave named Thomas Jackson in 1821, before he lived in this house. "There is a long and involved story about how we came into possession of these documents," Sue said, "but let's just say that the estate of an elderly neighbor was put up for sale, and many buyers had passed through that house that day in 2003. When I got inside, I found this accumulation of documents, many bearing the Schermerhorn name.

I bought them for a song, then brought them home." She and Dan had piles of those old deeds, indentures, diaries, etc., even young Simon Schermerhorn's writing book, laid out on the dining room table for my intuitive friend, Susan, and me to peruse on my second visit to the house. At least one of the papers was written in 1703, during the reign of Queen Anne—very valuable documents for a couple that wanted to research the house's history. We marveled at the cosmic coincidence that caused that portfolio of history to remain unsold when Sue got to the sale.

"There is also a tradition that the present house was used as a way station on the Underground Railroad," Dan said, "and some suggest the anxieties of the fugitive slaves might account for mysterious energies that erupt from time to time in the old house. One day, some neighborhood people, a man and a boy, were walking past when I was mowing the lawn. I overheard the man tell the boy that ours was a haunted house, and that there were hidden tunnels in the cellar. Well, I *did* find a strange cavity in the cellar, though I wouldn't call it a tunnel. It might have been a hideout for slaves, however, if the Sheriff came looking," he grinned. "I'll keep looking for the tunnels, in any case!"

"One day, at a baby shower, one of the women attending came up to me," Sue said, "and told of visiting the house during the tenure of the previous owners. Doors in the house often slammed spontaneously back then, causing the family's two daughters to blame each other. Only later did they conclude it was a ghost. I also remember coming home to do some laundry while we were at our camp. As I waited for the machine to cycle, I distinctly heard a conversation taking place at the top of the stairs. I listened for a bit, but couldn't make out the words or what the discussion was about, so I continued with my task, putting the wet clothes into the dryer." She gave me a big smile, and I could see that the couple really wasn't worried if individuals from other times occasionally manifested in their home.

However, both Sue and Dan were curious about what an intuitive might pick up there, so I made an appointment for my sensitive friend, Susan, to accompany me on my next visit.

We arrived on a sunny day in late spring, and Susan walked throughout the house alone, as is her style. When she returned, she asked Sue about the library room, though she didn't know that its door had a habit of opening. "I have a strong impression of a woman sitting in that front corner window," Susan said, "maybe reading, watching the road, or sipping tea. It feels like that was some woman's favorite corner for reading, thinking, or watching the world go by."

Then, the two of us walked throughout the house. My receptors weren't very strong that day, and I had only one image, that of a tall, thin man,

20

perhaps in early 1900s dress, standing in the front bedroom. I got the word "uncle." Susan was drawn to the energies in both upstairs front bedrooms, and continually was impressed by the feeling of at least one woman's energy in the house.

"She shows herself in a formal traveling outfit," my companion said, "and wears a hat, perhaps with a feather in it. She may also be using that image to show me that something she did (marrying an affluent Schermerhorn?) was a 'feather in my cap.' It seems clear, wherever I go in this house, that the lady loved her wealth and station in life. Probably, if that is Helen, Simon's wife, she may have enjoyed being just a bit better off than most people, and I suspect that her love of things keeps her here. Maybe she can't let go of all the finery."

And it would be hard to let go, as Sue and Dan have restored so much of the house to its former Victorian elegance. Antique fixtures and furniture are to be found in each room, and it was as if we had entered a home that is one hundred fifty years old, and the Schermerhorns had just stepped out. Both Susan and I marveled at the beauty of the house restoration, a house which is seldom opened to the curious or casual visitors.

I knew of the alleged shooting in the front foyer and asked Susan what she got there. "There is just a continual movement of children throughout the house, for one thing," she told me. "Did they have children?" I told her of the eight Schermerhorn youngsters who grew up there, finishing with Alice. There are three likely candidates for 'lady ghost' there: Maria, who was murdered, Simon's wife, Helen, and Alice, the last of the line who died unmarried and childless. When I asked about other energies there, Susan went back to the foyer and sat quietly on the front stairway, then returned to tell of seeing a man in Civil War military dress (none of us could identify him right away) and then sensing a tussle of some kind, and seeing someone wave a pistol, and even firing it, because she heard a shot!

I had told Susan nothing about the house at the beginning, though I was returning the Schermerhorn family photo (used in this story, and which may show Helen on the far right, wearing a *feathered hat*) to the Daytons. We then told Susan about the historic murder, and we all grimaced at the thought of some of that energy still remaining after almost two hundred years. Sudden death victims are usually the prime candidates for resident ghosts, though there may be more than one woman's spirit in the house. After we visited the house and had gone home, Dan and Sue found an old photo of Alice with a feather in *her* hat!

In the upstairs, Susan sensed that in a walk-through closet that Dan constructed as an addition to the adjacent bedroom, the overhead light must malfunction quite a bit. Dan immediately agreed. "Overall," she said, "my sensation is of the constant movement of energy throughout this house. Some of it may just be the remains of long ago, what you call 'house memories,' David." Though I kept it to myself, I wondered if Sue and Dan's expended restoration energy would one day be sensed by sensitives of a future era.

Sue Dayton said, "The Schermerhorns were important people." She showed us a topographical map which indicated what was likely Simon's race-track atop the hill behind the house. The couple also showed us a late 1800s photo with Simon, his two sons, the family dogs, and two apparent thorough-bred horses in the long ago side yard. Three women were in the background, and one wonders if the foreground-to-background placement indicated the family's priorities. Simon was on the board of directors of two Schenectady banks. His children, as adults, knew the famous people, the Edisons, the Steinmetzes and others who made the county famous. They were likely investors in many of those early enterprises, perhaps even General Electric Company.

As a *coup de grâce*, Dan brought out his photo album, showing the house as it looked in 2000, covered with cracked and dirty white paint, sur-rounded by towering dying trees that threatened to fall upon the house, and old barns with faded paint. There were interior photos of rundown floors, walls, and ceilings. Susan looked at me and I at her, and we realized that we really didn't want to *know* how many thousands of hours of sweat equity this couple had invested in the old homestead.

"But, you know," Sue Dayton said with a smile, "I think the ghost lady or ladies approve of our struggle to bring back the house to what *they* knew, and they are proud of us for saving so many old paper records. Lately, they've gone easy on us, and we don't have too many occurrences any more."

Mrs. Tilden

"I've never seen a ghost, and I don't believe I've ever personally experi-enced one," James told me. "Nevertheless, I have had friends who did so, and one of the most intriguing was the story of Mrs. Tilden, the alleged ghost in my friend's house."

In 1974, when he was twelve years old, James had a friend named Simon who lived in a five-story townhouse at 16 E. 76th Street in Manhattan. Sometimes, the chum was a bit nervous at school in the morning and explained his behavior as being the fault of a Mrs. Tilden who lived in his house. James accepted that until, a few months later, when it occurred to him that Simon lived in a *single*-family house. "So, just *who* is Mrs. Tilden?" he asked his friend.

Simon finally broke down and confessed that Mrs. Tilden was a former resident of the old building, but the fact that she had died seemed to mean nothing to her. "The elevator can be seen moving between floors. When the door opens, many times there is *nobody* inside. One of the neighbors told us that old Mrs. Tilden loved to ride the elevator when she lived there.

"The other thing that really spooks me," Simon related, "is that she seems to wait until I'm the only person in the house. Let's say I'm reading on the second floor. Suddenly I'll hear the toilet flushing up on the fifth floor. I absolutely *know* that there is nobody else in the house, but I have to tell you, James, I'm really afraid to go up there. I'm afraid I'll actually *see* her."

"So, Simon just had to live with all his anxiety until his family sold the house. I wonder if the residents there are still graced with old Mrs. Tilden's presence," James grinned.

The Grandin Farmhouse

When the Holland Land Company sold off the lands south of Lake Ontario, James and John Aesop purchased acreage in what is now the village of Williamson. Their plans didn't bear fruit, however, and the pair sold the parcel in 1808. A house was constructed in 1811 by the new owners, the Bristol family, and soon after, the structure became a refuge for women and children during the British invasion in May 15, 1814, what is today remembered as The Battle of Pultneyville. Three years later, the Bristols sold to Daniel and Ame Grandin.

The couple was still grieving the death of their newborn, Rachel, in 1812, but two years after buying the house, Ame conceived another daughter, who was likewise named Rachel. Unfortunately, this daughter also died young, expiring suddenly at age twelve.

In 1994, Chet Peters, local historian and storyteller, who had owned the house for many years, recalled to Rebekah Porray that one day in the 1960s, he had come home to make a phone call, and hearing scuffling and walking upstairs, assumed that Pearl, his wife, was doing housework. Preparing to leave the house again, he called upstairs to tell her that he was leaving. Receiving no response, he checked all the bedrooms but found no one else home. Puzzled, he came downstairs only to spot his spouse crossing the yard from the neighbor's house.

Old Grandin Farmhouse

Chet's son, Jay, and his wife, Sherry, took over the house in 1976 and have experienced many puzzling events, though Sherry has experienced the greater number of those. The couple has heard slamming doors, and Chet recalls hearing that sound during his tenure there, but he was always mystified as to which of the house's doors were banging. At first, Sherry believed the noises emanated from her children's bedrooms and that a youngster had gotten up in the night, but upon checking, she always found them asleep. Visiting friends have also heard the sounds and theorize that invisible former residents are just absorbed in living their lives in their own time.

Jay reported that the alarm times set on their clock somehow get changed during the night. The family has also discovered the television set turned on in the morning, as if some nocturnal guest had just finished viewing a program.

"One night in 1987, I awoke at about 1 a.m., sensing that something was wrong. I felt a strong presence at the foot of my bed, though no one was visible. I got up to check on the children and found my three-year-old missing from his bed," Sherry told me. "I went downstairs and through the kitchen, then saw his smiling face through the door in a back room where he'd wandered. The door had closed behind him and there was no way he could open the door to come back in." Had Rachel helped her avert any injury?

Sherry remembers that in 1993 she was ill and required surgery. As she recovered, she invited a friend to visit, and as the pair sat sipping tea one evening, movements could be heard upstairs. "Are your kids up?" the friend inquired. Sherry smiled and said slowly, "I don't *think* so." It seemed wise to make it a short answer."

24

In an interview, Sherry Peters told me that the presence was strongest whenever she was not feeling well, and it always seemed that the spirit was definitely a female. Then Sherry met Rebekah in 1994. After relating her experiences in the house to Rebekah, the high school senior did some research and informed Sherry about the early deaths of the two Rachels in the Bristol family of long ago. "That *really* made connections for me!" Sherry said with a laugh.

It is not out of line to suspect that a teenager of any historical period would remain on the earth plane "for just a bit longer," to enjoy family life with a happy family, after having her life so suddenly snatched away. If there is any sense of time for most ghosts, it seems they are always in *their* reality, in *their* time. Apparently, though her noises have been less frequent in the last ten years, Rachel continues to live just beyond the veil separating her time from ours. The girl's spirit seems not to trouble the Peters family, nor do they disrupt her enjoyment of this extra allotment of time.

Others

In 1967, Bernadette's mother bought the duplex, previously the home of the McCormick sisters, at 1311 3rd Street in Rensselaer, NY, and the girl grew to womanhood there. "When I married, my mom invited Steven and me to live upstairs, which was especially nice when we had our baby," Bernadette remembered. "Living there was very familiar to me and nothing out of the ordinary occurred until our baby, Stephy, was eleven months old." The child had her favorite teddy bear in the crib with her when she went to sleep that night, and Bernadette went to bed in her own bedroom.

"I was sleeping when I felt someone sit down on the other side of the bed; I thought it must be my husband. All at once, the bed started bouncing violently. Steven! What are you *doing*? I thought, and woke up. Without turning, I angrily said, 'Cut it out. It's 3 a.m.!' Then I looked, and nobody was there. Just then, I heard the door slam out in the kitchen, and knew *that* was my husband. But if it hadn't been Steven bouncing my bed just then, who was it? I angrily turned on the lights in each room as I went out—nobody was there. Going back to my bedroom, I noticed the baby's door was shut. What's *that* all about? I asked myself, and pushed the door open. Turning on the light, I saw Stephy was almost blue—she was choking on something!

"Frantically, I grabbed her, tipped her upside down, and squeezed her chest while groping inside her mouth with my finger. Out came a button from the teddy bear's face. I called 911, and we went to the emergency room. I hadn't been afraid, I realized, but then I *had* had some first aid training in my second job at a hospital. The baby was okay, but Steven kept asking me, 'How did you *know* what was wrong with her?' It wasn't easy to explain it to him. When we got back to the apartment, I was no longer scared, but I don't think Steven believed me about the bouncing bed. After all, in a locked apartment, who else could have tried to awaken me?'

Bernadette remembers that, soon afterward, she began to experience things disappearing from their customary places in her apartment. "I complained to my mom downstairs, but she told me not to worry. She has a lot of the old country in her and seems to understand such things. A while later, I began to find the missing objects in the downstairs hall closet. Mom wasn't scared, I decided, so why should *I* be?"

Two years passed, and then Steven, asleep on the bed for an afternoon nap, suddenly got bounced really hard. He woke up a bit groggy. What was *this*? Had Bernadette really been right? A bouncing bed? But that had all happened when Stephy was in trouble, right? And she was certainly okay this afternoon, right? And where *was* she? It sounded like Bernadette had come home, and he made his way into the living room. There was Stephy, contentedly sucking on her bottle, watching television. She was okay; was someone now warning *him*?

Steven later confessed the entire episode to his wife, who talked at length with her mother about the matter. It was as if there were one or maybe two other beings in the apartment, and they seemed to be like invisible nannies or baby sitters. Could it be that the McCormick sisters had stayed on? Her mother admitted to having experienced such things during most of her life, but she had come to take them for granted as being good things, so she seldom discussed them. Mainly, she told Bernadette not to worry. "Don't be afraid if you experience stuff ahead of time in your mind," she told her daughter.

Years passed; Stephy grew up, graduated and became engaged. Life was supposed to be easier now, but Bernadette's intuition had become even stronger. One day, she found herself quite upset when it came time for Steven to go to work. "Don't go in today," she implored him, after receiving a vision of two large plates smashing together and everything becoming covered with red. For various reasons, Steven didn't go to work. A few hours later they got a phone call that a nineteen-year-old employee working on Steven's machine had fallen into it and been squashed, splashing blood all over the area.

"Now that the job of motherhood is over, if it ever really *is* over," she told me, "life should be easier, but it isn't. My intuition is very strong, and I've seen ghosts or spirits where I work. Fortunately, my mom is still here, and I can check with her when I get these visions. Maybe someday I'll be able to play that role with *my* daughter," she said with a laugh.

Pine Grove Farm

Pine Grove Farmhouse

"Our home is almost two hundred years old," Colleen told me. "Jim and I came here twenty-nine years ago and have enjoyed every minute of it, even the presence of our ghost or ghosts!" Pine Grove Farm is not far from the village of Hamlin, NY, in Monroe County, an area of flat fields and beautiful orchards that enjoy the mild climate south of Lake Ontario.

"We purchased the farm from a young couple that had lived in the house for only a few years; in 1979, soon after we moved in, the incidents started. At first, we noticed lights that we had turned off were found lit again and vice-versa. We then discovered that our television set and radio often turned themselves on or off. On our first Christmas here, my teenage sister helped me set up the tree in the living room," Colleen told me. "I was underneath, twisting the turnbuckles that held the trunk, while my sister held it straight. All at once, my husband's guitar began to strum itself in the corner of the room. Somehow, it had moved from the other room into *our* room, and we could see the strings being plucked, making sounds but not much real music. It was almost as if an invisible someone had discovered the instrument and decided to test its capacity. My sister was suddenly under the tree with me, both of us scared at such an unexplainable event!"

After the tree had been set up, Colleen noted that "there was a residue of fallen evergreen needles on the floor, so I got out the vacuum and plugged it in. It turned on all by itself," she exclaimed. I told her that, for some reason, vacuum cleaners are easy for ghosts to manipulate, so her experience is quite common in haunted houses.

But there has been much more, she told me. One of the first renovation jobs for Colleen and Jim was to remove old plaster and lath walls and put up dry walls inside their new home. They also decided to eliminate one of the doors onto the front porch and sealed the space with dry wall panels. "At the time we had only one dog, but, since then, we have gained four others who never saw that old door, but they all do the same thing—they sit in front of the 'vanished doorway' and stare at the wall or at someone in the old doorway. They wag their tails, as if asking the ghost to let them out. The first dog might have remembered that old door, but *not the other four*!

"My husband works until late, so one evening, when he got home, the television station was signing off. The national anthem played, and then the screen went black. He turned it off and began to read a magazine. Suddenly, the TV went on again. He got up and unplugged it, unfazed by the ghost's desire for entertainment. The next evening, I sat with our baby and a neighboring teenager who came over to visit. I related Jim's experience from the night before as we sat in the kitchen, and then, instantly, I heard the TV turn on in the living room, and the volume began to turn up and up. The poor girl was scared out of her wits. So was I, but I had the presence of mind to yell at the ghost, '*Stop it right now!*' The TV went off immediately, and the two of us grabbed the baby and went next door to wait for Jim to return home.

"We have a rocking chair that sways by itself in an unoccupied room, and many doors open and close by themselves. Our family knows to be careful when using the oven broiler, as it will almost always set off our kitchen smoke alarm—but all of them? All at the *same* time? And even when we aren't using that broiler at all? It sure is a mystery," Colleen laughed. Of course, she and Jim and their children recognize these phenomena as normal ghost activity and often speculate about the individual (or are there several?) causing these episodes.

"Prior to the young couple that we bought the house from, a Mrs. Kruger owned the farm. Her husband had died of a heart attack in the area outdoors between the house and the barn. Strangely, though we often smell a cherry-scented tobacco smoke in the house, it always seems strongest in that area between the barn and the house," she told me. "Mr. Kruger apparently did some writing on a barn wall; we can just make out the pencil scrawls, though they really aren't very legible any more." I reminded her that the writing we leave on walls can sometimes be enough of a link for a departed soul to remain on the earth plane. It represents energy or thoughts that we expended at one time, and the departed spirit has to learn to disassociate from those acts before it can move on.

We talked some more about the family pets, as cats and dogs are usually more sensitive to presences than the humans in a house. "Oh, our poor last dog, who just died," she grimaced. "It was as if the ghost were pinching or goosing her behind. If I called to her, she'd walk around the entire perimeter of the room rather than cross the open space. It sure looked like she was being self-protective. Then she went into what we assumed were fits, as she'd shake and shake and run around the house looking upward, almost as if she was chasing an invisible person or objects. Our vet could find nothing wrong with the dog." Unfortunately, I said, most veterinarians seldom honor the pet's sensitivity and suggest a ghost might be at fault.

"In February 2006, some visitors came to the house for a candle demonstration party, and most of them were professional people. One of the women went to the upstairs bathroom and returned to warn me that the bathroom light kept going off and on, and that perhaps we had a short-circuit. When it went out, she'd turn it on and return to the toilet, but when she did so, the light extinguished. After three or fours such episodes, she simply left the light off and finished her business in the dark, with the door closed. The woman had never been to our house before and may never come again! During that group's visit, I had to shush the dog, as she kept looking at an empty chair and barking. Finally, I had to yell at both the dog and the chair-sitting ghost, '*Stop!*' And they both obeyed. I can handle the ghosts, but they sometimes have minds of their own."

The family has two grown sons and a younger daughter who recently reached adulthood. The young woman wanted to be sure her mother related to me the full litany of experiences that *she* had to endure in her adolescent years. The daughter had a television set in her bedroom and discovered that the ghost could turn it off and on whenever it suited him, even though the remote control device was on her bedside table. Many times in the night, she'd awaken to find the set turned on, usually set on Channel 109, a non-operating channel. She never did understand the ghost's attraction to the "white sound" that came from the TV.

As a teenager, she also had a touch lamp in a bedroom corner, though she seldom used it. Many times she would awaken in the middle of the night to find the lamp turned on, and one night the girl spotted a misty humanoid form standing at the foot of her bed. She guessed it was a male, though there were few recognizable features. Often, it was the sound of the wall light switch clicking on that awakened her, as they didn't have the silent solenoid switches.

"On one occasion, my daughter awoke to see the ghost coming forth from her bedroom closet and exiting out the door into the hallway. Another time, a friend gifted her with some Mylar balloons, which my daughter left inflated and floating at ceiling level. She awoke in the night, hearing the balloons scraping the ceiling in movement. Around and around the ceiling perimeter they traveled, as if the ghost had found a new sport. Upset at being awakened, she yelled out, '*Stop!*' and immediately, the strings on the bottom of the balloons went limp—they stopped!

"How much time do you have to listen?" Colleen grinned, "I can go on for hours. Everyone in our family has had experiences, as have countless visitors to our home. For me, one of the strangest experiences took place a few years ago. I had visited a psychic for a fun reading, and the woman told me that the ghost in my house would give me a message through a 'trophy' that I had. Well, we raise and show horses, and our house is full of such awards, so I asked the seer if she could be a bit more specific. The woman said I'd know it when it happened, so I went home.

"A friend had given me a little Hallmark Christmas ornament a few years before, which was a merry-go-round design featuring four circling horses. At about that time, I bought two nice riding horses, Ginger and Star. One day, as I was dusting the living room, I saw the merry-go-round on its corner shelf, where no one had touched it in some time. I picked it up and could see the lack of dust pattern underneath it. But there were several other old patterns around it too, as if someone had picked up the ornament and then replaced it at several intervals over the past year. As I held the little treasure in my hand, I noticed that each horse had its name engraved in small print on its blanket. The first name was 'Holly,' which was the name of my brother's wife! And the next two horses were named 'Star' and 'Ginger!' Well, I just about fell down with surprise! *There* was my message—the ghost could live with me, yet give information to the psychic."

Colleen told me that she had kept her daughter's old bedroom door closed to conserve heat since the girl has begun her career away from home, and, today, the room is only used for storage. The portal has a strong latch and it catches well, but on many occasions, she or Jim will find the door ajar in the morning. They close it firmly, but the next morning, there it is, open a crack again.

Many people living with ghosts nowadays have digital cameras, and Colleen is no exception, though she has several types of cameras. Not too long ago, she left a film camera on the kitchen table in between uses. When she finally finished the roll of film, she took the canister to the developer and was surprised to find a strange image in the returned pictures. "Here, in this picture, you can clearly see that it was shot from the table top, looking into the living room. That isn't a picture *I'd* ever have taken, but note the four vertical streaks of light in the photo. This has happened many times, and I'm pretty sure I captured some ghost energy." She paused and reflected that many years ago, when her daughter was six, the poor girl was sick and sitting on the couch when her picture had been taken. The resulting developed photo showed what appeared to be a small statue of Jesus sitting on the child's shoulder!

I believe it likely that, when one lives with denizens of the spirit world for so long, he or she can become much more sensitized to subtle energies, and Colleen seemed to be an example. One evening, when showing horses at the State Fair in Syracuse a few years ago, she sat near the steps of the family camper. "It was a nice, quiet, dark night, and I looked up at the sky. Suddenly, there were orbs of light, such as the ones I'd photographed once in the balcony of an old Boston courthouse on a school trip. The lights of the fair were refracted through those circles. Then I saw something like spider webs hanging down, but there was nothing for them to hang *from*! I sat there transfixed, watching them move aside for people to pass, then moving vertical again after the people had passed."

Though I am very serious about my ghost story interviews, I wanted to break the eerie mood by faking the theme music from *The Twilight Zone*, but I restrained myself. I read quite a bit of paranormal literature and am very familiar with orbs and their potential causes, but I had never before heard a tale of phantom spider webs. More than likely, these may be strings of energy, and I wonder if they have a consciousness attached to them, as seems the case here. It was a new one for me, though many ghost experiencers have told me that their walking *though* a ghost feels "like walking through spider webs."

Jim and Colleen have lived with an array of ghosts (Colleen believes that, beside Mr. Kruger, there may be one or two more ghosts who are usually well-behaved) for almost three decades. The family's three children have grown up with the specters, both visible and invisible, and it certainly has given them an introduction to the unseen aspects of Reality. The ghost or ghosts have been fairly well-mannered in allowing Jim and Colleen to use *their* house, it seems. But when ethereal push comes to shove, I'll put *my* money on Colleen.

Noises

"When we bought this house, we could see that there were many modifications from the original structure. It was built in 1792, and a previous owner added eyebrow windows and another one raised the roof to accommodate three upstairs bedrooms. Regardless, it's an old house that we love," said Michelle McConville about her home in Valatie, NY.

One might expect a ghost or two in a home that is two-centuries old. After all, Columbia County had European settlers before the Pilgrims landed on Plymouth Rock in 1620. That's a long time period in which people live their lives and depart. Nevertheless, Michelle and her husband didn't expect

McConville's House

any holdovers when they bought the old house. When the music started at night, she was sure that some neighbor had a stereo system turned up too loud. It sounded like old fiddle music, however, of a melodic genre not favored by young moderns who seek truth in volume. Night after night, the sounds wafted into her bedroom.

One morning, seeking a solution, she sat sleepily in the kitchen. It struck her that the nearest neighbor at that time was a quarter mile away and that overgrown orchards separated her house from theirs. The sounds *couldn't* be coming from neighbors. One day her husband commented on the sounds, so she knew they weren't her imagination. Later, her mother visited and commented on hearing the rustic tune at breakfast the next morning. Each family member recalled the same melody, though none of them could identify its title. Michelle and I talked about the fact that many old Hudson Valley homes certainly must have hosted "house dances" in the eighteenth and nineteenth centuries. Could these melodies be a ghostly playback of historic dances or concerts of a long-gone era?

"Another sound that irritated us was that of the big front door knocker banging at night, usually between ten and midnight. At first we hurried to the door to greet a visitor, only to find the doorstep empty. It couldn't have been a prankster, we decided, though the episodes did occur from three to four times per month." I asked if the frequency still continues. She paused to think for a minute and said, "We did replace that old wooden door with a new metal-clad door and assumed that would end the knocking sounds. We were wrong. The doorknocker continues to bang away at the same time and on the same

32

irregular schedule, but I guess we all just tune it out now!" Many folks living with ghosts become habituated to sights, sounds, or smells and just stop hearing them unless a conscious effort is made to look or listen.

"We have an old barn out back, and, though I'm not a fraidy-cat, I just choose not to go in there at night. We had horses when we first moved in, so I chose to take care of them in daylight. One evening at dusk, just as I was leaving the building, I felt a hand on my shoulder. I set a new speed record back to the house that evening!

"Every year my mother, aunts and a few cousins would visit for a 'girls' weekend.' One year, when my son was just a baby, we thought it would be intriguing to have a séance in the barn. But just before that weekend, my Aunt Irene was warned by a psychic friend about attempting that psychic activity, especially with a baby in the house. My young son was upstairs, so we cancelled the activity."

I told her that few *responsible* psychics favor doing séances these days as, unless the preparations and concluding ceremonies are done properly and spiritually, mischievous spirits can enter this dimension and then refuse to leave, causing not only mischief but also suffering to those involved. Séances are one of those "don't do this at home" cautions.

"When my son was quite young, my job caused me to be on the road for long hours. The baby was in daycare until my husband picked him up and brought him home," Michele told me. "One day, as I was leaving on a trip, I gave my house key to my husband and hit the road, expecting to see their two smiling faces upon my return. But when I got home after nightfall, the house was dark. I had no key and no way to get into the house. The poor dog was frustrated too, as he had been outside all day and was hungry. As I stood undecided about what to do, I heard the phone ringing inside the house (this was before cell phones). I was certain it must be my husband, and some awful fate must have befallen him and my son. I started to panic when the phone rang a second, then a third time.

"I hurried around the house and onto the side porch, hoping the side door might be open. It wasn't! I rushed around to the front door, then again to the back door, finally returning to the side door. All that while the phone kept ringing. The house was locked up tight. Finally, in desperation, I shook the side door handle and yelled, 'For God's sake, I wish *someone* would open this door for me!' The lock then clicked, and the door opened.

The dog, knowing dinner time was long overdue, shot inside, headed for his dish. He got only about three feet inside when he yelped, turned, and ran back outside. For the moment, I ignored him as I rushed to the still-ringing phone. It was my husband telling me that he would be late. After I hung up, I went to the back door, where the dog was barking, asking to come in. Once inside, he sniffed suspiciously, then hurried to his dish."

Michelle told me of a curious incident soon after the baby's birth, when they were given a flower arrangement with an "It's a Boy!" helium balloon attached. "I tied the balloon onto the baby's crib, but it tended to get in the way, so my husband untied it and just let it float toward the ceiling. We ignored it for a few days until my stepson told us he'd found the balloon at ceiling height outside *his* bedroom door when he came into the hallway. He ignored it until it dropped down and went through the doorway into *his* room. He'd never seen a balloon move on its own, and it spooked him, so he carried it back into the baby's room.

"Over the next few days, we watched the balloon float between the two rooms, almost as if it had a life of its own. There were other doorways to other rooms, but it never once went into any other bedroom. It usually floated between my son's room at one end of the hall, and my stepson's room at the other end—even as it lost gas, it continued to float back and forth. Finally, when it reached knee height, we put it out of its misery," she laughed. "We have never been able to get another balloon to duplicate this, not that we really *want* to!"

I asked Michelle where she sensed the ghost energy most strongly, and she said that the living room is the most energetic. "The fireplace is largest in that room, so we think it once was the house's Great Room, and it's likely the place where family members congregated at evening time in years gone by."

Then she smiled, reflecting on another mysterious event. "When our son was small, my mother, father, and Aunt Grace came over to baby-sit while my husband and I spent two days in Boston. They put the baby in his crib and then went downstairs to the family room. They had hardly gotten comfortable, when they heard a *very* loud crash from directly overhead, either in the baby's room or the master bedroom. My mother, father and aunt described how they ran frantically upstairs but found nothing amiss. When I asked what the crash sounded like, my father said it sounded as though a large dresser had fallen over.

"As I said," she told me, "so much has gone on here, though none of it has harmed anyone. Now we are oblivious to things that used to worry us; we know the sounds and tune them out. My son has grown up with the noises, and, at his present age, he seems immune to it all, as if thinking, doesn't *everyone* have such strange goings-on?"

And I guess that is the message here. Several layers of history seem to overlap in these old houses. Seldom is there a dangerous event. And many times, the living are assisted by "the others," as in this case, where warnings are given or assistance comes upon request. I'm sure Michelle would tell those in similar circumstances, "Ask and you shall receive."

34

The Homestead

**The Old
Nichols Homestead**

In 1986, Gordon and Joreen Van Lint bought the old Nichols Homestead on Route 149 in the town of Fort Ann, NY. The aged Victorian house was worn down and needed restoration. Looking at the building today, one can see the great amount of work and care that the new owners have lavished on the old farmhouse. "But that's only part of it," Joreen (Jo) said. She told my intuitive friend, Susan, and me about all the "sideshows" that have taken place there. This dialogue, of course, took place only after Sue and I had toured the building, listening, feeling, and intuiting who might be there.

As usual, we only knew that "stuff was going on" in the house, but we had no details. Sue walked through the house by herself, then returned to the kitchen to get me. Together, we walked about, waiting for our intuitions to be triggered. Hardly had we stepped into the living room, than I noticed a man, tall and lean, standing where a recliner chair stands today—both seemed to occupy the same space. I didn't comment at the time because Sue seemed anxious to go upstairs. She ascended first, then stood with a grin on her face, watching me walk upstairs. Three steps from the top, it was as if I ran into an invisible cushion and found myself walking backward down the stairs. Sue smiled and said, "I *knew* it." At that point, I returned to the stair top without incident, and we found ourselves at the door of a dark bedroom. "What's here," I asked myself, as Sue stood watching me. I knew that she'd already sensed someone or something there.

Then, there she was, half there and half not. A rather sturdy woman in an ankle length maroon dress with a white apron. Her salt and pepper grey hair appeared to be tied back. What caught my attention most was the sensation of a clenched jaw on her face. The figure seemed angry, perhaps resentful or determined about something. What does she want? I asked myself. I received an impression of acrimony and half-heard the words, "How could they *do* this to me? After all I did for them!" Then she was gone. I shared my impressions with Sue.

"Yes, that's exactly what I got, though I felt her hair was more shoulder length. Her energy comes at me in a rush. She's angry and upset, though I can't tell about what or at whom," she responded. We then moved to what we came to call, "The Dark Bedroom" because it was dark when we entered—an ideal atmosphere for a specter of some sort. However, we felt no abnormal energies there.

The Van Lints had almost completed restoring the bathroom, our next site, which was bright and inviting. Sue gave me another smile, so I expected to experience something, and I did. The modern toilet beside me suddenly gurgled and Sue laughed, "It did that when *I* walked in, too." This is too easily dismissed as a dysfunction of the plumbing system, however, and we didn't attribute anything paranormal to that, though Gordon told us later that the toilet didn't normally make that sound.

We returned to the downstairs and entered the first doorway, a room that we later referred to as, "The Roses Room" because of its wallpaper pattern. Immediately, the visitor can sense that it is normally a cool room, but Susan felt a very cold spot, often an indicator of a ghostly presence. Then she said, "I get an older woman here, but not the lady from upstairs. I think this lady died in this room." Jo later informed us that a relative of the first owners remembered an elderly relative being waked there before her funeral.

We then turned into a modern combination laundry and bathroom. Sue watched me closely as I entered. At first, I declined to tell my impressions, such as feeling something firm brush my left cheek and then half-hearing and half-seeing a word pass by me. Susan told of her first entry into the room and feeling a sudden energy near the doorway. "At first I felt as if I were walking through a vibrating energy field," she told me.

Then, I related my own experiences. When one intuitively hears words or sounds, it is often difficult to discern the source, or even to credit the sensation as being genuine and not generated out of one's imagination or need to "please" the house owners. My sensation was that of the word "twins" appearing on a rectangular piece of paper, like ticker tape, which floated quickly past my line of vision. We had agreed to say what we "got," or I might easily have dismissed this event. Jo got a big smile on her face. "See those hooks on the top of the door frame? When my nephew Andrew was a child, we had a swing here. He loved to swing and copy whatever I said or did. He used to say we two were alike, 'Just like qwins,' he'd say in his baby talk." I was amazed. Apparently I had picked up not on ghost energy but an event from a few years ago.

36

Sue's intuition operates differently from mine, I had learned from experience. She moved quickly to a door that opened into a stairway to the upstairs, seemingly "hot on the trail" of something. We climbed the stairs, and it became clear that she was hearing something that I couldn't hear or see. "Hear that?" she queried. "It's a baby crying." I heard nothing, but as we moved more into the center of the large room, something struck my left chest, near the heart. For a moment, I wondered if I had picked up on some prior resident having a heart attack there. Then Sue continued, "I *knew* there was a baby here. I could hear it yesterday."

That statement dumbfounded Jo and the others, including me, when we did a debriefing in the kitchen after our house tour. Susan has a unique technique of presensing a place during the day before we go there. Neither of us knew a thing about the Van Lints or their house, and Sue loves to test her intuition ahead of our trips by quieting herself at home, entering a meditative or receptive state, and asking for a clue. She fully expected, and experience has shown that her expectations are usually realized, a baby to be involved with the house when we got there.

We stood quietly in the sunny upper room, awaiting sensations. At first, I received a mental image of long logs awaiting cutting into smaller pieces, though I didn't believe such activities were a part of this room's history. Then Sue tuned more profoundly into the sensations of a baby. "I'm sensing a woman sitting here rocking a baby, and I hear the rocker creaking. But the poor baby cries and cries. I think the infant must have died in here."

There were only boxes and power tools there, but no bed, when we visited. "I see a wicker, old-fashioned baby carriage, too. Maybe the baby is in that, instead of a bed," Sue added. "The mother knew the baby was going to die, and after its death, she sat here and sobbed and sobbed." The strong emotion of her sixth sense moved us both. When we later did our debriefing on the day with Gordon and Jo, they agreed that they, too, had several times heard a baby crying upstairs in that room, though it was under construction and unoccupied. Then Jo smiled, reached into a drawer, and produced a photo of the Nichols family from the late 1800s. Prominent in the picture was a wicker baby carriage with a small child inside. Was this our crying baby?

When we descended to the kitchen, before we began our debriefing, we walked through the modern kitchen and out onto a closed-in back porch that runs across the rear of today's house. As we moved through the kitchen, I half-heard a narration, "Now we're going out to the ice house." I sensed that an open porch once ran across the entire back of the house, but Gordon said that the original house had no back porch at all. As to the existence of an ice house, nobody knew. I believed ice houses to be rather large, but there were only the foundations of small outbuildings behind the house. There *was* a large pond across the road and another way back toward the rear of the property, but whether or not these were ever used for cutting ice for storage during the winter, we were unable to know. Gordon said that there were apparently several buildings behind the house over the years, though nothing as massive as the traditional ice storage building.

Sue was also drawn to exit the back door onto today's porch, and, like me, she felt it had once been open. Apparently, today's porch was constructed entirely by Gordon since they bought the house in 1986. During our debriefing, Gordon and Debbie, a neighbor, told us of a tragic situation involving a former neighbor named Maggie who once lived far behind the old Nichols house in a rusted mobile home. "It's a sad tale," Gordon said. "She had two children, though she never married. The first one was given away for adoption, while the second one died (around 1944, we estimated) and was surreptitiously buried at the rear of the property in an unmarked grave. In the wintertime, when neighborhood boys revved their snowmobiles through her property, Mildred would open her door and scream at the boys, "Don't run over my baby!" So, in a way, two babies played a part in the house's past, to say nothing of Jo's niece and nephew.

Audrey, a friend of Debbie, was new to the process of investigating a "haunted house," and Sue took her through the house, teaching her how to sense energies. Before she finished, Audrey had sensed energies near Andrew's room and the upstairs "Baby Room." Most people need instruction in learning to use their sensitivity, but once they learn to quiet themselves and understand how to "feel," their talent can be improved.

"You know, David, where you sensed the man in the living room, my niece, Atajah, has often seen a ghost man. He waves at her, and she happily waves back," Jo told me. And the girl's brother, Andrew, has apparently encountered some phenomena in that room at the top of the stairs.

"Back in 1986, soon after we moved in, I saw a filmy lady just outside the 'Roses Room' near the wood stove," Jo told us. "She was more modern than the older ladies you saw, though, with black hair puffed out in the '50s or '60s styles. She had a bow in her hair, too. She just stood there. At that time, I slept in that room on a full-size water bed. One morning, I awoke while facing the other side of the bed. There was a guy sleeping there, with his face about a foot away from mine. I didn't know what to do. He had a fisherman's hat on his head! How did he *do* that, and where did he come from? He vanished after a while, anyway." I now sleep in the "Dark Bedroom," but not very well. It seems like once an hour all night long, I feel a hand touch my upper arm, and it always wakes me up," she said. Sue and I both told her that she might try talking (or complaining) to the ghost. "Tell him to stop, that you don't like it," Sue said.

"I always keep the porch light on when Gordon is out at night," Jo said, "and after dark one night in the summer of 2002, I looked out the front window and saw a man standing out near our driveway with his hands in his pocket. For a minute or so, I thought he was real, and I wondered who he was and what he wanted. Then, suddenly, I knew he was a ghost. He stayed there for about fifteen minutes before he faded out. He wasn't rich, as he had on a plaid shirt and work pants, probably the spirit of a farmer or workman. When Gordon came in I asked him, 'Weren't you just back there?' but he denied it. Anyway, the guy didn't look like my husband, but I had to *ask*."

Jo seems to be both amused and troubled by "the others" that she cohabits with. "One night I woke up and realized that I had to go to the bathroom, but I suddenly spotted a woman standing at the foot of the bed. I would have had to walk through her, and I didn't want to, so I stayed put until she vanished," she grinned.

"When Andrew and Natajah stay with us, they often sense some of those 'others,' too," Jo continued. "During the summer of 2004, hoping to get a night away from the ghosts, Andrew went over to Debbie's to sleep overnight with her son, Gabe. He returned home quite early the next morning, sleepy-eyed and complaining. "I had an awful night. That lady (ghost) wouldn't leave me alone. She'd stand in the doorway and wave." When Jo queried the boy, it seemed that he was seeing the lady from the '50s. On occasion, it seems that some of the ghosts migrate, if only briefly, to Debbie's house, which stands about one hundred yards away. Sue and I instructed all concerned as to methods to send the ghosts peacefully on their way. Talking often does the trick; the spirits need to know they are dead and that something better awaits them.

This spot, with just two houses, is an area of active ghosts, though they don't induce terror in the residents, as is sometimes the case with hauntings. "The whole thing may end up being a moot point," Gordon told us, "because what really scares us is that a big mining outfit has bought up most of the land and houses along here, over into the town of Hartford. Pretty soon, if they get their way, they'll be blasting so often every day that no self-respecting ghost will want to stay around. Maybe these two nice houses that both families have worked so hard on will be just a part of vanished history one day soon. The ghost people won't even have their old buildings to cling to."

Jessie

The Old Babcock House

Americans put a great amount of life's energy into their projects and homes. The American Dream is to one day have a castle in which to enjoy retirement, a concept unknown in much of the Third World. Though *The Bible* enjoins us, "Lay not up for yourselves treasures upon earth, where moth and rust doth corrupt, and where thieves break through and steal,..." it is still our national pastime. Thus, when the end of life comes, and often unexpectedly, it may be hard for the departing spirit to abandon a lifetime of striving. Here is a story from Stony Point, NY, that may illustrate this dilemma.

Eric and Maria Molders found a dream house at 563 Willow Grove Road in 1997. It was a solid and pretty house, and the real estate agent could trace its pedigree back to 1917, when Ernest and Jessie Babcock built it. Ernest worked on the construction with his two brothers. In time, Babcock and his son would build similar homes on adjoining plots of land. After Jessie's death, Ernest lived there until he died. The stone exterior of the houses came from rock quarried only across the road. It sounded like a real family house, Maria told me, and they were eager to move in.

"It was somewhat upsetting during those first two years that, though Eric and I both worked away from the house during the day, there were strange sounds during our time at home. Unaccountable squeaks came from the stairway, as if an unseen person were traveling up and down. It is a straight stairway up to the landing, then the steps jog to the left, and after one more step, one reaches the top. That landing, however, is a center of ghostly activity, we decided.

"I have pictures hanging there to decorate what would otherwise be bare walls. One day, I recognized that someone had been reorganizing the art work. Some frames were crooked, some were turned toward the wall, and others seemed to be hanging upside down or in a new location. I asked Eric about it, and he said he thought *I* was rearranging them to get the display just right. Not him. Not me. Then who? Also, there is a rather complicated mechanism for securing the Andersen window that the previous owner installed on the landing. One must first unlock it, then crank a handle to open the window—difficult enough for a living person," Maria told me. "Too many times, when we've been certain the window is locked at bedtime, we find it standing open in the morning. By 1998 we suspected a ghost."

While they were sorting out the stairway events, both noticed that the house's heavy, old wooden doors would slam themselves from time to time. "At first, it was easy to explain away as being caused by a breeze. But, after a while, we *knew* that wasn't it," Maria explained.

"Eric works in construction as a career, so the thought of completely rebuilding the stairs to end the squeakiness wasn't a bit daunting to him. He ripped out the old carpet and installed new oak risers and treads," she told me. "Brand new, no more squeaks!" Nevertheless, within a year the squeaks returned. Who or what was walking those stairs? "Our cats were wondering too," Maria laughed. "One of them often engaged the 'whoever' by sitting on the landing, looking upward and staring. *At what*, we couldn't imagine. From time to time, she would paw the air. The other cat sat at the bottom of the stairs and meowed. When Eric and I planned to be away for a week, a girlfriend of mine agreed to house-sit and feed the cats. When we returned, she told us that she moved out after three days, and only came in the house briefly during the rest of the week to feed the kitties. Slamming doors and squeaky stairs had unnerved her. Both cats have since died and now we have dogs.

"The oldest of our dogs won't go upstairs by himself if our spirit is active. He sits at the stair bottom and whimpers. He won't attempt climbing the stairs, and if we want him up, we have to carry him. Even so, he whimpers when we get to the landing. When upstairs, he won't go down either; he has to be carried down."

Maria told me that her sister, Gloria, stayed with them in 1998 and noticed, while seated on Maria's bed one day, that she could see a filmy mist out on the landing. Maria, herself, later saw the vapor. It never quite coalesced into a recognizable shape though, she said. I asked her whether or not she knew the sex of the ghost. I suspected a female ghost, as few male ghosts care to rearrange pictures.

"I had no suspicion which gender the spirit was at first, but after two years of that activity, I decided it was time to get some history on the house" she said. "We knew from the house title that the Babcocks built it, and neighbors soon told us that the couple had lived here until the late 1940s, when

Jessie died. Shortly thereafter, about 1950, after Ernest died, his family put the house up for sale. Though there had been other owners since the Babcocks left, the mystery seemed to center on Ernest and Jessie." Who is hanging around? Why? Maria wanted to know. The long-time neighbors usually looked around furtively before confiding the rest of the story to her.

It seems that Jessie's last months were painful ones, as she was slowly dying of an illness that most remembered as cancer. One day, she had gone to Ernest and told him she could no longer stand the racking pain and diminished capacity to move about. She begged him to shoot her or poison her or *something* to put her out of her misery, the neighbors said. But Ernie was a pretty upright man and couldn't accept Jessie's request at first. Nevertheless, as painful days became agonizing months, his heart broke at her suffering.

One day, the story went, as the couple stood at the top of the stairs, about to descend painfully, Ernest gave a sudden, forceful push, and Jessie crashed down onto the landing, then bumped and banged to the foot of the stairs, where she no longer moved. Her spirit passed. When the Coroner came to rule on the death, the word "*homicide*" never entered his thinking. It was an obvious case of accidental death, so he signed the death certificate and Jessie's funeral was held. For another year, Ernest tried to mend his shattered heart, and then put the beloved house that he'd built up for sale.

It all seemed to fit. The landing would almost certainly have been where Jessie would have received her first physical and emotional trauma, very likely a shattered bone of some sort. As she wasn't expecting to die at that time, there must remain some residue of astonishment or fear at that spot. Maybe she's trying to open a window of understanding on that landing. It is entirely likely that she doesn't know she's dead, and, of course, those who can't be certain that life has ended usually hang around trying to get life going again.

"A guy up the street jokes with me that I should put a cup of coffee at the top of the stairs because Jessie loved coffee. So far, I haven't given in to that," Maria told me, "but maybe someday. She's still here, and I talk to her as a friend. 'After all,' I say, 'it was *your* house, Jessie, so I'm not going to throw you out.' I've begun to think she evaluates our guests when they come over, too," she told me. "After visitors leave, the noises and banging are more frequent for a while. Maybe she just has little tantrums at having strangers in. Of course, Eric and I no longer count—we're *family* in her mind, I'm pretty sure."

Maria told me that a few years ago, she and Eric considered moving from the nice old house, and they put it on the market. When the first prospective buyers showed interest and came to view the house, they found a foot of water standing in the cellar. "Now that is *impossible*," Maria told me. "We have sump pumps down there, and they've *always* worked with even the smallest amount of water. And the day after the prospects refused to make an offer on our house, the water was all mysteriously gone!

"The next potential customer came, and as they toured the house that rainy day, they found water dripping through the roof. You couldn't miss the big stain on the ceiling. But Eric had put a *new roof* on just two years before! Those people left on the run. When we went to repair the roof the next day, we couldn't find any water, dampness, or even the ceiling stain. It was all just impossible, except that there were a number of witnesses. So we were full of hopes when the third buyer came.

"On that day, they looked into the backyard and were aghast at the overflowing septic tank, and the prospects made tracks right down Willow Grove Road! The next day, there was no evidence of septic malfunction. Shortly after that, I developed a medical problem that needed attention, and we cancelled the sale, taking the house off the market. Thanks *a lot*, Jessie! In retrospect, though, I think she just didn't want to lose us."

Eric and Maria have no children at present, and I wondered aloud what child visitors would do to the domestic atmosphere. "Strange that you ask," she told me, "because my sister has two children and when they visited recently, her two year-old girl did a lot of running through the house. Gloria asked her to please stop making a racket. 'But Mom, I want to keep playing with the lady,' the youngster pleaded."

I visited the family in early May of 2006 and enjoyed the warm atmosphere in the house. After I left, Maria e-mailed me that Jessie must have been listening in on us. After Eric returned from work that night, the couple discussed my visit and interview and the prospect of Jessie's suffering appearing in print. Suddenly, a wooden Indian axe that has been displayed on the wall for nine years, suddenly fell to the floor, missing the youngest dog's head by an inch, and broke into three pieces when it hit the floor. We assume that she still wants to call the shots and resume her role as mistress of the house.

Thus, it looks as if Jessie has finally found an existence free from pain and suffering, and things are looking up again. Wherever Ernest went, she now has a *new* family, and little kids come to play! And even the dogs can be counted on as companions, sometimes. What Heaven? She likely thinks she's already *there*.

CHAPTER 2
GRANDPARENTS

Gramps

Here is a story that some readers might find incredible, but veteran ghost story readers will read it with a knowing smile. Many times, the deceased appear to us in dreams because our conscious mind, which is full of self-protectiveness and doubt, is sublimated when we are in the dream state, so spirits can "get through" to us.

Frank Draganchuk was a hardy man who drove poultry trucks from the Warwick area down to New York City for many years, hefting the crates on and off the truck. In deer season, he tramped throughout New York State with his son, Frank, and other family members, almost always getting his buck. However, he never killed an animal that he didn't eat. He loved nature and fed all kind of creatures in his back yard: deer, turkeys, doves, songbirds, and crows.

He led a vigorous life well into his eighties, but his rugged frame slowly began to show its age. First, there were knee surgeries, then difficulties in his legs. Next, there was hip surgery. Eventually, he could no longer avoid using a walker, which became his constant companion in 2002. In the nursing home, he continued to request seed for the birds outside and spent hours watching the wildlife feeding in their freedom, which he envied. Medications began to take their toll on his overall wellness, and he took his last steps in 2004. Further difficulties made it hard for him to communicate as he lay waiting for his inevitable end. He kept asking his family when he could go home and, finally, on October 21ˢᵗ, 2005, he drew his last breath and made that journey.

This passing was difficult for his family, but they continued life as normally as they could. On New Year's Day, I received an e-mail from my niece, Denise, Frank Sr.'s granddaughter. I scanned it quickly because I thought it might be more ominous family news, but instead I found it a delightful tale that I want to share with readers.

"I hadn't done anything unusual the previous day," Dee wrote, "except to stay up a little later than usual. Then I went to bed, keeping an eye on my new baby, Emily. In the night, I roused a bit and became aware that Gramps was standing beside my bed. I was overjoyed to see him walking again. He began to speak and informed me that he was okay now and that I shouldn't be sad for him as he was in a good place. Everything he said to me made sense, and I felt relieved in a way that I can't explain. Then, I was amazed to find us dancing! What a treat for me and for Grandpa. It was a waltz, I think, and for a while I savored just being with him. Then it all faded, and I came to a different level of wakefulness and had to move Emily to her bed. That was when I noted the time—2:30 a.m. The sense of his presence was still so strong that I *knew* he had been there with me.

"When I remembered it so vividly in the morning, I even told my older kids about the experience. That Friday night my parents came down for the New Year holiday, and I just blurted out the story because I was so happy from the experience. When I finished, Mom had a funny look on her face. 'But, Dee, I had a very similar experience the same night!' It was such a nice feeling, and my heart has truly been at peace with his death since then. I had always known he was in a better, beautiful place, but this dream really confirmed it."

E.T.

Former Treta Apartment House

Ernestine Treta wobbled when she walked. This trait was the result of a horrible childhood accident that mutilated her legs. In her elder years, besides cardiac problems, she also had severe arthritis, especially in her hands. These handicaps, however, never slowed her down; though she needed a walker or wheelchair at times, Ernestine was constantly busy around her Lyon Place home in Utica. Her grandchildren affectionately called her "E.T." because of her unsteady gait. She bore the nickname with pride after a Spielberg film of that name was released.

Ernestine's adult son, Alex, (everyone knew him as "Uncle Johnny,") was handicapped by *spina bifida* and lived with his mother. Many times, people were fooled by his awkward appearance, thinking him severely handicapped, as he walked with his head down on his right shoulder and used a cane. Not hindered by his challenges, Uncle Johnny earned a degree from Utica College of Syracuse University and was employed as an advocate for the handicapped in the City of Utica. It was his campaign to make all public facilities accessible to the handicapped.

E.T. and Johnny lived downstairs in the house and rented the upstairs to tenants. One day, when Ernestine was out, Johnny, now in his late forties, maneuvered his wheelchair onto a power lift at the back door. For some unknown reason, the wheelchair tumbled from the platform, and Johnny fell headfirst onto the sidewalk. It was two hours before a neighbor spotted Johnny, who was unconscious, and the ambulance was called.

Granddaughter Juliane Lupino remembers that her parents were summoned to Johnny's hospital bedside. Johnny was on a respirator and the prognosis was poor. Johnny's brain had begun to swell and other medical complications developed. "It was a horribly difficult decision to make," Juliane told me, "but my mother, Sandra, had to make the difficult decision as to whether or not to keep Uncle Johnny on life support. The doctors recommended letting him die in peace. Mom finally agreed to that choice, though she had a very difficult time with it.

"Following Johnny's burial, Grandma lived alone in the downstairs. The upstairs tenants moved out when my mom and Aunt Judy decided to fix it up so that my youngest sister, Jinette, and her daughter, Kouryn, could live there. Grandma was very happy to have family upstairs and was thrilled to hear Baby Kouryn's feet scampering about overhead. However, Jinette soon began to hear strange noises in her apartment, though she kept her experiences to herself, so the baby wouldn't be upset.

"Nevertheless, one day Kouryn (who was two at the time) asked her mother, 'Who's here, Mommy?' The child told of hearing footsteps passing her on the hardwood floors. Jinette responded, 'No one, honey,' but she now knew that someone *was* with them in spirit. Jinette called her mother one night, begging her parents to come right over. The young mother had heard strange noises in the attic. Mom and Dad brought Jake, the family dog, to stay with Jinette and provide security. They clearly heard the slow footsteps overhead, but they decided not to go into the attic to investigate.

"That night, Jake became very anxious, pacing and acting strangely. The poor canine just couldn't stay still; every few minutes he'd shift position or jump to his feet to investigate the apartment. *Something* had his attention." Jake was so nervous in the apartment that the young mother finally had to call her parents to come pick up the dog, as he was as much a concern as the phantom walker overhead. On other visits to the upstairs apartment, Jinette's mother also heard not only footsteps but also doors closing when nobody else was there.

Jinette had many figurines on the large mantle over the fireplace, but they were placed far enough back from the edge so that Kouryn couldn't reach them. One day there came a crash, and Jinette found a bust of the Virgin Mary broken on the floor. There was no logical explanation for its falling. "In retrospect," Juliane said, "we're certain that the incident was caused by Uncle Johnny, attempting to let us know he was still with us. Jinette was frightened but accepted that if it was indeed her uncle, he would never harm the family."

Downstairs, Ernestine was having a difficult time physically and, because of her handicap, found it more comfortable to sleep in her old upholstered chair than in a bed. The family didn't understand that E.T. was developing congestive heart failure until a sudden emergency caused her hospitalization. The doctors discovered later that she was having many small heart attacks because of fluid retention. Her body was greatly swollen, and her heart was laboring mightily. Daughters Sandra and Judy asked the doctor to discontinue all of E.T.'s medications. With the use of a diuretic, Ernestine's blood pressure soon normalized, and she began to shed weight. "She must have lost 100 pounds," Juliane told me, "and I didn't recognize her when I finally got to visit her.

"One day as we visited with her, Grandma told us of an experience at home before her emergency. She had awakened from a nap and saw Uncle Johnny standing in the living room with a cane in his hand. His head was now erect and he looked healthy. It had been two years since he died. With a smile, Uncle Johnny beckoned and called to her, 'Come on, mama. Come with me.' But she knew she wasn't yet ready to go. She got better and was released to St. Joseph's Nursing Home on Genesee Street.

"Grandma spent the last four years of life there, happily involved in daily activities, crafts, and games," Juliane told me. "Many friends and family members came to visit, and they even planted a tree in her honor there."

Juliane was now a sophomore at the State University in Albany but came home to visit E.T. on many weekends. One weekend, Juliane asked her mother what time she planned to visit her Grandma. Sandra said that she had already gone earlier that morning. The girl was distraught, as she treasured each minute with her grandmother. Still, she couldn't understand why she was so upset, because her mother promised they'd visit together on the next weekend. Two days after she returned to school, Sandra called her to inform Juliane that E.T. had died suddenly. The funeral was very difficult, as was the necessity of returning to college immediately thereafter.

"Several weeks later," Juliane told me, "I was staying over with my friend Amy, a girl I knew from work in Albany, and I had a vivid dream. It began in a deli shop with high, glass-enclosed counters along the side of the

48

room and across the front. I remember a long line of older people in front of me, placing orders and being served their food. I remember fidgeting horribly and being incredibly impatient. And then, behind the counter, I saw Grandma, hobbling without a wheelchair or walker, preparing sandwiches and serving the people. I couldn't stand still and nervously kept looking around. 'Come on, come *on*,' I kept thinking. Grandma stopped and looked down at her hands, which she held in front of her. Referring to her arthritic swelling, she said, 'Oh, these hands!' I continued to be impatient for my turn to see her.

"Finally, all the others disappeared, and it was my turn at the counter. Grandma stood back and just looked at me. She said, 'What would you like, honey?' I was fidgeting horribly and looking all around the deli; 'Um, um,' was all I could say. I couldn't decide and didn't know what to order. Finally, Grandma said, 'Honey, it's *alright*. I'm okay. I'm fine, don't worry about me.' My fidgeting stopped at those words, and I made eye contact with her as she reassured me that she was fine, and I shouldn't worry about her—that I should *let go*."

Juliane remembers awakening and sobbing, feeling a great sense of relief, though still missing her grandmother. "I no longer harbor any guilt about not having seen her one last time before her death. *She* came to see *me*, to speak to me and let me see her one last time, and for that, I'm grateful."

So many of our loved ones return soon after their passing to assure us of their well-being as they enter the Next World, if only we can muster the courage to hear and see them as they begin their journey into Pure Love.

Isabel

Ghost stories told by children are some of the most provoking tales I've come across. Few young children are able to fantasize or confabulate believable stories, so here is one of my favorites, one which offers no easy explanation.

Helen Cackener, of Queensbury, NY, a wonderful Adirondack story teller, collected this tale from the Daly family, longtime residents of Washington County, NY.

In 1881, Isabel Henry Daly presented her husband Patrick Brian (P.B.) with a beautiful daughter, also named Isabel. The Dalys had farmed a piece of land east of Hudson Falls, along the banks of the Champlain Canal for years, and grew prize-winning potatoes. Their immediate area, called Dunham Basin, is the site of the junction of the old Feeder Canal and the sixty-mile-long Champlain Canal. After major rainstorms and the resulting water runoff, the area is prone to sudden flooding.

Canal fans remember that the present day Champlain Canal was re-routed by New York State in 1913, leaving the old original ditch abandoned, though it is still visible today. And it is near this old canal that these events took place long before the new channel was excavated.

Little Isabel had reached the age of eight at the time of our story in the springtime of 1889. It was a sunny spring day just a few weeks before the canal was to open for the season, and Isabel wanted to play with her cousins on the other side of the ditch. Promising her mother to be home before supper, the girl skipped happily over the rough wood bridge that spanned the water.

About 4 p.m., however, the cloud cover off to the west thickened and darkened, flashes of lightning appeared on the horizon, and a downpour ensued. It rained heavily for an hour before abating, and the water level rose dangerously as torrents of rain poured from the Feeder Canal and into the Champlain Canal, rising almost to the tow path at the top.

Patrick, Isabel's father, became concerned that suppertime had arrived, but Isabel had not. He decided to walk the path to the old bridge to see if he could see his daughter approaching on the trail to home. His heart skipped a beat when he reached the canal—the flash flood had swept away the bridge, and the water was dangerously high. Isabel didn't know how to swim—had a horrible accident befallen his daughter?

He instantly recalled how the child feared the booming noise and lightning flashes of thunderstorms, and he nervously scanned the canal banks. No sight of little Isabel. P.B. then began pacing the muddy old towpath. There was no way to cross the canal to search for the child, and he was greatly fearful for Isabel's safety. He was startled when he spotted his daughter skipping south-ward toward him on the path. This could not be! "Isabel, child, how did you ever cross the canal?" he begged.

"Why, father, I had no trouble at all. Grandfather Henry carried me," she responded happily. Patrick's brow darkened and his face grew hard.

"Now, child, this is no time to be telling me stories," he said sternly. He was well aware that Grandfather Henry had died over two years before.

"But father, he really *did!* I got to the canal and saw all the deep water, and that the bridge wasn't there any more, and I didn't know what I was going to do," the girl said earnestly. "Then I heard Grandfather's voice, and there he was.

"'Child, you seem to be in trouble,' he said.

"Because I was scared by the high water, I was so happy to see him, and I told him, 'Oh, Grandfather, I don't know how I'm going to get home.'

"'Don't worry, child, I'll get you across the water,' he said to me, and he carried me over. And here I am!" she said, looking quite pleased with the outcome of the whole matter.

P.B. didn't know what to say. Surely, his child stood before him. And, just as surely, there was no way to cross the canal for miles in any direction. Yet here was his precious Isabel, dry and happy. For years to come, after P.B.'s death, the Daly family repeatedly told the story in wonder of the apparent miracle. For her part, Isabel recounted the story until the time of her own death, never deviating from the facts of long ago.

Until his death, Patrick Brian Daly continued to puzzle over his part in a great mystery that he could not fathom. All he knew is that love had prevailed; he loved Isabel as much as Grandfather Henry had, and that was *that*. Everything else, even death, was just details!

Confirmation

"If I ever had any doubts about life after death, I sure don't now," Andrea told me with a laugh. A vivacious widow, she lives in Massapequa, NY, and works in the field of public education. When she was younger, in 1966, her grandmother died. Then, four months later, her grandfather passed over. On the night of his death, Andrea was in her mother's house and could hear her grandmother calling the grandfather's name. "That was pretty impressive," she remembers, "but I really didn't think of it as being *ghostly*, just a family love kind of thing."

In retrospect, it seems that the world of spirit was just warming up Andrea, preparing her for new horizons. One day in 1973, the now married Andrea was cleaning the room in which Grandpa had died. By then, all that remained in the room was Grandpa's old red recliner chair. Accompanied by her puppy, Pal, she began cleaning other rooms and, as she passed the door to Grandpa's empty room, she could hear labored breathing inside.

"I slowly opened the door to look, but I knew all I'd see was the old chair. Pal ran into the room and ran directly to Grandpa's old chair, circling it and barking. The loud breathing stopped, but I figured it must have been Grandpa, who had died of emphysema, just coming back for a visit," she said. Finally, the house was ready for my husband and me to move in. We had no children then, just Ralphie, our big English sheepdog, who always slept at the foot of our bed.

"That first night after we moved in, we'd gotten to bed around 10 p.m., and Ralphie was settled in his space on the floor. Then, just as we drifted off to sleep, there came slow and heavy footsteps out on the stairs. Ralphie shot under the bed, and I grabbed my husband, Lou's, arm. He was a big guy, but his size was no help against an intruder that couldn't be seen. Lou went down the hall to the spare bedroom, from which most of the noises came, and the sounds stopped, but he felt an icy cold. Was it Grandpa? Was it one of the Krichmars, the previous owners? We never figured out."

In time, that room became daughter Nicole's bedroom. In high school Nicole had a boyfriend named Joe, who was curious about some of the tales the girl told. One day when he came to visit, the boyfriend heard the phantom footsteps. When Nicole was in college and returned for a weekend visit, she had a disturbing experience. "You see, we carpeted the house when we moved in, but in Nicole's room, under the carpet, there was a loose board that squeaked when a person stepped on it just right. On Nicole's weekend, I awoke at 2 a.m., hearing that board squeak. I wondered if Nicole had gotten up to go to the bathroom, and I suddenly heard her shriek, 'Mom, there's somebody in my room!' She wasn't out of bed but had heard that sound, too. Lou ran into the room and found our daughter shaking, but nobody else present—nobody we could *see*, anyway!" Andrea told me.

"Another night, in 1995, Lou and I were at a party and it was about 3 a.m. Suddenly we got a phone call from Nicole, who was babysitting—she'd heard the sound again. We hurried home, but as you might guess, there was nobody else there. Nicole also told us that she had felt icy cold in the room from time to time, but Tina, who was five years younger, had heard nothing from *her* bedroom and wondered what the fuss was all about."

Andrea had so many stories to relate. One involved a smoke detector that she wanted Lou to install. One day, it disappeared from the shelf, and she assumed he had put it on a wall someplace, as she had requested. A few days later, as Andrea worked in the kitchen, something round shot past her head. Lou was outside barbecuing and a small amount of smoke had entered the kitchen. She looked at the floor and discovered the smoke detector. She called Lou inside and asked how the detector could fly. Sheepishly, he informed her that he had simply placed it atop the kitchen cabinet, propped against the wall, where it could function, though not be seen. "Flying smoke detectors? That was enough for me. I went to the Yellow Pages and looked for a parapsychologist! In the end, though, that guy offered no real help."

Andrea was stunned in September 1996 when her brother, Joe, a very sensitive guy, died in Daytona Beach, Florida. He had been in Massapequa only two months before, visiting all his relatives and had seemed so healthy. They had gotten together at Robert Moses State Park Beach on a beautiful day, and the family had a great time together. Now he had suddenly gone. "I often went to the beach at Moses State Park because it is so beautiful; the beach seems to stretch on forever. One warm day in April 1997, I went to the beach just to walk and think. Almost nobody was there, so it was perfect for my purposes.

All at once, as I walked along, I realized I was at the spot where Joey and I had our last conversation. I sat down and, closing my eyes, started to doze. Suddenly, something hit me on the leg—a grazing hit. I opened my eyes, expecting to see a sea gull, but nobody and nothing was in sight. Could it have been Joe, saying, '*See*? I'm still here. What a great time we had!' Aloud, I yelled, 'Joey!' There was no further response. Joe was a smoker, and, you know, sometimes when I'm driving, I still all of a sudden smell cigarette smoke in the car, and I wonder, is it Joey?

"These strange events helped focus countless other experiences that had only seemed odd at the time they occurred," she told me. In 1989, she and Lou had fixed up a basement bedroom for their son, Louis, when he was eleven. "He always said that he heard things down there, but nothing really scared him," she remembers. "One morning, I went to the door at the top of the cellar stairs and turned the doorknob. It came right off in my hand! What made *that* happen?

"1999 was a particularly strange year for us. Nicole was in college in Islip, and Tina was a junior in high school. Louis had joined his dad in the roofing business, and the two of them were usually up and out of the house before 6 a.m. every morning. One morning at 6:30, when I was pretty sure those two had gone, I heard someone running up the basement stairs. Must be Tina, I concluded, probably getting something for school out of the dryer. A minute later she emerged from the bathroom. 'What were you downstairs for?' I asked. 'I heard you running up the stairs.'"

"'*Me*? I thought it was *you*—I just got out of the shower!' Tina exclaimed. We never solved that one either."

In July 1998, just before her seventieth birthday, Lou's mother had a stroke and called Andrea. As Lou sped to his mother's house, Andrea told her mother–in–law to sit tight; Lou was coming. She then called the South Farmingdale Fire Department ambulance. Mom was in good shape when she reached the hospital that Monday night, and Andrea resolved she'd visit on Tuesday. Though Lou visited with his mom the next day, Andrea had too much to do but assured herself that nothing would prevent her from visiting mom the next day. As she prepared to leave for the hospital on Wednesday, Lou's van suddenly pulled into the driveway. Downcast, Andrea's husband emerged and told her that Mom had suddenly died.

"It was such a difficult period. I lost my dad in 1994, Joey in 1996, and Mom in 1998. We had Mom's letter saying she wanted a closed casket funeral, so I gave it to Lou to take to the funeral director, while I went over to Mom's house to clean out her refrigerator. I felt so bad that I had not gotten to see her one last time. Mom's wake was on Friday, then the funeral on Saturday.

I was exhausted and dropped into bed Saturday night. Then, strangely, I awoke around midnight. Something was up, even though I heard no sound. In our bedroom doorway, there was a soft golden glow, and in that light, I saw my smiling mother-in-law, looking relaxed and beautiful. Then she just vanished.

"The next day, as Lou and I were driving down Broadway in Massapequa, I told him I'd seen his mother the night before. I described her hair style and the blue-flowered button-down polyester blouse she wore with its top button open. Remembering the previous night's vision, I also told him she'd been buried in her jeans and white Keds. Lou pulled over and sat there stunned. He knew I hadn't gone to the funeral home with him to help pick out Mom's burial clothes, and he knew the casket had been sealed during the wake and funeral. He just couldn't believe I'd seen all that or that his mother had come to our house to let me see her one last time," Andrea said with a happy smile.

Not long afterward, in 2001, Lou died. His family grieved; he was just too young to pass away. Then, a few weeks later, as is often the necessity, the family gathered in the living room to sort out some of Lou's possessions. Suddenly the room was filled with the scent of cigar smoke, and they all smelled it. Cigars were one of Lou's passions—was he just checking in to let the family know he was still around?

Recently, as her house-sitter, Joe, was readying for bed, he heard the kitchen stove timer go off. "In thirty-three years of living here, that *never* happened!" she said. "And I haven't used the timer since Christmastime, when I was baking. Joe never uses the timer or the stove, only the microwave. And the timer is a very hard gadget to use, as one has to turn and push it really hard, so it's not likely someone jiggled it. Joe said it all happened after he heard footsteps, though he was alone there."

So, it continues in Massapequa, as it does elsewhere. The end of life is not the end of love. Andrea has had significant experience with the spirit world, most of it through family events. I surmise that The Creator is getting her ready to do some important work in helping others adjust to death, dying, and grief. So many times, it seems that our personal sorrow becomes a stepping stone to assisting others who don't have adequate resources to deal with Life's Last Great Mystery.

Old Timers

One of the most commonly seen ghosts is the grandparent, often a benign presence whose appearance usually conveys concern or love. Many times, the beneficiaries of these visions are children, whether or not the youngsters recognize the figure(s) or not. Here is a tale of one woman's experiences with grandfathers.

In 2004, Lauren Macchia began dating a guy named Jerry in Centereach. Watching television together one night, she tested her new man to see if he was as sensitive to the other world as she had always been. A few minutes before, she had just spotted a spirit gentleman in a chef's hat and wondered if Jerry would panic at the revelation. "Chef's hat? That's probably my grandfather," he answered unfazed. "Grandpa was a chef." A short time later, Lauren spotted a transparent man walking through the bedroom closet. Knowing it was a ghost, the pair did some investigation and discovered that the closet had formerly been a hallway and that a former deceased owner of the house had also been a baker, who died in a bakery accident. "That was a pretty good start, I thought," Lauren told me, "so I told Jerry the whole thing about my past. I don't think he even blinked once," she smiled.

At age nine, she told her new beau, she spotted a stranger in her house as she passed an open door in the hallway. She first noticed the man with surprise—was he a visitor? Studying the figure, she noted his spread-leg stance as the elderly man had clasped his hands behind his back while studying a photo of her grandfather on the wall. He didn't seem to mind being observed, so she took time to notice the grey/green color and the cut of his suit. Finally, curiosity won out and she asked her parents about the man she'd seen. At first, they believed she was making it up until she mentioned the stance. That *was* her grandfather, they finally concluded, though they had never seen his spirit. The strangely colored suit was the uniform he'd worn daily at his elevator operator's job, and that standing position had been his working posture all day, every day.

Jerry liked that tale, so she told him of her next, even more troubling, incident when she was twenty-three. Visiting her friend Dawn's house, she always got an uncanny feeling near a certain doorway in Dawn's hallway—almost as if someone invisible were watching her. It also became clear upon each visit that nobody in Dawn's family ever entered that room. One evening when Dawn was out and Lauren was washing dishes in the kitchen, there suddenly came the distinct imprression that she'd see someone staring at her if she dared to turn around.

She did a slow about-face and was startled to see a white-haired man in the doorway. He wore a blue smoking jacket with a black collar, but he had

55

no face! "Get away from here—you're frightening me," she exclaimed, and the figure vanished. Still unnerved when Dawn returned home, Lauren demanded to know about the apparition. The young woman sat and cried for a short time before telling Lauren that the man was her grandfather.

"That was his bedroom and he spent his last days in there when I was much younger," Dawn related. "He was always unhappy, and one day when he hadn't been seen for hours, I went in and found him dead on the floor. He'd shot himself in the face and there was blood everywhere!" After a while the young woman finished sobbing and took Lauren to another part of the house, where she uncovered a self-portrait of the man. That was *him* alright.

"Time passed, and in 2004, I met Jerry," Lauren said. "We lived in a rented house behind a funeral parlor, a place whose cellar the owner had filled with antiques—especially bikes and toys and dolls and so forth. One day I walked over to the funeral home to pay our rent and had hardly entered the back door when I could go no further. I told Jerry it was if there were a forbidding invisible wall in front of me. Somehow I knew that there was a murderer's body inside the building. I handed over the check and left. A few hours later, Jerry discovered that I had been correct—a murderer's body was being embalmed inside at that time.

"Our house was another matter. I often heard giggles and the sound of little feet running through the house, though Jerry seldom heard the noise. The name, 'Ryan' popped into my head, and I remembered that when we moved in, there had been a baseball bat next to the fireplace that used to move once in a while. On it, I had seen the 'Ryan' brand name. Other than that, however, I knew nothing of the house's history. One day, I spotted a youngster's legs running up the stairs, though I couldn't see the top of his body, so I came to think of the boy as 'Ryan.' Then finally, I spotted him coming from the downstairs hallway and into the kitchen, where I was cooking. Strangely, he wasn't running any more or doing anything joyous. He just walked into nothingness with his head downcast and with his hands jammed in his pockets—he just vanished! A while later, I recognized that the house was too quiet and that he'd probably left for good; I never saw or heard him again. Who he was and where he went, or even *why*, I'll never know. I suspect he might have been attached to the toys in the basement, and he was finally able to relinquish his attachment to them, his childhood, and to the life that he now acknowledged had come to an end.

"In 2005, we bought our present cape-style house in Centereach, and, almost as soon as we moved in, we began to experience strange events. The interior had seemed like a do-it-yourselfer's battleground because many attempts at renovation had been made by the previous owner, but few had come out right. So Jerry got a contractor friend to help us make it look nice again. As they worked, I kept hearing the name 'Harry' in my mind. At the end of a long day, when commenting on the botched renovations, the two of us would joke about Harry.

"Then it became a standing joke. If either of us had had a bad experience during the day, we joked about it being *Harry's* fault. After a few weeks, we met a neighbor who had known the former deceased owner, and the neighbor told us the owner's name *was* Harry! Then, shortly after that, in the midst of my joking about the man, I felt a hand upon my shoulder. It scared me, and I apologized to Harry, but that didn't seem enough. We were living in a finished upstairs apartment at that time, while the downstairs was being renovated, and many strange events occurred up there. When I'd climb the stairs, I could feel or hear Harry coming up behind me. Again, I got very frightened at being so closely followed, and both Jerry and I sincerely apologized again to the man. Finally, those episodes ceased, though we knew he was still around."

It was fascinating to chat with Lauren, as these phenomena just seemed to be an ongoing, no-longer-frightening part of her daily life. "We had trouble with an electrical circuit that kept cutting out, so Jerry decided to ask Harry's help," she told me. "One day, Jerry commented that the wind chimes sounded pretty. I paused to think for a moment and told him we didn't *have* any wind chimes. Yet, the pleasant tinkling continued, and we searched throughout the house to find the source. Finally, down in the cellar, way over near the electric circuit breaker box, we found the cause. A small travel clock stored with some other possessions was chiming away. How it got turned on, we'll never know, but to reach the clock and turn it off, Jerry had to go right up to the breaker box. It was there that he spotted a problem with the switches that had to be corrected. After that, we no longer had an electrical circuit problem—it *had to* have been Harry helping us out!"

Maybe it's because both Lauren and Jerry are sensitive to the other world that the phenomena continue. In April of 2006, Lauren saw a large man wearing a baseball hat, a big shadow really, standing in the living room doorway. At first, she thought it was Jerry, but discovered it wasn't when the figure suddenly vanished. Lauren told me that it gave her something to look forward to each day to have a new character there.

I noted that because she works in the medical profession and is a Scorpio, a sign often associated with healing, perhaps the spirit world is using her sensitivity to prepare her for a new capability to work with ill people, possibly in seeing their auras or intuitively diagnosing their problems. Lauren was right—only time will tell.

CHAPTER 3
HISTORIC BUILDINGS

Caretaking

The Merchant's House Museum

"The distinction of the Merchant's House—and it is a powerful one—is that it is *the real thing*. One simply walks through the beautiful doorway…into another time and place in New York." So wrote a *New York Times* reporter at the time of the museum's rededication in 1990. Enthused as she was by the beauty of the old house, the writer may not have realized how appropriate her choice of words *was*.

My friend Shirley McFerson *did* simply walk into another time there. She was a Renaissance Woman, fascinated with life: art, dance, architecture, folklore, civil rights, travel, and education. Our paths first crossed in May, 1999 when I interviewed Shirley on the subject of ghosts that she had encountered. Retired from her post as librarian for Lake George, NY's, Public Library, she went everywhere and did what her heart desired most. "I've had plenty of experiences with ghosts right here in Lake George," she told me, "but the one experience that moved me the most was at The Merchant's House Museum in New York City. I was visiting The American Ballet Theater that summer, and heard that the beautiful old Tredwell House at 29 E. 4th Street in Manhattan had finished its restoration and was capping it off with a ceremony. How could I miss *that*?" she asked with a smile.

"I got there a bit early, before the ceremony, and spoke to the docent at the door. As soon as I entered, I could feel the presence of others who had no physical form, so I turned and asked the girl if the building was haunted. Very seriously, the young woman replied, 'Definitely *not*. I work here, and if there were ghosts, I'd *know* it!' Well, I was willing to be convinced, but I had this inner knowing, so I chatted up a workman standing in the back. He responded to my question with raised eyebrows. 'Well, I don't know about ghosts, lady, but there *is* something or someone here that *I* can't see.'

"He told me that the Museum had sought a night watchman or caretaker to prevent vandalism during the final months of the restoration, but just couldn't keep a man for long. When each one started his shift in the evening, something happened. I don't know if it was a sight or a sound, but none of them wanted to stay after 3 a.m., the man told me. He said that the museum employed a plumber to modernize some of the piping in the cellar, and, though the man had recently completed the job, he complained loudly every day about 'being watched,' though no one was ever there when he turned around. I told that workman I used to have that *same* feeling in my family's old restaurant in Lake George, so we got along very well.

"Then came time for the ceremony to begin, and everyone gathered in the front parlor area. The new museum director stood facing the front of the double parlor, and behind him, facing the dignitaries, stood the many volunteers who were thrilled to finally be opening the restored room. One costumed woman seemed to arrive late, descending the stairway behind the director. I appreciated her authentic 1800s morning dress costume, and I was surprised that she didn't seem to mind interrupting the ceremony one bit. She seemed to be in her own home as she walked over behind the dignitaries.

"There are two tall windows on the front wall of the house, with a long mirror between them in that parlor. I looked toward the mirror and noticed something very strange. My peripheral vision kept track of the woman walking behind the dignitaries who were reflected in that mirror. But *she* wasn't in the reflection! Back and forth, I scanned. In the room, but not in the mirror—how on earth could she *do* that? But, of course, I knew—she was a ghost."

The old Federal style Tredwell House near Washington Square dates from 1832, having been built by Joseph Brewster, a hat maker who became rich speculating in real estate. A few years later, Brewster sold it to hardware merchant Seabury Tredwell, whose family lived there for almost a century more.

With his wife, Eliza, Tredwell produced two sons and six daughters. The youngest child, Gertrude Ellsworth Tredwell, was born in the house in 1840, and, as she never married, she became the last of the family line to inhabit the place. She died in 1933 amidst period furniture and countless family possessions that have been on display since the museum opened in 1936. It's not that a museum was created there; it was simply *retained* there. Everything was already in place, and provisions only had to be made for visitors—many visitors.

It is my estimate that Gertrude understood that she was the end of the line. She couldn't avoid dying, but she did have control over whether or not to leave that house. I believe that after her death, she discovered that she could remain in the old Greek Revival parlors and walk, with more ease than she had recently been accustomed to, up the stairs to her bedroom each night. Though the servants no longer answer their summons bells, she must be happy to have visitors shown in daily.

60

I have found no other museum so filled with the palpable spirit of American family life, and I am not surprised that Shirley McFerson discovered a higher dimension of that energy than most visitors experience. It is the one home in New York City where one can simply *walk in* upon nineteenth century family life. It's all there: the Duncan Phyfe furniture, the rare antique gas chandeliers, and the display of Tredwell women's ornate dresses spanning America's years of growth.

When I visited in early 2006, I wished my friend Shirley had been able to accompany me, but, since her passing in December 2005, she seems to be off in the universe, researching another dimension of beauty. *Somebody* has to jazz up Heaven!

The Hat

Mike loves history, especially Civil War history, and he recently shared a strange story with me. He has a fascination with antiques, especially military items, and he heard that the honorable discharge papers for a Union soldier from Washington County could be purchased in Pennsylvania. Mike was interested in the service record of the man from Ft. Edward, NY, who had served in the 123rd New York Regiment. At the last minute, he was unable to attend the sale and asked a friend who was going there to buy the documents for him.

The soldier, who mustered into the Union army in Kingsbury, had fought in a number of engagements, specifically the Battle of Gettysburg (July 1-3, 1864). He had seen furious action in the battle area called Culp's Hill, which had always intrigued Mike.

A few years later, on a trip to the battlefield, he had a chance to meet with other Civil War re-enactors gathered there, and before they left the site, a group photograph was taken atop Culp's Hill. The print showed a Union army kepi, or uniform hat, in mid-air over Mike's left shoulder. Was the ghost of a long-dead Union soldier standing there?

The Lost Mohawk

One of the strangest historical tales in New York State is that of Eleazer Williams, born of Mohawk parents somewhere in the New York-New England area around 1787. His birthplace and date weren't recorded at the time, and therein lies the genesis of our story.

He hoped to become a Congregational Church minister, but found his "Indian appearance" to be a detriment in white congregations. What can be said authoritatively about Eleazer is that he took part on the American side in the War of 1812, transferred his religious allegiance to the Episcopal Church in 1815, then sought to lead a group of Central New York State Indians (Oneidas, Mohawks, and Stockbridge Indians) into the Wisconsin wilderness, where he hoped to form an Indian "empire." Though he did create a small reservation near Green Bay, WI, he began to lose the affection of the Oneidas, and then the Episcopal bishop withdrew all ecclesiastical powers. Throughout the period, Williams made fabulous claims of ranks he'd held in the army and titles he had been granted from the U.S. government, though he was unable to document any of it.

Williams entered a new era of self-promotion in 1841 when, after a certain amount of rejection by the Indians he'd hoped to lead, he took a steamboat voyage in Wisconsin. On the boat, he met Prince de Joinville, son of French Emperor Louis Philippe. The men were drawn to one another and conversed for much of the journey. Williams emerged from the tête-à-tête with an audacious claim: that he was the lost son of Louis 16th and Marie Antoinette, and that the Frenchman has sought him out to inform him of his noble birth. Eleazer Williams, after so much ignominy, was the Lost Dauphin of France! That is what he wanted people to believe, though there was not a shred of substantiation, and de Joinville had returned to France.

Supporters at Akwesasne, thrilled to have a Bourbon in rural northern New York State, rallied to his cause and subscribed funds to build an ornate chateau for the pretender at Hogansburg. In order to support his charade, Williams denied his Mohawk birth by Mary Ann Williams, who was devastated by his rejection, and his forging her name to a document stating that she had adopted Eleazer. He lived for some years in what became known as "The Lost Dauphin Cottage," and did some teaching in a Mohawk Reservation school. He provided historian Franklin B. Hough accurate histories of major Mohawk figures, which Hough incorporated into his *History of Franklin and St. Lawrence Counties*. Williams died quietly on August 28, 1858.

The tall A-frame "Lost Dauphin House" aged and became run down. "It was in horrible shape when I bought it in 1978," Phil Tarbell told me. "Whether or not it was ever owned by a Dauphin, I sure put a king's ransom into restoring it," he quipped. In any case, it seems that Phil has at least one ghost in the historic house. Whether the wraith is old Eleazer Williams or another figure is open to conjecture.

"By 2004, the noises and missing objects in the house needed to be explained, so I asked a Canadian psychic, a channeler, to visit us and see if she could shed light on the cause. The woman arrived with a reporter and they toured the house. Then, what was purportedly a spirit speaking through the lady, claimed to feel a sharp pain in the back, as if she'd been shot. Her demeanor was that of a young man in his early thirties, but I just couldn't place such an individual in tribal history," Phil remembers.

The psychic then described another male presence in the house, giving a description that Phil immediately recognized as his deceased grandfather. In another room, the woman gave a physical description of a woman Tarbell recognized as his sister, who had died a year earlier. It was quite a revelation to the former educator that *his* family members were cohabiting the old house.

"As they left," Phil told me, "the woman gave the date of May 1, 1990 and said a young man had been shot and left here to die. I immediately remembered J.R. Edwards, one of the two men shot during the time of the 1990s barricades on the Reservation. Edwards was an innocent bystander at the time of those incitements, and it is plausible that he wasn't ready to depart from the earth at that young age.

"I know your question, David: Is *Eleazer Williams* here also?" Phil offered. "And I can't say that he is. I had no way of knowing the identity of any of the spirits here until the sensitive lady described them to me. Williams lived a troubled life. His desires for fame never were gratified; even his own self-promotion failed. His major contribution to us at Akwesasne is the first-hand historical information that he supplied to the historians. It allows us to raise our young people with the certainty of great heroic men among their ancestors. Eleazer Williams wasn't up to that task, but he did help us *know* our past, so we're grateful for that."

I had to agree with Phil. Many ghosts are deceased individuals who still feel shamed at their supposed failures or inability to reach earthly or egoistic goals. In the end, The Great Spirit may care more about the *quality* of the lives we choose to live than the real or imagined honors we accumulate. It seems that the disquiet in people's souls reverberates for centuries before they can forgive themselves for their imperfection and can accept the invitation of the angels to "come up a little higher at the table."

Susan?

In September 2005, my new friend, Helise Flickstein, sent me an e-mail. A transplanted Long Islander, Helise is passionate about the Suffragettes, women who led the fight for political and social rights for American women during the early 1900s. Flickstein and historian Debbie Craig have embarked

The Anthony House

on a venture to save the Susan B. Anthony house, east of Greenwich, in the hamlet of Battenville.

I had often passed the old house when I drove to and from Salem and remembered the "For Sale" sign that seemed to sit forever on its front lawn. Helise told me that the owners were desperately trying to fend off foreclosure and hoped a non-profit group would purchase the place and donate it as a women's museum. Nice, I thought, but I'm trying to write a ghost book. Then Helise dropped her ace: "Here is a photo I took in the upstairs hall," she told me.

The photograph shows a column of light rising in the upstairs hall near the banister. In that light, some viewers claim to see the lower half of a human figure. I have many photos of orbs given to me, but, as they are so numerous and hard to understand, I tend not to use them. But the proffered photo seemed to indicate a genuine ghostly energy, and I made an appointment with Helise to explore the house with my intuitive friend, Susan.

Helise and I picked up Susan, and as we drove to the house, Sue (seeing our direction and remembering a recent story about the house in the *Post Star*), asked, "It's the Anthony House, right?" I had to confess, yes, it was. Sue told us that (as she always does) she had meditated about our jaunt the previous day. "I kept getting the impression of an old abandoned house." Helise responded that "Yes, that would be Susan's sister Guelma's house, which is next door. Susan B. told in her autobiography that she had been in love with her sister's husband." That is all the information we gave her.

A few minutes later, we parked along the side of Route 29 and went to the house, where one of the owners, Paul Franke, greeted us. Our normal procedure is for Susan to tour the house alone first, and she did so while I talked with Helise and co-owner, Paul. When Susan descended the stairs at the end of

64

her upstairs tour, I noticed moisture on her cheeks. This was uncharacteristic of Sue, who is an upbeat woman. "You okay?" I asked.

"Yes, you'll see later," she responded.

Then, as usual, the two of us toured the house. In the cellar, I heard the word, "parasol," though there was no context for it. I heard wood being chopped, though Susan didn't. As we looked at the steep hill immediately behind the house, I heard or imagined the word "trumpet," followed by the term "forward-looking." Again, no follow up, no apparition, or any other phenomenon occurred.

Finishing the downstairs, Sue and I walked up the main staircase. As we wandered through today's bedrooms, I heard "Morgan" and "ordinary ways on ordinary days." None of this seemed connected to anything else. So we approached the top of the stairs, where Sue heard a "Shhh!" in her right ear. She told me that all during her solitary tour of the house, she had felt a strong urge to look out at the house next door. At the top of the stairs was a window from which we could do just that. This was near the position of the light column in the photo (which Susan had never seen), so I took my lead from her. "What do I do now?" I inquired.

"Make a turn to your right, around the banister, and go over to that window," she instructed. I did as directed, but could see little of interest outside. Perhaps fifty yards away was an old derelict house that I'd seen many times from the road. "Guess that's it, Sue—nothing," I told her.

She came over to the window and related her first experience there. "I walked to this window, almost *drawn* here when I came up alone," she said, "and as I stood looking at the old house, I felt tears running down my cheek. It didn't make any sense; why cry over an old house? Then I heard, 'I really loved him. I loved him so much.' That was it—doesn't make any sense, does it?"

But it did make sense. We knew who Susan B. Anthony was, and Helise had told us that Susan B. had spent the years from 1826-1839 in the big house and, with her family, lived in the Greenwich area until she was nineteen. We knew that her father, Daniel Anthony, had lost the beautiful, now restored house in bankruptcy in 1839, along with his mill across the road. Was this the ephemeral spirit of Susan B. weeping for a lost house or way of life?

We returned downstairs and, as usual, did a de-briefing with our escorts. When Sue mentioned the tears episode, Helise brightened and got a big smile on her face. "Well! You know that house next door? That's the one that belonged to Guelma, Susan B. Anthony's older sister. And *she* married Judge Mclean's son, Aaron, from across the road (she pointed across Route 29) and then the two moved into that house where they lived as man and wife.

"Susan B. Anthony, in her biography, tells that *she was also in love with Aaron*, and many of her biographers believe that this unrequited love led the Suffragette to remain single throughout her life," Helise told us. As a young lady, Susan had dubbed Aaron "The Prince of Battenville," and Helise said that "no other suitors could ever compare to the boy she fell in love with at age six." A heart rending tale. Susan, the intuitive, hadn't known these points of the Susan B. story, and she reminded us that when she had meditated the previous day, she had known nothing of Aaron, Guelma, or even Susan B's love for her neighbor. Apparently this love, or the energy from it, had transcended the grave and remained in the house, accessible to a sensitive visitor.

One could commiserate with Susan B. Anthony, but what had the intuitive Susan run into at the upstairs window? Was it the ghost of a nationally-famous woman who died in Rochester, NY, in 1906? Or was it the powerful energy that a younger Susan B. Anthony often likely expressed at that spot? Did this sorrow remain in the house during a succession of occupancies by other families? Is that sadness *still* there, able to be discerned by a suitably sensitive person?

This is always a hard choice for ghost hunters to make: active ghost or quiescent energy? There is almost certainly an energy there, though it doesn't appear to move, which would be the normal activity of a ghost. There was no apparition except light, either. Sue and I voted that this was most likely a remnant of Susan B's heartbreak of almost one hundred seventy years ago.

There was heartbreak aplenty for women in Susan B. Anthony's youth. She experienced it in the unequal wages of the women workers in her father's cotton mill across the road; she saw it when those working women had to turn over their earnings to husbands on payday. She knew it in the inability of women to hold property, and she saw heartbreak in the fact that the mothers, wives and daughters of presidents, congressmen and senators were given no vote on election day.

One wonders if heartbreak, though its effects can last years or even centuries, may be the necessary impetus for great social change, such as that engineered by Susan B. Anthony and her companions, Lucretia Mott, Elizabeth Cady Stanton, and so many others.

The Old Magistrate's House

Clayton Townsend moved his family into a beautiful old Greek Revival house at 49 South Main Street in Newark Valley in 2000. It was a stately historic structure that had once been the home of a Tioga County judge and the

Old Magistrate's House

center of neighborhood life. In its day, many community leaders, upper class people, and lawyers must have frequented the place, doing off-hours consultations with the judge.

"Neighbors watching us move in warned that the house was haunted, but we figured they believed those things simply because the house was old and had been vacant for a while. Since then, however, we're inclined to believe it is so," he told me. Many of the old timers told him that the building dated from the early 1820s, which wasn't inconsistent with the architectural style, but the oldest legal records they could find dated the place at 1855.

"Maybe my scariest encounter with the former residents happened soon after we moved in. It was late at night, about 2 a.m., and I slowly walked up the front staircase. All at once, I became aware that someone accompanied me up the stairs. I couldn't make out all the details, but it surely was a man in his thirties or forties, not old, who walked with me. I don't even know if he was aware of me, as he walked with his hands clasped behind his back. His face was in the shade, but I clearly saw his long hair pulled back. Intuitively, I'd say he was upset about something and was deep in thought. I don't know who he was, but his appearance was a powerful introduction to the ghosts."

Since that time, Clayton noted, the family dog, looking up the stairs from the bottom, barks. He considered the possibility that the dog might also be seeing the old master of the house taking his upward walk. The ghost man's hair and clothing styles suggest a date earlier than 1855.

Clayton told of tearing down the old barn behind the house because of its poor condition. Underneath the floorboards, they found neatly-stacked piles of old whiskey bottles, with the cork tops put back in place. Perhaps the old building was a place for secret drinking sessions by a former owner; the end of the parties seemed very neat, however, with the stoppers returned to all the bottle tops. However, the oddest issue with the barn is that the space beneath it was filled with great depths of golden sand, a material not native to Newark Valley. "We had to hurry to finish our work, so when bones turned up in and around the sand, we assumed it was the burial of a dead horse. But the stone foundation of the barn went much lower than we had time to dig. Where did that colored sand originate and what secret does it hide?" he asked.

"We found an axe head hidden underneath the kitchen door to the outside, and under a large slate near the corner of the house, we found the barrel of an old cap and ball pistol. For a moment, I wondered if someone had considered shooting the old magistrate. We also found a hand scythe buried in the center of the backyard, and I suppose there are still hidden items for us to find. Those objects were all part of someone's life once upon a time, and we don't know what vibrations or memories they still carry.

"We have sought out all the old documents relating to the history of this house," he told me, "and though there are no grave markers, it seems certain that at least two children were buried in the backyard. My guess is that, if it's true, they lie under the old lilac bush. Two years ago, my daughter said she was sometimes awakened at night by the sound of a child crying, so I wondered if *that* might be one of the dead children.

"On top of all this, recently I sat in the master bedroom and suddenly, in the doorway, I saw a little girl in a white shift peering around the corner at me. Then, just as fast, she disappeared. I jumped up quickly and went to the hallway to look, but nobody was there.

There is also an old man that resides with them. "Visitors to the house were the first to alert us to his presence. I noticed that the cellar light often was turned on after I had definitely turned it off. We have a switch at the top of the stairs, but the light can also be turned on by a pull chain on the fixture in the cellar. The cellar spirit, an old man who never makes a sound, seems to be in a contest with us to keep that cellar light on. I'll turn it off at the switch and even at the pull chain, but within hours, it's on again. My wife, Lise, resists going down there because she just doesn't like the atmosphere. Who is the cellar man, and what is he doing downstairs? We met a psychic woman who volunteered to take a tour of our house. In the cellar, she claimed, there *was* an old man, and one of his issues was his surprise that we didn't put up or can our food, putting it away for lean times. The woman suggested that we leave a piece of fruit down there as a token response to his concern. After that, all the noise in the cellar stopped. Then, as if to substantiate all that, when we tore out an old cellar stair way, underneath, we found many broken Mason jars in the cellar soil." It seems that one concern of the man is shortages or lack of food from his long ago days.

"Another spooky feature of the cellar is that the workmen found a mummified cat under one side of the house. Its back was arched, so it looks like it went out fighting," he laughed. Clayton told me that a former female resident of the house is alleged to have poisoned all stray cats that ventured onto her property, so there is a likelihood that the kitty was one of her victims.

He told me of a small bedroom in the house with a curious wooden floor. It is constructed with thick floorboards, but they are angled in such a way as to form a spiral toward the center of the room. Is there something about that shape that causes a spirit energy or presence to remain? "We've had many visitors who have slept soundly in that room—couples do fine, men likewise, but women who sleep alone in there always seem to have a disturbing dream.

"Such a single woman slept there shortly after we moved in and was horrified in the night to dream of an incident that seemed very lifelike. A man with long black hair manhandled a woman, biting her on the breast. Our visitor was glad to see morning come, but we tossed her dream off as exhaustion on her part. Then, three years later, a visitor from the South, a very religious woman, slept in the room and was equally terrified to *experience* the attack by the same man on her own body! She hasn't returned," he noted, "though *I've* slept in there many times, and sleep like a baby."

The old house is nearing its two hundredth birthday. With certainty, it was used to shelter escaped Southern slaves on the Underground Railroad network before the Civil War. Friends come there and go and love the old house. But is something else at work here beside the ghosts? When entertaining visitors at evening cook-outs, Clayton says with a straight face that "fairy lights" are seen wandering through the lawn or grasses. "And it's still too early for fireflies, and we have no swamp gas," he laughs. One wonders just what energies and personalities remain near the old magistrate's house in Newark Valley.

Ft. William Henry

Lake George, NY, has many historical spirits still active in the community. The oldest European dwelling site is on the grounds of the British fortification Ft. William Henry, built in 1755 to command the southern shores of the lake and prevent France from taking any more land to the south. Two years later, the French army of the Marquis de Montcalm descended on the site of today's village and defeated the British forces, permitting the vanquished redcoats to retreat south to Ft. Edward. James Fenimore Cooper, in his famous

Ft. Wm. Henry, 1755-1757

novel *Last of the Mohicans*, recounts that many of the conquered soldiers, along with their wives and children, were savagely massacred by France's Indian allies before they could reach safety. Montcalm's army then burned the fort and retreated north to their stronghold at Ticonderoga, taking Ft. William Henry's cannons with them.

The battle site remained a charred, abandoned ruin, except for British Maj. Gen. Jeffrey Amherst's brief encampment of forces there in 1758 as he prepared to counterattack Ft. Ticonderoga. Well into the twentieth century, the site remained an abandoned, overgrown field until an archaeological study was done in the early 1950s, anticipating the fort's two hundredth anniversary. Under the inspiration and investment of the McEnaney family, an almost exact reproduction of the fort was constructed, aided by old maps and records. Ft. William Henry gained recent publicity again in Michael Mann's 1992 film, *Last of the Mohicans*, though the filming took place elsewhere. The fort site is now a must-see Adirondack summer attraction for both casual tourists and historians. Young adults are employed as "character guides," offering visitors an understanding of life on Lake George almost two hundred fifty years ago. Many of these guides have come to understand the role of those historical figures at the log fortress quite well.

From time to time, usually in the early morning hours before the fort opens, a uniformed guide hears "The Limper." One young man, unlocking a barracks door in the east wall, distinctly heard footsteps on the rampart over his head. Thud, *thud!* Thud, *thud!* came the footfalls, as if someone walked on the overhead ramparts with a limp. The guide entered the casemate and then paused, remembering that it was only 9 a.m. and nobody else should be there until 10. Sprinting out the door and onto the parade ground, the lad looked up at the rampart, but nobody was there. Over the years, these footsteps have been heard many times when the parade ground is quiet.

It is tantalizing to consider that, during the archaeological dig in the 1950s, five graves were found in the charred ruins of that old east wall casemate. An archaeologist determined that many of the soldiers had osteoarthritis when they died, and one had endured *a leg amputation* before death. It is also notable that one of the bodies lacked its head, causing researchers to remember a scenario written by a French missionary after the fort had surrendered—an Indian joyously running out the gate with a human head held aloft. Perhaps The Limper seeks his head during his endless roaming. Any of these soldiers could conceivably be the unsettled ghost with walking difficulties.

The same guide, about a month after first hearing The Limper, noticed mist rising from rain puddles along the northeast corner of the parade ground before the fort opened one humid day. The fort was about to open, and he and his fellow guides were readying for visitors, standing in a uniformed group along the southeast corner of the Parade Ground. Suddenly, one of the young men gasped and pointed to the misty area. There, a ghostly arm beckoned from within the mist, as if begging for help. There was no body attached. Could the spectral arm be a residue from the horrible massacre of long ago? None of the young men dared venture over to see. The mist then dissipated, and along with it, "The Beckoner's" arm. This phenomenon has occurred several times since the early 1980s.

On another morning before opening, a nineteen-year-old guide sat in the courtyard finishing his morning cup of coffee. He looked at the morning mist rising from the ground, a result of the previous night's thunderstorm, and, suddenly, the stunned young man saw the outline of legs walking toward the west wall within the ground fog along the south wall. Nothing solid—there was only the outline of the legs, gently moving the mist aside as they walked. "The Strider" vanished as he entered the west wall, leaving the lad wishing for a drink stronger than coffee!

While some apparitions are seen in early morning, others are viewed in the late evening. In August, with summer just about gone, it turns dark around 8 p.m. One night, after 7, with the approach of dusk, a guide walked toward the north (officers') barracks, ready to secure the upper doors for the night. The interior lights had been extinguished and only the western sky's diminishing light illuminated the parade ground. Readying himself to climb the stairs to the Officers' Quarters, the young man looked upward to a window that overlooked the left stairway. He clearly saw a tall man looking out at him. The figure was arrayed in a tricorn hat and a soldier's red uniform which, strangely, had orange facing decorations. The guide reflected that the only uniformed personnel in the fort were the guides, but these young men had *yellow* facings on their uniforms. To make matters worse, nobody could have been looking out from that window as, in those days, the entire window opening was sealed with a panel just four inches inside the glass panes. The startled lad secured the doors and quickly left the scene.

This same stairway was the scene of another phenomenon. Again, it was late evening, and the day's visitors had left the fort. Several guides had hung their uniforms inside the southeast bastion dressing room and, upon exiting into the parade ground, were surprised to see several apparently costumed soldiers running up the twin stairways toward the Officers' Quarters. Suddenly, the soldiers scattered and disappeared from the stairways, as if wafted away by a breeze. The next day, after the young guide queried the fort historian, the man related that during the six-day siege of the fort in 1757, several British soldiers are known to have died on those stairways, likely blown apart instantly by a mortar bomb exploding just above the Parade Ground.

My perception of the foregoing incident is that these figures were not genuine ghosts, but more likely "memories" or energy patterns within the fortification. All people have a psychic capability, some stronger than others. It seems that this ability, on occasion, allows our consciousness to transcend time. We can see an historic event that took place on the site long ago. Einstein said that there is no time, so maybe this phenomenon is occurring yesterday and today, and a perceptive person will experience it again "tomorrow."

While the parade ground, scene of many ghastly deaths, is the center of spectral activity, the spirits seem to enjoy provoking modern people indoors as well. The guides refer to one of these spirits as "The Slammer." A poltergeist character, The Slammer has a devilish sense of humor. Several employees recount that just as they are about to cross through a doorway, the door suddenly slams on them, sometimes bruising a nose. It is difficult to understand this phenomenon, as the fort's safety regulations call for all public doors to be locked into the open position, so that even a strong wind cannot move them. It takes a concentrated effort to manually release the restraining pins. Somehow, The Slammer seems to accomplish this. Several times, after traversing the fort and opening and securing the doors in readiness for that day's visitors, guides will find the doors behind them closed, necessitating another effort to secure them in the open position. Also, after the fort is closed and the interior offices are empty, doors to those same offices are heard slamming. Investigation never turns up any miscreant.

Another unseen entity is a formless woman who calls out the names of men who work at the fort. When his name is called, the employee looks to see who might be summoning him, but no one is ever spotted. This unknown female ghost could be one of the camp followers who perished during the massacre, or the dead wife of a soldier. There were also some prostitutes attached to the garrison in 1757, and many women are recorded as being massacred on the old military road as the British retreated to Ft. Edward after the surrender. It is alleged that a spectral woman's head occasionally shows up in tourist photos taken near the parade ground well, leading guides to speculate that the spirit is that of a woman who suffered decapitation during the fighting. No one has yet determined how "The Camp Follower" knows the employees' names or what she wants from them. In the summer of 2005, a photo taken on the northwest rampart, showing two tourist girls and two "soldiers," was developed and showed a featureless face blocking some of the group's details.

Then there are the orbs. Orbs of light are a fairly common phenomenon at haunted sites, perhaps a visual representation of the spirit energy or consciousness remaining in the spot. At Ft. William Henry, orbs have been seen to pass from the southeast bastion across the parade ground and toward the northwest bastion. It is noteworthy that, although today's main entrance is on the western curtain wall, the fort's original entrance *was* along that southwest wall. Perhaps the conscious energy of some long-dead soldier is still doing his duty, possibly bringing the fatal message from the commander at Ft. Edward that he cannot reinforce British Commandant Col. Monro, thus sealing the doom of the outnumbered British garrison in 1757. Such a traumatic realization by the British forces may have taken the form of a visible energy, still occasionally playing out on the hilltops overlooking Lake George.

It is not only ghosts from the distant past, but also at least one entity from recent history that occasionally appears on Route 9 outside the fort. In the archaeological study period of the early 1950s, a village dog named "Beamer" loved to frequent the dry moat excavation where soldiers' skeletons were being unearthed almost daily. One day, Beamer became fascinated with one spot and began digging furiously. Tourists and archaeologists together were stunned to see the dog raise a bone, an arm bone, it appeared, from the soil. Beamer then paraded past the stunned crowd, proudly carrying the bone with shreds of ancient red uniform cloth still attached. One of the excavators quickly seized the dog and rescued the bone for later reburial. Daily, Beamer returned to the excavation searching for *his* bone. It wasn't fair; they took it from him when all he was doing was digging, the way the humans were doing!

After a year or so, the dog was no longer seen. It was rumored in the village that Beamer had died, which was welcome news to the diggers. That should have been the end of it. Nevertheless, there has been a series of panic stops every few years by motorists along Route 9 outside the Fort Entrance ever since that day. Drivers claim they almost hit a big dog that appeared suddenly in the road, almost as if by magic. All the startled motorists describe the same dog, and he's always headed toward the Fort. Beamer, the ghost dog, seems to be persistent in trying to retrieve his prize.

What is going on at Ft. William Henry? If none of the historic buildings or fortifications of 1757 remain, how could the ghostly energy survive? Isn't two hundred fifty years enough time for the souls of British and French casualties to depart?

Many of these things are unknowable at this time, but if there *were* traumatized souls still lurking about the fort site in 1957, the rebuilding of an exact replica fort on the original site may have reenergized them. Each of those unquiet souls now has an individual battle on its hands—how to move on from the beauty of Lake George to a Greater Beauty that has no "tourist season."

Southampton Spooks

The DuPont Mansion

"I'm interested in science," James told me, "so whenever I hear a purported ghost story, I try to reconcile the events with what I know of cosmology, and many times, the stories just don't wash. But I'll tell you a few stories from Southampton that I still haven't been able to attribute to the normal workings of the universe."

Most residents of the village of Southampton know of the old Henry F. DuPont Mansion on Meadow Lane because it has recently been the subject of a heated architectural and zoning dispute. This story, however, predates Barry Trupin's present ownership.

"The owners of the house back in 1978-79 bought the big old home because of its beauty," James told me, "but they couldn't afford to furnish it in the style of the DuPonts. So they lived simply in just a few rooms, enjoying the spaciousness and splendor of the original design. They quietly told friends, including me, about a ghost in the house. Longtime neighbors implied that the earthbound spirit likely originated from a deranged DuPont family member who had been kept locked up in a "secret room" at the mansion, and who likely died there years before.

"When visiting my friends and touring the house, we passed through a large room decorated only with Chinese coolie hats arranged on the wall," he remembered. "As I passed by the display, all the hats tumbled off and hit me—not hard, but they did strike me. My friends apologized, picked them up, and rehung them on the wall. The host mumbled something about the ghost being responsible for the incident. He said it with a straight face, so I assume that *he* believed it."

Maybe Mr. Trupin's current efforts to redesign the home into something more fabulous will uncover an energy that has been hidden for years. Usually, when there is a ghost in habitation, any new construction or renovation will bring the spirit forth, if only to examine the changes taking place. Ghosts don't understand change, I believe.

"Ten years later, I visited Southampton once more," James confided. "I knew a woman named Kate who lived in a newly-constructed building at the corner of Pleasant Plain and Somerset Avenues. My wife-to-be, another couple, and I visited Kate, who had furnished the apartment with furniture that she had inherited from her grandmother.

"As Kate showed us around, we paused for a moment in a hallway. My friend Peter stood next to Kate, and as they talked, the pair moved toward me, as if choreographed. Then they stepped back. It was like a strange, old dance. 'What the heck were you guys doing?' I asked. Both looked blankly at me, and I had to call attention to their just-finished movement. 'Oh, somebody just went by,' Kate said. I could see my fiancée, Peter, his girlfriend, and Kate—who or what *didn't* I see?

"Peter spoke up and noted that all the hairs on his arm were standing straight up—a signal that something uncanny was afoot. Both he and Kate agreed that they had noted, in their peripheral vision, a woman wearing a white lacy dress in the style of the late 1800s pass them. 'I guess we just made room for her to go by us,' Kate said sheepishly."

Afterward, as the small group discussed the issue, they agreed that the deceased grandmother must still be present, linked to this plane by her attachment to some former possessions. It is very common for such attachments to physical objects to continue on into the spirit world, until the soul of the former owner has passed completely beyond this physical plane of existence. So often, that process requires a letting-go of all that which seemed "real" in that period of the universe's unfolding which we call our life.

People called *psychometrists* can often feel the energies (and some can actually provide physical descriptions) of the former owners just from holding or touching these objects. When the details of the ownership are very emotional or intimate (a treasured ring, cameo, gem, for example), it may take the deceased quite a long time to relinquish the attachment and thus stop appearing as a wraith.

In this second story, Kate's house was almost new. It was the emotions and memories that her grandmother had conferred upon those old possessions that generated her ghost.

Horatio

Pultneyville, on the southern shore of Lake Ontario, was a major embarkation point before the 1860s for escaped slaves on the last leg of their journey to freedom in Canada. Avid abolitionist Horatio Nelson Throop, a mechanical tinkerer, ship captain and ship builder, offered free passage for these escapees.

The Throop House

His beautiful old cobblestone house, built in 1832, can still be seen at 4184 Washington Street in that village.

Whether it's the captain or some other previous resident making the fuss, it appears there is an unquiet spirit in the building. When Jim and Carol Doty owned the house in the 1980s, they experienced the sound of furniture moving about on the second floor, but they never found anything out of place when they investigated the noises. They also often heard footsteps on the wooden hallway floor at the top of the stairs, but they never saw anyone descend. Many past residents and some visitors had the uncanny feeling of being observed, though no spectator was visible.

In 1994, high school student Rebekah Porray (now Loveless) visited the house seeking information on the ghost. As she entered a room at the top of the stairs, "the energy was very strong, and I felt someone watching me intently," she said, though no one was there. She later discovered that Throop's nephew, also named Horatio (or by his nickname "Raish") Wilcox, had died of tuberculosis in that upstairs room. Rebekah won the coveted Hoffman Award given annual-

76

ly in Wayne County, for her ghost research, and I am indebted to her for that effort.

That particular chamber continues to be a hotspot of activity. Jim Doty's stepson once slept in the room and announced at the breakfast table the next morning, that he'd had a curious dream of "a man in old-fashioned clothes doing something with windmills." The lad couldn't have known that old Capt. Throop loved to study wind power and often experimented with gadgets that permitted such study. In addition, Mr. Doty once hoped to make the bedroom into a music room, but when he placed his stereo on a strong table there, it unaccountably collapsed, apparently permitting the Captain's ghost the quiet needed to contemplate and innovate.

It turns out that Throop had a favorite dog, an Italian greyhound named Japa, and, upon moving in, the Dotys found a heavy metal statue of the animal and placed it on the room's windowsill. One day it suddenly fell to the floor and broke, though no cause could be determined.

Wayne County was one of the early centers of Spiritualism in New York State in the 1800s, and the Dotys, when remodeling the house, were only mildly surprised to find two "witch bottles" secreted in that room's ceiling. These objects were thought to torment or drive away witches; perhaps the old Captain favored such fetish objects, though local historians know of no former witch activity in town.

For many years after the Dotys left, the home operated as a bed and breakfast, though that operation has now closed. As Throop's old house has returned to the status of a private residence, I suspect that young Horatio Wilcox now roams the upstairs more freely, seeking to understand why his life was apparently cut so short.

CHAPTER 4

RESTAURANTS & LODGING

A Sour Note

Country Club Motel

Knowing the history of a place can often help identify at least the time period from which a ghost comes. Here is a story with more questions than answers at the end, but it can illustrate how my story-gathering often takes place.

Just before Halloween in 2005, I met up with Robin Carnevale, a former student and old friend. "You'd better come over to the motel," she said. "It's coming down soon." She referred to a longtime fixture in the city of Saratoga Springs, the Country Club Motel on Route 9N. Built about 1950, it sits just north of the city line, across from the Saratoga Golf and Polo Club, once the exclusive domain of the well-to-do and well-connected in this resort city.

From the late 1960s, the drive-up motel was managed by Emily Doyle, who then turned the reins over to her son, John, slated to be the last owner. By the early 2000s, it became clear that the rather small rooms no longer offered the ambience of luxury that so many more modern hotels and motels in the city offer. Renovation would be too costly, so in the summer of 2003, at the end of the racing season, the "Closed" sign was hung in the window. From 2003 on, Robin Carnevale has lived there as the watch-person until the sale was completed. According to plans, a more modern multi-story office and residence building will take its place by 2007.

Robin brought some especially treasured mementos and pieces of furniture to adorn her manager's apartment where she sometimes cares for her granddaughter, Brooklynne. It was these furnishings that finally helped us make a breakthrough in diagnosing what has been a rather recent haunting.

During our Halloween conversation, Robin wondered aloud if her ghost wasn't a military man, as the gentleman had appeared three times in a uniform. "I went online and searched several military sites," she said, "to see if I could identify what kind of soldier he was, but nothing that I found seemed right." The first appearance took place downstairs behind her apartment's rear door, a lower level where there is storage space and access to the furnace, washer, and dryer.

"I had just come up the stairs and turned to make sure I'd turned out the light, when, all of a sudden, there he was—at the foot of the cellar stairs, standing and looking up at me. He didn't move, so I was able to note the details of his outfit. First, most prominently, I spotted the brass buttons which ran up the front of his tunic or tailored jacket. The clothing was dark blue, but it had areas of grey or black up near the shoulders. His slacks either terminated below the knees, or he didn't exhibit any lower extremities—for a minute I thought the thirty-something man

Face on cellar wall

wore knickers. He had no facial expression, just a stare that might have indicated curiosity, as if to say, 'What are *you* doing here?' I shot him a verbal 'Hello there,' and scurried into my apartment, closing the door tightly behind me. I was pretty sure he was a ghost, but I couldn't understand why he was *here*."

Robin and I discussed the possibility that the man had been a soldier in life, but the 1777 Battles of Saratoga had taken place a dozen miles further east. Why would he hang out on outer Church Street, near a busy intersection? I told her that the uniform's description was unlike the Revolutionary War, War of 1812, or even Civil War uniforms I'd seen, but I suggested that she might visit the New York State Military Museum across town. There she could view many of our nation's military uniforms that are displayed to see if any of them looked familiar. It seemed to me that there must have been other uniforms in Saratoga's past. Typically, if the ghost individual's death didn't take place at the site of the haunting, the spirit must have migrated to its present location because of a close connection to a living person there, or it had arrived attached to some object. Haunted objects were dealt with in *Ghosts of the Northeast.*

Construction on the motel's site was of rather recent vintage, only post-World War II. Considering the previous owners and uses for the land, nothing seemed a logical cause for the haunt.

I then asked about objects, as there were some nice pieces of furniture in the office. She showed me the antique druggist's cabinet with its many drawers. While it is possible that the cabinet was connected to the soldier, few druggists I knew of had ever worn a formal uniform. "What else do you have?" I inquired.

"There's this fairly large old wooden bed that I keep downstairs. It was my grandmother's, and she got it from the old Grand Union Hotel over on Broadway when it was torn down around 1950." Robin told me of her grand-mother's work as a hotel housekeeper for many years, so it was logical that she'd want to take a piece of her job home with her when the Grand Union was razed. Then, it hit me—The Grand Union!

One of my favorite Saratoga stories involves Monty Woolley (1888-1963), the famous Hollywood character actor who grew up in that hotel, as his father was the Grand Union's manager in the late 1800s and early 1900s. As a child, according to legend, Monty got to conduct the piazza orchestra on the opening day of each summer season. And no small ensemble it was. The regular conductor of many years was beloved American musician and composer Victor Herbert, with a sixty-piece orchestra.

I also remember reading a 1952 *Saratogian* interview with Harry Foster from Round Lake, NY, who had been the Grand Union Hotel's bell captain in the late 1940s. He maintained that one often encountered a ghost woman in the vast hotel cellar. Garbed in a long black dress and sporting flaming red hair, she was remembered by old timers as a long-ago suicide there. But, that's another story.

Once we got onto that mental track of hotels and resorts, I remembered that Saratoga, especially at the height of the summer thoroughbred racing season in the 1800s, was a magnet for the rich and great personalities from Europe and the U.S. To keep the public's interest when the horses weren't running, the big hotel keepers or The Casino hired brass bands to play daily concerts, and Broadway was often the scene of impromptu parades by competing musical groups each afternoon. The most famous bands in America, especially Gilmore's and John Philip Sousa's, were annual attractions. Lohan and his Musicians, Joyce's Orchestra, The Florentine Mandolin Band, John Lund's Orchestra and Gartland's Band of Albany were also regular performers in the city.

Each musical organization consists of individuals working in a group, in concert, so to speak. So, as the city's gambling was wide open, liquors flowed abundantly, and bawdy women were numerous, who is to say that at least one bandsman among the thousands may not have found his personal Gethsemane in Saratoga when the baton was laid aside? Performers, musicians, and other creative people often have disordered private lives of sorrow or addiction because they are unlike the common, unimaginative people. If his death were sudden or sorrow-filled, this purported bandsman ghost may have been unable to leave the physical plane. Did he move into the Country Club Motel just a few years before with Robin's bed?

Back to our entity: Robin told of seeing him twice more. In 2004, while checking the dry linen room downstairs, she spotted him over near the furnace. Again, the figure just looked and didn't move, so Robin offered another quick "Hello," before hurrying upstairs. "The third time I spotted him, he was *upstairs*, walking past the apartment's rear door, toward the office," she said. "He looked in at me and kept walking. By then, I knew the building's days were numbered, so I went down to the cellar one last time. I couldn't see him, but told him aloud that the building was coming down soon, so he'd better find a new lodging. Since then, I've had no sense that he is still around. He seems to have come here with *me* for a while, and, he's moved on now." Just in case, I told her, she should make one more trip dowstairs and tell the uniformed man that he has, in fact, died, and that he is now free to move into The Light.

Bringing with me my intuitive friend Susan, I came back one more time. "There's an old woman with a walker there," my friend pointed as we entered the parking lot. "She has a black cat with her." In the end, no one familiar with the motel could identify the old lady. When we entered, an employee escorted us through the building in order for Susan to soak up the atmosphere, which she found quite heavy when we reached the foot of the cellar stairs. "There are two males down here, I'm sure of that," Susan declared. "I get the name 'Burt or Bert,' and perhaps one of them has to do with landscaping."

We turned the corner into the linen room and our guide turned on the light. "Yes, there is a young male here, alright," Susan said. "He has shoulder-length long hair." Then, I spotted some artwork on the concrete block wall and asked our guide to pull away containers stacked in front of the design, so that I might photograph it. "Oh, that's terrible!" Sue exclaimed, as a flaming skull picture came into view. All at once, the negativity became too strong for her, and she had to leave the room. I could see other uncolored and only partial designs drawn on other walls, which I photographed. Then, to be sure I had photographed all the soon-to-be-destroyed imagery, I returned to the motel one more time. Robin helped me pull aside the storage containers, and finally, we had some understanding of the drawings. The legend "Grateful Dead," was drawn beneath the pictures. Clearly, the mural was fairly recent, and it was apparently giving off negative energy that Susan had felt. All we had left to do now was decide if *all* the energy (and the long-haired man) emanated solely from the drawings.

As we discussed the matter upstairs, we wondered if a long-ago employee or visitor at the motel had done the artistry with some malicious intent. Ordinary motel guests would never have been allowed in the cellar, suggesting that the inscriptions were done by someone who owned the motel or who was related to a previous motel owner. None of that information came to us, and John, the motel owner, didn't know anything about the art's origins.

So, what did we have there? Robin's old bed from the Grand Union stood inside the linen room. Did the negativity come from the bed alone, or just from the wall designs? Or both? Might one of the spirit men of the cellar be my hypothesized musician and the other be a troubled, more modern type still attached to the demonic world portrayed in the skull photo? Had there been a landscaper Dead fan there once? There were no firm answers, either from the spirit world or the historical records. By the time you read this tale, the motel will be no more, and a modern office building will be under construction at the site. Will the spirit remain?

Collecting ghost stories often leaves me with a lot of loose ends when the tales finally have to be written down. It's always questionable how much energy I should devote to apparently minute details of a haunting or its location. As a creative type, I'm more fascinated with people's personalities—living or dead—and why they behave as they do. What keeps a soul attached to the impermanent realm that we all occupy (calling it *Life*) is fascinating; it is just as intriguing as wondering what event can cause the spirit to finally "give up the ghost" and depart for The Unknown Region.

Illumination

The Montaukett Indians lived along the hilltops and beaches of eastern Long Island for over 10,000 years before they encountered their first Europeans in the 1630s, probably Dutchmen. Explorers found the natives friendly, except in their tribal wars with the Naragansett and Pequot people who often raided across Long Island Sound from Rhode Island. In 1636 the great Montauket chief, Wyandanch, met English Capt. Lion Gardiner, and a friendship grew, creating good will on both sides. British trade goods became common among the Indians, who sold plots of land to British settlers who then created the settlement of Maidstone, later renamed East Hampton.

But the European allies were nowhere to be found when, in 1653, the Naragansetts sent a powerful war party onto Long Island, and a great battle was fought on and around what came to be known as Signal Hill. In the valley below the hill, hundreds of Montauketts died violently, and in time the place became known as "Massacre Valley." After the Rhode Island tribe withdrew, the locals buried their dead atop the hill in the usual flexed body position and in gently marked graves. Wyandanch died six years later.

Montauk Manor

Readers surely understand that the European occupation of the island rapidly expanded, as it did throughout the colonies, and through trade, threat, alcohol-induced treaties and intermarriage, the influence of the local tribe waned. In the end, a dedicated band moved to the Mohawk Valley near Oriskany, and later, cheated of their land by the New York Colonial Assembly, they decamped to Wisconsin, where they have land today. Only a small number of Montauketts remain on Long Island today.

By the 1800s, the hills of Montaukett were covered with farm animals and the gardens of white Americans. On occasion, ancient Indian graves were accidentally uncovered, looted for the burial artifacts such as bowls or beads, and then destroyed. Preparing for the Spanish-American War in 1898, Long Islander Teddy Roosevelt held war games, leading mounted charges with his Rough Rider troop on and near Signal Hill. When quite a number of those soldiers died of yellow fever or typhoid, they were quickly interred atop the hill, even though these temporary burials sometimes disturbed Indian remains. Later, with more disruption of the ancient graves, those military burials were exhumed and sent to the white man's cemeteries, where they received honors and perpetual care. The Montauketts received neither honors nor care for their grave sites.

Perhaps the greatest insult to the tribal spirits came in the Roaring Twenties, when Carl Fisher, the developer of the Miami Beach waterfront and the Indianapolis Speedway, turned his attention to Signal Hill and visualized an English Manor Style resort on its heights. In a time of a runaway stock market and great financial speculation, Fisher finished his resort, complete with swimming pools, a golf course, a yacht and beach club and glass-enclosed tennis courts. Opened in 1927, the Montauk Manor hosted the greats of politics, entertainment, sports, and the world of commerce. Business was great!

Soon after Black Friday in October 1929, however, finances became tight everywhere. The wealthy, struggling to remain solvent, had little time to visit the Hamptons and stayed home. By 1930, Fisher's corporation had to shutter "The Castle on the Hill," creating a haven for bats, and perhaps permitting the quiet protests of the Montaukett spirits to finally be heard.

Then, in 1933, another entrepreneur appeared, re-opening the Manor as a hotel. The receipts were adequate throughout World War II and for a few years afterward, but the reservoir of patrons dried up by 1963, and Montauk Manor closed again, and it wasn't until the early 1980s that the tread of patrons was once again heard in the lobby of a modernized resort. Having stood vacant and vandalized by local miscreants, the old building apparently began to consolidate its spirit energy.

Even though a new corporation modernized and restored the resort in a twenty million dollar rescue, something vital seems to have remained. Desk clerks frequently heard strange tales from patrons and staff. The story of a nine-year-old girl from nearby Fort Hill spotting an Indian in full headdress atop the mound was repeated by housekeepers. Then came the story from a guest rooming on the first floor of the hotel itself. She spotted a Caucasian ghost in her room, followed by a rain and sleet storm *indoors*, though there was no moisture to clean up later. The ghost allegedly told the woman that he *had* to be indoors, as if he were outside in the weather, he would melt! Then came verification from a former maintenance employee: he, also, had encountered an Indian ghost who made the same claim. Subsequently, three more pale faced ghosts appeared. Staff might easily have attributed such an outlandish tale to the woman or employee over-imbibing at one of the resort's bars.

But then, incidents were reported from all parts of the hotel, especially after Labor Day, when the Montauk Manor has a seasonal quiet time. One morning in 1991, the head housekeeper sat in her office reading a report, then she looked up to see a brightly-lit tall man passing the door and peering in to look at her. As she composed herself, she remembered the gentleman had long, flowing white hair. Not one of *our* employees, she reckoned, and she entered the hallway to apprehend him, only to see him vanish in mid-air. Later, twice during the winter season, the woman (who resided on the hotel's second floor) heard knocks at her door, but found no one outside when she answered the summons. It was her considered belief that these sounds were generated by an Indian. The flowing hair sounds suspiciously like a description of old Chief Wyandanch himself.

In 2001, reporter Amanda Star Frazer, working for the *East Hampton Star*, interviewed Manny Gomez, a former employee at Montauk Manor, who provided her an amazing anecdote. He had met a woman resident of the fourth floor who said that "while in her bed, she was lifted five feet off the floor." Frazer also reported that a resort workman took before and after photos of a project he worked on. He claimed one of the prints showed a wispy, smoky form in the middle of the picture, an object that he *knew* wasn't there at the time he snapped the shutter. Many assumed he'd gotten a picture of at least one ghost.

Gomez also told of a resort night watchman who discovered a pump running at the nearby cemetery, flooding the lawn. He spotted the pump handle gyrating upward and down, as if energized by an unseen hand. Hurrying to inform his superior, who returned to the site with him, the man found that the well was dry, and there was no moisture anywhere around that location.

And so it goes. From time to time, ordinary working people are sometimes surprised by extraordinary experiences. Employed in luxurious surroundings, they occasionally are required to struggle with the aftermath of past generations' insensitivity.

How does one explain that if the dominant ghost energy is Native American, why are apparently white people's ghosts commonly seen? Remember Teddy's Rough Rider deaths? And then there is a most esoteric suggestion, offered to me by a psychic friend. "There was a vortex of outrage created on that hill long before there was a United States or a Carl Fisher. The spirits can't rest, and as long as that negative energy persists, the energy field will continue to attract discarnates from the spirit world that have a score of some kind to settle, though they never died in East Hampton."

The psychic advised me to notify the Montauk Manor management to secure the services of a good and holy person, Indian or not, and hold a blessing ceremony, whereby old grievances can be addressed. "It's all in God's good time," the man told me, "so it's *never* too late to apologize." I think I'll pass that on.

Look on the Bright Side

In the 1880s, as adventurers, miners, railroaders and hunters thronged the Adirondack wilderness of northern New York State, Joe Bryere convinced his lady love, Mary Agnes Gooley, that they could make a good living entertaining city people in the wilderness. They married at St. William's Church on Long Point on Raquette Lake in 1884 and immediately began the construction of a large guest house called Brightside on the opposite shore near "The Crags," a rocky hill favored by rock climbers. For a year, until the hotel was completed, the couple lived a rustic life in a tent and then a rough shack.

As the large lodge was completed, the Bryeres began construction of amenities that would ensure a steady stream of vacationers. An ice house and

Joe & Mary Agnes Bryere

water tower were erected, then a large boathouse and separate guest cabins. A generator house was built to provide electricity for the summer season. Tennis courts and a small golf course were ready when the first guests arrived in the early summer of 1891. Doing much of the hard physical labor themselves, Joe and Mary hammered, cut, trimmed, dug, and sawed away at the forest.

With his friend Seth Pierce, Joe constructed a carpenter shop over the boathouse and began building rustic Adirondack furniture, some of which is on display today at the Adirondack Museum in Blue Mountain Lake. Seth, with his chest-length white beard, was a local curiosity when he donned his Civil War uniform on holidays, leading guests in raising the American flag at the dockside flagpole.

Though the Bryeres raised four children at Brightside, none of them stayed on after reaching adulthood, and Joe, Mary, and Seth did most of the seasonal work for years. One night in a cold 1930s winter, Joe passed out (legend says the event was alcohol-aided) on the lake ice, and by the time he was discovered, he had a badly frostbitten leg, which required amputation. As a result, until he died in 1941, Joe Bryere was trundled about the resort property in a wheelbarrow.

After her father's death, daughter Clara returned to Raquette Lake to help her mother run the hotel, and after Mary's demise, Clara remained proprietor until she retired in 1957. The resort continued as a resort for a few years, and then it passed to The Light Connection, an optical fiber company from Oriskany, NY, presided over by Frank Giotto. Today, the old hotel and its outbuildings provide seminar and training space for Giotto's FIS optical fiber operation, and many times good customers are invited to visit and enjoy the forested splendor.

At times when the resort isn't entertaining, company employees spruce up the buildings, readying for the next business group. And it is during those quiet times that the year-round residents make themselves known. Many of these anecdotes were given to me by employees and guests.

Brightside, it should be noted, is inaccessible by land, so the motor of any approaching visitor's boat would be heard by those inside. In the summer of 2005, Frank's assistant, Devon, worked with John in cleaning the hotel, readying for a new season. The two were alone and hurrying to complete their tasks. As Devon cleaned in the downstairs, she heard footsteps ascending the stairs and walking about on the second floor. Must be John, she mused. Then, looking out the window, she spotted him at

Brightside

the boat dock. On another occasion, she heard a male voice upstairs and suspected John was calling her. She went up and asked him what he wanted. John responded that not only had he *not* called her, he was deep in thought and hadn't even been humming to himself.

On another occasion, John began changing bed sheets in an upstairs room that is famous for its many ghostly events. After tucking in three corners of the fitted sheet and heading for the fourth corner of the mattress, he collided with an extremely frigid draft, though the windows were open and the August heat permeated the room. He later shared the event with Erin, another employee who often changes the bedrooms while wearing her CD player headset. "Yes, that's the place all right," she told him. "Whenever I clean and change sheets in there, I lose all volume in my earphones. As quickly as I return to the hallway, I get all the sound back." To employees and long time guests, the room is simply called "The Ghost Room."

At another time, a guest named Wayne placed his camera on the bed in this room. He stepped aside, only to have the camera take two flash pictures on its own. Someone in spirit was likely fascinated with creating his or her own light!

Colleen, a frequent guest from Pennsylvania, experienced a similar cold draft while waiting for a group portrait to be taken on the side porch in August 2005. "I stood with my back to the clapboards of the house. There's no way anyone or anything could have been behind me," she told me. "Nevertheless, I kept looking back, anyway, trying to see if maybe there was an air conditioner vent there, but Brightside doesn't have air conditioning at that spot."

These events have been experienced over and over since FIS purchased the old hotel. In fact, the experiences were so numerous in 2001 that a staff member invited Joanne O'Dell from the Mohawk Valley Ghosthunters group to visit and examine the premises. Her work, using infrared devices and digital cameras, turned up an amazing number of light orbs moving throughout the house. Unfortunately, none of them had a face, so one must guess at the identity of the spirits. In the Brightside guest book, Joanne wrote of opening a guestroom door and entering, only to have the door gently push back at her. Recognizing a spirit entity was present, she turned on her digital recorder, hoping to get a sample of the ghost's voice if the being chose to communicate.

Electronic Voice Phenomena (EVP) is a relatively new and fascinating tool used in exploring ghost sites, and many times apparent human voices are heard, sometimes with an appparent message. O'Dell's machine clicked off ten seconds after she set it to record. She restarted the device, but again it turned itself off. Her digital photographic investigation found an orb inside an antique phonograph that was playing on the second floor. Later on in the probe, she set up a video monitor on the first floor and told guests to watch the image to see what happened as she descended the cellar stairs inquiring "Who's down here with me?" There was no audible response, but viewers spotted several light orbs rapidly encircling her as she walked.

This is just a sampling of the ongoing strange events at Brightside. As in so many similar instances, nobody seems scared, though John, my guide there, told of Mike, a recent guest in the "Ghost Room," having the bed suddenly start heaving up and down. Certain that one of the staff was playing a joke, he tore off the blankets and mattress, all the while yelling that a prank was being played on him. The poor guy found nothing amiss. Present at the time of my overnight stay, John joked that maybe I'd have a similar experience, as they had assigned the room to *me*. Well, I did. The bed's movement was very slight; no heaving and no noise. I likened the encounter to the vibration one might notice if living alongside a railroad track—not scary at all. And, to be truthful, it lulled me to sleep. Is it possible that Joe and/or Mary wanted me to have a good night's sleep if I was to write of my adventures there?

Justin, a company engineer, stayed overnight at Brightside and, preparing for bed, saw a small orb of light atop his blankets. Suddenly the other pillow flattened out, as if someone had just lain down, but of course, nobody was visible. Justin said it took some self-talk before he could voluntarily turn out the light and relax.

Often, employees come to Brightside alone in order to ready their part of the operation for the arrival of guests. One of those is Mike Latreille, the cook. Arriving by boat and carrying groceries in the early summer of 2003, he unlocked the kitchen door at the otherwise-vacant hotel and was stunned to see a still-wet muddy spot or puddle between the stove and shelf. Someone had recently stepped in the damp spot with a right foot, but the resulting print was almost eight feet away, near the table. Examining that footprint, Mike then saw the wet imprint of a left foot six feet away from the first, near the doorway into the next room. In pursuit of the long-striding entity, he found more footprints circling back through The Great Room to the other kitchen doorway, each impression was six to eight feet from the previous one. Nobody was able to explain the phenomenon.

Other than the energies moving through the bedrooms and kitchen, this is not an especially scary place. The old Adirondack décor, complete with stuffed animals, old snowshoes, and antique furniture, is decidedly relaxing, as if one has returned to the ambience of Joe and Mary's time. Joe was a legendary tough guy. It is alleged that he once strangled a bull moose with his bare hands, and that he did the work of three men. Perhaps it is his spirit that lingers most strongly at Brightside, attempting to compensate for the work he could not complete during his later handicapped years.

Brightside is aptly named, and it is a wonderful experience to see the sun rise over the misty lake each morning, and to hear loons calling to one another in the distance as gentle waves slap against the rocks. It is a place to regain one's perspective on the beauty that The Creator placed in nature, a peace that has invited Adirondack visitors for almost a century and a half.

Still Managing

The hill country of Rensselaer County was a major travel and trade route through the Berkshires between Massachusetts and the Hudson River, and for years stage riders made the trip on a regular schedule. But once stage-coach service was established, there needed also to be regular way-stations, small hotels, or rooming houses where passengers could wash up, refresh themselves, get a room, and new teams of horses could be hitched. A notable place, built in the early 1800s by Phillip Upham, was Upham's Tavern on Crooked Lake in the Town of Sand Lake. Following a fire in the late 1850s, the hotel was rebuilt by James M. Mosher, who provided room and board to travelers until he sold out to the Brown Family in 1881.

The Browns renamed the place "Brown's Crooked Lake House" and began entertaining and putting up not just travelers, but also the well-to-do visitors who came to the hills on vacation. Other visitors were managers from the mills in Troy, seeking temporary relief from summer's heat and the noisy factories. Most prominent among those Albany-Troy executives was Theodore Roosevelt, who first lodged with the Browns in the 1880s when he was elected

BROWN'S CROOKED LAKE HOUSE

Brown's Crooked Lake House c. 1888

to the NY State Assembly, and TR continued to visit when he became New York's Governor in 1899. With quite a collection of mounted animal heads accumulated from his years in the western Badlands of Dakota Territory, Teddy introduced the bison and pronged-horn antelope to the Browns and gave them several mounted specimen heads with which to adorn the tap room and dining rooms of the hotel. Brown's was a favorite place of respite for Teddy and his family until he became President McKinley's Vice President in 1901, and then President, when McKinley was assassinated six months later.

Mabel Brown finally sold out to a Mr. Wendell, who renamed the property "The Wendell Inn" and owned it for a number of years. During the late 1920s, Eleanor Roosevelt often lunched there when FDR was Governor. Then, in 1935, Al and Theresa Coon bought the famous hostelry and made many modernizations that drew more tourists and many of the big bands that were touring the nation—it was a popular place to dance. The inn had already achieved legendary status during Prohibition as a place where good food and booze were readily available.

In 1957, the Coons added a motel and added a heated indoor pool, five years later. In later years, Marc Hammond became the manager, and during this time I heard about "the picture." At that time, I was becoming fascinated by stories of ghosts and other things that "shouldn't be" and made a half-hearted attempt to get to the Crooked Lake Inn, as it was then called, to see the famed photo. However, the place closed and other things got in my way.

Then, as I began this book of New York State ghost stories, I knew I had to track down the picture in order to share it with you, the reader. Unfortunately, the original, which used to hang in the Inn, has come up missing, but a fair copy remains, along with several other photos shot a few minutes before the formal portrait in question.

Judy Rowe, Town of Sand Lake Historian, custodian of many old

The Picture

photographs, provided me with these historic photos to inspect.

Let's set the scene. It is a hot summer day around 1890 and an itinerant photographer has come to the resort house to stay briefly, and under the influence of good food and perhaps good drink, he offers to take a picture of the Browns and their assembled staff. The first three photos in the sequence show seven employees, one man and six women, gathered at the left end of the hotel's front porch. They laugh and carry on and one woman embraces the man; maybe those are the Browns. Finally, the photographer has the light he wants, and, calling the group into a formal grouping, he ducks under his black cloth and hoists his flash. Poof! The magnesium flare powder explodes, providing enough frontal lighting to show good detail on all assembled. He then takes the glass slide negatives to the developing booth within his wagon and brings the images to life.

And there they are, all eight people—some smiling and all but one looking at the camera. Wait a minute—eight? Who's the lady on the right? *She* wasn't there! The staff members peer at the just-printed photo. Then, there are oohs and aahs as they recognize the mystery lady. She was a former manager known to them all; she was employed by the Browns, but she no longer worked at the hotel. Everyone knows that *she died* a few years earlier! She simply isn't quite finished managing yet! That fact sank in and, dazzled, they went back to work, while the photo became a local curiosity.

There are a number of such photos all over the world, where a deceased family member or individual of a team or military organization can be found in the group photo, and this is the first such photo that I heard about when I became interested in ghosts. I knew you'd like to examine it, despite its poor quality. Go ahead, rationalize it. How else could it have happened, especially as all present *knew* who she was and also knew that she was dead?

Meantime, the Crooked Lake House is back in business, hosting weddings, bar mitzvahs, and parties while offering great dining for travelers. In reopening the old landmark, the pages of history are being reopened. Maybe Teddy or Eleanor still drops by to watch the dancers. Maybe the old manager is still there, too, after a century. Check it out, and bring your camera!

Emily

"The White House on Route 20 was scary to me as a child. Growing up in the Village of Bridgewater, I feared it, not so much for the house's different Italianate style as for Mr. Rogers, the owner," Juanita said. "He was mean to neighborhood kids and seemed to fear they would sneak in by night and steal his fruit. And they *did*," she said with a laugh. "Now, who would have ever thought I would one day buy that old house and make it my own—a place of business and a treasure for Oneida County?"

On a warm August afternoon in 2005, Juanita Holmes Bass was reminiscing about the combination soul food restaurant and bed & breakfast that she operated for thirteen years. Her dad, Everett T. Holmes, had been the first black mayor in New York State, and Juanita accomplished a number of firsts in her own life. "When I decided to create a soul food restaurant in 1988, I looked at the old house and immediately felt comfortable inside, almost as if I were being welcomed by an invisible hostess. When we investigated the attic, I found old Mr. Rogers' sign, 'White House—Berries,' so we gave our restaurant that name."

The soul food fare immediately captivated the palates and imaginations of central New York State diners, and show business luminaries often traveled hours from New York City and Philadelphia just to partake of Juanita's culinary skills. I recall visiting there in the early 1990s, meeting Juanita, and being captivated by her catfish with black-eyed peas entrée. Little did I know then that the restaurant had guests upstairs that evening, and not all of them were living.

"Overnight visitors would sometimes come down to breakfast inquiring if we had spirits here, and I'd laugh and tell them it's just Emily. I can't remember exactly when I first discovered her, but it was soon after we opened.

Things began to be moved. For example, I had a teddy bear on a small chair in one of the twin bed rooms, and every afternoon I'd find it on the bed. I asked the chambermaid if she moved it, and she denied it, saying, 'I always find it on the little chair when *I* come to work.' Then someone in town asked if I knew the story of Emily. I said no, I'd never heard of it, even having grown up in Bridgewater," said Juanita.

The friend then told her of a jilted bride named Emily, who was one of the earliest residents of the 1874 house, and whose family name is now forgotten. The young woman had apparently hanged herself in one of the upstairs rooms. "Well, she seems to have gotten her spirit back," Juanita laughed. "Now she just moves things and sometimes hides them for a while, but they always turn up…though sometimes in the most curious places. My cleaning woman one day set down her pail and turned a moment later to find it gone. We scoured the house for quite some time before we found that bucket hidden behind the bathtub. Now, *nobody* would have done that—at least, not anybody living," she joked.

"Then there was that dinner party I had for fourteen friends a few years ago. One of the wives suddenly sat bolt upright and stared at her husband. He gave her an innocent look, and she accused him of tickling the back of her neck. He denied it. A few minutes later, another wife across the table had the same sensation. We knew the husband was innocent of the charge; he couldn't reach *that* far. So I 'fessed up and told them all about Emily. I'm not sure that comforted them very much, but at least they stopped accusing one another. And Emily ceased her joking, for *that* night anyway.

"One evening in 1997, I told my cook, Michael, that the only reason I had bought the house was the massive three-foot-tall oak Victorian medicine cabinet in the bathroom, a truly Victorian piece of wall furniture," Juanita reminisced. "Then I said that I was considering having a big auction, selling all the contents of the house and closing the restaurant. Immediately, we heard a terrific crash in the bathroom. Hurrying to investigate, we found the entire cabinet had fallen from the wall—an item that had been affixed there since the house was built. The cabinet's back remained fastened to the wall, but the entire front and its contents were on the floor. It's curious that very few items broke, but we felt Emily had weighed in on the sale issue. So I kept the White House Berries Inn open a bit longer!

"Emily was good at that disruptive behavior. Whenever a waiter dropped a dish or cup, they immediately piped up, 'Emily did it!' And we all laughed." Juanita Bass said that all lightly, but I remember that her dinnerware was all fine china, and too much breakage would have been expensive. "One evening a waiter was walking to set a table, carrying a full tray of china. For no reason that anyone could figure, the tray suddenly flipped in mid-air and all the dinnerware crashed to the floor. There goes tonight's profits, I thought glumly, but a scientist seated in the dining room told me that only three plates had broken; he could tell *by the sound*. Well, that's strange enough, but even stranger, he was right! Then we all thought back to what we had said or done that might have gotten Emily upset. We couldn't figure it out. But, in retrospect, I think Emily knew we were going to close the restaurant, which I finally did in 2001.

"Something positive about having a haunted B&B and restaurant," she mused, "was that most of the neighborhood kids were scared of the ghost. On Halloween, when neighboring houses were smeared with eggs or soap or had their yards strewn with toilet paper, the White House Berries Inn remained immaculate, so I suppose Emily had her value. I always knew when she was around; often I'd see a shadowy form moving, or sometimes I'd feel just a little prickle of my skin, but that was it. I never saw her clearly and don't know of any guest who did either. I was never afraid, because on many stormy winter nights, I slept there rather than drive home on snowy roads, and I slept better *there* than at home."

So a marvelous old building has now closed its doors to guests and is stripped of its antique furniture and chinaware. The commercial kitchen has been removed, and it looks as if the old house is headed for residential use. Juanita Holmes Bass is still busier than ever, however, at www.juanitassoulclassics.com, where she offers lip-smacking soul food recipes, a barbecue sauce hot enough to make Texans envious, and a wonderful allspice seasoning. Expect a recipe book on the market soon. And, when all is said and done, Juanita will likely dedicate it to her old "silent partner:" Emily.

Park Row

In the center of Clinton, NY, is a small park, a vestige of the affluent 1800s when Oneida County's farms, railroads, and canals were thriving. It was a genteel time and place, and lawyer Othniel Williams built a Greek Revival home on the park's west side in the mid-1820s. Following his death in 1832, his son, also named Othniel, rose to fame as a Clinton lawyer and judge, and he soon became involved in small business enterprises. He also endowed his alma mater, Hamilton College, just a few miles away up the hill. During its heyday, the old brick Williams house entertained leaders in American business and politicians, such as President Grover Cleveland, who visited the community in 1887. Members of the Williams family called the old place home until 1938, when it became a Utica attorney's house.

O'Connor's Alexander Hamilton Inn

From 1942 to 1945, the building was the Hotel Ades, then it was purchased by local investors, The Kirkland Properties Group, and became the Alexander Hamilton Inn, taking its title from the college's namesake. Whose energy remains to mysteriously taunt the Inn's staff from time to time? It seems certain that a whimsical and dedicated ghost or two is present.

Pat O'Connor, from Oriskany, NY, bought the Inn in 1998, adding his family name to the sign, "O'Connor's Alexander Hamilton Inn." He has since assembled plenty of evidence, certainly enough for old Judge Williams to accept it as *prima facie* evidence, that spirits abide there amidst the thousands of mouth-watering meals served each year.

My interview at the Inn began with Ruth, an employee who has worked at the Inn for six years, and one who has had several personal experiences. "I'm pretty sure I know who our main character is," she told me. "George Traub was the manager after 1948. He worked hard at making this a fine restaurant and worked personally with his staff. Too personally, perhaps," she smiled. "He fell in love with a housekeeper, and, one dreaded evening, he went upstairs to tell his wife, Martha, that their marriage was over. Nobody really knows what happened, but the next morning, George was discovered dead in the driveway beneath the one-story addition. Martha told investigators that George had gone out a window onto the roof and must have slipped. The police must have bought that tale, but none of *us* who know the story believe it for a minute."

Pat, the owner, Ruth, and I sat in a quiet pre-lunch dining room, inviting other staff members to share their ideas and experiences. O'Connor

96

remembered a patron who dined at the Hamilton a few years ago. The man (now a priest) identified himself as a former employee who bussed tables at the Inn. He said Martha was a horrible boss after George died. She was mean to the staff and often emptied the ashtrays on the leftover rolls and breads so that the employees couldn't take them home at night's end. She barked orders rather than talked, he said. Pat told me, "Our present coat room used to be the coffee room, and Martha got very upset when the saucers weren't piled *exactly* thirteen high. What do you think *that* was about?" We all acknowledged the myth of the number 13 being unlucky. Was Martha trying to push George's ghost away?

"When I first came to work here in 2000," Ruth told me, "I found the upstairs lights often flickered on and off, as if someone was trying to get my attention. We had no electrical problem because that was checked. Another time, I was folding napkins—we do a fancy fold on those—and put them into a large plastic tub to await the next table setting. I had just about filled the tub, when I had to turn and look at something else. A few seconds later, I turned back, just in time to see the tub move horizontally and then crash to the floor, spilling all my hard work. George? Martha?

"I saw a figure I believe is George twice," Ruth continued. "The first time, I stood at the desk in the front hallway, and caught a movement out of the corner of my eye. A tall, thin man stood in the living room. A second later, he evaporated. Then, a few months later, I saw the same character on the landing of the stairs to the second floor, where we have guest rooms and a small dining room. Only his dark suit was remarkable, otherwise I couldn't pick out any details."

Denny Blacek, another long-time employee, remembered the time that he and Pat stood at the front hall podium greeting diners. "Things were slow right then, and we had just two senior citizens seated at the bar. Suddenly, we heard piano music from the dining room, just chords, as if a pianist was warming up. We didn't have a pianist at that time of day, and I hurried in to see who it was. All at once, before I could get to the doorway, the music stopped, and no one sat at the piano when I looked in. The other strange episode, the one that shook me up the most, occurred near the rack where we store dinnerware waiting for the washer. A glass that sat there unmoving suddenly exploded and fell in pieces to the floor. None of us had an explanation for that event, though I did offer a weak suggestion of some infra-sound vibration. I don't think any of us believed it."

Sarah Stancato, who has worked at the Inn for two years, heard other staff members casually chatting about George and told me with a smile that she thought she'd *never* get to see him. But then, in April 2006, "As I walked through the hall and doorway into the main first floor dining room, I spotted a white-haired man seated at a table in the dining room. I went to ask the bartender if the man had been greeted, and the bartender asked, '*What* man? We don't have any customers right now.' So I quickly retraced my steps but found no one sitting there. Other than that," she said with relief, "I've only had the impression of being watched, and *that* I can handle!"

"Just when we try to blame everything on George," Ruth interjected, "I've also seen a woman. In 2003, we were ready for lunch, though it was a bit early yet. As I walked down the hall past the dining room, I spotted the back of a woman seated at table four. I asked the bartender if she had been served; he responded with a strange look and told me no guests had arrived yet. I couldn't believe it and hurried back to the dining room but found only the chair pulled out from the table. No woman was present. The second time I saw her was just after I returned from vacation in 2004. When I came in to work, I walked down the hall and saw a woman in a skirt and sweater standing at table four. Then, suddenly, she was gone. Do you think it was Martha?

"Now, explain this one to me," she grinned. "A few years ago, we had a tall waiter named David, and the two of us stood at the work station sharing information. Suddenly, his head jerked to the left. He turned white and told me he had just been slapped—hard! I could see that no one else was there."

Pat, Ruth, and I sat in a state of perpetual smiles at the table. The longer Pat and Ruth thought about these matters, the more they realized that the unusual was the usual at the Alexander Hamilton. Old incidents, easily forgotten at one time, began to surface, and it became quite a history of spirit events. "I remember closing up one night with two other staff people," Ruth told me. "In this room, we can turn out all the lights with just one switch," she showed me its operation. "Everything was dark as I locked up, and we all headed for our cars. Just the small light next to the piano broke the darkness of the interior. I started my car, looked up, and discovered all the lights in the Inn turned on! The other girl and I walked up to the windows and looked in and saw nothing and nobody. But we had no key and had to wait until Pat came later to turn the lights off. Thankfully, they all *stayed* off that time!

"And then there are the orbs. Lots of times they show up in people's photographs, but I sometimes see one live. From time to time, I spot one about the size of a lemon, turning the corner and coming down the hallway. I had seen them once before in a friend's haunted house in Grant, so they really don't scare me," Ruth said with satisfaction. "Whose ghost do you think that one is?"

Pat remembered sitting at the bar with the cooks one night after closing. "There was a single wine glass on the bar near the beer tap and Clint, our bartender, was washing glasses as we talked and joked about a long day's work. All at once, the wine glass began to move slowly toward the edge. I was so mesmerized by its movement that I couldn't speak. Just as I finally yelled out,

'Clint!', the glass went over the edge and shattered on the floor. The cooks all looked at one another, got up without saying a word, and left."

"That's just like the time I was carrying in a load of linen and an invisible something just hit the whole pile, throwing them out of my hands and into the air," Ruth recalled. "I had to just walk away from *that*. I also remember the time I was closing up and heard water running in the men's lavatory. I went in and found water gushing full-blast in the sink. That faucet had been off a minute earlier!"

"I sleep on the third floor," Pat told me, "and one night I heard a cat's loud yowl. I got out of bed and went into the hallway, where I found our cat with his head stuck in a hole in the drywall—a hole that wasn't there when I went to bed! He was just able to support himself on his legs and was in danger of strangling, so I broke away the plaster and freed him. Just then, a picture flew off my bedroom dresser and out into the hall. *That* got me thinking!"

I had to marvel at Pat. Many owners of inns might not want to tell of such goings-on. But we live in different times today—many Americans are interested in that called "supernatural." Television programs take people on ghost hunts, and well over 50% of Americans have had unexplainable events. Pat is a history buff from an historic old battle site village. So, here is some "*living* (pardon the expression) history," if you will—an old historic home with some former residents, albeit cranky ones, still at home.

"Oh yes," Ruth added, "did I tell you about the little girl with her cat on the staircase? One of our guests came inside late one evening to tell his party about seeing a child leading her cat on a leash outside. Charmed, they all went to look, but she wasn't there!" Pat remarked that he'd come across information about a child's death in the house years ago.

So, the events at O'Connor's Alexander Hamilton Inn can be almost comical at times. A beautiful old mansion from an earlier time, George and Martha still at war with one another and their own spiritual selves, things flying about or breaking, a little girl occasionally greeting visitors outside, and it's all *normal*, just history playing out every day and night on West Park Row. Despite it all, every time I visit the Alexander Hamilton, the meals just seem to get better and better. It must be the "spectral seasoning."

The Bloody Bucket

In early 1999, Vance Agee, an officer in the local Rotary Club, attended the weekly meeting, this time in a new location. On Center Street hill in Lewiston, NY, stands a building that once housed "The Bloody Bucket," a

The former Bloody Bucket/Village Inn

notorious waterfront bar that long ago catered to laborers, river men, and, I'm told, riff-raff. By the time his Rotary Club meetings were held there, it had become "The Village Inn." Likely, the former gruesome name evolved from the history of bar and street fights that once were common on the river end of Center Street, where the river boatmen from barges and sailing ships on the Niagara River sought relaxation and worked out their frustrations.

Sally Schoonmaker, who owned the establishment and lived upstairs for many years, told me, "That name was awful, and I kept trying to get away from it, so people would be more disposed to come in for a nice relaxing dinner. But the name persisted, unappetizing as it was." Village Historian Margaret Laurie also reminded me that the fabled Iroquois "Western Door" stood nearby at the waterfront on Center Street. For that reason, it might also be considered a mystical place where spirits and souls would congregate after closing hours.

The old building, constructed about 1850, had seen not only the fisticuffs of the river rats, but also the violence and murders of the Prohibition era, when liquor smugglers plied their trade across the international boundary of the Niagara River and were often met in shoot-outs by revenuers and FBI agents.

It was a new meeting site, and Vance and his companions were eager for a different ambience. And straight off, they got what they were looking for—perhaps more. "The waitresses told us right away that the restaurant was haunted by five ghosts, all of whom they had actually seen at some time, and with whom they even talked."

The first of the specters most often appeared in the kitchen near a thick wall that was actually a superimposition of five walls, each from a different era. Once they are sealed up, such walls may hold in energies from long ago, as many ghost fans know. Another spirit seemed to frequent the outside front balcony. Still a third wraith seemed to be that of a young woman who sits on the staircase in the foyer, awaiting a fiancé or beau who never shows up. Patrons of the restaurant often experienced the figure seated there, a woman who suddenly vanished when looked at.

Agee continues, "One night we arrived early and the staff explained that one ghost was in a bad mood," so the early arrivals moved to the restaurant's interior. "Suddenly we were jolted by a loud crash and discovered that a huge old wooden china cupboard had fallen over flat onto the floor in the entrance way behind us, along with the newer coat rack!" Hurrying to investigate the strange phenomenon, the men discovered not a soul nearby. It took two of them to lift the cupboard upright, yet when they did so, they found only a few pieces of china had broken, as the cabinet had fallen onto a rug.

Agee says that he was both angered and fearful at the unexpected and irrational crash, and after the other men left, he blurted out, "If you do anything like this *again*, I will bring in an exorcist to send you on your way to a place from which you will never return!" Agee is not a firm believer in ghosts but seems a very spiritual man. There was no answer and no indication that the ghost or ghosts had heard him.

When he returned home later that night, after the meeting, he discovered that an old lamp in his house had unaccountably fallen or been pushed over, and he found the glass globe broken. He reasoned that, though the family had a dog, it was a small animal and in no way could have upset the lamp. What if he had brought some of the spirits' resentments home with him? Then, he figured what his error had been.

"Please just imagine with me what it could be like," he said. "If ghosts are not evil spirits but, instead, are the souls of dead humans who just have not let go of this world and are trapped in a dark land between two worlds!" He instantly felt pity for such souls and admitted that he could not even fathom the anguish or feelings they might have, trapped and cut off from normal, living humans. He felt guilty about his arrogant speech to the discarnates at the Bloody Bucket.

From his Christian upbringing, he recalled that, following the Crucifixion, Jesus had gone down into hell, Sheol, or the underworld, to free those souls trapped there. Vance came to believe that he, himself, should have spoken more in accord with the Golden Rule, putting himself in the position of the trapped and lost souls at the restaurant. He knew what he had to do.

On the next meeting night, he says, he got to the Bloody Bucket early and stood alone in the foyer facing the stairs. "Guys," I said, "I'm sorry for what I said. I *love* you guys!" With his expression of Love there was no bitter cold reaction, which some patrons have experienced at that spot. "Instead, a warmth spread over me," he reported. "And, as long as we held our meetings there aftterward, I always greeted whoever was in the front entrance way when I came in." When no one else could hear, of course.

A few years later, the restaurant closed and the building's future is now in doubt. To Vance's knowledge, no clergy or professional liberator has ever gone to the old bar and restaurant to free all the souls trapped there. In time, perhaps, the building will be torn down—an activity that often, but not always, frees those entangled between the worlds of spirit and earth. It would be a loss to Lewiston for such an old building with "character" to disappear. Agee reiterates my own prescription for such haunted sites: pray for the deceased, that they will *see* the White Light and enter it. Such illumination is a bright portal to The Beyond, where *no* soul is in chains.

Who's There?

"For a number of years, my husband and I had a nice old restaurant called 'The Homestead' in Niagara Falls," Mary Grisanti told me. Now a retired grandmother, Mary remembers the Homestead on Niagara Falls Boulevard as if it were yesterday. "My mother-in-law, Jennie, chose the name and started the restaurant in 1952. Then, my husband, Tony, and I took over from her later and kept the name because the building used to be an old farmhouse, and there were woods out back when we lived and worked there."

The Grisantis lived upstairs over the restaurant, which had an "old part" and a "new part," with the older section apparently having been the farmhouse that dated from the mid to late 1800s. "I guess my family was the first ones to hear the strange sounds," she told me. "I remember that one night, I had gotten the kids to bed and was cleaning the floor. I heard slow, heavy footsteps coming up the stairs, so I got up and opened the door for Tony, then got back down on my knees to scrub the floor. The door stayed open but nobody came in. I got up once more to see what was keeping Tony. Looking down the stairs, I saw nobody. When he finally came upstairs after closing the bar a half hour later, I asked him why he'd come up, then gone back down. He told me that it wasn't him!"

She remembers that, some evenings, when she put the children to bed, they would wake up and complain that the movements in the hallway were keeping them awake. This reminded her of her own experiences as a younger woman, when she heard a repeated clicking sound in the hall. Only her mother was in the apartment, though, and was way down at the other end of the hall. *Nobody* was outside her door.

"About that time, another strange thing happened, though not at the restaurant," she told me. "Tony had eye surgery and had to stay in the hospital for a few days. I went to visit one evening, along with my son and daughter-in-law and sat beside his bed in a chair that touched the curtain that separated us from the other bed. As I sat and chatted, I became aware that someone on the other side of the hospital curtain was tugging and tugging at the cloth. I thought that was rather impertinent, and when we stood up to go, I looked on the other side of the drape. The other bed was empty, and nobody was there!"

A few years later, we sold our restaurant to a man who dramatically changed its appearance, painting the outside with large polka dots and changed the restaurant's name to 'The Crazy Horse.' He cut down the trees out back and made a softball field, hoping to attract team business after the games. It didn't work that well, however, and the Grisantis had to foreclose on his loan. Mary's nephew, Tony, then reopened it, gutted the old upstairs apartment, finished off the cellar, demolished part of the old structure on the front, and returned to a similar name, "The Homestead."

Nephew Tony, an enterprising man, created a dinner theater, which prospered for some years. When I interviewed him as to his memories about a possible ghost, he demurred. "What I'll never forget," he said, "is being asleep in the upstairs apartment and having a very vivid dream of my mother's and aunt's faces." Then, and he's not sure if it was in the dream or an actual event, the phone rang, and he told the person on the other end that he was beat, tired

Captain's Cove Restaurant

out, and couldn't come to the hospital. He hung up and went back to sleep. Shortly after he awoke, the phone did ring, and when he answered it, the caller informed him that his aunt was dying in the hospital. He hurried there, but wondered just what part of the previous experience had been "real."

In early 2006, I sought out the old restaurant, only to find it radically changed both in name and structure from Tony's memories. The new owner, Don Boland, invited me into what had been the old dinner theater, now called "The Captain's Cove." Where the stage had been was a well-stocked bar and pretty barmaids, and in the corner was the regular Friday night blues band.

Busy with overseeing his business, Don was amused that I came seeking ghosts. But after the schedule got into its nightly flow, he sat with me and a former waitress, Debbie, and the pair reminisced for me. I related the Grisanti stories, and we all laughed. Debbie then told us of the many times she had come to work and heard noises in the front restaurant section. Investigating, she never found anybody there. "It has been kind of unnerving," she said. Then, Don recalled the evening that they closed late, and Debbie had gone home. He checked all the locks and machines and returned through the restaurant bar, only to find that someone had poured a large draft beer and a glass of wine. Sometimes, in reviewing the day's business, he and Debbie would have a drink before heading home, but not this night. Debbie had *gone*. "Anyway, why would she pour drinks for the *two* of us, when she was going home?" he asked. Debbie spoke up and denied having done so at that time.

Then, certain memories clicked in Don's head. "Here's a funny story for you," he offered. "Several times, when I first took over the restaurant, I heard loud noises in the front. I'd come into the restaurant and find a pile of ashtrays spilled onto the floor. One night, I found several trash cans tipped over. I was determined to find the troublemaker, whether or not it was a ghost. I set a trap and caught a raccoon, which had somehow gotten in. But that was just that once. Now, you've got me thinking maybe the animal didn't do all the damage."

He took me into the cellar, which Tony Grisanti had modernized, and showed me the one thing that he hadn't changed when he bought the place. It was the old dinner theater dressing room. Inside, we could see the signatures and graffiti that the actors and actresses had put on the walls and ceiling. Signatures, production titles, little wise sayings, and copious lipstick kisses. I thought the latter might have brought Don some good luck, but reminded him that signatures are sometimes a last earthly restraining link for those who have passed on.

He told me he had kept the graffiti in case one of the players became famous someday and returned, and he could then show the world that the star had begun a career in Niagara Falls! "But," I asked, "how would he know if one of the old performers had died and was in the process of letting go of their earthly past?" He responded, "Guess I'll hear them banging around down here, won't I?"

We returned upstairs and rejoined Debbie. All of a sudden, she had begun to remember a list of objects that had mysteriously disappeared since she began working there.

This seems to be a place to watch for future developments. And one can get some great music and even better pizza and wings while waiting!

The End is Near

"If you ever get to Southold on the North Fork of Long Island," my friend Helise told me, "be sure to take a look at the General Wayne Inn, an old restaurant that has seen better days. It *looks* spooky," she said, "and maybe it *is*." When I visited Southold, I made sure to seek out the elusive building on Cedar Beach Road. She certainly was right; the old place must have once been elegant, but it was now more an eyesore than a presentable historic relic. It appears that The General Wayne's days are numbered.

In an upscale area of summer houses, the old establishment sits in an untended field with dumps of trash and broken furnishings strewn throughout the old parking lot. Overgrown trees hang over it, and weeds are everywhere. I found parts of the roof caved in and the rear door flat on the floor. So I walked in.

It is an old building, to be sure, as the large timbers supporting the oldest, center part of the house were put there to last. I discovered that the first part of the structure was built in 1784 by Maj. Gilbert Horton, a blacksmith, farmer and Revolutionary War officer, as a present for his bride, Keturah Terry. Many additions and modifications have been made since the Horton family gave up the house, instigated by a series of entrepreneurs, starting with Edwin Brown during the Depression, who attempted to operate it as a restaurant. One of its past names was "The Cedar Beach Inn," and the last investor/owner called it "The General Wayne," though there is no historical connection between the general and Cedar Point. For some reason, maybe its remote location, none of the owners have made the inn a profitable concern, and now it stands in limbo, begging a well-heeled lover of history to rescue it from oblivion and entropy.

Not much here now, I mused, as the looters and vandals have stolen or destroyed anything usable. I don't see any objects moving or hear voices, so a haunt isn't likely. Nevertheless, I settled down to meditate, and all at once, I became aware of an energy more than a movement. I looked toward the front

The former Gen. Wayne Inn

window, and my mind created a large round table where only broken plaster and dirt are found today. Seated at that table was a curious man, almost a Fred Astaire look-alike, but with jet black hair. I asked him telepathically who he was when he lived. He shot back two names, "Slick" and "Speed" or "Speedy." He told me he loved to play the horses but hadn't done so for some time. His entire "life," if one can call his present existence that, is focused on looking out the window, awaiting the arrival of a car. He showed me what the vehicle looked like, and my impression was that of a car from the late 30s, boxy and black.

The energy from this man was hyperactive, and, though he reclined against his wooden chair, one would not say he *sat* in it. In his black suit or tuxedo, he was straight as a board, and I assumed he was hopped up on some drug. Calling himself "Speedy," at times, might have been a clue. In death, he had but one goal—to await that car's arrival. My guess was that he might be in withdrawal from his drug of choice and was awaiting a re-supply. That's all I got from him.

There was a woman in her fifties there, too, but she seemed as much an observer as me. I asked her name, and she gave me, "Margaret." She stood immobile, dressed in an off-white dress, with a small apron that appeared to be azure or green. I asked why she stayed there in spirit, and her response was tentative, just that she, too, was waiting for something to happen. I had the impression that she emotionally protected the man in the chair, though I'm not sure he even knew she was there. Her employment there was in the 1950s. In a sense, the entire scenario seemed like walking onto the set of an old Bogart film, maybe *Key Largo* or *The Petrified Forest*.

106

I returned to the back door, near what must once have been a busy bar. Then I became aware that there was one more man, perhaps named Lance, who sat on the last bar stool. He didn't move and was more of a cardboard cutout, which I associate with a "house memory," a soul's remembering rather than his actual energy presence. He sat looking toward the old center fireplace, with a beer half-raised to his mouth. He came to watch one of the waitresses but wouldn't give her name or any information about himself. That's all I found there in the spirit world.

I have interviewed Helise and Alex Wipf, who both have invested time and energy in attempting to save the old Horton House. The Horton family has long ago gone to their glory, and the beetles, vandals, snow, and rain are trying to push their once-elegant old home and its residual ghosts into its own grave.

The Old Library

The Old Library Restaurant and Bed & Breakfast

In the 1880s, George V. Forman had a house and law office at 116 Union Street in Olean, NY. Forman, who amassed a fortune in the oil business and the legal profession, could afford to be generous when he donated the property for a city library, and in return, the library board dubbed the structure, "The Forman Library." Then, in 1909, contemplating the construction of a larger facility, the board sold the building to Mr. Stillman, a construction man who dismantled it and recycled all the parts into new buildings. Later, with a donation from the Andrew Carnegie Foundation, the city's new library was built on that lot and opened in 1910.

Olean's population and prosperity grew, and by the early 1970s, the library board was again in need of shelf space. Rather than destroy their fine old building, the board donated the library in 1974 to the Olean Historical

Society, which used the building for office and lecture space. Included in the new configuration was office space for the local Department of Aging. But in 1982, the city school district, the property's new administrators, decided it was time to sell the old structure.

Local entrepreneurs, named Louis and Mary Barbara Marra bought the old brick building and made it into one of the finest Italian restaurants in Cattaraugus County. Louis died in 1990, and his son, Joseph, and wife, Susan, became the management team, continuing the tradition of fine dining and adding a catering business. They envisioned a high quality bed & breakfast near-by and had previously purchased the beautiful old 1895 Victorian house next door. In its time, the residence had been owned by a city oil man and a city physician, and it became Olean's first bed & breakfast inn: The Old Library Inn.

Ghostbusters aside, in most instances, libraries tend not to generate ghosts, so there are but a few anecdotal tales from the restaurant. The same, however, can't be said for the old house that now serves as the Inn.

In October 2004, newlyweds Dominic and Kate Dudley-Perry attend-ed a friend's wedding in Olean after having driven from central Pennsylvania. They knew they'd be exhausted at day's end and, as both were graduates of St. Bonaventure University, they had always sought a good excuse to stay at the beautiful old Inn. *Now* was their chance. They had checked in and prepaid before the wedding, and, all tuckered out after the nuptials, they returned late to their lodging, fatigued after an evening of dancing at the reception.

"Dominic fell into bed and was asleep immediately," Kate told me. "I thought I was just as weary, but for some reason I just could not drop off to sleep. I couldn't understand my wakefulness. Each time I was about to drop off, I heard a pounding. Someone in the hall, I guessed, and I got up to quietly open the door and look. No one was outside—my imagination? I returned to bed, got comfortable and reached the edge of sleep once more, only to hear the pounding again. I couldn't understand why Dominic didn't wake up. I tried to rouse him, but he was fast asleep," she smiled.

This sequence of events was repeated throughout the night. As she lay half asleep and half awake, Kate kept trying to isolate the source of the rapping noise. Kate wasn't fearful, as she sensed that, if a spirit was causing the sound, it was simply a mischievous one. The noises weren't coming from outside the room she concluded, so she turned her attention to the interior, though she could clearly see in the room's dim light, that nothing was moving inside. Finally, after getting up once more, she discovered that the sounds seemed to emanate from the small desk in the room, though the sounds seemed to issue from *within* the desk rather than its top. Could the desk, itself, be haunted?

"The closet door next to my side of the bed was mirrored, but for some strange reason, I felt a strong compulsion to avoid looking into the reflection," she told me. I responded that it was just as well she didn't. Mirrors are often thought to be potential portals to The Other World, and many suspect that Lewis Carroll was writing of such an experience in *Through the Looking Glass*, the original *Alice in Wonderland* story. Kate and I also chatted about the ancient custom of *scrying*, looking into a reflective surface as a way of entering the *alpha state*, where extra-sensory perceptions are common. Readers might wish to consult the works of Dr. Raymond Moody, who has a "psychomanteum" facility in Georgia, which allows clients to meet with deceased loved ones. Consult his book *Reunions*.

"In the morning, I told Dominic about my sleepless night and the knocking or pounding sound. As we packed to leave for our home in Pennsylvania," Kate told me, "I resolved to question the desk clerk about any resident ghosts when we departed. But no one was at the desk, and, as we had prepaid, we hit the road for State College, PA. Some time later, I ran into a college friend, JT, and I told him about our adventure. He laughed, 'The Library Inn? For goodness sake, I used to *work* there! Don't you *know* that it's the most haunted place in Olean?'" Kate hadn't known. When I interviewed her, she suggested I contact her friend for confirmation of the experience.

"I had only had one previous experience with ghosts," JT told me, "back in Saugerties, when I was growing up. I experienced strange sensations on the stairs in a buddy's house, but I considered that maybe it was just one of those adolescent things."

JT attended college at St. Bonaventure and befriended Kate during their undergraduate years. Afterward, she went on to post-grad work in England, while JT and his wife, Kelly, remained near Olean, where he took a job as bartender at The Old Library Inn and Restaurant. "At nights, after the B&B hostess left for the night, I was responsible for all the money and had to put it in the safe before closing the bar. I also had to turn out all of the restaurant lights and the lights at the B&B. That's when I began to think I wasn't alone.

"The Inn is a big old Victorian house with three floors. As I did my jobs there, I often felt watched, as if someone invisible were observing how well I did the tasks. Sometimes there were abnormally cold spots, but I tried to mentally write those off as drafts. There are two wine cellars in the basement, and I had the darndest time getting the cellar lights to stay off. All the switches are dimmers, though you can turn them off simply by pushing in. So many times, I'd push the button on the cellar lights and start up the stairs, then turn back, only to see the cellar lights turned on again. It was frustrating having to repeat the operation.

"One evening, I noticed that as I passed each pay phone, the handset would fall off, and I had to replace it. Strange stuff! So by the time I got down to the wine cellar, I was a bit spooked. I punched the lights out and went upstairs to be sure the lights were also out in the upstairs banquet room—they were. Turning once more, I looked toward the cellar. I could see bright light shining from down there again, not dim illumination, but *bright*. I ran down to turn them off, but then I headed for the door and *ran* as fast as I could to my apartment several blocks away!"

JT remembers hearing an employee commenting about the Inn's uppermost rooms being cold and figures that Kate and Dominic had one of those. At other times, there would be stories from the employees in the restaurant about hearing slammed doors when nobody else was there. "Several times, I stood in the dining room at day's end and heard silverware clinking away in the kitchen. When I walked in there, the noise stopped and nobody was present. Today, JT is a teacher near Kingston and finds the antics of the adolescents he teaches at least predictable. "But I still have fond memories of the Old Library Inn and Restaurant," he said. "I'd have a dinner there in a minute!"

JT felt, as did several other employees, that the spirit of the whole operation was old Louis Marra, a man who worked so hard for years to present quality, appetizing meals to diners. How could such a conscientious guy just drop the satisfaction he got from all that effort and run off to the other world? He may not be ready for a while yet. JT assures me that your appetite will appreciate a visit to the old restaurant, even if all the other diners are real. However, you might just encounter some spirits at the bar—not just the kind that JT used to serve!

Hospitality

The first thing I missed was a large gold-lettered sign in front of the house. I double-checked the address on my notes—6 Main Street, Candor, NY. Yes, this is the place all right, but why no sign? How can these folks, the Musgraves, hope to draw the attention of passersby to their bed & breakfast? I didn't realize that I'd missed the sign at a nearby road intersection. Later, I discovered that they don't *have* to be overbearing in presenting themselves. There is such a wonderful feeling of *home* there, and I learned from the proprietors that they have very many repeat guests. And maybe a ghost or two.

The Edge of Thyme is aptly named for a number of reasons, but first, let's look at its history. The house was built in the 1860s, but was later purchased in 1906 by Dr. Amos Canfield and his wife Rosa as a summer house.

The Edge of Thyme Bed & Breakfast

Amos was a native of Tioga County but chose to practice medicine on Madison Avenue in New York City, where he met the attractive secretary to John D. Rockefeller, Rosa Murphy, an Irish immigrant. For a secretary, Rosa had done *very* well, investing her income in stocks and bonds that John D. recommended. When she met Amos, Rosa was seeking a refined gentleman as her husband but, as her income was ample, she discouraged him from working very hard. The Canfields lived the good life, traveling each summer to Candor.

Their village summer home had to be exquisite, they decided, and the old Queen Anne style house they bought was converted to the Georgian style with simulated Doric columns on the façade and Grecian urns in relief on the fireplaces inside. A side sun porch with beautiful leaded glass windows designed by L'Hommideau from New York City was added on the side of the house where the former owners had a large wrap-around porch. Parquet floors were then installed throughout the house.

A staff of specialists helped the Canfields enjoy their leisure, and among these was a Japanese gardener to care for the perennial and shrubbery gardens behind the house, a cook, servants, and a chauffeur, who had his own specially-built car wash in the carriage house. Sometime during the renovations, Rosa wrote her name on a cellar beam, where it can still be seen today: Rosa Murphy Canfield. As readers know, handwriting can maintain a spirit's attachment to a house, and by her signature, Rosa certainly considered the house was *hers*. The estate on Candor's Main Street became known as "Canfield Gardens," and the couple entertained the cream of American society, including one President, there. Dr. Amos only practiced medicine in Candor for a few years.

Rosa died in 1934 and Dr. Amos followed her into Eternity eight years later. There were other owners, but none who are officially recorded as suffering any apparent trauma and thus remaining as ghosts, before Frank & Eva Musgrave bought the old house in 1983. "We made just a few changes here and there," Frank told me, "and then opened for business a year later."

Frank is a PhD. in Economics and has taught at Ithaca College for 36 years, and Eva Mae Gifford-Musgrave is an RN, BA in History with a minor in Religion, Business and Art and Architecture. She has also been a teacher and financial advisor. The third permanent staff member is Fred Bassett, a genial basset hound that they rescued from being tied to a tree for a year. Fred spends considerable time seeking petting from guests and engaging in meditation.

"At first, it was touch and go in attracting guests," Frank told me, "as there are over four hundred B&Bs in the tri-county area. But The Edge of Thyme stands out because of the laid-back atmosphere that is also sumptuous, that we've created here, and soon, we were regularly filling our seven guest rooms." Because of the elegance inside, we've hosted several murder mystery weekends, and High Teas are conducted on a regular basis. "It's just a nice place to stay," Frank said, making me wait just a bit longer to hear about the ghosts. Then he was ready, and Eva joined us, having just brought a fresh batch of muffins from the oven.

"From time to time we, or our guests, hear footsteps descending the wooden front stairway. But there is a problem," Eva smiled, "our stairs have been covered with carpet for almost twenty years—one should not be able to hear footsteps. From time to time we hear the back door slam, as if a servant has just gone out to the garden or garage. But the back door is locked, so we look at one another and nowadays just shrug."

Frank added that the upstairs rooms are named after family members and one of those, Scott's Room, is often the location where guests report seeing a blonde woman rocking in a rocking chair. "We don't know if she was a member of the Canfield family, though Rosa and Amos had no children, or a long-ago Canfield guest. The lady is harmless, she just rocks and smiles. Some folks don't expect to see her there in the night, though they usually just go back to sleep. Our first dog used to sit outside that room's door and stare at it, as if waiting for someone inside to let him in. Then, one day, he decided either nobody was inside or it just wasn't worth it to wait, and after that he never stood around there any more." Now, the Musgraves have a younger basset hound, Fred, as their earlier dog is off exploring the universe following his death a few years ago.

Several psychics have visited the house and one told the Musgraves that there is a Civil War soldier in the house, and he won't leave because his blonde wife (whom the psychic saw dressed in a long white dress) was buried in the base-ment. Such a surreptitious burial, if true, must have occurred long before the Canfields owned the house, and certainly wouldn't have been legally recorded.

Eva told me of the many careers she had before they bought The Edge of Thyme. Add to those qualifications that she is an excellent cook and recent-ly finished publishing her cookbook of drop-dead-delicious-recipes. Again she smiled. "One other non-degree thing I've learned in our twenty-three years here is *never leave a perfume bottle in the bathroom.* The ghost or ghosts steal it. After having several guests complain that their perfume disappeared from that room, I tried a test and put a nice little bottle of Chanel No. 5 on the shelf and, when I came back later, it had vanished. None of the missing perfumes has ever been returned," she said.

It occurred to me later that, as so many ghosts do pranks because they simply want recognition of their presence, maybe Eva needs to *demand* their return. Often, even the most dedicated wraith will give up what they've "bor-rowed." I will recommend that to her.

"Maybe the most persistent taunt from the spirit world is that we keep finding a sun porch window on the front open," Frank told me. "Look at those fasteners, sliding bars that can't be influenced by gravity," he said. "Yet, we come downstairs in the morning and too often find one open, and in the win-ter *that* runs up our fuel bill. One thing I've noticed, though, from what a vis-itor told me, is that on the original house, the corner steps onto the old Queen Anne porch were right at that window's location. Therefore, probably *the ghost* knows how to come in, and wonders what's wrong with Eva and me? However, the specter probably finds the present "door" a bit smaller than he or she remembers it.

"About a month ago, one of our cleaners needed to be paid and I sat down with my check ledger to write her a check. I have a record sheet in the ledger but I couldn't find it. It *had to* be there, and I went through the check-book page by page, but the sheet had vanished. I am *certain* it wasn't inside, though ten minutes later, when I looked, there it was!"

While we attempted to find a rational explanation for the returned record sheet, Eva took me through the spacious rooms. It was if the Canfields had just stepped out, as each room was done in turn-of-the-Twentieth Century furnishings, though the bathrooms are modern. "See that elevator there inside the closet," Eva opened the door for me to look. "Amos and Rosa added that for President Franklin Roosevelt, so he could travel up to his bedroom without discomfort when he visited them." Wow, I thought, *I*'d have a couple of his-toric signs out front, but Frank and Eva just aren't into ostentation, and the house speaks quietly for itself.

"Maybe the ghost lives in the attic, I don't know," she continued, "because when Frank or I go up there to get some stored item, we find things moved from where we left them. And we are the only ones who go up there. I don't *disbelieve* in ghosts after our experiences here, but I don't find them a hindrance if they really *are* here—the alleged two in the cellar, the soldier and his lady, never give us any trouble." I asked if she'd ever encountered ghosts before moving to town, and she said yes. She and a friend had a pact that whichever one reached Paradise first would let the other know. "So, there I was in the funeral home, dearly missing my friend and not even remembering our agreement, when suddenly somebody tapped me on the shoulder. I turned quickly but nobody *visible* was there," she beamed.

I asked if the ghosts ever trouble the guests, and the Musgraves could only remember one case in over two decades, on a night when two guests announced they were going to hit the sack early. "As I was closing up around midnight," Frank said, "I saw the two of them with packed suitcases, hurrying down the front stairs. The wife claimed to have seen a ghostly woman dragging a baby (or was it a doll?) across the upstairs floor. Well, *that* was a new one on us," he grinned. "There are still many surprises awaiting *us* here too, I'm sure. After all, we've only been here a bit over twenty years. Rosa and/or Amos, or maybe one of their servants have over a half-century head start on us!"

Ghosts, it occurred to me, live at the edge of time, still working out what is important to them. Eva's kitchen, filled with herbs, spices and those wonderful muffins, more likely partake of thyme. It was a busy weekend for both the proprietors and me. They were catering to a house filled with Cornell parents attending graduation, and I was attempting to finish up a three-day trip around the state, visiting source people who had previously just been voices on the phone, so I had come to Candor in a hurry.

I found it strange then, that at the end of my visit, I had to make a genuine *effort* to rise from the interview table, pack my notebooks and camera, and hit the road. The Edge of Thyme had, in less than an hour, become my home, and I just wanted to settle in. And maybe perk up my ears for subtle sounds.

Knocks

The average person would become exhausted by reading the biography of Charles Briggs Knox. Born in 1855 to an ambitious family in Mapleton (Montgomery County), NY, he eventually held positions as grocery clerk and wagon wheel factory worker in the Mohawk Valley, lumber inspector in Michigan, sheep herder in Texas, Texas Ranger, and then he returned to his

The Knox Mansion

father's flour and feed business in Johnstown, NY. Once back in Fulton County, Knox became a traveling glove salesman, which led to an interest in glue manufacture, and he finally hit on his life's purpose—the development of the best food gelatin in America. Before 1900, the Knox Gelatin factory was the largest business in Johnstown.

He married Rose Markward from Ohio in 1883, and in 1898, they built one of the largest mansions in the city, "Rose Hill," at a cost of $1.2 million. He continued to take an active interest in Fulton County's social, financial, and religious organizations and was known for his philanthropy. He and Rose had three children, two boys and a daughter who died in infancy. Charley Knox, as he preferred to be known, died suddenly on a Canadian fishing trip at age fifty-three. Townspeople expected Rose to sell the family holdings and retreat from public life. How wrong they were!

As new owner of Knox Gelatin, Rose listed her young son, Charles, as the company president, then went to the plant to do the job herself. She began with the managerial staff, entering each office and demanding, "Do you have any problem in working for a *woman?*" Most turn-of-the-century managers and department heads, in fact, *did* have a problem, and Rose fired each in turn, until she had a core of cooperative and energetic executives and employees.

In an early 1900s photo of the top corporate executives of American business, there sits Rose in the front row, the only woman executive in a room of over a hundred men. She was Charley's Rose and loved to travel and bet on the horses with him, sometimes to the tune of twenty-five thousand dollars per bet, and the couple also had a racing stable of their own. Rose didn't surrender easily to age, but finally succumbed in 1950. Much information about her life can be found on www.johnstown.com/roseknox.html.

"It will be thirteen years since I bought the old Knox mansion," Marty Quinn told me. "Thirteen was a lucky number to Charley Knox, and he had it built into the house design. Here, look at the fireplace—thirteen tiles across. And that is just one place that you will discover it. When I found the old house for sale in 1993, I raised every penny I could to buy it. It is absolutely gorgeous, mainly because I've put a lot of my resources into its restoration. That day, as I prepared to close on the property," he grinned, "the real estate agent disclosed that there had been a suicide here. That would have been the previous owner, old Doctor Larrabee. He had an extremely painful cancer and couldn't alleviate the pain, so he shot himself." Marty isn't sure if the doctor is the prime ghost in the place, "because there are so many here," he laughed.

Marty Quinn is good natured about all the spirit phenomena in the Knox Mansion Bed & Breakfast. I have seldom encountered a building so filled with anecdotes of ghostly activity. Most of it is just plain fascinating and some of it is poignant.

"Soon after I moved in, I heard a vase break," he told me. "Then I found a heavy object on the mantelpiece moved. I've had lamps smash during the night, and most of my friends who come to visit sense 'the others' here," he told me. "I started finding the downstairs rug flipped over when I came downstairs in the mornings. Somebody wanted to be recognized."

A good deal of the activity takes place in the master suite, a delightful large Victorian room on the second floor. Getting to the second floor, however, is a slightly spooky excursion in itself. Walking up the main stairway, one sees portraits of both Rose and Charles on the wall. "Take your time going up," Marty instructed me, "look at their faces." Though he didn't tell me what to expect, I readily saw that each subject seemed to follow me with their gaze as I climbed upward. The two of them seemed to look directly at me wherever I was, and once in the upstairs hall, I saw Rose's face undergo a strange transfiguration. You'll have to see that effect for yourself.

In March 2006, a guest was making a phone/camera picture of the master suite to show to folks at home and found a mass of spirit energy on her screen. "I hadn't told her about the ghosts. I try not to tell guests what to expect, and many leave here knowing nothing at all about our spirits," Marty laughed again. "The woman told me that the power in the room had gone off at 3:30 a.m. and then turned back on, though she saw and felt nobody. This is a room where guests sometimes feel a cold breeze, even though all doors are shut, and the storm windows are closed tight. One of my daughter's boyfriends, walking in the hallway between the master suite bedroom and its Jacuzzi room, had his hat blown right off his head. My daughter, walking just ahead of him, felt no breeze at all.

"For me, and for my two daughters who grew up here, it sure has been exciting. I've had blankets pulled off my bed during the night and felt the bed shake," Marty said. "Often, when sitting in the dining room, I hear the back door open, then close, and then there is the sound of footsteps moving through the kitchen or laundry room, though nobody is there. And I have had too many peripheral visual sightings to remember. Many times an androgynous voice calls my name, even when the house is empty.

"We have school groups come to tour the old mansion, and several times youngsters have told me of seeing a man standing at the top of the cellar stairs. One of these students, a boy, later told me that a photograph hanging on the wall was the man he saw. It is a portrait of Phil Ulrich, former Knox family gardener, who died in 1950. Many people have spotted a man dressed in a black coat standing or walking in the kitchen area, though I'm not sure it's Phil. One individual saw the man walk through a solid wall.

"And then, there is the child, or maybe children. We know Helene, the Knox's daughter, was born and died in 1895, so the entity might be her. But living here for over a dozen years, I have asked myself many questions about the public and private details of the Knox family's life. I have a theory," Marty said. "As there is some retardation in the Knox family, I suspect there was another *unpublicized* child, possibly a handicapped or retarded daughter. I suspect she was kept in her own quarters on the third floor, near the servants' rooms. There is a room up there with its lock on the outside. Inside, there is a small door that gives entrance under the eaves, and I've thoroughly explored that space and found old-fashioned, empty food containers in there and down inside the wall. Who would have eaten meals up there, especially when there was a bounty of food in the dining room?" He showed me a relief ceiling decoration that Mr. Knox favored, a design of four wreaths. Marty theorizes that the design is symbolic of four children. One of the symbols is flawed, not having a ribbon where the other three do. Is this Charley's silent tribute to a child that was abnormal and who died quietly without reaching adulthood?

"Children's voices are sometimes heard when none are present, and one guest saw a blonde-haired girl about age nine who quickly vanished. Of course, Rose hosted many children's organizations and clubs in the house. Here," Marty showed me, "look at this handwritten booklet of club rules that I found under the stairs. Would this object be powerful enough to retain a child's consciousness in the house after she died?

"We have so much fun here on Halloween," Marty Quinn told me. "We have statues of ghouls and old codgers standing in the foyer's dim light when the kids come through trick and treating. Some of the children enter here only by sheer determination, as they've heard legends about The Knox Mansion. Some of our staff members are costumed, but for the more fearful kids who can only make it as far as the foot of the stairs, I have girls in regular dress, ordinary teens, handing out the goodies. It is wonderful to see the children's expressions!" It occurred to me that Marty was happily carrying on Charley Knox's tradition of generosity to the community.

Debbie, the B&B's secretary and chef, has had her own experiences there. "From the time I came to work for Marty, I've felt watched—not really in any danger, but just observed. My boyfriend, Erik, stayed over one night recently. Feeling that I was up, he called out, 'Be right there, hon!' But when his eyes focused, he saw a woman dressed in black standing and observing him. It wasn't me; I was down in the kitchen at that time. I was also one of those who saw the black-coated man near the laundry room and called out to him. But he wasn't there when I went to look. I feel strongly that Rose is still around, as she loved the house.

"We had a blackout of sorts in January of 2006, and a guest's husband came downstairs in the night to locate some candles. As he stood in the dining room, the man saw a woman walk through the library and into the greenhouse, where she vanished. I showed him a photo of Rose Knox, and he identified her as the woman he had seen. But there seem to be so many others here who just don't want to let go either. A Mexican guest at breakfast one morning asked if we had a ghost. He had awakened during the night to see a ghost man standing beside his bed, and in his hand, the man held a doctor's black medical bag. That had to be Doc Larabee!"

Debbie said that Erik had also spotted the black-coated man with a black hat walking through the kitchen, and Erik theorized that the spirit might be the old family chauffeur. Marty Quinn joined our conversation, suggesting that this may be the same spirit who pulled an afghan off him as he lay on the downstairs couch watching television one day. Nobody was around when Marty jumped up to look.

"I escorted a new guest named Gary and his wife along with their ten-year-old daughter, up the front stairs to their room. At the top of the stairs, both the girl and I heard, 'Come here' whispered in a child's voice. We looked at one another and said, 'Cool!'" he told me. A salesman from Texas visited the house, and as we walked along in the hallway, the man informed me that he didn't believe in ghosts. I told him it was okay not to believe, but then he got the strangest look on his face and asked me, 'How did you *do* that?' I asked what he meant, and he said that someone or something had just rapped him on the forehead. Of course, *I* didn't see anyone else," Marty grinned.

Quinn generously permits local fashion companies to do photography for their catalogs in the house, with its unique fireplaces and antique black walnut paneling. On the day I interviewed Marty and Debbie, there was another such group moving about, taking portraits through gauzy curtains and posing in the greenhouse/atrium. What a delightful group of young people, I mused. I'll bet Rose is delighted to have children here again. And maybe the little ghost girl is enchanted with the models' jewelry and trendy haircuts. I have been in no other house that seems so designed for enjoyment, both for those residents of the past and the guests of the present.

There is no other B&B that I can recommend so highly for those seeking "a little invisible something extra" for their weekend away from home. I left there thinking it should be called "The Knocks Mansion."

Stay Here!

The Old Furness House

In 1993, Sue visited Saratoga Springs, to relax and spend time away from her downstate teaching job. Before she left a restaurant, she heard a child's voice say, "Stay here!" There was no youngster around at the time, but as she walked to her car, she pondered the words. The region around Saratoga Springs often exerts an attraction to first-time visitors, and Sue was not immune. Could she really give up her well-paying teaching job and move to a town where she knew nobody? Yes, she could. And she did so with a sense of certainty that the universe wanted her to move. She wondered what new lessons awaited.

There were many years of struggle in the 1990s, as she moved from one temporary job to the next, even going to California for a while, though she returned in 2004. That decade had been a period of exploring her burgeoning intuitive nature. In 2005, she found a position as innkeeper at Union Gables, a delightful Queen Anne style bed & breakfast on Union Avenue in the city.

Visitors to that old house today immediately spot the green and white plaque above the porch, designating the building as "Furness House." It was a dormitory for girls attending Skidmore College in the city, and it was a beloved part of the campus before Skidmore built a new campus on North Broadway in 1970 and put many of its old Victorian homes on Circular Street, Spring Street and Union Avenue up for sale. Just a few blocks from the world famous Saratoga Thoroughbred Racecourse, the greats of American society have passed Union Gables for over a century. Maybe more than a few have stayed behind.

Dry goods merchant George Crippen built the stately home in 1901, employing famed architect Newton Brezee as the designer. Brezee had designed summer homes for many of America's wealthy on fashionable North Broadway. There was a strong feminine influence in Crippen's life, as he was raised by an aunt in Glens Falls. After selling his Broadway store, he built a factory to design and produce women's coats in the early twentieth century. Following his death in 1920, the house was sold to Charles Furness, owner of the *Glens Falls Times*.

The Furness family lived a genteel life at 55 Union Avenue, the high class route between the downtown hotels, the Casino and the Racetrack. Mr. Furness was an avid fan of thoroughbred racing and had a box in the grandstand there. In 1936, as the women's college named for Lucy Skidmore expanded, Furrness sold his home to the college for a dormitory. Then, in 1970, after the college no longer needed the big house, it was used as a group home for seventeen years and then sold to a local man, who renovated the building and created the bed and breakfast.

The interior design is exquisite, and on the day I came to visit and interview Sue, I was struck with how comfortable and peaceful such a large house could be. My hostess revealed some strange experiences that I also found impressive.

Tom Fox, who owns the building, has arranged a virtual computer tour in the foyer for those who enter, so that prospective guests can choose a room without climbing the stairs. "On my first day at work as innkeeper, in the interior shot of an upstairs guest room, I suddenly saw a group of men sitting around a table, smoking and playing cards," she told me. She had to blink twice because, as quickly as the scene appeared, it was gone and the attractive décor of the present room (with no inhabitants) remained on the screen. She remembered that one onlooker at the card game had lathered his face and, holding a straight razor, was about to shave. He turned at looked directly at Sue through the screen and their eyes met.

In a short time, one of the chambermaids complained to Sue (now the innkeeper) that an upstairs room door was sometimes sticking and required quite a bit of force to open; at other times it opened easily. Sue accompanied the woman upstairs and discovered it was the room she had just viewed in the foyer. She tried the door, and it opened easily; as expected, the room was empty. However, Sue and the other woman could smell the strong aroma of shaving cream (maybe Barbasol) inside, as if the men had just departed. "I had to sniff several times to make sure my nose wasn't playing tricks on me," she said. Were the ghost men still there playing cards?

Several months later Sue gave potential guests Mindy and Ron a tour of the upstairs, stopping in the "shaving cream/gamblers room," now called the "Bill Room." Ron entered and stood almost at the spot where the gambling table had been in the vision. Suddenly, Sue saw a man in a dark suit stand up from nowhere and put his hand on Ron's shoulder, though Ron apparently felt nothing. All at once, Sue felt compelled to tell him of the specter that only *she* could see, and announced, 'He says he knows you from the railroad." Ron, not a believer in ghosts, was amazed. A close member of his family, now deceased, *had* worked for the railroad!

A few months later, around Halloween, Sue stood in the kitchen, washing dishes. All at once, she heard running and a door slamming upstairs. The sounds were repeated, and at first she thought trick or treaters had somehow entered the house, gone upstairs, and were acting up. She moved swiftly up the back stairs and paused in the middle of the stairway. In her mind's eye, she saw a scene that must surely be taking place in the "Cindy Room" at the top of the stairs.

In the vision, there were five young women in a room with old-fashioned décor. They giggled and laughed, having just washed their hair. One girl was putting her hair up using hair pins. The back door facing George Street was open, and one of the girls was ogling some handsome men on horses on that back street. Then, apparently, one of the men spotted the girls in the upstairs room and pointed. Laughing playfully, the girls dodged inside and slammed the door, having a great time, and then darted into a smaller anteroom.

Sue opened the room's door and found it empty and returned to its present-day décor. At her feet was an old-fashioned hair pin, which she retrieved and saved. "I put it in my pocket and thanked the girls for giving me the images and the pin," she said. In January of 2006, Dr. Hollis Palmer, famous Saratoga author (who writes of old time murders, involving the reader in the evidence and trials), was conducting one of his regular walking tours of the city's ornate homes. Sue stepped onto the front porch just as Hollis stopped his group on the front sidewalk to deliver his spiel. "Oh, hello," Susan said.

"Please, everyone, come on in. Let me show you the house." Dr. Palmer, enthused at the opportunity to escort his group inside the ornate old home, took her up on the invitation.

Susan escorted the gathering through the interior, telling anecdotes about her employment in Union Gables. Then, she took the visitors upstairs and offhandedly told them about the Cindy Room while opening the door so the travelers could view the room's interior. As she described the hair pin incident, she pointed to the floor. There was *another* old-fashioned bobby pin at that spot! Sue was speechless, but picked it up to share with the visitors. How could it have happened *again*? How many times had that room been swept and vacuumed since it became a B&B? Surely, if the Skidmore girls had left such objects behind in 1970, the items would long ago have been discovered. There was no way Sue could have "salted" the room to impress visitors, as she hadn't known she would entertain them until she went onto the front porch on a whim.

Two male friends came to visit her that night, and, instead of laughing at the improbability of such an event, they stood with mouths open, looking at one another. She asked them why they were so silent. One man said, "Sue, we saw a hair pin on that floor when you first showed *us* that room, but we didn't want to mention it, as we know you like things *just so* in this house. So, I just picked up the pin and pocketed it." Sue suggested that the girls surely were again flirting with *these* young men, and they all laughed.

During my interview, we went to the room, but the coeds hadn't left a souvenir for *me*, so Sue donated one of her growing collection of bobby pins, and it now resides on my desk.

By the time you read this tale, Susan may have moved to another job, as she is currently finishing her Doctorate of Arts in Humanistic Studies. She is smart and sensitive and has learned some lessons that aren't in college textbooks—not in the old tomes used at Skidmore, and not even in books of today. Life and good times *do* go on and resonate through the years in Saratoga and elsewhere.

"Stay here!" the child's voice had said to her. And that has been Susan's motto for guests at Union Gables. Few get to meet the gamblers and pretty girls of the past, but, do stay here, because *all* guests get pampered in one of the city's finest old homes.

Stoneleigh

As with many of the famous lawyers in Elizabethtown, NY's history, Francis Smith came from New England and took up residence in Essex County in 1865. Joining his wife's uncle, the Hon. Robert Hale, in a law firm, he soon

The Judge Smith House

made his mark. Within ten years, he had become County Judge and then Surrogate Judge. Later on, he was elected President of the NY State Bar Association. A man of reputation and a man of means needed a distinctive home, so he and his wife, Julia Scott Smith, bought an elegant house called *Stoneleigh* on River Street, a building filled with architectural details copied from the work of famous Boston architect, Henry Hobson Richardson. They later adopted a niece, Louise Scott, giving her the name Smith. Following her parents' deaths, Louise lived on alone in the mansion until her death in 1950.

In 1951, new owners severely modified the building, especially in the center hallway, by adding partitions and panels that obscured a third story stained glass window and beautiful wrap-around spooled banister, in order to accommodate a nursing home. For almost two decades, patients (some bunked six to a room) came and went, many of them leaving through death's door.

In 1969, a Long Island family, the Remingtons, Ronald, Rosemarie, and their daughter, Rebecca, found the house deserted and on the real estate market at an extraordinarily good price. Despite Ronald's intuitive reservations, it became their home, and, over time, the panels and partitions were removed. Missing sections of banister were replicated by a local wood turner and the building assumed most of its former elegance.

"My dad hated this place from the time he laid eyes on it," said Rebecca. "On our first visit, he looked in the window and saw everything inside covered with dust. Entering, he could see the footprints he left as he explored the house. All at once, there was a huge grey cat seated in the doorway of the library, as if in greeting. Dad took a step, and the cat disappeared. Going into the library, Dad found not only no cat, but no paw prints in the dust either—he came out shaking his head.

"A few weeks later Dad saw the same cat on the stairs. When it spotted him, it sped upstairs, and he pursued it. A thorough search of the upstairs turned up no animal of any kind. Was it real? We wondered. Then, another day, as we cleaned up the interior, Dad glanced out a window and saw the same large cat sitting smugly in the driveway, looking at him standing in the window. Apparently satisfied with what it saw, the animal rose and swaggered into the bushes. None of the neighbors knew who owned it and nobody ever saw the cat again."

As I interviewed mother and daughter in the spring of 2005, the conversation was matter-of-fact. Rosemarie clearly remembered the events as they came to mind, but didn't consider her beautiful home to be haunted, perhaps just "different." "I remember when my granddaughter, Jessica, was small and her crib was in the suite bedroom. One day we saw her standing in the bed and throwing her ball at something invisible over her head. Jessica was very serious about hitting whatever it was, but we couldn't see a thing. When we first came to town in 1969, some people downtown told us we'd bought a haunted house, but we figured that was *their* belief because the house had been vacant, and empty old houses *look* haunted, don't they?" she inquired.

"Now that you mention it," Rebecca said, "nothing out of the ordinary ever happens in the rear section of the house that was added in the 1920s." But in the house itself, which has the appearance of a glamorous Victorian mansion, things are different. After Ronald's death, Rosemarie converted the stately residence into a bed and breakfast and now lives in the rear section. "Oh yes, there are those ghostly footsteps on the main stairway. And it's funny, but the only people who ever report them are the male guests. No woman, to my knowledge, as ever heard them, and the steps are always coming *down*," Rosemary continued.

"One night before we took in guests, our family sat in the suite, as it's a comfy living room. All of a sudden, our dog, Archie, who had been asleep on the sofa, awoke with a start and jumped down. He ran quickly to the pocket doors opening at the foot of the stairs and peered upward. Then, the hair on his back suddenly stood right up straight, and he *backed up* to the couch, where he cowered the rest of the night. Well, he's a guy, too!" Rebecca added with a grin.

A year previous to my Elizabethtown visit, I had been telling ghost stories at one of my regular "story dinners" at the Saratoga Rose Restaurant in Hadley, NY. I had never heard of Stoneleigh until I met Mary Ann from Gansevoort, NY. She told me of meeting another visitor on the restaurant's

124

front porch during a break that day, and the discussion had turned to ghosts. Mary Ann told him her favorite getaway spot was Stoneleigh, the old Judge Smith house in Elizabethtown. "Why the Judge was my great-great grandfather," the man exclaimed. Thinking this too much of a coincidence, Mary Ann later told me I should investigate Stoneleigh.

Before venturing to Elizabethtown and its historic buildings, I thought it best to hear of her experiences. "I go there several times a year," Mary Ann said, "because it's beautiful and quiet. I had just gotten to sleep in the Suite Room, during a visit two years ago, when a cat suddenly walked across my bed. I could feel each foot as it depressed my pillow, but the room was too dark to see him. That was all—just a cat walking. So in the morning I asked Rosemarie if she owned a cat. She denied it, but I did remember reading that the old spinster, Louise Scott Smith, owned many cats. Rosemarie said no other guest had ever mentioned the phenomenon, so I decided to forget it.

"The next time I went to Stoneleigh, Rosemarie was waiting for me with a smile," Mary Ann remembered. "Three weeks after I'd left, she told me, another guest inquired whether we had cats. She had stayed in the suite room and had a cat traverse *her* pillow! You know, haunted or not, I just can't stay away from this house. It's so beautiful, almost like an old castle. On another trip, my husband came along, and we walked the grounds quietly. I had a Polaroid camera and took a picture of him in front of the building. A short time after we went inside, I opened a drawer in the library to get a game and found an old photo of Louise Smith sitting in her carriage at that very spot eighty years ago. Coincidence? I got the shivers!"

On yet another trip, Mary Ann searched the cabinet drawers in the Library looking for playing cards. Instead, she found a box labled, "Cremains of Ronald Remington." That *also* spooked her. When I read my "Mary Ann Notes" to Rebecca and Rosemarie, they both broke into smiles. "Oh yeah, *that!*" said Rebecca. "We've got to do *something* with Dad's ashes. He always wanted to be buried in California. Guess we'd better get him out there."

But apparently, there was more to the ashes story. Mary Ann told me of going upstairs to bed after finding the ashes. "If you knew me," she said, "you'd know that I sleep like a log—*nothing* can wake me, but that night I woke up every few hours, hot and burning, as if I had a fever. My body was in great pain, and I was covered with sweat. The next morning, though, I felt okay, and since Rosemarie wasn't around when I left, I didn't tell her then." As I related this incident, Rosemarie and Rebecca looked at one another and shrugged. Was it possible that Mary Ann had taken on the condition of Ronald Remington just before he died painfully of cancer?

"But that's it," Mary Ann concluded. "I never see anything when I'm up in E'town. There are occasional shadows, little things I see out of the corner of my eye, but when I look, nobody's there. Nevertheless, I'm going back soon!"

That's the way ghost hunting *should* be, I thought to myself as I left Stoneleigh. Friendly and happy people, a beautiful historic house filled with light and antiques, and strange goings-on that they never told us about in science class. One last time, I scanned the yard for big grey cats, but, finding none, I headed home.

Timothy

The Ancestors Inn Bed & Breakfast

A Syracuse friend told me of a delightful bed & breakfast in the nearby village of Liverpool—one with a ghost or two, so I had to check it out. I was met at the door by a smiling Mary Weidman, who with her husband, Dan, has owned the Italianate Villa style home for eight years. Entering the hall, I was transported into the décor of the 1850s.

The quiet atmosphere reflected the relaxation available to modern guests, but also the upper-middle-class values of George Bassett and his wife, Hannah. Bassett, it seems, made his fortune in a number of businesses in Liverpool and Syracuse, the primary one being the salt industry in which he served as a supervisor. Syracuse became a rich community first in producing salt, then as an important stop on the Erie Canal, and later, the New York Central Railroad. Then, in the 1870s, as salt deposits waned, George continued in business both as a cigar maker and merchant.

126

Today, the Bassett House's 1852 builder is no longer known, but curiously, the Weidmans had a tentative contact with him, or at least, one of his workers. "Our son was ill and came home from college to recuperate in his downstairs room," Mary told me. "The boy ran high fevers and had to take medication at regular times during the night. Early one morning, he was shaken awake and spoken to."

"Time to take your medicine," said the black man at the foot of his bed. Groggy, the young man complied and took his pill. A glass of water seemed to be extended to him, so he drank, then immediately fell asleep again. The next night, the still-dizzy lad was again awakened when it was time to take his medicine, and once more beheld the black man. This time, the boy had the presence of mind to ask the apparition just who he *was*. "I'm Timothy Bassett," the figure replied. "I came from Virginia with the builder." The young man noticed that his visitor wore a white cloth shirt and vest, a likely outfit for a servant or builder's helper. Whatever his role had been in life, Timothy stayed with the boy a while longer until he could wake himself at the appropriate times and take the prescription. He wasn't seen directly after that.

The Weidman family was tantalized by the thought of a long-ago servant who considered himself a member of the Bassett family. Perhaps, they thought, old George might have adopted Timothy, thus giving him the surname Bassett, though no records to that effect have been discovered. It also seemed unlikely to the Weidmans that the builder (possibly Timothy's father) might also have been named Bassett. Was Timothy a slave refugee from southern plantations who stopped in mid-flight into freedom in Canada, choosing to become a freeman laborer in central New York State? It was common for freed slaves to take the surname of their former owners. It is also known that many branches of the Underground Railroad ran near and through Syracuse, even though assisting escaped slaves violated federal law before the Civil War. Or was Timothy's use of the Bassett family name just an affectation?

"During our years here," Mary said, "we have come to suspect that Timothy may have been in love with Hannah Bassett after George died. We invited a local psychic to visit us, and she picked up all the high energy spots where we have experienced curious events since we opened on Halloween in 1998. She, too, felt that Timothy was in love with Hannah, though he likely showed his love by working and helping to manage the house, and it probably was an unrequited love.

"The sensitive found strong energy in the northeastern second floor bedroom, a place where we saw a light several times before we moved in," Mary said. "We knew the house was empty when we bought it. At other times, when we had no guests upstairs, we often found the lights in that room turned on when we came home. In the back guest room on that side, our visitors sometimes hear the doorknobs rattle, as if someone is about to enter, but no one comes in. And if the visitors open the door to look, nobody is standing there.

"It is as if there is an inhabitation from another time taking place right alongside *our* family and the guests," she said. "On the upstairs south side, lodgers sometimes tell us that they have heard loud walking in the attic overhead, though we *never* go up to or walk around in the attic when we have guests.

"Our daughter, who is now twenty-seven, visited recently and was putting on some lotion in her bedroom. She put the bottle down, left the room for less than a minute, and returned, only to find the bottle gone. She looked everywhere, but it never turned up. What she *did* see, however, was the bathroom light flickering and a strange shadow on the wall." The light never flickered before or since. As in so many such cases, these shadows are uncanny, as they appear on the same wall as the light source, or seem to move through midair. Several such incidents are recorded in other stories in this book.

Mary smiled a big smile and told me of the curious experience of some other guests. The visiting couple was seated in the restored front parlor and noticed a well-dressed elderly man enter and sit. He looked about, and they tried not to stare, but he seemed a kind, grandfatherly type. After a few minutes, the man stood, nodded to them and left. The guests were so charmed by his old-fashioned ways that they asked Mary which room he was staying in. "For a moment, I drew a blank," my hostess said, "then I realized not only that we had no senior citizens with us that day, but also that they had *probably* witnessed George returning to survey his mansion."

Up to that point, I had heard nothing scary. Haunted houses are *supposed* to be scary to the uninitiated, aren't they? Then, I heard it. "Well, there is only one spot in the house that I *don't* like," Mary told me. "It's a corner in the cellar where I had Dan install a light with a pull-string, so I can illuminate the area whenever I have to go down. You know, he's pretty much the skeptic, but one day I saw him come back upstairs with a very concerned look on his face, saying he'd seen a movement in the cellar, and there was nothing physical there to stir. But he tries to stay objective—even when his screwdriver occasionally disappears from the desk drawer where he keeps it." Mary had a "See?" smile on her face for him.

She took me through the beautiful large dining room in which candles were all ready to be lit for the following morning's breakfasters. What a wonderful short stay in the early Victorian era, I thought to myself—why, *of course*, a ghost would be happy here—it's all so luxurious and yet homey. Maybe all the invisible presence would have to do to earn its keep would be to *readjust* an item here or there, just to notify guests and owners that "Hey, I'm still here—how can I be of service?" Timothy, unable to find Hannah Bassett any more, may be waiting for you, to come and help him fulfill his new profession of concierge.

Furniture or Servants?

"There's the nicest place to stay when you go to visit Niagara Falls," a friend told me. She whispered, "And they've got a strange *ghost* there!" Such a comment is usually all it takes to whet my appetite for an interview and get me packing. Tom and Louise Yots, who bought the old house in 1992, are the proprietors of the Park Place Bed & Breakfast at 740 Park Place in Niagara Falls, only a few blocks from the famous world wonder.

Park Place Bed & Breakfast

"I suppose you can consider this 1913 house historic," Tom told me, "because it was built by James G. Marshall, the founder of the Union Carbide Corporation. It was constructed in what is called 'the Craftsman Style' of building, which some call 'Arts and Crafts.' Louise and I bought it from St. Peter's Episcopal Church, which had used it as the rectory for many years. We were overjoyed to find that most of the original décor survived, especially the large Steuben Glass chandeliers and wonderful woodwork, though it all needed refinishing. We thought it odd that the elevator ran to the third floor, which was traditionally the servants' quarters, but in *that* lies a story," he smiled.

"You see, Marshall was very good to his servants. There was a Dutch couple who served him for many years. Soon after the domestics arrived, the woman became pregnant, and Marshall would not hear of her having to march up and down the stairway between the second and third floors. He spent a great deal of time and money designing the elevator so this servant wouldn't have to trudge up and down! Marshall also did considerable construction in order to install a bathroom on the top floor, just for that expectant mother. Since he enjoyed that couple, he made another adjustment for them. Marshall normally preferred to eat dinner at 6 p.m., but after discovering that the homesick couple loved to tune in a short-wave program on Radio Nederland at that hour, he had dinnertime moved up to 5 p.m. just to accommodate them. He was a nice guy."

When they finished their restoration work and opened the bed and breakfast in 1993, Tom and Louise Yots acquired many pieces of period furniture in order to provide an authentic atmosphere for the B & B. "Where did the ghosts come from?" I asked. Tom smiled and said that, as a former chemistry major in college, he had a hard time believing in spirits. Nevertheless, many of the phenomena seemed to involve the third floor where the he and Louise now sleep. The alarm system on that level often has ongoing glitches that are unexplainable from a scientific point of view.

"Marshall's great-grandson once visited here, and, after he returned to Toronto, we had a great number of strange noises throughout the house. You'd be interested to know that the family has contacted us, and the California branch even donated Marshall's original oak dining room furniture to us. Once we got that in place, even more little things have happened. First, shortly after those relatives departed, the alarm circuit for the basement windows began to flash. We almost never open those windows, and I rushed down to check. Sure enough, one of them was open, but we were certain that all those window latches had been locked. Was some unseen presence trying to protect us? In addition, we have a psychic friend who often visits us, and, each time she comes, she insists that she feels a female presence, but she can't tell if it's Mrs. Marshall or the servant woman."

Not having an intuitive companion with me when I visited, I was unable to make that determination either, though my money is on the Dutch servant woman. One might suppose that at least one of the Hollanders was treated so well during her years of service there that she just doesn't want to depart. I'll bet this individual creates the malfunctions just to let the current owners know they're continuing to receive affection and protection in return for the care shown to her a century ago. Love can last an awfully long time, as these things go.

As I drove away, still filled with the care and attention lavished on me by the lovely Park Place Bed & Breakfast, I sided with the ghost, wondering why *anybody* would want to leave this quiet neighborhood.

Fun and Games

"I grew up in Fulton, NY," Diane Bednarek told me, "and always hoped to have a bed and breakfast in my hometown. Imagine my excitement to find an old Italianate Villa from the 1840s for sale! I went over and took a look and absolutely fell in love with the house. Unfortunately, I hadn't known

Battle Island Bed & Breakfast

the previous occupants, and in a house *that* old I could never know them *all*. So, maybe in the light of what's happened since 2004, I should be thinking that they are slowly introducing themselves to *me*," she said with a big smile.

The Battle Island Inn Bed & Breakfast takes its name from a nearly-forgotten battle during the French and Indian War. Philip Schuyler and troops from Schenectady had just reprovisioned Fort Ontario in Oswego and were returning home via the Oswego River, when they were set upon by a band of French and Indians. The Americans took refuge on an island in the river and successfully fought off their attackers, returning home as heroes. Since then the island has taken the name of its biggest historical event.

This is not to suggest that the unseen residents of Diane's inn are military people, though one can never tell.

"I have always been fascinated by ghosts and eerie stories of the afterlife," she told me. "When my father and grandfather died, I heard voices and had visions of them both after they passed. So I knew it was possible for the worlds of the living and the dead to mix at certain times.

"Two weeks after we opened, I was replenishing the towels in a certain room on the second floor. Just as I turned the key in the lock, right next to me at the foot of the stairs that goes up to the cupola, I heard a woman speaking. 'Hello,' she said in a cheery voice. I knew no one else was there, and I dropped the stack of towels and washcloths and fled downstairs. A lot has happened since then, and now I don't even bother to turn my head at the voices. I usually just reply in kind, 'Hello!'

"That really is an interesting room, as it turns out, and there's likely some interesting history to it, but we haven't discovered that as yet. I have children's books and games in the hallway outside and, often, when I'm getting the room ready for a guest, I find a book in an unaccustomed place inside or a game box moved. Of course, I ask myself who could have switched it. From time to time throughout the house, though most commonly in the hall near that room, I hear a child's voice calling, 'Mom!' There is never a reply, but I'm certain that at least one of our permanent guests is a child."

Another curious experience that she recounted had to do with a girlfriend helping her clean one August day in 2004. The girl went to the porch and shook out her cleaning cloth. On the ground, she spotted a playing card from the *Secret* game. Picking it up, she found it inscribed, "The last time I was involved with the supernatural was…." "Amazed, as the girl knows some of the events in the house, she brought the card to me, and, straightaway, I knew exactly what game it was from," Diane said. "And the game box was located in the 'Hello Room'. Had some child visitor thoughtlessly tossed it out the window? It didn't make sense, and it couldn't have lain there long, as the lawn had been cut just the day before. We puzzled and then forgot the incident for a while.

"Then, in September, I told my daughter-in-law about the incident as we were walking toward the back door. We went outside and found *six more* cards from that set on the lawn! We retrieved them and took them upstairs, trying to rationalize that a breeze might have carried them out an open window. But when we found the game box, it was buried under three others. There was just no way the cards could have been blown away! Some months later, a neighbor came over to help me fix the boiler in the cellar. When he went outside, he, too, found a card from that game on the grass!" Diane and I both surmised that, indeed, after three such incidents, a former resident of the house enjoyed games and was trying nicely to make his or her presence known.

When I interviewed Diane about her stately house, we talked about the property and she off-handedly mentioned that on the back boundary line there are several tombstones that someone culled from the Seldom Seen Cemetery in the back lots. I paused at that name. Yes, that's what they are— seldom seen. Diane noted that several of the epitaphs are still readable, and the burials seem to date from the early 1840s, and at least two of them are children's stones. Again, considering the playfulness of her ghosts, I had to wonder if one of *these* youngsters was the playful one inside, though the child may or may not ever have lived in the house.

"Sometimes it gets quite busy in our house," Diane commented. "There are quiet footsteps going up the stairs—you know, just a quiet creak of the old steps, nothing scary. Then there are sneezes that seem to come from

NEW YORK STATE GHOSTS

nowhere but everywhere. I just say, 'Bless you,' and keep on with my work. One of the ghosts seems to like the laundry room. At one time, it would close the door at least once a day. I patiently went back there and asked aloud for the spirit to cease doing so. To assure that they did, I put a stopper under the door. And that fixed it," she grinned.

"Several times, when I've been vacuuming the rugs, and you know how noisy that can be, I hear a voice shouting, 'Phone!' I turn off the vacuum, and every time the phone *is* ringing. So, I suppose," she said ruefully, "they *are* earning their keep here."

"I can see how that's helpful," I said.

"Yes," she responded, "but explain this. Many times the electric alarm clocks in the guest rooms go off. Okay, I could understand this if a guest had left it set, and it went off the next morning. But, every so often, the alarms that go off are in rooms that haven't had a guest in three or four days. How does *that* happen?"

As is often the case when investigating ghost phenomena, I was without a rational explanation.

Diane continued on to tell me that in early January 2006, she encountered a confusing situation involving her decorative Christmas jingle bells on the front door. One day, as she worked on the computer in the office, she heard a cacophony of jingling bells, as if an impatient guest was seeking entry. "I hurried down and found the doorway empty, and there were no footprints in the light snow covering outside. Want to try explaining *that*, too?" She laughed.

Some guests at the Battle Island Inn love to hear the litany of ghostly events that have occurred there, and many have tales of their own to tell. Others, who have no eerie experiences, still are a bit taken aback, because Diane doesn't advertise the spirits. Her aim, her purpose in opening the beautiful old residence, was and is to provide a beautiful, restful journey back into another century, to a time when "home" was a reality and not just a concept.

There are three wooded acres for guests to stroll and several parlors filled with period antiques to admire and enjoy. There is a nearby golf course and the lazily-moving Oswego River passes by across the road, next to the state park. What nicer place could a soul find to relax? I asked myself. It occurred to me that perhaps *this* is why the former residents have been so slow to move on.

CHAPTER 5

HAUNTED HOUSES

Bear Care?

"When I was younger, I was aware of strange events in our old house, but when I turned fifteen, things really began to happen. One day that winter, I was alone, reading in my room upstairs, and the family dog, Bear, was sleeping in the living room downstairs. The front door opened and closed, and I heard footsteps crossing the floor into the living room. An unfamiliar male voice said, 'Hi, Bear.' Who could it be? I knew it wasn't my father or even a family friend. Next, I heard someone stirring up the wood fire in the fireplace. I didn't dare go down! After a while, it was silent again. I never heard the stranger leave or the door close, but when my parents came home, I went down. They were the only other living people there," said Theresa.

Now a grown woman, she still puzzles over the events that she has observed in the 150 year-old home in Berlin, NY, where she has lived all her life. "I'd really like to get to the bottom of it all," she said. "All kids are afraid of the dark when they are little, and I know I was always afraid of that living room in the dark. But, even when I was no longer afraid of the dark, I still was reluctant to enter that room because I felt a presence there. As I thought about it, I figured the spirit was very unhappy and sat or stood by the couch, just as one enters the living room. When I vacuum that room, the spirit seems more energized.

"In the summer of 2003, we moved the couch to a new position in the room, and now the couch ghost seems to occupy the far end of the couch, the end nearest the entrance. I noted its new location that fall, when I sat on the couch watching television. Since then, especially when I'm home alone and the house is quiet, I can hear noises that sound as if someone invisible is just carrying on life along with our family. And the energy seems stronger upstairs now, with doors closing and footsteps moving to and fro. When I was upstairs a few months ago, I went to the bathroom, which is next to my bedroom. When I went in, the hall light was on. I thought for a minute I'd turn it off, but I didn't. When I came out, it was off. That upset me, and I said, 'Please don't do that any more!' It hasn't happened since."

Such experiences are upsetting to Theresa, as they would be to most readers. However, they are commonplace in homes around the world. Somebody's spirit has simply declined to leave the earth plane and is continuing to work out unfinished elements from his or her lifetime, or is attempting to do so. Though we experience living in a single dimension, a big part of our unconscious mind, some would say our soul, is tuned in to other dimensions of cosmic life. We believe we perceive reality and make countless decisions based on that perception each day. And yet, how little truth we have.

Benjamin

Benjamin's House

The Erie Canal had not been completed for long when European immigrants thronged the plains and valleys of western New York, where excellent farmland was available from the large land companies. Among the early settlers was British immigrant Benjamin Lee, who owned a large farm on Bridge Road in Kent, Orleans County. The soil, a prehistoric lake bottom, was fertile and deep, and the Lees prospered. In time, Benjamin raised four sons, three of whom farmed the land long after Benjamin's death in 1911. Death, however, seems to have been a temporary inconvenience to the old Englishman, and it appears he has stayed on in his old house to supervise the newcomers.

"When we bought the house, I immediately felt somebody traveling through the house or yard with me. Sometimes the individual was behind me. It took a while to sort out all the phenomena and isolate the fact that this was an overseer or manager. He kept me informed of his presence by knocking pans from their peg-board hangers just inside the laundry room door," Wendy told me. "They hang on hooks and have to be *lifted* off if they're to be used. But, bang! They hit the floor at regular intervals. Once, a heavy frying pan did likewise. While on the phone with a friend one day, I mentioned Ben's tricks, and immediately, a pan hit the floor just a few feet away, and my friend heard it."

Wendy's husband, John Becker, nonchalantly suggested that Ben, as a farmer, was naturally an early riser and probably was just getting his own breakfast. "But he takes little things, too, and it can be a long time before they are returned," Wendy continued. "I have a little decorative pin from the Gulf War, and it disappeared from its place in a box on my dresser. It was months later that it finally reappeared in its normal spot."

She told me of filling in at the Town Clerk's Office when the Town Clerk went on vacation. One of her jobs consisted of getting the office mail and opening it, then handing the communications to the individual who could best attend to the matter. "One letter was sent by a Lee family from California. Believe it or not, they were descended from old Benjamin Lee, and they were seeking family information about his descendants. '*I* will deal with this one, I told the other clerk!' In our office records, I found Ben's marriage and death certificates and sent copies to the California Lees. But I also made copies for us, and brought them home to hang on our refrigerator door. I told John and the kids about my proud discovery.

"That night, my daughter, Sarah, screamed and ran upstairs and into the bathroom. 'Get that stuff off the fridge,' she yelled. It seems that her run upstairs was prompted by Ben chasing her. We discovered that Ben died in our other daughter, Emily's, bedroom. One day when she was growing up, Emily had a sleepover with a friend. During that evening, the girlfriend screamed, reporting that she'd just witnessed a man wearing what appeared to be a denim coat, standing in front of the television set, punching its buttons. I never actually saw Ben," Wendy added, "but one morning when I got up early, I saw something cloudy or misty shoot past the foot of the stairs."

Daughter Sarah had a collection of music boxes, and Ben, it seems, loved to turn them on and enjoy the music. Once, it was all too much for the girl and she shouted at the otherwise empty room, "Stop that! Leave them alone!" Instantly the music ended and did not resume. Emily also remembered something strange that she witnessed when she was in third grade. As she lay across her bed, doing homework, she could see her bedroom window ledge, which was decorated with small decorative cans. Taking a mental break from her lessons, she noticed movement near the window and could see the entire collection of cans levitating, as if held up by a phantom hand. Then, a moment later, they all settled into their normal location on the ledge and remained still.

"Do you like coincidences?" Wendy asked me. "Here's one for you to ponder. When my mother grew up in Hilton, a nearby town, she lived in a house that was formerly a funeral home operated by a *son* of old Benjamin Lee. Now, we're spending our lives in *his father's* house!"

Her daughters are now grown and live away from their childhood home, and Wendy reports almost no activity from Ben. He may have been attracted to the youngsters or may have thrived on their energy. Having raised sons, he may have been curious about adolescent female energy. As for Wendy and John, they are both quite happy that the house is quiet now. Perhaps Ben is out in his fields, planning his next crop. Or perhaps his next prank.

Dorothy

Outwardly, Huntington Village is one of the peaceful areas of central Long Island, but there is some disquieting activity by unseen forces there. "We were drawn to the beautiful 1920s house in June 2005," Beverly told me. "The baby was three months old, and we wanted our own first house, and this one looked like a wonderful old New England or Long Island residence, even having an historic cemetery way in the back, behind the trees."

The owner, who showed the young couple the house, said that an elderly woman had lived there for many years, surviving into her nineties, and she hadn't been happy that she finally *had* to move on into the afterlife. Beverly and her husband, Henry, were ecstatic with the beautiful woodwork and large rooms. They made an offer on the building, which was accepted.

"The night before we moved in, Henry and I picked up the key from the owner to take one last look around before our belongings arrived. We intended to live in just one room and unpack only necessities until we got the interior painted. We let our imaginations run wild as to what we'd do with this room and how we'd furnish that one. We walked into the attic, and that is where the experiences began. Henry heard scratching sounds, and we couldn't figure where they originated. Then I heard someone walking around on the hardwood floors downstairs, probably on the second floor. 'Who's down there, Henry?' I asked. He couldn't figure it out, and we both went down, but nobody was there. We went down to the first floor and found that space empty too. We looked at one another and laughed—nervously.

"Returning upstairs, I felt watched by some invisible being. I also felt a powerful energy and began to regret that we'd signed the sales contract. In any case, we tried to be blasé, but when the owner pulled up out front as we were leaving, I told him I thought the house was haunted."

The man responded honestly, telling Beverly that he and his partner had bought the house not long before, and he filled them in on old Dorothy, who had been a forty-year resident there. "My partner and I felt nothing after *we* took possession, so I honestly couldn't tell you folks there was anything wrong, but it sure could be the old lady. We did feel watched, as you say, when we packed up to leave but chalked that up to our imagination. I'm sorry for this. Do you want to back out of the deal?" The young couple said no, gritted their teeth, and awaited the moving van the next day, when all their belongings went into the one room they'd occupy until renovations were complete.

"Right from that first day, both Henry and I felt a strong presence, and I got weepy at our misfortune. Henry saw two bright lights out in the dining room, but they vanished when we looked again. Maybe we just can't live here,

I considered. But before surrendering, I decided to invite a priest to come do a house blessing, though we aren't Catholics. The painters had just finished and the house now seemed brand new, and, for whatever reason, we didn't tell the priest about the ghostly encounters.

"In retrospect, it's hard to say what effect his visit had, but a few days later as I sat on the couch nursing the baby, I felt something touch my leg. Wow! I wasn't ready for *that* either. All during July, whenever I went to the second floor, I felt that powerful energy in the air, and my arms tingled. The sensation of being watched also continued, and I was very emotional and at my wit's end. The power was especially strong in the room that was to become the baby's nursery and I feared for her, hoping this wasn't a negative energy. When I finally got downstairs again, I prayed to God: 'I just *can't* live in a haunted house.'

"Henry soon enough had his own experiences," she told me. "We have really gentle, nice dogs, and one day Henry was outside walking one of them, Hillary. Out of nowhere he heard an unseen woman's voice say, 'Hi, Hillary!' He asked me about it later, but I told him it wasn't *my* voice. Nevertheless, he remained cool about it."

One day, the pair was visited by another young couple, and Beverly stood inside the house talking to the woman. Suddenly, Henry and the other man entered from outdoors. "'What did you want, Bev?' Henry asked. Outside, both men had heard a woman's voice summon him, but it clearly wasn't me, as I was chatting with the other woman. So now we had independent confirmation that Henry and I weren't crazy; someone *outside* our family had heard a voice. And then I thought back on an offhand comment made by one of the departing painters. I had said something to him about the color of a wall, and he responded, 'Never mind, you don't know how long you'll live here anyway.' Now, I began to wonder if he and his partner had had some experience that *they* didn't want to share with us," she exclaimed.

Shortly afterward, following a series of small noises and other sensations, Beverly confronted Henry and said emphatically that they had a ghost. Her husband admitted that there had been strange events but, "curiously, Henry was never as upset as I was; he was pretty matter-of-fact about the situation, telling me that I need not be afraid. 'Fear is the enemy here, not some spirit! So what if it's the old lady? Maybe she is just having a hard time letting go, but she hasn't hurt anyone or done any damage.'" The husband took a rational course and told Beverly that no matter what or who was there, *she* was stronger than any energy that might remain from previous residents. And that calmed Beverly, giving her a new assessment of the situation, making her less anxious for the baby.

"Nevertheless, I knew I had to grapple with the situation, and one day I went upstairs. I stood in an apparently empty room and spoke aloud. 'I know you're here—I can feel you, and I know you're strong.' Henry had said that nothing in the house could hurt me, but at the instant that I finished speaking, the house fire alarm went off! It had never done that before and hasn't done so since. The entire event made me laugh, as it was almost like old Dorothy's response to me—'Maybe you *think* I'm powerless!'"

Beverly has a friend who visited and stayed overnight, taking photos of many rooms downstairs in the house. The woman talked to whoever was there, then snapped a picture. Some of these photos contained orbs, which, as you know, some folks think show a ghostly presence. Finished photographing the downstairs, the friend went upstairs and found her camera had completely malfunctioned; it just wouldn't work! Another friend helped her validate the eerie presence, discovering after researching the house back to its construction, that a man named Edward had built the place in the 1920s and had conveyed the building to Dorothy in the 1960s. Many times it helps to know the former residents' names.

While holding the baby one day in August, Beverly felt a gentle touch on her shoulder and wondered if perhaps Dorothy was mellowing, finally understanding what motherhood was about. "And after that," Beverly told me, "there has been almost nothing. Our home has been absolutely quiet. Maybe Dorothy just needed to have us recognize her presence and validate her attachment to our new home.'"

Almost a year later, I checked in with Beverly to see what's up. "It's been quiet for ten months," she replied, "until last night. I thought I saw something float from the dining room into the kitchen, then the dishwasher went on, and one of the kitchen light bulbs blew out. It sounds more dramatic than it was in real life, but it sure kept me awake for a while. Curiously, just before all this happened, there was a very sweet smell in my daughter's room, though I didn't at first think the events were connected."

My response to Beverly (as I have at least one such visitation event in *my* life currently) was that someone is likely watching over the child. One immediately thinks of deceased family members projecting their care and love. To resolve these episodes, try identifying the spirit, think about whose aftershave or sachet or perfume it could be. When you do, say hello and thank the spirit for watching over us. One such scent immediately disappears from my car when I send my love to the departed loved one.

This fairly laid-back scenario may seem a letdown for avid ghost story readers, but it is probably the norm for many or most visitations which never appear in print. A new family will buy a house or rent an office, have many experiences, and then, after a period of "becoming acquainted," the phenomena taper off or cease entirely. It seems to me that the residual personality of the individual still in spirit wonders why there are strangers in "their" house. Then, realizing that these are new occupants or owners, and (in the best scenario) that they must be dead and no longer in need of an earthly abode, and perhaps also recognizing that the new tenants love the place, they turn their attention to "What *else* is there, then?" And, at that point, they become aware that more developed spirits, ancestors, or even angels are there waiting to guide them into The Beyond.

Driving Miss Helen

The Rider Mansion on East Avenue

In 1965, Andrew Bauridel was hired as chauffeur for Helen Ryder, a well-to-do single woman in Rochester, NY. Helen, who was never married, had a nice old mansion at 1399 East Avenue in the city, having inherited the estate of her father, Thomas B. Ryder. During his lifetime, Mr. Ryder was the prosperous and well-known president of the Sibley Department Store. "Helen was accustomed to the best," Andrew told me, "and I drove her around the city in a big golden Fleetwood Cadillac. Another part of my job was to supervise the other help: the cleaning lady, the cook, and the gardeners. It was a dependable job, but there were other aspects of that position that made me uneasy.

"My wife at that time, Marlene, worked the second shift until midnight at the phone company, but one day, when she had the day off, I came home to find her screaming that an invisible man was in the living room. From time to time, she said, she could just make out his hazy shape. Eventually the activity stopped, and she calmed down. Soon after that, however, I was down in the cellar and heard a man call my name. Neither Marlene nor Ms. Ryder was home. I yelled out, 'What?' but there was no response. Then Jim and Karl, the gardeners who had just arrived to work, came down the stairs and asked what I wanted. I was shaken up because the voice was loud and clear as a bell."

Sometime later, the longtime cook moved away, and, while Ms. Ryder was visiting a friend in Boston, Andrew interviewed a replacement candidate, a stout Dutch woman. He went over the schedule and duties, then escorted the woman through the house to familiarize her with the layout. They ascended the rear staircase and he took her into what was called "the work room," containing sewing materials and a mannequin. Then he escorted her through Ms. Ryder's bedroom and to the "French Room," decorated in French Provincial style furniture. Traditionally, the bedrooms were locked if no one occupied them. Just as the pair reached the French Room door, there was a resounding crash inside. Andrew fumbled with the key and then unlocked the door, suspecting that a section of ceiling had fallen. Inside, however, nothing was out of place save a small framed photograph of a Ryder female ancestor, which had fallen to the floor. Only a small corner of the gold frame was bent. Bauridel suspected the applicant could see something else invisible to him, as the woman scurried through the hallway and down the stairs, all the while screaming that she'd *never* work in the place. As it turned out, Andrew and his wife, a frequent visitor to the house, experienced many strange events in the upstairs during Andrew's employment.

One December, as Christmas approached, Andrew went up the back stairs to the large storage closet that held the Ryder family Christmas lights, ribbon, and ornaments. As he walked to the rear shelf, he saw the door close behind him—something it had never done by itself. No windows were open to create a draft; when he turned to open the door, it wouldn't budge. He twisted and twisted the knob to no avail. In the dim light, he retreated a few steps to stare at the door, trying to decide his next move. All at once, the door clicked and swung open of its own accord. Andrew scratched his head, mumbled to himself a bit, then quickly exited.

In 1967, Marlene became very ill, and Andrew stopped working at the Ryder Mansion in order to spend more time with his wife, who died just three weeks later. Andrew then returned to Mrs. Ryder's employ.

Helen Ryder had a small poodle, Gigi, and the dog had free run of the house. One morning, during his walking inspection of the building, Andrew found the Green Room's bed linens disturbed, though nobody had slept there and the door had been locked. He told Jo, the housekeeper, to remake it. The following morning, as he looked in, he found the bed again in disarray. He told

Jo to remake it, but he also asked who had been there. How had this happened? She didn't know and suggested that he ask Ms. Ryder. Helen dismissed the matter, theorizing that Gigi was the culprit. Andrew reminded her that only he and *she* had keys to the room, but Helen didn't seem concerned. Andrew began to suspect that his employer knew more than she let on.

On the third morning, when Andrew again found the bed disheveled behind a locked door, he once more brought the matter to Ms. Ryder's attention. Briefly, he suggested that a ghost might be the instigator. She denied that ghosts existed, but then grew pensive and confided to him that she once *had* seen her deceased mother in a chair alongside her bed. It is important to note that Helen slept in the bedroom that was formerly used by her parents. As she watched, the woman rose from the seat and to the ceiling. "But, of course," Helen said, "it was my imagination. I'm a Christian Scientist, and we don't believe in those things."

A short time later, Andrew escorted Freddy, the security guard, through the house, seeking an explanation for the episode. They exchanged possible causes while Jo remade the bed. In front of Freddy, Andrew locked the door. With their employer and Gigi away for a few days, nobody would be using the room overnight, so the two agreed to meet outside Helen's room the next morning. At that time, Andrew unlocked the door and found the bed once more disheveled. "We were just stumped by it all, but I started to believe a ghost was present," he told me.

Andrew also remembered a time when Marlene was still alive and visited the Ryder house overnight. Marlene and Helen were with him in a rear upstairs room, when Helen decided she'd like a milkshake, and she asked him to make one in the kitchen downstairs. As he left the room, she added, "Oh, yes, I left my purse in the living room. Would you bring that back with you?" Downstairs, Andrew quickly assembled the milkshake ingredients, and, with the blender humming away in the kitchen, he walked into the dimly-lit living room.

He was startled to see a woman silhouetted against the large front windows. "She didn't move, but I could see her black dress and a face that was covered by a black veil. As soon as I looked directly at her, thinking she was a visitor who'd come in unannounced, the figure began to become foggy, then broke into parts, and, thirty seconds later, she vanished. Running to the kitchen with Helen's purse in hand, he poured the milkshake and took it upstairs. Excitedly, he told Marlene and Helen what he had experienced.

In many instances, such apparitions remain unsolved, but in this case, there soon came a solution. A few weeks after the aforementioned event, Andrew and Marlene sat in the upstairs work room with Helen, who was sewing. As conversation waned, Marlene picked up an old Ryder family album that was stored there, and she and Andy scanned the old photographs. Paging through the collection, Marlene stopped at a photo of Helen's mother, and Andrew excitedly identified the woman's shape as that of the ghost he'd seen, though he'd been unable to see a face of the recent apparition.

Months later, after Marlene's funeral, Andrew Bauridel returned to his employment at the Ryder Mansion, and continued to have strange experiences. One weekend, as Ms. Ryder prepared to leave home to visit friends in Boston, Andrew asked permission to invite two friends to stay over. Helen agreed, and thus Mike and Adele came to stay for a few days. Andrew put them in the French Room, which had two large twin beds on opposite sides of the room. He was curious if either one would experience anything extraordinary.

At breakfast the next morning, Adele was animated and told of awakening in the night and feeling someone blowing hot breath on her neck. She thought for a moment it was Mike being playful, but she looked across the dimly-lit bedroom and saw him asleep in his bed. She quickly scurried over and jumped into bed with him, where she spent the night. Hearing her experiences, Andrew then related the story of the mysterious crash in that room.

A year later, Andrew was shopping at the Red & White Market a few blocks away and encountered Mrs. Guici, a Christian Scientist friend of Helen's. They exchanged pleasantries, and then the woman told Andrew that she'd never entered Helen's house again after a frightening experience. "One night, I stayed over in that French design room upstairs, and, in the middle of the night, somebody or something was breathing right on my neck. I was petrified!" Also a disbeliever in ghosts, the woman stayed away from phenomena that might contradict her rigid beliefs. Nevertheless, it provided an independent confirmation of Adele's experiences—and from a non-believer at that!

When I interviewed Adele about her experiences, she also remembered seeing a shadowy woman passing a window with a lit candle when she, Mike, Marlene, and Andrew were conversing in the back yard.

Upon Helen Ryder's death, the classic Italianate house (according to the owner's will) passed to the Rochester Historical Society. It would have been a wonderful headquarters, but the organization had its own offices and later sold the building, which is now used as a non-profit building. Non-profits often have ghosts of their own to deal with, mainly financial ones, but one must wonder if Helen has now joined her mother, adding another ghostly resident to the old mansion at 1399 East Avenue.

Coping

Today, Stacy lives in Endicott, NY, and when we first met, she told me that she believes she has been psychically sensitive throughout her life. "In the 1970s, when we lived in Chicago and I was two, I sometimes talked to my dead grandfather in the backyard, my mom told me. And I told her what he looked like and correctly described the clothing he'd been buried in, though I had never met him. Later in life, I knew ahead of time when my father-in-law was dying."

She told me that when she was seven and living in Elmira, the windows in her home playroom used to go up and down by themselves. "I was frightened by that, and so was my Mom, who wanted to move out," she said. "But my step-father just dismissed it as imagination. So I went to live in another town with my dad, while my sister moved in with my grandmother. Mom, who used to care for the elderly, often said she felt followed by some unknown being. Then, a few years later, we came home one night to find my father, stark naked, sitting on a stool in the dining room, saying he was the devil. He'd been drinking, but we wondered what had gotten into him.

"A year or so later, I went to open my bedroom door and a heavy dresser slid across the floor and blocked the door. I was trapped and scared to death. I called my uncle, who came upstairs and chopped the door open. That was the last straw—my mom sold the house to the Wallace family for one dollar, and we moved. I later heard that the new owners had just as much trouble there, and that they soon left. In the summer of 1989, I lived farther up that street with my dad, and we heard police sirens and fire trucks, and they all pulled up in front of our old address. Neighbors called authorities to say that every light in the house was turned on, though there was no electrical hookup to the house! I lived with Dad until I turned thirteen, and that was a fairly quiet time, but then I moved back in with Mom, who briefly ran a bar in Elmira."

As with most sensitive and troubled teenagers, Stacy had few confidants in high school. Who could understand the strange world she lived in? Stacy found no support for her susceptibility in either church or school. Soon after high school, she married and started a family. "He was a good man, and we had some good years living in Binghamton. The house was quiet at first, but one day I found a watch on our entertainment table. No one in our house owned it, so I mentioned it to our neighbor, who gave a strange smile and admitted it was his. 'This has happened before,' he assured us. 'Somehow this watch often gets taken over into that house where you live!' He was trying not to scare us, but he *knew* our house was haunted.

"The kids' toys began to make noise during the night. I'd pull out the batteries, but they still functioned. Our stuffed Ernie kept awakening us in the middle of the night, saying, 'I'm sooo sleepy!' Then, one of the talking dolls began to talk—even without batteries." Stacy revealed the strange events to her mother, who asked her to take photos of the house, especially the kitchen. In one of those photos, they could see two little girls in bonnets playing on the floor. Of course, the girls weren't present when the pictures were taken.

"As I passed a row of wine glasses in the hall one day, they flew off as if someone was trying to hit me with them. Then, my sister swore she saw a woman looking down at us from the attic window, and the name 'Ava' appeared on a wall in another photo, though it was invisible to the eye," she told me.

The previous tale is a typical result of action not quickly taken. But then, when are we ever told that one day, in a house with negative spirit energy, we'll meet unfriendly ghosts or spirits, and we must put our foot down *immediately*? Call them what you will, there are souls in the spirit world who aren't anxious to go *anywhere*; they don't seek Heaven and are afraid of Hell. Much of their time is spent in invading human homes (or even bodies!) and attempting to savor the physical pleasures that captivated them when alive.

Those who live lives of lust and search for sensation often find it impossible to let go of those cravings when they reach the afterlife. So they attempt to keep the party going endlessly, far short of Heaven. Because they are prisoners of their lusts, they *are* in a hell, but resist knowing that. Individuals such as Stacy are simply ignorant of what needs doing, mainly because churches, schools and government do not empower the average citizen. It's up to you if your Uncle Charlie still rocks in his favorite chair. If he's okay and you enjoy one another, let him stay a while, but *unfriendly* spirits *must* be driven out of the house before they build up a familiarity with the living. Like spousal abusers, these spirits just get bolder and physical assault (psychic assault) can result. A full-blown tantrum on your part is recommended, starting with "Get out *now!*" If you don't defend yourself with prayer, house blessing ceremonies, smudging, exorcisms, or at least the daily blessing of self with White Light, the "evil spirits" *will* gain greater control of your life. As an undefended person, nice as you may be, you are buzzard-bait for the uglies.

All these things I explained to Stacy, as she is now worried about her children's emotional futures.

She told me that Prof. Gary Truce and a team from the Science Department at SUNY Binghamton came to visit her former house a few years ago and discovered countless cold spots. They spotted orbs in the digital photos they took and filmy shapes around Stacy. Gary felt that Stacy's daughter might also have been temporarily possessed by one of the beings.

Then, Stacy's husband underwent a major personality change, drawing inward, not shaving and sitting alone in the dark bedroom. He complained of being followed by someone he couldn't identify. The man said he was being constantly watched by a woman or man. It sounded like a major psychological break was coming, though Stacy's family didn't know how to diagnose such symptoms. One night, she returned to the house with her daughter. The little girl scampered toward the bathroom. Stacy looked briefly through the door, then immediately grabbed her daughter and threw her across the room. Slamming the bathroom door, she grabbed her daughter by the hand and left the apartment. Her husband's body was hanging inside the bathroom.

"We moved out that night and never went back," Stacy said. Her little girl was traumatized by the sight and emotions of the suicide for several years. Stacy's husband had been bright and happy when they first married. Eventually, the house, or whatever malignant force dwelt there, possessed him with its negativity, until he, unprotected by spiritual disciplines, was submerged in its darkness. One suspects that Stacy and her children may also have picked up some of that negative energy.

For several years, the young mother and her daughter lived alone in Elmira, and then she found a wonderful new man and remarried. "When we came to our present house it was wonderful to have the peace and quiet. But, you know what? A few months afterward, while I was doing the dishes, I felt someone or something touch the back of my neck. When it happened again, I heard breathing behind me, though nobody else was there. Afraid, I told my landlord about it. He didn't dismiss it, but doesn't comment about it much, either."

Stacy told me that, although the landlady has several locks on the attic door, she and her new husband often hear whispering sounds and walking overhead in the attic. A short time ago, as she descended the stairs, she felt a push from behind and now will not use the stairs unless she has a firm grip on the handrail. One night, she felt someone or something sit down between her and her husband, David, on the couch. "David talks to the spirit, but I haven't done so," she told me. "One day, before we left the house, we placed a pad of paper and a pencil on the floor, so the spirit could write to us." Not a good idea, I countered, as it is just encouraging familiarity; one needs to separate herself from the spirit's consciousness, not encourage it. If she is to stay there, she needs to take action *now*, to put that entity at bay or drive it out. Her children are becoming afraid because their blankets are sometimes yanked off them in the night.

"Recently, my daughter was taking a bath upstairs," Stacy told me, "and claims she heard me come upstairs and enter my bedroom. Drying off, she walked into the room because she heard the door inside slam. No one was there. She was surprised to find me downstairs and asked me why I slammed that door. I told her I'd been downstairs the whole time, though I, too, had heard the door slam upstairs. I thought *she* did it!"

The child has seen a curly-haired woman in her mother's bedroom and often thinks it is her mom, and the little girl's sensitivity to the spirits is increasing. She experiences having her hair pulled at night and is increasingly nervous, Stacy told me.

"Kids shouldn't live in fear," I told her. "Neither should you or your husband, for that matter." I advised her to go down the street to the Catholic Church, though she isn't a regular communicant there. This two millennia-old institution calls itself the "living presence of Christ on earth." It's time she gave them the opportunity to live up to that claim. "Ask the priest to come and do a house blessing with holy water," I instructed her. "That's a first step. If that doesn't drive the spirit out, the priest may have to come back several times, if needed." I also told her that, in my experience with parish priests, not all of them are proficient at casting out the bad spirits. She may have to get the diocese exorcist (though the church doesn't use that title any more), and his work may involve exorcising both the house *and her family*.

Readers might want to read Tick Gaudreau's book, *Spirit Rescue*, which explains how easily *any of us* can pick up spirit parsites. He and David Darrow both have plenty of wisdom to pass on. Few moderns, who think themselves sophisticated would take the concept of daily prayer for protection seriously, but that *is* what many need to incorporate into their lives—a regular and humble link to a Higher Power.

What can the average person do to prevent such possession, whether the attachment is minor or major? First, *each* person in your home should start the day saying at least an informal prayer to The Creator, or whomever (s)he believes that Entity to be. Before retiring at night, the same prayers for protection should be said again. Children should be instructed in this activity also. A hundred years ago, such spiritual activities were common, but as huge segments of the American population no longer worship or take any kind of advanced religious instruction where traditions can be passed down, it is no longer common sense to think of prayer when we get into troubles such as this. Each person should also learn to encircle himself or herself with The White Light of Protection or the Christ Light, if you prefer. Visualize a brilliance surrounding you from head to toe and in the space surrounding you. Ask for protection from evil and darkness each day.

Stacy was not raised with such precautions and, to date, hasn't practiced them. Several of her homes have obviously been haunted and people in them have suffered. She agreed that she cannot permit this to continue. Is there any bright side to this story?

Any of us can turn our tragedies to triumphs if we will *use* what we've learned. In our conversations, I found Stacy to be a peaceful and loving parent and wife, who wants the best for her family. As I often do, I did a bit of numerology and astrology for her, and I discovered that her soul intended to become a humanitarian in this life. There's still time. She has a goodly amount of psychic ability and can use that force to benefit both her family and others if she will get some training. In our talks, I also discovered that she is a potential healer. "Yes, my hands sometimes get very hot," she said, and I told her that a loved one of mine used to have the same difficulty. That loved one had to go touch another person in order to release the healing energies flowing through her. I urged Stacy to consider taking a course in Therapeutic Touch or Reiki, so that she can begin doing her good works.

One thing about her troubled life thus far: it sure has taught her how miserable life *can* be for some. "And I don't want to continue that way," she said. I also urged her to visit Lily Dale, a small spiritualist enclave south of Fredonia, NY, where she may have to shop around a bit, but she will find both healers and seers who can give sage advice for dealing with discarnate entities. This story may yet have a magnificent ending, if this woman will reach out for her potential. Others will be grateful.

Emma

In 1978, Patrick McCarthy took the job of police chief in Canandaigua, NY. He and his wife hailed from the New York City area and were charmed by the countryside and the nice old houses of the Finger Lakes Region. They visited many houses, but none was quite right. Then they drove by a boarded-up house that had recently had a fire. "And I knew that was *it!*" said his wife, Patricia. "Even though there were scorch marks and plywood covered the windows and door, I fell in love with the old mansion. And it didn't take long before we made a purchase offer to the Keehn family, which they accepted, as the house had been vacant for the previous twenty years.

"We could see that it needed a lot of restoration, but we were only the third family to own the 1871 house at 171 Howell Street, so we were thrilled." When I interviewed Patricia (who is also known as "Pat," but will be called by her given name in this story to avoid confusion between the two Pats), it was a dreary January day in 2006, but she was sunny and full of excitement about the house that is just about fully restored today. She told me that Mr. Gillette, an

The McCarthy House

attorney and the builder, loved the Second Empire architectural style which was then the rage and could afford to build it. The Gillettes had servant help, though the McCarthys didn't know about this bit of history at the start.

Patricia is sensitive to vibrations from other realms, having sensed a long-ago murder on a road she walked in Pennsylvania when in her late teens. It would not be out of order, then, to expect her ability to blossom later in Canandaigua. "Soon after we moved in and began the renovations, I started to feel presences, and not long after that I began to catch brief glimpses of a ghost woman. She wasn't frightening to me, but I was frustrated that she wouldn't stay around long enough for me to get a really good look. That took time. Eventually I had her full image: a stocky, older woman with grey hair pulled up, who always wore an apron. What should I call her, I wondered, as she was more of a companion than an intruder in the old house? Finally, the name 'Emma' came to me. She seemed to be a domestic, which tallied with my perception that she only was seen in the rear of the house, which must have been the servants' quarters."

In time, as she met neighbors and introduced herself, Patricia asked questions about the previous residents. She learned about the Keehns and then discovered that old Mr. Clarence Van Zandt Keehn had employed a cook named *Emma*! And, yes, the servants' quarters, indeed, *were* in the rear of the first floor!

"The house was often filled with plaster dust, but I could always tell what filmy part of it all was Emma. She apparently was a bit petulant, as sometimes my candle would seem to jump off the kitchen counter," Patricia continued. "Several times I also heard my name being faintly called, but I always had a hard time locating the source of the voice." Laughing, she told me that once, it seemed as if the sound was coming from inside the microwave oven, and, in an effort to hear the voice more clearly, she actually opened the microwave door, though it didn't help. We both chuckled at that. "Probably it was Emma, trying out my name, as she was the most frequent visitor," Patricia concluded.

"Once, however, my daughter, who was sixteen at the time, came home from school and walked into the room we use as a library. There, seated on the couch, was a man in a brown suit, seemingly waiting for something. As soon as he saw my daughter, he vanished. That's the only time he appeared, and we have no idea who he is or was. Our son, who lives on Long Island and is a confirmed non-believer, has had his experiences here, too. There are parts of the house, especially the attic and the root cellar, that none of us feel comfortable in entering at night. We're not scared, just cautious; we don't *need* to meet more former inhabitants.

"In October 2005, my husband sat in the living room and heard the sounds of heavy furniture being pushed or pulled across the floor upstairs. He knew he was alone and stayed put, he told me when I came home. He's a bit more logical than me," Patricia said. "He's lived here long enough to know we have other residents. And he *knew* he was alone. So, why bother? He knew if he went upstairs that he'd find nothing moved."

I first met Patricia in the summer of 2005, and she remembers that, not long afterward, the house lights went through a phase of turning themselves off and on. "We have a big double-door freezer, and for quite a while I'd find the produce in the bottom frozen solid—ten times in just two weeks! I thought my husband kept turning up the setting because of the warm weather, as I always found it quite high, but he denied doing so. I got angry and, standing alone in the kitchen one day, said aloud, 'That's *it*! You have to go. Leave this house *now*!'

"Well, the trouble with the fridge stopped and so did the blinking of the house lights. I was pretty proud of myself, getting the spirit to behave. We weren't sure, however, if it was Emma, since she had always been so docile. One of my workers named Sue had died shortly before, and I wondered if it might have been her. In any case, it stopped.

"Then, shortly afterward, I was talking on the phone to my friend Dagmar, a European woman who lives a mile and a half away. I told her that I believed I'd chased the spirit out. Dagmar laughed, 'You sure did. She came over *here*. Now I have that trouble in *my* refrigerator!'" The two women figured that the instigator must have been Sue, just trying to notify them both that, though dead, she was still around and had successfully crossed the gulf between the living and the dead.

As is so often the case, living in a haunted house is an exercise in patience. The resident spirits, unless you want to evict them, and the living have to get used to one another. If, indeed, the culprit in the latter episode *was* Sue, it only illustrates the fact that individuals who die bodily are suddenly exuberant that their consciousness is still intact and that their real self did not perish. The spirits of our loved ones, enthused by this new reality, strive to contact those of us who are emotionally or psychically open to such a notification. It appears that such relatives, friends, or loved ones don't hang around much longer after they have notified others of their successful passage. Once this loving task has been completed, those who are ready to move on, do so.

A Ruckus

Children are quite perceptive of spirits, perhaps because there is a native psychic ability in their early years, though most youngsters seem to lose the talent around the ages of seven or eight. Here is a typical tale of such an experience.

In 1983, Dan Alexander and his wife, Gayle, purchased a house on Big Creek Road in Hornell, NY, where he worked for a publisher. One of five built by a local contractor, the house was built in a contemporary style. The Alexanders were parents to a son, Dan, who was seven at the time they moved into their new home. The previous owner, also a publisher, told the newcomers that "stuff always happens in that house." For example, the dishwasher was always dying, he said. But *some* events are always taking place in a house, Gayle reasoned, so why attribute anything mysterious to the house itself?

On the day the Alexanders took up residence, there were immediate problems with the water supply. Next, the television cable went dead. Soon after, the refrigerator went on the fritz. As these issues were attended to one by one, little Dan seemed restless and stayed close to his mother in the kitchen.

"Dan, we put all of your toys in a nice place downstairs under the stairway. Why don't you go down there and play while I'm straightening things out?" Gayle asked.

"I don't want to," the tyke replied. "There's a lady down there." When Gayle questioned the boy in detail about the stranger, he replied that the woman wore a pink flowing gown, but he still didn't like her and didn't want to go downstairs while she was there, and, furthermore, he didn't want to talk about it.

"That was one more problem that I didn't need," Gayle told me. "I decided right then and there that this was going to be a happy house, and we'd all enjoy it. I stood for a moment in the kitchen, surveying the cupboards and ceiling and said out loud, 'House, I know you've been abused for years. I'll take care of you and love you, so don't worry.'" After that, all the problems stopped, and little Dan ceased to see the ghost lady.

As I've advised so many times, if you live with ghosts, most are disruptive because they crave recognition of their survival. Many who have passed on are anxious about the people and property that they have left behind and create a ruckus. The new owners can reassure the spirit that everything will be fine, and often that is what the ghost most needs to hear. It helps clear their minds, so they can search for greater light and beauty.

Four in a Row

Kellogg Street House

Bill Eichinger and Cindy Dardano were very much in love, and looking for a cozy home that would be just right for them when they would soon marry. In 1999, they found a delightful 1832 home that the long-time owners, Lavern and Virginia Norton, had just listed for sale on Kellogg Street in Clinton, NY. It took no time at all to conclude the sale, and, within months, Bill and Cindy married.

"When we first looked at the house, I knew I *had* to have it; I *had to* live there, and I have never been sorry for that feeling," Cindy told me. "Our story isn't much as far as phenomena go, but it nevertheless caused us to question many of our old beliefs.

The Nortons were in their 90s and needed to live in a more structured environment, and they moved to the retirement community where Cindy was

153

employed. Because of their ages, the Nortons hadn't been inclined to put much more money into the house. "It did need some modernizing, and Bill was worried that getting the house back into good shape would be costly," Cindy told me, "but he loved me and agreed we *would* fix it up and live there.

"One thing became clear after we moved in. I always felt the urge to check through the house every night before we went to bed. It wasn't really an anxiety, but just a task that I felt compelled to perform," she continued. "One morning at 5:30, I awoke suddenly and couldn't figure why. I went downstairs and, to my astonishment, there on the counter beside the stove, I found the four electrical burner elements and their protective pans all pulled out of the stove top and *lined up* in a straight row!"

At first, she concluded that Bill had done it as a joke of some sort, and, as soon as he got up, she asked him. He denied taking out the elements. Cindy went to the stove and looked over the situation again. Everything seemed okay, so she replaced the pans and burners into the top of the electric stove. Bill mumbled to himself that a logical solution could be found, but he then went back upstairs. Cindy, however, figured that if the arrangement hadn't been her doing or Bill's, then the only other logical solution was that they had a ghost.

"After Bill went upstairs, I started talking to whomever was rearranging our kitchen. I said, 'You are welcome to stay here. It's really okay if you stay here, but it's *our* house now; *we* are here. And if you ever scare me again, I swear I'll go get a priest and have you sent on your way. Got it?' There was no answer."

Later that day, the couple again discussed the odd event. Bill suggested that someone had broken in and then departed. "What? Cleaned our stove and *then* left?" Cindy retorted. It didn't make sense. Burglars aren't common in Clinton, and the ones that the Eichingers had heard of never did domestic chores.

The best possibility was that one of the Nortons had died and returned to their old home. But Cindy saw them both each day at work, so she asked them if they had had any strange experiences in the house. "They didn't seem to know what I was talking about," Cindy said, "so the entity might well have been an earlier owner or resident. It's a little macabre, but Bill found some bones in the cellar walls one year. He waited until Halloween, then brought them upstairs to my girls, Marie and Nicole, and me. We all screamed and ran upstairs, but none of us believed they were human bones, as they were too small. Likely they were food scraps or animal bones that a prior owner had tossed there, so we never reported it to the police.

"And, to date, that is the only other odd experience we have ever had here," she added. "I have so much comfort in this old house. When Bill is away, I feel protected and watched over, as if by some strong and kind force. Bill? He's still searching for a logical explanation for the burner arrangement. But me? I'm still very happy that we found this house and that I got the spirit on *our* side!"

Sights at Two Sites

"When I was a little girl living on Long Island, my grandparents had renovated an old farmhouse on Dunnigan Road outside the village of Salem, NY, up north in Washington County. When we went there to visit, I noted that there was one second floor back bedroom that nobody in the family would set foot in. I glanced in there once and saw a dark-hooded individual with red eyes sitting on the bed inside. That was enough for *me*! I never looked or went in there again. Even when we'd be outdoors, walking around the house, I would look up and see the figure parting the curtains to look out at us. It was always a special scare to go up to Salem because Grandpa Cuozzo used to tell me about seeing 'an evil black cat' that hid and wandered in the back field. I tried never to go back there either," Carol Manno told me.

She also remembered seeing, on one visit to the farm, a vision of a Long Island neighbor woman, Mrs. Messina, who had died. "I could see the funeral being held inside her living room back home, who attended, and even how they had dressed her body. I came downstairs and told my mother, who immediately disbelieved me. But when we returned to our Long Island home, the neighbors confirmed everything I had seen. I guess it was that sensitivity to spirits and ghosts that made me a different person to my peers. Little did I know that, in a few years, my entire family would move to Salem!"

The Mannos moved into an old farmhouse atop Riley Hill Road, an area with which I was familiar, as I, too, had lived in Salem once. She told me of being immediately afraid the first time she set foot in that house, and she retained that fear until the family sold the house in 1974. "Years later, my mother confided to me that she was also afraid to enter the house which my father had purchased. Sitting alone one night, she had seen the chandelier begin to swing violently. Suspecting that what she was experiencing was caused by ghostly activity, my mom stood her ground and yelled at whatever force was there, 'This is *my* house now, and I'm *not* leaving!' The light fixture stopped its gyrations, and it never did that again.

"I hated to be alone in that house," Carol said. "One day when I was fourteen, I came home from school, and no one else was there. In the hallway, I heard a seductive male voice calling out, 'Carol! Carol Lynn Manno,' and I was pushed from behind. I beat it out the door and didn't go in again until another family member came home. Sometimes I'd awake in the night to find a grey uniformed soldier sitting on the foot of my bed. He didn't do or say anything; he just sat there staring. Grandma Cuozzo said she saw him, too, but that he'd tried several times to push *her* down the cellar stairs."

As Carol related one strange event after another, I wondered if the old farmhouse hadn't actually become a haven for ghosts from everywhere. Sometimes a ghost can be easily identified as a former resident of a building. At other times, the figures that are seen differ greatly from any former activity or known former resident of the house. In such instances, an investigator should suspect the spirit has arrived through an attachment to some item of furniture or antique.

Then there are the far-less-common "wanderers" of the spirit world, individuals without a body who, for whatever reason, have refused to accept the fact of body death, and who seem to cruise that ethereal realm, content to officially be neither alive nor dead. Many of these wanderers are malevolent and should be cast out by an exorcist or expert in spiritual cleansing. In this case, however, the soldier might have originated in a brief occupation of the hilltop by the Charlotte County Militia at the beginning of the Revolutionary War, as they erected a stockade there, garrisoned by Vermont and New York Colony soldiers.

"We'd hear footsteps walking up and down the stairs all night long almost every night. The dogs used to howl during the night, and I'd keep my bedroom door closed tight because I was afraid. I guess I was born afraid. As a little girl, I had told my mother that I remembered being in her womb. Even before I was born, I hated my father and knew he didn't want me. When I got older and discussed this with her, I told Mom that I used to kick and kick inside her when I'd hear him come home. She was astonished at this memory because she vividly remembered my kicks. Mom was afraid of him, too, and I remember her sitting there, wringing her hands with worry that we'd never be able to pay the bills. In the end, I quit school and got a job in order to help out."

The more we talked, I became aware that Carol had been a sensitive individual right from the start, more open to the spirit world than many other folks. Psychic ability, unless it is trained, can often be a burden that certain individuals carry throughout life. When worked with in a disciplined way, psychic ability can be a blessing to many.

Carol continued, "My mom said that a family named Olson used to own that old house, and that it had had some connection with the Catholic Church; two nuns had died in what became my bedroom. Nice!" she grinned. "Apparently, the house was also a station on the Underground Railroad, and I wonder if those escaped slaves left some fearful energy there. When they sold us the house, the Olsons told my mom that it was an unhappy house, as so many people had died there. I sure agree on the unhappiness."

Other phenomena used to intrigue Carol. "One night, I sighted a strange girl with long hair who ran right *into* a solid wall. Later, we learned that there had been a fire there years before, and that the house had since been rebuilt. I guess I know where at least one of the old doorways was," she quipped.

"Then there was the Chinese chef," she told me. "I used to think I was seeing things when I spotted him emerging from the back of the house with a big knife in his hands, so I shut up about it. Years later, when I worked in Greenwich, I met a UPS man, and we started talking about the old house on Riley Hill Road. He told me that he never made deliveries there without calling first, to be sure someone was home. One day when he was making a delivery, a Chinese cook suddenly emerged and chased him. I was sorry to hear that about him, but it comforted me to know someone else had seen the guy," she told me.

In later years, Carol married and moved to Long Island. When she first arrived, she found a wonderful old apartment house on Route 25 in Southold on the island's north fork. "It was such a happy house, even though it was filled with spirits. I had my Manx cat, Hazelanne, with me, and we loved it so much. One night, I heard children's voices—laughing and giggling. I looked up and saw two little blonde girls having a ball and playing with my cat. The next day, I asked my landlord, John, about them, and he told me they were his aunts. For some reason, after their deaths, they decided to return to the house and be little girls again, at least for a while. John told me that he had inherited the house from his uncle some years before.

"I rented the upstairs apartment, but the downstairs was vacant. I had a key and could go down and enter that apartment whenever I wanted. And I often wanted to. When I'd open the door, I'd hear wonderful, happy conversations taking place all around me. I could smell wonderful foods cooking—toast, eggs and bacon, and there was laughter everywhere. After my residence in Salem, I felt that this was my reward. I'd tune in on men's conversations, and they always seemed to be talking about fishing. At night, I'd hear kids running upstairs and downstairs, having such a good time and playing with my cats. Finally, I had to ask John about this. He gave a big smile and said, 'Why, of course, Carol. My uncle and his family *were* fishermen—all their lives. *Of course,* that's what they used to talk about constantly.'

"One night when I was in bed, I felt small hands running fingers through my hair—not enough to scare me though, as I knew who it was. Then the girls giggled, and I heard one say, 'Come on, now, let's go play with the cats.' I also had a musical, wind-up cat's toy, so I'd wind it up and set it on the floor to run around. But as the music played, I could hear a woman humming along with the sound! Oh, it was such a wonderful apartment!"

Carol remembers that John stored some of the family's furniture in the house, and I reminded her that the happy vibrations of family life can "stick" to those items.

"One day, John came over with a long face. 'I have to tell you, Carol, that I sold the house. The new owners will be coming soon, and I had to promise to move you out.' Oh, I cried and cried. He just *couldn't* take this treasured place away from me! But, of course, he could; it was his property. So I had to pack up and move. I'm still in Southold, but there's nary a ghost to feel or see here in my new place."

My interview with Carol was one of the scariest yet most wonderful ghost experiences that I've collected. She is quite sensitive, and I urged her to continue using this talent for the good of others. What a ride it has all been for her! So far.

CHAPTER 6

PERSONAL EXPERIENCES

Turned On

Many Americans have had ghost experiences. Yet, if the spirit entity was simply smelled or heard or communicated by touch, the observer might not realize that it was a spirit. And many people too easily dismiss vivid dreams of the deceased, though most of those are ghost contacts too, *spirit* contacts. Too many people think a ghost must be *seen* to be a valid encounter. But what do you think it would be like to have such experiences *at will*? What would one experience if he or she could just decide to see who's there? Here is the story of an extraordinary woman I've met. She is extraordinary first in that she revealed a great range of experiences, but secondly in that she was perfectly comfortable in sharing them with others. I told her that many of those now termed "Indigo Children" among my readers will be grateful for the knowledge.

Camille England lives today in Pleasant Valley, in Dutchess County, but she has lived in many parts of the world in this lifetime. "I was born with *sight*," she told me. "Even as a child, when other children were watching television, I didn't. I found it more gratifying to look for lost souls; I've always known about The Light and wanted to help the lost ones reach it. Thus, I've always been able to communicate with those who have passed over because I can meet many of those forgotten or lost ones in meditation.

"Not *everybody* that you meet in the Land of the Dead is a nice individual, however. Some are just as dark and mean in death as they were in life— death doesn't change that. I've met some real bums there, but I learned very early in life that such excursions into Spirit are like walking down a sidewalk made up of different blocks of concrete—many of them you'll like, and many others you *won't* want as friends. Still, I try to help and heal those who welcome such assistance."

A forty-five-year-old woman, Camille remembers living in Pine Plains in 1981, when she had to drive her sister to the airport. She noted that her neighbor had a male visitor before she left. "It was a long drive back from New York City, and it was early morning as I approached home. Suddenly, I wasn't alone in the car. I had a spirit visitor riding with me. He told me that he had a message for the man visiting my neighbor. I said I'd pass it on, but he insisted on riding home with me, and on the way, he identified himself as 'a brother in the service who had died in an explosion,' so I didn't send him away."

When she got home, the spirit delivered his message, offering information for his brother, the male visitor next door. The sum of it was that the two of them had once dated the same girl, and a fight had broken out between them over her. That resulted in a history of hostility between the two, but the spirit man simply wanted his brother to know that he harbored no animosity and still loved him. Then he disappeared. "What would my neighbor think about this strange message? So I sat on that communication for a few days, but I couldn't sleep and finally sent the message," Camille told me. "Then, a week later, a tearful man came to my door and thanked me for the words. He was the brother, you see, and he told me that all the heaviness and guilt that he had held toward his dead brother was now gone."

Camille related this not as the first, but as one of many opportunities she has had to use her spirit world contacts to bring healing to troubled people for whom death has brought a calamity. She said that during the previous year, 1980, she had a similar event when she and her sister visited their mother in California. As they drove their mother around the city, the sister remarked that a girlfriend's father had died. "Suddenly, the father was riding beside me in the back seat," Camille remembered. "He had information that he wanted delivered to his wife: when his family had gone on vacation one year, he hadn't accompanied them, as he had work to do at home. While they were away, he built a little cut-out storage area in the back of a closet, where it wouldn't show behind the hanging clothes. He had placed his important papers there, but he had died without being able to reveal the storage place. I told my sister the story, but she felt I'd be infringing on the family's grief if I passed on *that* unlikely information, so I didn't send the message. Years later, I heard that their family sold their house and, only then, after emptying their closets, did they find the hideaway. And in it was an expired insurance policy that would have greatly helped their family finances. That was the year I resolved to pass on *all* messages I received, whether or not it upset people!"

In another instance, the husband of Camille's friend's friend committed suicide. "Up to that time, I had relied on my former religious teaching that all suicides are consigned to a place of darkness until they were released. The dead husband and his wife both had children from previous marriages and were deeply committed to one another, so the wife was absolutely grief-stricken and felt betrayed. Nevertheless, Camille let it be known through her friend that she'd welcome a visit from the widow.

"When the tearful woman arrived, I noticed that her husband was suddenly there in spirit, too. He wasn't in some dark spiritual dungeon, but very much bright and present. Through me, he explained that a terrible event had come up in his life, one that was going to be exposed if he had lived. He felt suicide was preferable to subjecting his new family to the shame, as it would be too traumatic for these loved ones. 'So I left,' he communicated.

"The wife had a sudden recognition of the statement's truth, and told me that she understood perfectly, and she left my home uplifted by her spouse's love and caring for her and her children. I learned so much from that experience," she told me, "because I know that God is *all*-forgiving; it's people who can't forgive! And I now know that one cannot judge all suicides the same—it's a very *individual* set of circumstances in each case. But suicides *can* be prayed for. Some time later, I checked in on the husband and found he had been released from whatever darkness he'd temporarily been in.'"

Camille worked in the Social Services system for many years and relishes all the clients that she was able to get out of that bureaucracy. We shared ideas about people finding it so hard to let go, as I have some such issues in my own life. "People come in all vibrations," she mused. "So many times I've met the nicest people—they are absolutely *wonderful* individuals...until they take that first drink or pill. Those substances suddenly separate their consciousness or spirit from the physical body. You've heard of people being in a blackout? Well, that is an apt name, because their soul just has *fled* the body! When and where there is light, these people *can* return to their bodies, so never give up praying for them. Should one of your readers suddenly find themselves dead, they should remember to *look for The Light*. You'll tell them that?" she asked with a broad smile. I assured her that I would comply.

"There *is* an angelic realm," she said confidently, "but it is peopled with individuals without wings, unless the living person really *needs* to see wings, then they manifest them. But I see the angels as multi-colored, shimmering lights. They are capable of instantaneous adaptation to whomever or whatever needs them. And, the average person can never tell when she is among the angels," Camille revealed. "I've often seen them working among the homeless. Think how many people pass by a homeless person, not understanding that they've just ignored one of God's finest creations!"

Camille smiles often. Her outlook on life is anything but grim. "Sometimes I do have unusual experiences, though," she said. "One night when I was living in Ohio, I couldn't sleep, so I began to read a book, but that was suddenly interrupted by a blood-curdling scream. Wonder who *that* is? I pondered. As I put my book down, I discovered it was a woman that I'd once known; she was not in a good place and was dead. I heard her say, 'I am murdered!' In my mental conversation with her, I discovered that she wasn't ready yet to enter The Light and she wanted help escaping from the horrible place in which she found herself. I helped her a bit with that, but I didn't want to get involved in a murder.

"When I returned to New York State, however, I was still bothered by the situation and contacted a friend who was a policeman. I told him my story, and he revealed that there were currently many missing women, often prostitutes, around the nation and many of those were presumed murdered, though their bodies had not yet been found. Then, just a short time after that, I saw a story on television about a missing woman from Poughkeepsie. I asked my policeman friend if I could help with the disappearance. In my mind, I made a beam of light from the police to the spirit of the woman who had contacted me."

Two days later, she told me, the policeman called to notify her that authorities had found traces of the missing woman. It turned out that the serial murderer was a college student who invited women to his family's home when they were away. He then murdered the women and disposed of their bodies. "After I knew that the woman's remains had been located, I sent her spirit into the Light," she told me.

"My sister has been the closest person in my life, even though we had the typical rivalries and problems growing up. We always expected to grow old together and become The Snoop Sisters, investigating life's mysteries," Camille said. "But suddenly, there we were in mid-life, and my sister got cancer and died. I was devastated, despite knowing about the world of spirit and God's love. I hadn't expected her sudden death. And I was so sorry that my sister never wanted to know much about the other worlds that were so open to *me*. There was so much I could have told her, so much that *I wanted* to tell her.

"I remembered that when we were girls, we had made a pact that whichever of us died first would get back to the other one with a message. Now, as I visited her deathbed, seeing her sinking so fast, I asked her to renew that promise. She smiled and promised, but after her funeral, nothing happened. I'd listen for her voice or feel for her presence. Nothing. What had gone wrong? Why didn't she communicate? I was so filled with grief because I missed her so much.

"Months later, I had one of my first good days. Things had gone well at work," Camille reminisced, "and it was bright and sunny out, and when I slowed down to reflect, *there she was*! I asked her what had taken her so long to contact me. She seemed very happy and replied that I had a dark cloud of sadness around me for *so long*, and my grief prevented her from making herself known. 'Let's get a cup of tea,' she teased me.

"We had a long conversation, and she wanted some information sent to various living people, and I agreed to do it, though some of them might scoff. One of those people, her doctor, was absolutely thrilled with his message. Another communication was for her favorite aide at the hospice, who really appreciated the information. I hope you will tell your readers that the dead don't always look the same as they did in life. More than anything, I could *feel* my sister, then I *saw* her appear as light. That's what she is, you know—light. That's what *we all are*, if we'd only learn it!"

Camille offered another story, not necessarily a ghost experience, but one that involved her use of spiritual powers in her healing ministry. "I was visiting people who were watching a football game on TV. One of the players was injured, and the commentator said the medics on the field determined the man's spine was severed and that he would be paralyzed. After immediately asking for help from the angels, I found myself transported to the injured player in my spirit body, and I used Light to visualize his spine reconnected. Then I pictured his spinal cord wrapped in what I'll call 'an etheric calcium wrap.' That's all I could do, so I returned to my body. My friends might have thought I'd dozed off for a few minutes. A few days later, a television reporter said the original diagnosis had been a mistake, and that the player would be fine. I have no desire to prove this, nor would I take credit for his cure, but I know that I did what I *could* do."

It is easy to become immersed in the phenomena in this story, but Camille stressed that her main focus is not on mere contact with these souls, but, instead, on *healing*, in whatever form that takes. While the previous events are stories of communication, one must spiritualize such contacts by healing and helping the discarnates.

This meeting with Camille was one of the highlights that I experienced in the many interviews I've done. In my estimation, the future will require many such "open people" who are just as willing to help a needy neighbor, homeless person, or stranger who calls out from The Other World. Each needs help, and those who claim to live religions of love should see the spiritual gift in those opportunities. We all will be Over There one day, too.

Tom's Tales

Tom Hathaway is a Mohawk Indian residing at Akwesasne, the Mohawk Reservation near Malone, NY. The Mohawk Nation leaders work hard to inculcate the traditional wisdom and values in their children, and yet provide them the education needed in a modern world. "Sometimes the traditions and folktales of the elders can seem like fables created to enchant children," Tom told me, "but I have lived with some mighty strange experiences that I know non-reservation folks experience, too. Unfortunately for them, *they* don't have Mohawk elders to help them interpret what is really taking place. Then, all those people have is fear of the unknown."

Spirit beings have always had their place in Mohawk folktales, and were often used by the teachers to show the young a proper respect for cosmic energies. "I grew up hearing the elders speak about nature spirits, for instance, little creatures about two feet tall, that scamper through the forest. I heard tales of people using their spiritual energies to overcome physical obstacles that frustrated non-Indians," Tom continued. His heritage is that of a twentieth generation member of the Bear Clan, the medicine people of the Mohawks.

"As a boy, I remember hearing the approaching hoof beats of Col. Louis Cook's horse." The Colonel was a great figure among the St. Regis Mohawks, as he aided the Americans in both the Revolutionary War and the War of 1812 and was a military friend of Gen. Washington. The Americans commissioned him as a Lt. Col. of Cavalry, and his derring-do in battle kept him as a legendary figure among his people, a leader who continues to ride as a spirit along the roads at Akwesasne. "As kids, we all heard about Col. Cook, who mysteriously rides along Raquette Point Road but is never seen. But I'd actually *hear* the clip-clop of the hooves on the pavement at night, and, just as it sounded like he'd appear, the noise stopped. I never figured that out.

"The St. Regis River was a sacred spot to our ancestors, as were many rivers and streams, and I remember, as a child, seeing "ghost lights" moving through the woods along the riverbank. These weren't fireflies; every Mohawk kid knows what *those* look like. No, these were larger globes of light that seemed to move with some intelligence. One old timer suggested that they were the spirits of the dead."

Tom related another strange story from his twelfth year of life. "It was Christmas Eve, and I still hoped there was a Santa Claus, though my belief was getting weaker each year. I remember cuddling up with my pet cat that night, hoping to fall asleep and find presents in the morning. Just as I began to drift off, I was suddenly awakened by a tiny ball of bright light that came underneath the back door of my bedroom. It came directly to my bed, as if to look me over, and then shot out into the living room. I know I wasn't dreaming because my cat suddenly sat upright and jumped as if he was trying to catch it. Nobody could explain it to me in those days, so I just kept the memory, but when I was older, I asked an elder about the experience. He told me that, because the light was tiny, that it probably was the spirit of someone who was dreaming and had left their body for a while, but it was okay, they'd go back. When you grow up with what many people could call 'magic' you don't find the spirit world to be strange at all," he smiled.

I had the idea that he knew much more than he wanted to tell right then, but he got me to wondering about what the lives of children would be like everywhere if their elders understood that the basis of all life is consciousness and energy. In that case, why would anyone be afraid of ghosts or the spirits of loved ones?

What's in a Name?

"When I was little I lived in Yonkers," Jessica Politano told me. "At about age three or four I began to see others in our house. When I told my family, they smiled and told me, 'How nice, you have an imaginary friend!' But I knew these were *real* people, and I wasn't making them up. There was one in particular, a man in a military uniform, and he was my friend. So I called him 'Ghost.'"

Jessica described her chum as a beardless young man who wore no hat. He sported a grey or light blue uniform with silver buttons on the front; he carried no weapon. He was just there, whenever she looked. "Ghost was almost always there before bedtime," she remembers. "Just a good friend, a presence that I could count on being around as I grew older. Once, when I was a young teen, I had a dream in which Ghost informed me that my boyfriend, Damion, was going to tell me that he was in love with my best friend, and, in just a few days, that's *exactly* what he told me!"

Now, as a young woman, she experiences Ghost less frequently, but when he comes, she knows he brings her a warning or information about coming events. "When my Mom was single," she recalled, "I saw Ghost one daytime, and that night I had another dream. This one involved a man named Bob, and Ghost told me that Bob would soon be dating my mother. I told my mother about the dream the next day, and said that I believed Bob would be good for her. Well, they married, and he became my step-father, but he was *not* good, and he's out of Mom's life now," she grimaced.

Ghost was like a guardian to her, especially before age five, Jessica remembers. Sometimes he would play with her. I asked what type of games Ghost liked to play. "Well, they were sometimes spectacular," she responded. "One day I was home alone and went to my room, where I saw my stuffed animals flying around in the air. One of them, my Care Bear, was a favorite. I have to believe Ghost caused this to happen, maybe to entertain me. Maybe it showed me how he felt most of the time. Then, there were other occasions when he'd just bounce a ball with me. To an observer, it must have looked strange, to have a ball bounce one way, then suddenly stop and bounce back without hitting anything."

Whether it was her experiences with Ghost or not, Jessica is entering adulthood much more sensitive to the spirit world than she was as a child. "Now, I go various places and can feel the spirits. Many times there is a chill, and sometimes I pick up emotions and get feelings that I know aren't mine," she smiled. "I've come to think of Ghost as my spirit guide, because that is what he *is* for me at this time in my life. He helps me, and I think it is his influence that causes me to immediately recognize the people who are good and those who are not in my workplace."

Jessica works in a restaurant in Kingston, and meets many people each day. Most enter her place of employment deep in their own worlds, and Ghost sorts them out for her. One might suspect that Jessica created this entity early in life to compensate for some person or quality that was missing in her life. Maybe Ghost is a part of her unconscious mind, though she still gets glimpses of the handsome young soldier. "He has stayed the same age as always," she said, "only now *I'm* getting to be as old as *he* is," she laughed.

Maybe a closer friendship will develop now. Perhaps Jessica will integrate Ghost's best qualities into her personality soon, and use her heightened psychic abilities to help others. Then, perhaps, Ghost can head off to his own spiritual battlefields.

The Sensitive

People have different kinds and amounts of sensitivity. Some are more likely to respond to their outer world through touch or sight, while others are especially open to odors or sounds. And even others have an exquisite receptivity to tastes. Then there is a less-readily identifiable awareness, where certain things just *are*, and one knows them to be true, though they cannot be explained fully. Here is an example of a woman that has been sensitive to the spirit world all her life, though no one has identified her as a seer or psychic.

Catherine Gawelko has taken all the experiences in stride, accepting that, although she often cannot know the cause, she is free and able to deal with the result. "I was born in Brooklyn in 1934 and lived at 1570 Bergen Street in a three-family home, in which all the families were relatives. It was an older house, and I'm sure others had resided there before our family came, which might explain some of the events that happened there. Until I left home in 1954, I had several unique encounters with spirits but, since then, I've read about other people's confrontations, and I can see that mine weren't that unusual.

"I remember always feeling observed or watched there. But still, it was a shock when someone invisible sat on my bed one night when I was five. The movement woke me fully, and I screamed out for my mother, but she didn't come. That only happened once, but that was enough.

"Then, when I was about eleven, I remember standing in our living room with its high ceiling, and combing my hair in front of a large mirror. I was grumbling to myself because I had spent all my money at the school bazaar. All at once, I heard my name called, 'Catherine!' in my ear. While I was deciding what to do, it came again firmly, 'Catherine!' Boy, was I scared! I dropped the comb and ran out of there and stayed outside until my mom came home. When I told her of the event, she just brushed it off, 'You're nuts!'"

The episode that frightened her the most occurred when she was sixteen. She went to her grandmother's apartment downstairs to stay for a day and fell asleep on the bed. All at once, Catherine was startled by the sound of Grandma's rocking chair. "It made a definite sound whenever it rocked; you couldn't mistake it for anything else. I looked at the chair and saw nobody in it, but it was picking up speed. It rocked harder and harder—what was I to do? Just then, I heard my dad come in. He always stopped in to Grandma's apartment at night to say goodnight. As soon as Dad came in the door, the chair came to a halt. After Dad left, the chair started up again, back and forth, faster and faster. I couldn't stand it any longer! I called a quick goodbye to Grandma and fled back upstairs to our apartment.

"So I guess the chair must have stopped. Grandma was a widow, so it never occurred to me that it could have been my grandfather keeping her company—I was just scared! A few years later, after Grandma died, my uncle offered me the rocker, but I told him there was *no way* that I wanted it.

"Not too long afterward, my father found employment upstate, in Salem, NY, and we lived in an old house there on Riley Hill Road. Soon after we moved in, my dad started saying how much he regretted buying that old house. (See "Sights at Two Sites.") It was such a busy house for ghosts, and the one thing I remember most was hearing a great crash one night. We went downstairs to find our big 36" x 36" mirror on the floor. It had a strong frame, and all the hanging wires were intact. Somehow, it had fallen over a shelf and down to the floor, resulting only in a diagonal crack in one corner. Some strong force sure moved it, but we could never figure out how it came off the wall, unless a ghost did it. He sure got our attention!"

By that time in life, she was married and had a family, although her husband was mentally ill and a divorce followed. One night, Catherine told me, her mother-in-law came to her in a dream, asking if she'd ever go back to the husband. "The woman looked terrible, all frowsy and unkempt, and that wasn't like her at all, as she was always neat and trim. I was also surprised that she was speaking perfect English, something she couldn't do when she was alive. I told her, I'd *never* go back to her son and explained why. She nodded in agreement and faded out.

"She came to me once more, a few years later, and she was back to neat as a pin, not a hair out of place. All she said to me was '98!' and then she left. We played with it as a date, such as September 8th, but nothing notable happened then. We then watched to see if 1998 would be a significant year, but it wasn't, so we never did get her message."

Catherine remarried and moved to 603 Front Street in Greenport, Long Island. "It was a nice old Greek Revival house that was easily one hundred fifty years old," she told me. "It was very quiet and a wonderful place to live, but my second husband died less than two years after we moved in. One night a few months later, I'd been out and came home, walked into the living room, and, suddenly, heard footsteps passing through the dining room, into the main hallway, and then climbing the stairs. Our curious cat followed the sound and we both looked up from the bottom of the stairs. I told kitty, 'It's okay. It's only Henry.' She seemed to understand."

Henry stayed around for the next six years that Catherine lived in the house, working out his attachment to unresolved problems. "One day when I was in the basement, I heard him pacing upstairs, so I yelled up to him, reminding Henry that if he had problems in the afterworld, it's because *he* made them here in life. 'It's *your* problem, so *face* it!' The pacing sound ended and never happened again. Nevertheless, he stayed on until I remarried and sold that house. I hope he left when I did," she smiled.

Then she moved to Montana but remained open to the spirit world out there, too. She and her new husband bought a one-year-old house and have been happy there. One day, however, she did see a strange light moving across the surface of a door. "And in it, I could see what looked like a man. A few days later, I caught myself excusing myself to nobody and nothing in the hallway. I became aware that I had been trying to move around someone or something that I couldn't see. Hmmm.

"Then, one night I went to bed before my husband came upstairs. All at once, I felt some gentle force snuggle up to my back; was it the cat? No, and it wasn't my husband either, so now I was mad! I stood up, turned on the light and yelled, 'Get the hell out of here! I don't *want* you here, so get out of this house!' It hasn't been back since, I don't think, though one night a few years later, I awoke because someone was standing beside my bed. I opened my eyes and saw a bride, all in white lace from head to toe. I couldn't shake the impression that inside all that lace was a skeleton, so I sent her on her way, too. My husband awoke to find me still steaming!"

It seems that after a lifetime of contact with the spirit world, Catherine is tired of being the victim of anyone or anything. "I think I've learned," she said to me, "if you encourage these things, they just settle in and get stronger. Let them go somewhere else." Now living in the Big Sky Country of Missoula, Montana, she is ready to see what else the big skies of spirit are going to throw at her. One thing's for sure, though, she's *ready*.

Mercy at Last

This story is more for an understanding of the dark side of the spirit world than for entertainment, as most ghost stories tend to be. Though I have a degree in Counseling Psychology, I'm not in clinical practice, and this interview was the most emotionally difficult story for me to write because of my compassion for human suffering. Readers should, at the outset, recognize that *all* humans have powerful emotions. Almost always these are fragile sensitivities, and sometimes they help us perceive the world of spirits and ghosts. But, if not handled responsibly, they can open an inroad of great damage to a person's soul and sense of well-being.

"I was born in 1964," Mercy told me, "and when I was five, my family moved from Mamaroneck, NY to a new multi-family house, a little farther north. It seemed creepy inside, and even though my sister and I shared a bedroom, we were often afraid in the dark. I first became aware of a tiny dark figure on the wall, something like the cartoon character, Jimmy Cricket. I'd see him move about, scratching at first, then tapping the wall. Then, there were vague whispers coming from either my side of the room or my sister's side. After a while, the two of us decided to sleep with the light on.

"One day, I sat with my bedroom door closed, playing with my dolls in the center of the floor. I heard the taps and whispers, but then something tickled my head and neck. I tried to get up and flee into the hall, but I seemed blocked or paralyzed. It took hours to break the spell.

"That night, I awoke to find my Aunt Betty sitting beside my bed and stroking my head, running her fingers through my hair. 'Mercy,' she said, 'I will always be around you, and I will always take care of you.' She smiled, got up and then walked through the wall and out of sight. When I awoke in the morning, I asked my mother why my godmother, Aunt Betty, had come to our house. Mom strongly denied Aunt Betty had visited. Just a few minutes later, the phone rang. It was a relative, telling Mom that Aunt Betty had just died."

Emotionally and spiritually, conditions in the household soon began to deteriorate. Home is a place where family members should care for and protect one another, but for complex reasons, Mercy began to lose any sense of security; everyone failed her. "I was five at the time, and a few days later, my older brother called me to his room upstairs. I was on guard and didn't want to go, but he pulled me by the wrist and pushed me into the bedroom, flinging me at the closet door. Inside the closet, when he opened the door, I saw something that I still can't believe. I can only describe the entities; they sure didn't seem to be human. They were grotesque, almost life-sized figures—one red and one blue. They zoomed around the closet interior, and then shot out at me,

covering fifteen feet of space in less than a second, and then they just dissipated into the walls.

"I was absolutely terrified, and my brother was laughing hysterically. I
screamed for Mom and she came immediately, but by then, there was nothing
left to see. The creatures were gone and she didn't believe me." In retrospect, it
seems that Mercy's mother was either unwilling or unable to mentally, physically, or spiritually support her daughter, and therein lies some of this story's
evil.

Because his business was doing well, Mercy's dad bought the house
next door for a new home and converted their old house to an income property. "I was glad to leave there because that house had so many bad memories,"
Mercy told me. "My brother used to go into the cellar where there was a tall,
thin spirit that resembled Abe Lincoln. Even though he was more of a shadow
than real, I was terrified of him, so I was glad to move next door. We didn't
understand my father, and he drank. He verbally and physically abused my
mother and us kids, and that was only the beginning because Mom couldn't
stand up to him. For some reason, my father chose me as the family scapegoat,
so I suffered whenever one of his plans didn't work out."

Mercy (not her real name, but one that I chose for this story) then told
me of the terrors that she lived through for the next dozen years. Her father
befriended some strange men who rented their multi-family house next door,
individuals involved in a cult or pedophile ring. One of them was a clergyman
who remained on good terms with her parents. It seems that one of those
neighbors, a member of the diabolical group, sexually abused Mercy over and
over. Her new home seemed filled with paranormal phenomena: knocks, whispers, strange sounds. Were these part of the house's energy or projections from
Mercy's violated essence? Were the demons inside or outside? Did it even matter any more? "After a while, I just paid no attention to any of it. I developed
bedwetting. At age ten and a half, I remember knowing that everything I
believed in had been violated. Is this *all* there is to life, I asked myself—*pleaded* with myself."

She finally stood up to the molester from next door and told him she
would no longer go to his house. The man then went to her mother and, apparently paid the woman a great sum of money to continue enjoying the little girl's
favors. After that, when Mercy complained to her mother, the woman ordered
her to go to the house next door for their "parties." Noises continually assailed
her at night and dark forms darted through the bedroom. Her body spontaneously developed scratches, and her bed shook from a strange vibration at
night. She became numb to it all.

Sometimes, her father would beat her up, and Mercy remembers one day being unable to go to school because of her injuries. Looking into a mirror and seeing her black eye, Mercy knew she had to cleanse her life and spent the next few hours cleaning, sweeping, straightening, and ordering her bedroom. Finally, it looked perfect, and she went downstairs to get a drink. Five minutes later, when she returned to the room, it was a total mess, blankets were torn from the bed, pillows were yanked from their pillow cases, clothing was strewn from the dresser drawers, and all her labors had been in vain. Her mother looked in and castigated Mercy for her messy room.

That night, Mercy reached her breaking point. She flopped upon the bed, amidst more knocking sounds in the walls. She sobbed and sobbed and spoke angrily to God: "Why do you let this happen? How can you be God and not *stop* this?" Her heart pounded in her chest, and she dared God and the angels to come get her, to remove her from the hell she inhabited.

"And then," Mercy told me, "the room became a creamy white color and a misty cloud came over me. In that mist, I could see Aunt Betty's smiling face. I closed my eyes and felt Betty's warmth come into me and flow from my head to my toes. The atmosphere in the room changed totally. Whatever spirits or energies were in the room departed. I was never attacked again before I got old enough to leave home and be on my own. Some years later, after I got out of there and learned to drive, I had just entered my car when an authoritative voice came from the rear seat: 'Put on your seatbelt—now!' it said." Mercy stopped her car and obeyed. Within just a minute, another driver cut her off and there was a collision. Mercy walked away unscathed.

Now in her early forties, Mercy has made major changes in her life. Today, Aunt Betty is more of a fond memory than an actual presence in her life. "Though I now have a small clerical job, I have developed new talents and practice Reiki healing. I have the ability to help others both with my empathy and in a practical way. Recently, I have had a new path open for me, and I'm going to take it."

Clearly, Mercy was a sensitive child and likely had some native psychic ability that, at first, ushered her into the lower regions of the spirit world, where she became prey to the darkness brought upon her house by other family members. She grew up at a time when child physical and sexual abuse weren't as high-profile as they are today, and even though those in her family whose duty it was to protect her failed miserably, she somehow survived. The depths of her psyche are clearly scarred, as we had some difficulty in concluding the interview. At the end of it all, however, Mercy and I agreed that her suffering from childhood must not be in vain. More than most members of society, she knows both terror and the redeeming power of love.

There are no ordinary ghosts in this story, except the failed spiritual lives of those who were tasked with Mercy's protection. Those individuals never became what they might have been, and they are likely working through horrors of their own in their present spirit state. They may well become ghosts after death unless they can find forgiveness.

Not all contacts with spirits are happy ones, and I include this story to discourage the casual experimentation with darkness that is so often a fad among unsuspecting thrill-seekers. Evil attracts evil; selfishness attracts selfishness. It is therefore no small miracle that Mercy, denied love and kindness and safety in her youth, is now able to extend mercy and compassion to others.

Buckle Up!

"In the 1970s, when my boys, William and James, were small, we drove to Brooklyn, to visit their Aunt Cath, who was a good cook," Gerry told me. "It was a birthday party for Cousin Eileen, and, boy, did we feast! Then came dessert—Jell-O. James passed it up because he really hated Jell-O. Then, ten minutes later, Aunt Cath brought out the big birthday cake. After the candles were out and the birthday song was sung, Jim held out his plate for cake, but Aunt Cath, who was kind of a strict woman, refused. 'You didn't eat your Jell-O, so you can't have cake,' she said, and stuck to it. James was so angry that he could hardly speak. All weekend long, while we were in the New York City area, he grumbled and mumbled about Aunt Cath and how much he disliked her."

Two years later, in June 1979, Gerry, got a phone call from Cousin Eileen—Aunt Cath had died suddenly. It was early morning, and the boys were eating breakfast before heading to school, and Gerry decided not to share the bad news with them. She was preoccupied with planning her trip to the funeral and finding someone to watch over the boys while she drove from Schenectady County to Brooklyn. She almost tuned out James' comment.

"Hey, Mom, I had *the greatest dream ever* last night," he bubbled. "I saw Aunt Cath. She came over and gave me the biggest hug I ever got! And you know what? I'm not mad at her any more." Gerry was astonished and asked the boy what happened next. "Oh, she just floated out the window and was gone," he chirped, digging once more into his bowl of Cheerios. "I had no problem about worrying the boys after that, and I happily sent them off to school," Gerry told me.

That was just one of the marvelous experiences that Gerry has had with "the other world." She is an intuitive and accepts that the world of the present and the world of the hereafter often blend, leaving the living puzzled.

"Here's maybe my best story," she said to me recently. "We bought our old 1857 house in Scotia, NY, in 1971. Some of our happiness was dampened by my husband, Bill's, father, also named Bill, being in the hospital with a heart condition. My father-in-law was a master carpenter and had looked forward to seeing our new home. Unfortunately, he never did, as he died four days later. Bill was a big-hearted and compassionate guy, and his family was his life. We were all so sad, and my husband took it very hard."

Their boys were three and six at the time and full of fun, and Gerry and her husband, Bill, had a new home, but Bill was depressed and couldn't enjoy life when he returned from work each night. Gerry seemed unable to perk him up and busied herself in housework each day. Two weeks later, she stood in front of the kitchen sink, washing dishes.

"Behind me, I heard the squeaky second step on our stairs give out a squawk. That startled me, as I knew nobody else was home. I turned, and there was old Bill, standing in the kitchen doorway and smiling at me. I knew it was my father-in-law, even though he looked so much younger—maybe twenty. He was very handsome, and I saw his dark, wavy hair. He wore a white shirt and black slacks, which were held up with a belt. What caught my attention most, though, was the light glinting off the belt's silver buckle. It kept shining at me, and I noticed his initials on it.

"'Oh my God,' I exclaimed, 'don't leave! Billy will be home anytime now, so please wait for him. He'll be *so glad* to see you!' Bill looked slowly around the kitchen, seeing it for the first time, and probably making some carpenter's evaluation of the fix-up work that needed doing, and then he turned to me.

"'Take care of my Billy-boy,' was all he said. Then he turned, and the silver of his belt buckle glinted again in the afternoon light. He moved toward the stairs, I heard the step squeak, and then he was gone. I thought to myself, Okay, Gerry you must have imagined this, but I looked down and saw the detergent bubbles on my hand, so I *knew* I was awake and doing dishes, but what should I do *now*? A few minutes later, the front door opened and my husband, Bill, came in. I told him the whole story.

"'I have to call my mother,' Bill said, picking up the phone. He called my mother-in-law, telling her 'Dad was here.' She told us to come over.

"'Why did he come to *you*, Gerry?' she asked when I told her the story, 'Why didn't he come to *me*? I was his wife!' she said, after I related my experience. I could see that she was hurt, but also overjoyed at the details of the vision. 'There is something that neither of you know,' she began. 'When your dad and I were married and honeymooning in Niagara Falls, I bought him a beautiful monogrammed silver buckle for his belt. But within a day or so, he lost it. We searched high and low, but it never turned up. When we returned from the honeymoon, we were so discouraged that we never told anyone else in the family about our misfortune. And now,' she smiled, 'he's got the belt buckle *back*. That was a token of my love for him, and he's *found* it. That makes me so happy!' she exclaimed.

"We were so overjoyed about the incident that we forgot what Bill, Sr. had said: 'Take care of my Billy-boy.' Only years later, when my Bill became ill, did we discover that he had the same heart affliction that his father had died from. Way back then, in 1971, Bill's father *knew*, and he tried to warn us. My Bill has since had two heart attacks, but he's okay now, and he's right here while I tell you about it all," Gerry said gratefully.

I love this story, as it has so many dimensions to it. First, the reappearance of the elder Bill. Second, his wearing of a love token in the apparition, a lost buckle, knowing that Gerry would understand and communicate the symbolism to her mother-in-law. And thirdly, he offered as much of a warning as he could for the health of his son. So many times, the spirits of the departed return to help resolve problems, not to scare the daylights out of us, as Hollywood would have us fear.

It is never clear why the deceased don't appear directly to the loved one they want to inform. Years ago, an old psychic lady told me, in the midst of my own similar experience, that we who receive such visions should be happy. We are like a mailbox that is "open" at the time. If the message isn't for us personally, we are still obligated to deliver it to the right person. I'm satisfied with that.

Healing

James is a fifty-seven-year-old professional man from Binghamton, NY, who has a journey scheduled for him, perhaps sooner than he'd wish. Now on disability insurance, he is HIV positive and expects, perhaps even welcomes, death. "I've been under a death sentence for twenty years, but I have had some amazing experiences during that time," he told me. "And, because I haven't died, I suspect that I'm supposed to learn something new, and perhaps teach it to others."

When he was seven, James told me, he had a vision of an old monk, who told him, "Remember who you *are*!" He pondered that experience for many years without fully understanding it. As a young adult, he worked in the business field. Eventually, however, he accepted that he wasn't entirely like everyone else, as he discovered a talent for seeing into the world of spirits. And he also recognized that he was gay. This latter realization, and his verbalization of it, was hard for his parents to bear. His mother found a way to work through it with love, but his father, who follows a rigid religion, distanced himself, alienating James.

He found a good friend in Robert, and they lived together in Binghamton, along with James's dog, Nick. After a number of years together, Robert suddenly died, followed a few years later by Nick. This double blow depressed James, who was by then expected to die of AIDS.

Soon after Robert's death, however, James began to experience more vivid extra-sensory events. More clearly than ever, he began to see what he calls "dead people." Each one seemed covered over with a black electrical field that zapped and sparked at times, an opaque covering that obscured the fine details of body shape or facial features, yet he knew who each one of these figures had been in life. It came as no surprise to him that Robert was soon among those spirits, but with a slight difference. His former housemate didn't know yet that he was dead but instead continued to roam the house carrying a coffee cup, as he had in life. And wherever his friend walked, Nick was only a few steps behind. Robert's former bedroom is now James' den, and James watches his friend and Nick walk that path from kitchen to den.

A few years ago, James felt great distress in his abdomen, almost as if he had appendicitis, but the doctors could find nothing wrong. Then came the day when he felt his appendix burst, and he got to the hospital with no time to spare. An MRI showed peritonitis and three large blood clots in the abdomen. The doctors told him he probably would die soon, and his parents were called from New England, and they came to say their goodbyes.

James remembers lying in his hospital bed, awaiting the doctor's findings of the test results, and wondering how, should his life be short, he could *ever* remember "who he *was*," as the monk instructed. Eventually, he came to believe that the monk was a part of his present personality—an ancient part. So many of his beliefs had undergone changes in recent months that he suspected reincarnation must be true in some form. His essence had taken form upon the earth many times before and would do so again, he now believes.

As he awaited his end, he became aware of a misty cloud of energy near the ceiling above his hospital bed. The cloud moved and sparked, much like the energy fields he'd seen around deceased friends. Suddenly, the energy lowered until it enveloped his body. "There were little tingles all over my flesh," he told me. "Then my contact with the cloud felt prickly, and all at once there came a whooshing sound, as if a storm were moving over me from head to toe. When the last contact with the cloud dropped off my feet, I suddenly heard a loud voice cry out, 'Behold the Lamb of God, who takes away the sins of the world!'

"I was absolutely shaken, though I felt cleansed or cured," he confided, "and I cried through the rest of the night. In the morning, the doctors and nurses came to tell me that they could no longer find an infection in me; the blood clots were gone, too. I felt both forgiven for my life's mistakes, yet also reborn as I left the hospital. I knew I wasn't going to die anytime soon, and I'd have to get at the task of fulfilling my life's purpose, if I could only discover it."

When I interviewed James, he told me of having recently met a physician who was quite psychic, a man associated with the Lily Dale Assembly in western New York State, who gave him hope for the future. It occurred to me that I also knew this man, Dr. Neal, and I suggested that James form a stronger relationship with the man, and let the doctor teach him about the spiritual world in which he lived. Dr. Neal told James that he was very psychic and should use the talent.

We also talked about methods for releasing Robert's ghost by first telling him he had died and then sending his old friend on the remainder of his soul's journey into Light. Then, as we talked about the special person that James was apparently destined to become, I shared some insights about his spiritual role from my knowledge of Numerology.

The door to the other world is already open in his experience. He visualizes the deceased as conscious fields of active energy, which is what they *were* in life, encased in physical bodies. He has faced his own death and reconciled to that, as an end must come to each body. He has received much insight relating to spiritual patterns established in what may be his past lifetimes, and these help him understand both the blessings and trials of his present life journey. Thus, James now is liberated to develop his psychic or soul abilities with no fear. He has gained a more profound understanding of love and humility and has come to understand that there is no seam between the world of the living and the dead, except one's willingness to live in the love of Something Greater.

CHAPTER 7

CHILDREN AND YOUNG ADULTS

Child's Play in Utica

In 1992, Russ Roberts worked as a maintenance man at St. Elizabeth's Hospital in Utica, NY. Most of the time he worked within the hospital, but one evening when he reported to work, his supervisor asked him to fill in for another cleaner at the Foery Drive Family Practice Building, operated by St. Elizabeth's.

The old three-story building had first floor offices and exam and treatment rooms on the two upper floors. Starting on the third floor, Russ worked methodically. The building was quiet, and he supposed all staff had left for the day. Suddenly, his reverie was interrupted by a small boy, about nine years old, running through the hall and into various rooms. The child sported a coat and baseball cap with a team insignia. At first, Russ took this to be the child of a doctor who was working late. But as time went on, it became obvious that the child was unsupervised. "Hey, kid!" he called out.

The child kept up his noisy maneuvering in and out of offices, as if to initiate a game of tag. Worrying that the child might break some of the medical equipment, Russ chased after the boy. "Hey, kid!" he yelled again and dropped his broom, starting down the hall to intercept the child. The laughing boy fled down the long hallway, seeming to enjoy Russ's hot pursuit. He felt he was gaining on the boy when, all of a sudden, in mid-stride, the child vanished!

Russ ran on through empty air for a few more feet but, looking back, he saw nobody. "That really unnerved me," he said, "I looked down the spiral stairs, and there was nobody there either. I thought to myself, how could he have gotten downstairs so fast? I scoured the building, checking every room and closet, but the boy had disappeared." Russ returned to work, and shortly thereafter a doctor appeared. Russ asked the woman if she'd seen anybody else in the building, but the woman hadn't. Russ, trying to comprehend the strange event, tried to persuade himself that it had all been his imagination, though he knew it hadn't been. He finished his work and went home.

The following night when he reported to work, the supervisor once more asked him to return to the Foery Drive work site. Unnerved by the previous night's experience, Russ refused to go alone. The boss then assigned Paul, a co-worker, to help him. The two went to the medical building and began their work. At the first floor waiting area, children's toys were strewn about from the youngsters who had visited various offices during the day. Russ stepped over them and moved to clean the first room.

As he stepped through the doorway, the wall phone rang. He answered it but heard only silence. Hanging up the phone, he cleaned that room and moved on to the next. As he entered that room, too, the desk phone rang. And, as in the first experience, he heard only silence when he picked up. This phenomenon continued in each room he cleaned that evening. As he stood in the hallway trying to comprehend these strange events, the hallway pay phone suddenly rang. As in the other instances, there was only silence on the other end when he answered.

Suddenly, Paul, who had heard of Russ' experiences of the previous night, bolted out the door and was gone. These strange goings on were more than *he* wanted on the job. Russ, somewhat unnerved by it all, stayed on. He called the hospital and the administrator sent security guards Wade and Jim to search the building. They found nothing out of the ordinary.

Russ knew that he was sensitive to "the other world," having seen filmy shapes in a Remsen, NY, cemetery in previous years. He knew also that there was more to life than that which could be seen, though he couldn't understand these unusual occurrences in Utica. A pragmatic man, Russ removed all the handsets from the wall phones until he had completed his cleaning, and there was no more ringing that night. But he was puzzled as to the cause. Could the boy be a ghost? Who was he, and from what period of history? Russ decided to consult an old timer.

The next day he found Sister Ellen, an elderly hospital staffer, and asked her about the building's past. "That was the old convent, Russell. We had no boys in there, you understand, unless they were the altar boys who came to help the priest say mass. But they always left right after mass was over." Could this have been a young altar boy who had died, and who now found himself free to joyously play in a formerly restricted area?

Today, the Foery Drive building is shuttered and closed. No doctors examine the ill there, and no therapists give treatment any more. It is up for sale, and it seems clear that whatever spirit remains in the building is going to need some help in order to leave. "But that job is never delegated to night maintenance men," Russ smiled.

The Child

"I'm a nurse, so, of course, I'm compassionate with children," Jennifer Edens told me. "In 2000, my husband and I rented a single-family house at 1101 E. 2nd Street in Jamestown. "We had a little boy, Christopher, then, and when the ghost phenomenon started, I often thought he was the cause at first. When we moved in, my husband and I spent the first four nights in sleeping bags on the living room floor, while waiting for our furniture to arrive. Each night, around 2 or 3 in the morning, we were awakened by sounds of children laughing and happily playing. If it hadn't been the middle of the night and an interruption of our sleep, it might even have been enjoyable to just listen. Even though we recognized that *many* children's voices were present, I still went upstairs to the baby's bedroom to check, but he was always fast asleep. Where did the noises come from?

"By the third night, I had to find the source, and even though I was tired, I got up and wandered the entire house, finally discovering that the sounds came from one corner of the dining room. But there wasn't anything to be seen there! It was like being in surround-sound of some kind, but with nothing to see," she told me, still marveling at the spectacle beyond science.

"A week later, my mother visited, and when I told her about the episode, she remembered a family that had lived at that address when she was in junior high school, and Mom recalled that their three-year-old daughter, Julie, had suddenly died. Might that deceased girl be part of the sound phenomenon? Shortly after that, I saw Christopher, who was two at the time, looking intently across the dining room, staring at the corner where the sound originated. Then, he pointed to the top of the stairs as the two of us were walking up, 'Mommy, there she *is!*' he exclaimed. I didn't doubt him, though I wished I could have seen the child," she said.

We chatted briefly about the many incidents where a group of children are heard in happy play. Though just a single child was known to have died at that address, others in spirit seem to have found her and engaged little Julie in jubilant games. There seem to be playgrounds on another realm where little kids' spirits can play with others similarly deprived of a full life. Then, perhaps when that period of play is gratified, the child's soul can then turn to an evaluation of its cosmic purpose, which was fulfilled in just a short span of years.

Jennifer remembered another strange incident at the old house, which occurred a few weeks after they had moved in. "Suddenly, one day, we heard loud hammering from the cellar, though I knew nobody was down there. We also began to find the back door open every morning when we awoke, and I told my husband that we just *had* to get a new lock. But the lock already *on* the door was a good one, fitting tight, and I don't know how it could open after we'd locked it the night before.

"Shortly afterward, I met a psychic and invited her to visit our home to see what could be learned about Julie or the person who pounded and then opened our door. Could Julie be responsible for both events? When the lady came, she sat for a while in silence, then described a man named John who was a woodworker and who had lived in our rented house some years before. The spirit told her about his love of fishing and how he enjoyed walking a few blocks to the Chadakoin River to catch his breakfast. So though he must have been responsible for the open door and a ghostly woodworking project in the cellar, I never saw him. Whenever I went into the cellar, it was dark and quiet."

The Edens family only lived at the house for two years before moving, and with the move, ghosts departed from their home life. Jennifer didn't know who rented the house next, but noted that the building is in pretty bad shape today. Perhaps the owners gave up trying to rent to people who would be unable to have a quiet home life. If so, one wonders where John is—still at work in the cellar? Or, when the old building finally surrenders to gravity and age, will he be released to cross over to the other side of the river of Life, perhaps dropping his hook once or twice more in transit?

Not Dunn?

Fultonville, on the south bank of the Mohawk River, was a favorite rest stop for travelers on the old Erie Canal. Immigrants moved westward on "Clinton's Ditch" through this Mohawk Valley gateway and into central New York State, then onward to Buffalo, before voyaging through the Great Lakes to new American homes and jobs in the Midwest. The flow of traffic past Fultonville brought prosperity, and the evidence of the good times can still be seen in beautiful old Greek Revival style homes, such as the one at 44 South Main Street.

The builder and first owner was N.B. Gardinier, a commissioner for the Erie Canal, who served as the village postmaster and built his hillside residence in 1835. By the late 1830s, the house passed to a succession of his relatives: Ostranders, Donaldsons, the Wiles family, Emma Edward, Jennie Wiles, and finally to Alida and David Dunn, who resided there with two adult daughters from 1920 to 1941. Because of their long period of residence, the building is known today as "The Dunn House."

In 2002, I published my third book, *Ghosts of the Northeast*, and the longest story in that work was called "The Dunn House," about a structure in Johnsburg, NY, near North Creek. It came as a surprise, then, when I received a letter two years later from Stella Gittle, who owns the old Gardinier/Dunn house in Fultonville with her husband, Steven Helmin. "I was astounded," she wrote, "that there are two Dunn Houses in New York State, both Greek Revival, both built by prominent business people, and both apparently harboring spirits. Minus the wrap-around porch of the Johnsburg house, ours seems an exact duplicate. Also, two sisters named Dunn were among the last residents of the house before new owners came!"

Intrigued by Stella's story and her suspicion that their ghost was a little girl (a fact which I initially kept from my intuitive team), we set out to explore the old building on a sunny March day in 2006. The house appeared suddenly on our right as we drove uphill, eliciting a "Wow!" from us all. "What a beautiful home," someone exclaimed. Sharon and Sue approached the house and looked upward, where Sharon saw "something" in the fan-shaped attic windows. She took a photo that later revealed what may be a woman's face. When we met Steve and Stella and toured their home, we found our preliminary evaluation to be true—it is a wonderfully restored home.

As usual, once inside, Sue, Sharon, and Adrienne separated, each making her own way through the old house with no preliminary stories or explanations. Each paused, looked, and listened in the many rooms, seeking vibrations of the long ago residents. We prefer to work in this manner so as not to prejudice ourselves about what might be found.

I got a bit of the home's history from the owners before I, too, began my tour. It is an extensive house, and there were many rooms to explore. The large living room or front parlor contains several sealed frames or display cases for old Indian arrowheads and seashells collected by Stella's ancestors. I received no sensations there, but I later discovered that items inside these cases are, from time to time, moved by mysterious forces that dislodge and relocate specific items. Because this movement seems playfully done, Stella suspects a child ghost might be the culprit.

When our group debriefed at the end of the day, Stella told me that she and Steve occasionally hear loud crashes from the front room where the artifacts are stored and displayed. "It sounds as if a picture has fallen from the wall," she said. "But we never find anything fallen. However, this is the room where we set up our biggest tree at Christmas, and *ornaments disappear* from the tree at times. Later, we find them in various vases or pots on shelves in the room. We have two smaller trees set up in the middle parlor, but ornaments are never taken from those trees."

Before I knew all this, as I glanced around the room on my initial tour, I caught sight of a long-ago square spinet piano, but there was no way of knowing if such an instrument had ever graced the room. This would have been the likeliest room in which to make music, I think. I seemed to hear the terms "jingle bells" and "drum roll" near the big front door, but there never was any confirmation that those terms related to the foyer.

It was a fairly unproductive day for *my* intuition and most of my "results" came in the form of words that I heard or imagined in certain places. I felt a strong presence of Indians, but not an active involvement, simply that of ancient observers watching over the house. In the back driveway, I thought

I heard a voice saying, "Martin (or Morton) is watching over you," but again, these names rang no bells with the owners.

Adrienne felt a shiver in the front foyer and also the certainty that the former owners (Gardiniers or Dunns?) knew who *they were* in the social or business life of the community. It was as if they had the responsibility to act according to *their place* in the community's life.

Susan, who (on the day before our jaunts) usually meditates as to what she'll encounter, had visualized the portrait of a woman in a dark, scoop-necked dress, with someone's hand placed upon the shoulder of a woman who was very sick with a high fever before she left home. She heard the name "Tommy" and saw a boy in a nightshirt. Also, crossing her meditative field of vision was a ball of light that moved down the upstairs hallway from the back bedrooms toward the owners' bedroom in the front.

As Susan walked slowly through the attic, she visualized phantom travel trunks and wondered if they contained papers with information about the house or its former owners. It occurred to her that these *may* have existed once and had been already found. In the trunks, she sensed, were old 1800s dresses. Alongside one spectral trunk, she spotted a woman dressed in such attire, holding up one of the old garments, though these objects no longer existed in the attic. Then, as she toured the cellar, she again sensed "something hidden." At one point in the upstairs, she heard a small voice say, "Hello" in her ear, but there was no one to be seen.

Behind the classic style front section of the home, there is an older-appearing section, and it was here that the intuitives seemed to have the strongest experiences. Susan heard a child's voice calling, "Mama" as she entered what was the only unrestored part of the house in the rear upstairs. She entered those rooms just as Sharon arrived there, so they entered together quietly. Both spotted a small, moving light inside a closet to their left. Bluish in color, it moved, and then disappeared. Both tried to compute how the exterior afternoon light might have been reflected or refracted from the small side window to create the apparition, but there was no logical way for this to occur.

Both women agreed that the strongest energies in the house were perceived there. Susan visualized a young mother (almost certainly a servant) with a young baby who was restless in that room. "I feel this young mother was torn between her duties to her employers, the owners of the house, and her responsibilities to her needy child. There were chores to be done downstairs, but the woman's heart was drawn to her baby's demands."

Using her digital camera, Sue took a series of pictures in those rooms and later showed us a small spot (as opposed to the usual orb) of white light that was blurred along its edge, suggesting that it was moving when photographed. An instant later, she again snapped the camera and found the light in a new place. Then a third shot showed no light at all near the doorway location. Had the energy of someone or something passed the women by?

Stella later revealed to us that this back area hasn't been restored because she just isn't comfortable in the space, so it sits, unused, much as it must have looked one hundred years ago. She especially avoids the closet where Sue and Sharon observed the blue light, but isn't sure why. Adrienne also strongly felt anxiety in that area, and as her profession involves sensing such energies, she is probably accurate in making that assessment.

Steve noted that, many times, he observes their cats watching something unseen move through the bedroom—the felines move their heads as if tracking someone's passage. There is another, smaller room upstairs that our team chose to call "the ship room," because of Steve's historic ship models there. Steve noted that the lights in there often go off and on by themselves, as if a ghostly someone is trying to notify the living of its ongoing presence.

Adrienne felt that the servant lady and the woman of the house continue to go throughout the house, still tending to the tasks that occupied them in life.

Although many of the families who lived in that home had children, there was nothing to distinguish the ghost child or children that our intuitives perceived, making the young spirit's identification almost impossible without using the services of a trance medium. Stella told us of meeting an elder woman of the community who remembered coming to the house as a youngster during the Dunn sisters' occupancy. "They held teas for the girls of the neighborhood," she related, so perhaps the child ghost might originate from the memories of such a youth.

As our entire group debriefed in the parlor at the end of our house tour, each person contributed his or her information. Sharon audiotaped much of that discussion, and as we talked about the sensation of a small voice saying, "Hello" upstairs, the voice repeated itself twice more, audible afterward on Sharon's tape. Maybe the child, who probably was of a past owner's family, wanted to be *sure* that we knew of her presence. What a nice touch to our day!

Stella also told me that her mother (who lives with them) broke a toe and chose to sleep in the downstairs rear parlor (where there is a display of antique firearms) rather than climb the back stairs to her bedroom. Awakening during the night on two occasions, she spotted a man standing in the center of the room. The next night she chose to endure the discomfort and slept upstairs in her bedroom. "That squares with my own feelings," Stella said, "because I've always thought more of a male presence here in the back of the house, and not the female energy that the intuitives got."

"This house was in pretty bad shape when we purchased it in 1989," Steve told us. "We discovered that before we bought it, a town truck coming down the hill swerved off the road, bounced up the little front hill, and turned over in our driveway, hitting the front, south corner of the house very hard. The passenger in the truck died in that crash. We often wondered if that accidental death has played some part in the house's shifting energies."

In a follow-up e-mail, Steve wanted us to know that while our group visited that Saturday, he had turned the thermostat up twice, hoping to warm the apparently chilly house. Only after our group left, did he find the house comfortably warmed. Upon reflection, he wondered if the chill was caused by the manifestation of the spirit energy attending our visit.

The Dunn sisters apparently were of different personalities, with one being extraverted and the other introverted and retiring. Yet, their family line maintained a social and political position of involvement in Fultonville for over one hundred thirty years. When the second sister died in the early 1960s, the house passed out of their line of descent to a new family. The old home hadn't been kept up and slowly declined over the next twenty years.

It is heartening to see what a beautiful restoration has been done by Steve and Stella, correcting most of the yesteryear blemishes, though they have not yet evicted the busy memories of those who lived and worked there long ago.

Lost Child

"It is amazing to me that one can live for ten years in a place and not fully know what is really there," Kiki Waldron told me. As a young mother, she lived in a housing development not far from Shoppingtown Mall in DeWitt, NY. "I had three young daughters at the time (ages ten, six and one) and we had bought a fairly new house, the former home of an elderly, single woman who taught piano lessons and lived with her dog. One day, the woman collapsed and died, but she wasn't found until a few days later. It was a sad story, but we felt none of that sorrow when we moved in. If her spirit was there, we never experienced it.

"Each morning, I did housework and picked up the kids' toys, putting them in their proper places before the older ones returned from school. One day I finished the task, and, while the baby took her nap, I went to the kitchen for a cup of tea. When I returned to the living room, there was a doll in the middle of the floor. I put it away, thinking I had somehow overlooked it a few minutes before. But then a few days later, my middle child complained that someone kept moving her toys in the bedroom."

One night, a friend stayed over and, after walking through the hallway past the oldest girl's bedroom, expressed surprise that my daughter had a friend sleeping over. "She doesn't!" Kiki replied. "Well, somebody is in that top bunk," the friend replied. Kiki investigated but found nobody in the bunk beds except her daughter. With her husband on a long business trip a few weeks later, Kiki awoke in the night to see a little girl in a white nightgown standing beside her bed and calling her "Mom." At first, the young mother thought it was her daughter, but she suddenly realized it was not. Panicked at the unreality of it all, Kiki jumped out of bed and yelled, but the little girl had disappeared. Sleeping uneasily for the next few nights, Kiki sometimes heard a child calling her in the dark, but the caller was elusive and never showed herself. Even after her husband returned, the young mother could hear the child's voice calling in the night. Once, it seemed that the little girl was just outside her bedroom door, so Kiki got up and opened it, but no one was there. Of course, her husband never heard any of the commotion.

"We had a tradition that I'd make each girl the new dress of her choice on her birthday, as I'm a pretty good seamstress," Kiki told me. "My middle girl asked me to make an old-fashioned outfit for her that year—a high-necked, long, narrow-waist dress with puffy sleeves. A strange design for a little modern girl, I mused. Additionally, my daughter wanted me to hand-make a rag doll for her.

"As I began cutting and stitching, the little ghost girl came to my mind. She had initially called me 'Mom,' and I *was* a mom, so I invited the child to speak to me and tell me what she wanted. The next time I felt her presence, I tried to deeply sense her needs. You understand, David, that I'm intuitive and sensitive, so I figured I could help the little girl. I sensed a lonely, confused child who continually searched for her mother, and who didn't understand that her body had died. Mentally, I asked for her name and received 'Jocelyn,' a name I had never heard before. She was unable or unwilling to give me a last name or the date of her death, but I did pick up the date 1870, which must have figured importantly in her life.

"Pretty soon, I found my life becoming *quite* unusual," Kiki said with a laugh. "I never told anyone in my neighborhood about Jocelyn, not even my eldest daughter (until years later). I had a dream soon after those intuitions, and in it I saw Jocelyn's mother, who told me her name was Ruth. She then showed me scenes depicting a sad life story. Her abusive husband was a big man, a drunk who was especially vile to Jocelyn, who was a simple-minded girl. Maybe that state of mind was caused by physical abuse from the father, who was an itinerant laborer employed by local farmers when there was work to be done. The family lived in a multi-family house where one night, when the husband was drunk and violent, Ruth had wrapped the child in a shawl and took the girl to a favorite tree in the nearby apple orchard where she loved to play. Jocelyn feared to stay alone, the mother said, until Ruth bribed her with the promise of a new dress if the child would stay there, out of harm's way, until her father sobered up."

The tragic tale continued with Ruth returning to the house where the drunk husband raved and ranted and eventually locked her in a closet. The house then caught fire, and Ruth died of smoke inhalation, unable to rescue Jocelyn the next morning. But by then, the little girl had frozen to death in the cold night, lulled into an everlasting sleep by the dream of a new dress. Even in the spirit world, it seemed, the mother was obstructed by the father's spirit from reaching the dead daughter who had slept into death and didn't understand her fate. In that other world, Ruth was still attempting to rescue her daughter and take Jocelyn into The Light. Kiki decided to facilitate the liberation.

"I brought a psychic friend who can communicate with spirits to my house, and he got more details of the story. Though Jocelyn had a chronological age of ten, her mental development was only at about age five or six. She feared men, especially bearded ones, and told the psychic simply that she waited there for her mother, but dearly missed her rag doll."

Kiki decided to seek historical confirmation to validate the scenario. Research showed that the area of Butternut Creek, near which she lived, had once been covered with an apple orchard, and indeed, many of the homes present there in the 1970s still had gnarled, old apple trees in the yard. It seemed reasonable that Jocelyn's father *would* have found seasonal work in helping local farmers load their crops onto canal boats plying the old Erie Canal. And yes, there had long ago been a multi-family house that burned there in 1876. Thus, at least part of the drama resonated as true.

Then it struck Kiki that her six-year-old daughter must have made an unconscious connection with Jocelyn, as her daughter's new dress seemed like a clothing style from the 1870s, and it would be easy to understand her own daughter's motivation to own a rag doll, if that was what little Jocelyn so badly missed. "My daughter really got into the story when I shared it with her. She no longer fussed if her toys were out of place, and even drew pictures of toys and other objects for Jocelyn to enjoy. Then, as suddenly as it began, after Halloween that year, the little girl's presence seemed to fade.

"It was springtime when I tried to set Jocelyn free. I got together a group of friends who are experienced in this kind of soul release work, and we attempted to guide the little girl into The Light. We made a circle, blessed the space, then invited Jocelyn to enter our safe place. We pointed her to the

190

gateway into The Light that we hoped she would see. We told her to see her mother waiting at that portal. What we didn't realize at that time is that one of the men in our group is bearded, and he sat too close to the gateway location. Apparently, *that* frightened Jocelyn, though she couldn't have known that he, though large, is a very gentle soul. In our ceremony, we assumed she'd crossed over. But that wasn't true; in the fall, she was back.

"We brainstormed our ceremony and hit upon the bearded man factor, so we conducted a new service with an all-female group. That *seemed* to do it, and, not long afterward, my husband and I sold the house. It was a few years later, in conversing with our former neighbors, however, that we discovered that the new owners were experiencing 'little girl phenomena' and that neighbors had seen a small girl running in the yard, though no child lived there. I had never mentioned our child ghost to others.

"I decided to take care of the matter myself, as I've been training in Shamanism ever since that time. In the Oriental, Native American and Siberian traditions, a shaman learns to travel (in deep meditation) to the world of the dead and help in releasing trapped souls, or even discovers how to bring healing diagnosis from that world to a suffering person on this level.

"My spirit guides and spirit helpers accompanied me to that house, and, sure enough, Jocelyn was still there. I have a wolf companion in that other world, and it was only the wolf's offer of a free ride on his back that convinced Jocelyn to abandon her itinerant existence and venture into The Light. *This* time I made sure that she went all the way to meet her mother, Ruth, who was waiting. Now, almost one hundred thirty years later, there is peace in that suburban section of DeWitt—and in a mother's and daughter's hearts.

Kids

Oneonta is a small college town, and one of the nicest communities in upstate New York. As with most Catskill Mountains communities, its early industry centered on forest products and farming. Those industries attracted stores and, eventually, the railroad, which, in turn, drew more residents. In 1888, the Oneonta Normal School, a school for teacher training, became the second school of higher education in the community, alongside Hartwick Seminary, which later expanded into Hartwick College.

As locals and students mixed with businesspeople, the village continued to expand, and in 1905, a group of new houses was constructed along Central Avenue. The first of these was built by and for the Cross family.

"That's the house my family moved into in 1963, when I was five," Tom Robinson told me. "It had been a duplex, but with the six children in our family, we needed all the space. So my dad had it restored to its original configuration. Not long afterward, my older sisters, who were in high school, had the first experiences. Three of them shared an upstairs bedroom, and they studied up there in the evenings.

"One night, with the bedroom door open and the hall lights off, they heard a swishing of women's skirts in the darkness. First, there were scraping sounds, and then the sound of someone deliberately coming upstairs in what seemed a secretive way: taking two steps at a time, then pausing as if to listen. Then two more steps and a pause." Understanding that these were not normal house sounds, and wary of the dark, eerie hallway, the girls slammed the door and called out for their parents. At first, Mom and Dad didn't hear. A moment later, the girls' bedroom doorknob turned. Frightened, the girls stood and waited to see who would enter. Nobody did, so after a few minutes, one girl snatched the knob from inside and pulled hard. There was no one outside.

"Somewhere in there, I began to have very vivid dreams of an older woman in a grey Victorian dress," Tom said, "and I couldn't figure out why she wasn't there when I'd awake. Then, about a year after the first scary incident, our parents were out of town, and I was home with two sisters. It was Sunday evening and one of my sisters, who had agreed to babysit me, took me upstairs to put on my pajamas. The stairway had a landing, and as we turned that corner to go up, we heard a little child's voice call out from up on the second landing, 'Mommy, is that you?' My sister and I fled back downstairs. We had both heard it and knew there was no child present except me. We checked outside to see if anyone had come in without us knowing. There was no car in the driveway and nobody on the porch. We never figured out that one!"

Maybe the Robinsons got used to the ghost lady or vice-versa. The next two decades passed rather quietly. Had she left? In 1996, Tom's New York City cousin got caught in a snowstorm on his way back to Syracuse University. The cousin, who stopped to wait out the storm at the Robinsons', was accompanied by a sensitive friend, and in the morning, the young man, wide-eyed, said, "Did you know this house is *haunted?* In the middle of the night, I saw a woman walk out of the closet!"

"Needless to say, my cousin and his friend were anxious to be on their way as soon as the snowplows cleared the road the next morning," Tom laughed.

An adult now, Tom is still fascinated by ghosts. In our interview, he remembered visiting newlywed Oneonta friends, John and Gayle, who lived in a small "railroad house" near the Valley View Elementary School. They spent time fixing up the house before moving in. At first, didn't know the full story about the previous family, who had all died tragically there. "Father, mother, and son were all alcoholics and died of the disease. After the father's death, the mother and son lived on there, but when she succumbed to alcohol poisoning, the son was too drunk to notice, and it was only several weeks later that her body was discovered. The son died some time later in a local hospital," Tom said.

"I was helping John fix up the old house in the '80s and we heard many noises from the attic. At the time, we brushed it off as being squirrel activity though, later, when we went up to look, there was no evidence that squirrels had ever lived or played up there. On another occasion we heard what was definitely *walking* up there, but we chose to ignore it.

"John was a drummer and was doing a demonstration for us in his bedroom one evening. I stood with my back to the attic door and watched him. Suddenly, there were three loud knocks on that attic door behind me. We *knew* that nobody was upstairs, and it scared me into my next lifetime! My friend nervously said, 'I guess I'll have to stop now because Fred (supposedly the son of the previous family) is not very happy!' So John stopped, and the knocks did likewise."

Today, Tom is an afternoon radio show host in the Capital District, and his life is manageable and fairly predictable. Nevertheless, those memories of Oneonta in the old days occasionally return to him. "When I think back on those times of ghost contacts," he told me, "I sometimes wish the spirits wouldn't be such strangers nowadays, but my new home is quiet, and my family is happy about *that!*"

Kidding Around

"I'm a newspaper reporter, and I'm concerned, day in and day out, with facts. I want to see some verification of the claims that my sources provide to me. Nevertheless, I have lived with some facts that I'm not sure any newspaper would want to print," Rob Snow told me.

"In 2003, soon after I got out of the service, I came to Potsdam and found an apartment on Waverly Street. The building was old, built about 1900, and it had been converted from a single family to a duplex. We lived on the right side at number twenty. Amanda and I were engaged at the time, and one evening we sat in the kitchen playing cards. It was a slow and friendly game and we were relaxed. Beside us was the kitchen counter, which had a little raised lip around the edge, and on that counter was a glass dish. Suddenly, the dish was propelled off the counter and crashed on the floor. It happened so quickly that neither of us had the chance to catch it. It wasn't a valuable piece, but we were shocked at how quickly it had happened. I guess that was our introduction to the ghost house on Waverly Street," he grinned.

Rob then told me of another series of strange events that took place within the next week. Semi-awake, he had been aware that Amanda had gotten up several times during the night, but he had drifted back to sleep before he could question her. In the morning, he asked her about her discomfort.

"It's really strange, Rob," she said. "Twice during the night, I was awakened by the sound of a child crying and sniffling. On some unconscious level, I decided to get up and go to the bathroom for a piece of tissue to wipe the child's nose. When I returned, because there was no child anywhere, I fell into bed and went right back to deep sleep. As I said, this happened twice. The second time, it hit me—*there isn't any kid here*! What do you make of that, Rob?"

"What could I say?" he responded, "We had a ghost? A ghost *child*? That was hard to believe," he told me.

The next episode, he explained, was "when we decided to paint our bedroom. After we finished painting one wall, we took a break. When we returned to the room, we found three letters and some numbers drawn in the still-wet paint. Amanda and I tried to figure the meaning of the letters and came up with nothing reasonable. In retrospect, I think they might have been somebody's initials, but we've now forgotten what they were. We also tried to make sense of the numbers by adding them or subtracting them, but it was as if they were just random digits.

"We have cats, and when we lived in that apartment, our pets refused to go upstairs without one of us to accompany them. Many times, they'd sit at the foot of the stairs and just stare upward, as if following someone or something that was invisible to either of us. At other times, we'd catch the cats staring at certain walls, as if they could see something that we couldn't," he told me.

The couple eventually moved out in October of 2004 and bought their own house. "Before we left," Rob told me, "our neighbors on the other side of the house told us that when they returned from a trip to California, that their goldfish were all dead. You know how hard it is to kill goldfish?" he asked me. Rob thinks the fish had "help" of some kind in crossing over to the Great Bowl in the Sky.

"After we left, the landlord began renting to Potsdam College students," Rob told me, "so maybe you could ask them what is going on nowadays." That sounded good to me—maybe Potsdam holds a non-credit course that these young adults will never forget.

A Pall for Paul

Interviewing Scott Schneider on another story, I asked him when he had his first encounter with "the other world." He got very serious and was quiet for a minute before he began.

"On Long Island, when I was a junior in high school in 1986, I had a lot of friends, especially Jeff and a girl named Shirley, who was dating another guy I knew, Paul. We hung out together that summer and had a lot of fun. Paul and Shirley were a couple, but I never thought it was *that* serious, and I wasn't surprised when Jeff became interested in her. I think all of us understood that it had become more than a friendship—all of us except Paul. I guess he was the last one to figure it out, and, boy, did he get depressed."

Scott said that Paul was humiliated at being "dumped" and drove to Shirley's house one evening to talk about the matter with her, but she wouldn't see him. The next day nobody could find Paul—he wasn't at his usual hangouts. Then Shirley found a note from the boy in her family's mailbox. It was very morose and seemed to be a suicide note. Surely it was just a play for attention and sympathy, the friends concluded. But Paul wasn't anywhere to be found. When Shirley showed the note to Scott, he, in turn, showed it to Jeff, and the trio discussed what it meant.

"He might have gone over to the bluffs at Rocky Point," Shirley ventured. "At one time that was *our* special place to sit and talk." Though it was completely dark, the three drove to the bluffs and, once there, searched for the rickety, old wooden stairway down to the beach. "It wasn't in that good shape," Scott remembered, "and we had to pick our way carefully. On top of that, there was no moon, and it was misty along the shore, so we had to watch where we were going. When we got to the bottom, Shirley, Jeff and I spread out along the sand, calling Paul's name. All we could hear was the surf. There was nobody else there.

"We started back up the stairs, which were very steep, with me bringing up the rear in the pitch black night. When I got halfway up, I felt someone aggressively pushing me in the back. I couldn't complain to Jeff or Shirley, as they were all *ahead* of me! It was a real pressure, and I moved very rapidly up those steps, pushing the other two ahead of me, maybe helped as much by fright as by that invisible force. Who was it? *What* was it? Nobody was visible behind me. Suddenly, having reached the road, the force on my back stopped. I turned to look at the other two who had just reached the top ahead of me. 'Did *you* feel that?' I asked in a shaky voice. 'Feel *what?*' they asked."

It was already 2 a.m., and the teenagers knew they were missed at home, so they returned to the car and went home.

The next morning, the full story spread all over town. The neighbors along the bluffs said that, during the night, they had heard a loud noise and called the police, but the cops had other, more urgent tasks, and it was dawn before they got to the site of what they were sure was just another alcoholic beach party. What they found, however, was no party.

"Near an old log, within twenty feet of where we had stopped our search for him, the cops found Paul's body, shot once through the right temple. In his humiliation, Paul had shot himself with his father's hand gun and died there. I reflected on the force that pushed me up those bluff stairs, and it sure seemed angry and aggressive.

"Years later, when I thought back on it all, it sure seemed to me that this was the spirit energy of Paul, still enraged at what he felt was his girlfriend's betrayal, pushing anyone he could on that old stairway. The pressure was on me, I'm sure, simply because I was the last in line. That was my first experience with the paranormal, David. It was scary at the time, but it has made me ask a lot of questions about life and death in the years since," he said.

Ascension

Ken's family was friendly with the Sinnots in the Greene County hamlet of Prattsville, NY, and one October evening in 1961, the two families met in the Sinnot's house for a meal and conversation. Ken, the youngest of the boys in his family, had no Sinnot boys his age to play with, but he got along well with their daughter, Monica, age seven. She had been ill the last time he saw her, and she wasn't at the gathering that night. Without a playmate, he wandered around watching the others. The parents were playing cards in the kitchen at the back of the house while the Sinnot children played outside. His brothers were busy spinning 45 r.p.m. records on the front porch, and he thought it might be fun to look in on them.

The Sinnot house was large, and to get to the front porch, little Ken, also age seven, had to walk through a large front room, almost a ballroom, which was unfurnished. As he walked toward the porch, he caught a slight movement from the corner of his eye. Turning to his right, he was puzzled to see a figure standing at the foot of the stairs to the second floor. He stopped and looked directly at the apparition. He could see it was a hooded figure wearing a grey robe, but no facial features were visible. As the two looked at one another, the figure motioned slowly for Ken to approach. For a moment, the boy suspected one of his older brothers of playing a prank on him, but he discarded that theory: the figure was too tall. Then, he panicked—this wasn't a member of the Sinnot family either!

Ken moved hurriedly toward the porch. Nearing the front door, he looked back and saw the figure standing halfway up the stairs. It paused and once more beckoned him upward, but, when Ken didn't respond to the summons, the figure climbed to the second floor and Ken lost sight of it. The boy shot out the door and onto the porch to the safety and companionship of his older siblings. Who or what was it? Could that have been a ghost? He'd heard his elders use that word from time to time, but he wasn't sure he'd really witnessed one.

He looked back into the room: nobody was visible, so he scampered through the large room, through the swinging doors, and into the kitchen, where his parents were still playing cards. He walked to his mother's elbow and asked what the figure could have been. She smiled and told him it all was surely his imagination. He couldn't believe that; it had all seemed so real.

A few hours later, his family headed home. At bedtime the telephone rang and his father answered it. There was a brief hushed conversation; his mother joined his father, and they talked in somber tones. After a bit more conversation, they hung up and told their children that the Sinnots had just received a phone call from a New York City hospital informing them that Monica's leukemia had finally ended her life.

Ken remembers his sadness mixed with wonder at the night's events. He hadn't understood that his little playmate was gravely ill. In later years, he pondered the synchronicity between the ghostly, robed figure ascending the Sinnots' stairs. It all likely took place as Monica lay dying downstate. Today, he has concluded that the figure was likely related to Monica's spirit departing the body, or else it was a heavenly escort who came looking for the girl in her house, but then found her in a hospital one hundred miles away.

Charlotte

After the dangers of Indian attacks and invasions ceased, settlers moved rapidly into the Adirondacks, following the rivers and ancient water routes of Lakes George and Champlain. By the mid-1800s, there were many small settlements in the Town of Caldwell and Town of Queensbury on Lake George's southern end. Many of the "next to nature" shore points became summer resorts. One of those was Assembly Point, named for the religious church tent meetings often held there after mid-century.

Following World War I there was an upsurge of summer camp building that rapidly developed the shoreline of "The Queen of Lakes." Many camps were built at Assembly Point, which no longer hosted summer revivals. One of

Camp on Assembly Point

the more modest camps had two owners before the year 2000, when it was purchased by Christine and her husband, full-time residents of Loudonville. "We did major renovations here," she told me, "and maybe that was the prelude to what came afterward. At first, I didn't suspect a ghost. We had a beautiful, winterized, and remodeled camp close to the lake, and it was our place to relax."

During the first year of residence, she told me, there were just a few glitches. "One of these was a closet light in our bedroom, with the switch next to the water line shutoff. Yes, it had the original bulb we'd put in during 2000, and sometimes I'd switch it on and it didn't work, causing me to think the bulb was going. However, five minutes later, I'd flip the switch, and it worked fine. We figured it was a fault in the wiring, but an electrician found nothing out of order. In addition, our ceiling fan simply quit once in a while, but then abruptly turned itself on again. We didn't have to look at the matter seriously, though, until my sister-in-law and her two boys visited us in the summer of 2001 and stayed in the little guest house next door.

"One morning, my sister-in-law, Erin, came in from our guest house, and said, 'Chris, I think you've got a little something in the guest house.'" Christine, a mouse phobic, feared for a moment that Erin was talking about a rodent, but she referred to a *spirit*. Erin had felt someone or something invisible push past her in the cabin, and then spotted a wispy form with a white object on its head.

The next night, around 11 p.m., Christine's daughter lay on her mother's bed with the dogs; shortly thereafter, the girl ran into the kitchen. "You have a ghost in your bedroom, Mom!" The girl was distressed and told her mother that she'd watched the light switch raise itself, turning on the light, then fall again, shutting off the light. And no human had been nearby. Christine noted that the dogs lay nearby dozing, and she assumed that the ghost, if that's what it was, wasn't harmful.

Christine told her sister, Susan, about the episode, and Susan said, "That's easy. I have a friend who's psychic. Want me to invite her up?"

Shortly thereafter, in 2002, Christine met Carolyn, an intuitive woman from Greenfield who provided a psychic reading that seemed genuine, so Christine invited her friend, Carolyn, to visit the camp to see what she could "get." Carolyn came to Assembly Point and entered the camp, reacting immediately after entering the back door. "I spotted a young girl wearing a long dress, apron, and a white cap on her head. 'Hello, I'm Charlotte,' the child said." Carolyn added, "It was just that quick! The hair stood up on my arms!" Psychically, the woman had a conversation with the girl, who appeared to be eleven or twelve years old.

Carolyn inquired, "Do you know when you lived?" The child responded with imagery that suggested colonial times.

"Can you tell me your name?"

"Charlotte."

"Who are your parents?"

Charlotte responded, "I don't want to talk about that."

As Carolyn told me of that response, I wondered if the child was a "trickster" of the spirit world (not a genuine ghost, but a playful spirit who, in the end, might *not* be so playful) or indeed simply the spirit consciousness of a long-ago dead girl.

"Why are you *here*?" Carolyn inquired.

"It's warm," Charlotte told her. "It was so cold where I was," she continued. "*Please*, may I stay?"

"Why are you at *this* house?" Carolyn asked.

"Because I like to play with the other children." That response was interesting; Erin's sons had no idea they were sharing their toys with a ghost girl, but apparently little Charlotte thought *she* was taking part in the boys' games. She told Carolyn that she was trying to get the boys' attention and interact with them—the first children she'd seen in a long time. It is worth mentioning here that Carolyn had no knowledge of other children at the site when she received this information. In any case, the child ghost seemed harmless, and so like Christine's daughter, so Chris asked Carolyn to tell the girl, "Okay. You can stay."

Over the next two years, however, lights and the ceiling fan worked when it pleased Charlotte to permit them to. One day in the summer of 2005,

Chris went over to chat with a neighbor. The man seemed irritated and told Chris that he'd been dozing on his porch swivel chair, when suddenly someone whirled the chair around in a circle. He had opened his eyes and found nobody else around. The man was clearly upset and noted that his house lights snapping off and on was bad enough!

Later that summer, with Erin, her husband, and two boys visiting in the guest house again, Christine's ceiling fan light came on with full illumination. She turned off the switch on the fan fixture and returned to bed. It happened again. She shut the switch off again. Finally, after the *fifth* time, when she turned off the wall switch to the fixture, she said, "Charlotte, that's *enough!*" And it stopped. The next morning, Erin's husband came over for coffee, and Christine told him of her tussle with Charlotte. The wide-eyed man told Christine that in the guest house, too, the ceiling fan had to be turned off *five times* before he could cease having to throw the wall switch.

Shortly thereafter, the neighbor told Chris that his porch light also refused to work on occasion, much as her closet light had. He, likewise, had gotten a new bulb to insert, but trying the switch one more time, he found that it now worked perfectly. It seemed that the light worked only when Charlotte wanted it to. Was the ghost girl pranking the whole neighborhood? As an afterthought, Christine considers that the neighbor has a new three-year-old grandchild, and she wonders if the child is the big attraction for Charlotte at the neighbor's house.

In the fall of 2005, I began working with Cable Channel 8 (WNCE) in Glens Falls to videotape historic locations and tell the ghost stories associated with them. I enjoyed working with Mike Carnevale, retired policeman, Reiki practitioner, bow-hunter, and outdoorsman, who hosted the program called *Adirondack Journey.* Our first video project had taken place on Graphite Mountain near Brant Lake, and after getting good public commentary, Producer Ed Gazel wanted to do another story. Program host Mike had recently met Christine and heard her story, and that was *that.* We had the material for a second program.

In March 2006, Mike and I came to Christine's Assembly Point camp, which now was being lived in year-round. Then Carolyn and Christine's sister, Susan, arrived, followed by Ed and Jack Hojohn, the station's cameraman. Mike began by interviewing Christine in the living room overlooking the lake, while I offered commentary on her responses. Then the crew took a break while setting up the next shot—an on-camera interview with Carolyn.

Off air, Christine told of another strange event. One recent evening, she had walked down to the dock by herself and found a tiny feather on the steps to the dock. Cute, she thought, and picked it up and pocketed the quill.

A bit later, back in the camp, as it started to drizzle and got dark, Christine went inside and decided to change the window covering. She climbed onto a step ladder to pull some tacks. As she extracted one of the tacks, something flew out of the wall and hit her hard on the forehead. Bug! she thought. Then, looking down at Lucy, her dog, stretched out on the floor, Christine saw a small feather landing near Lucy's paws. Wonder how that got out of my pocket? she pondered. Finishing the task, she absent-mindedly reached into her pocket. The first feather was still there. She picked the other from the floor and discovered it was a twin for the one she had found on the stairs. Was this another message from Charlotte? She remembers her husband calling her on the phone the next morning. As she talked, she walked to the bedroom closet and threw the light switch. It didn't work. Christine said aloud, "Okay, Charlotte, I know it's you. Thanks for the feather!" Again, she flipped the switch, and the light came on. On the other end of the line, her husband tried to process all the improbable events he was listening to at his camp.

During that videotaping break, we slumped on the couch and chairs, sharing some good-natured banter. Producer Ed jokingly commented about the possibility of the Tiffany table lamp beside him going off. Immediately, one of the three bulbs inside the lampshade *went off*. One of the lamp's three pull-chains then began to swing, not idly, but quite strongly, through a six-inch arc. We were astonished and spent the next five minutes, as the chain continued to swing, trying to rationalize what could cause it—Charlotte? We verbally teased her, "Come on, Charlotte, make another chain swing!" And one of the other chains *did* begin to swing very slightly, but then stopped. However, the first chain remained swinging quite vigorously for another ten minutes, seemingly defying the laws of Physics.

Someone suggested the movement might be caused by a draft through the window, but there were good, modern storm windows on the outside, and, besides, if one chain swung, wouldn't the other two do likewise? Another person thought it might be a ground movement beneath the house. Again, then why weren't the other two chains moving? Someone else suggested maybe the bulb had died a natural death, but how could we know? Our conversation then turned to other matters, and, suddenly, the extinguished bulb turned itself back on again. Nervously, Ed said, "Well, guess it's time to get the second part interview!" And that broke the spell, but maybe little Charlotte was laughing at us know-it-alls.

Because we had the cameras off during the light phenomenon and Christine's feather story, before resuming our work, Ed and Jack recreated and filmed an activity similar to the phenomena we had just witnessed with the table lamp and with the ceiling fan, which was also part of our story. We then moved to the kitchen table, Carolyn had her microphone put on, and we resumed. Mike, in his signature camouflage jacket and hat, smilingly persuaded Carolyn to verbalize *her* experiences in the house. "Carolyn, do you think Charlotte will talk to me?" he asked.

"I don't know why not," the intuitive responded. She closed her eyes and settled a minute, and then Mike asked if the girl wanted to talk. From Carolyn's mouth came, "Why are you wearing that funny hat?"

Mike looked up at his head covering and blushed. Mike seldom blushes. He responded, "It's who I *am*." Mike then inquired if Charlotte was tied to the house or the property, and asked if she would remain there if Christine sold the house?

Charlotte's response through Carolyn was that she was unsure. She liked the house because it was warm and cozy, and she enjoyed the company of other children when they came to visit.

I joined in and asked if Charlotte was aware of others who have passed over. The response was (and perhaps this offered a clue to Charlotte's activity in the spirit world) that there are many *wanderers*. "They're not here all the time, as I am," she answered. I had begun to suspect that this ghost girl had originated from some other place and had been drawn to Assembly Point by the happy atmosphere of Christine's family life.

Mike asked how long Charlotte had been on Lake George and the response was "Way, way back." Charlotte was unsure. She then confessed to being a wanderer herself, and said she had found *family* in Christine's home. Again, Mike, the humorous outdoorsman, asked the girl (from her vantage point along the lake) to tell him how good the fishing was near the Point.

"My family used to *haul* them in," emanated from Carolyn.

Mike then concluded the interview by asking the child if she would tell us about her former life in the body. The response was that it was always cold there. The voice became sadder, and we thanked the girl and ended the interview. This should be an interesting program for those interested in the possibility of the afterlife mixing with our plane of existence.

What to think? I'm always curious about such encounters, especially when they are purported conversations. Two weeks after our videotaping, I was called to the station by Ed. He and Jack were amazed to find during their program editing, small light orbs moving about during the table lamp simulation. In the footage of the ceiling fan, vague images could be seen moving past the fan blades. We tried and tried to explain these rationally, but we had to agree that Charlotte had been playing with us even during our storytelling. We had to do some new "voice-over" explanations for the viewers to show them the activity that had been invisible to our group during the shoot.

In summary, there is no question that winters around Lake George have always been cold. Charlotte's dress seemed to resemble a colonial American girl's outfit, if she originated in America. It's known that spirits can move from country to country, also. Children from long ago often had no knowledge of geography and knew maybe only the nearest town, where they might go to buy necessities or sell farm produce. In colonial times, the only educated children were those from privileged families on great estates or in cities. Also, I'm told that, when in the spirit state, time is either immaterial or nonexistent. Therefore, the little girl's confusion that Carolyn passed on to us could be accurate.

In the meantime, new forces are gaining recognition at the Point. Modern camps, at least two, are pestered by a mischievous girl, and Christine talks to her when things get "busy."

Coming Home

He couldn't stand it anymore. Charlie Dumar knew it had to be done, and his heart wouldn't let him delay any longer. Soon after midnight on June 1st, 2005, he swung out of bed and had his mother, Catteen, drive him to the over-pass on Route 9B in the northern village of Cooperville, NY. A sensitive like her son, Catteen was a necessary part of the project, as she was to be guard and guide.

On June 1st, 1968 at 2:05 a.m., Charlie lost his best friend, a teenager named Ellen Fisher, his babysitter until he was eight. Ellen died in a high-speed car crash while going home from a party after her high school prom. Police and witnesses at the death scene stated that Ellen was riding on the lap of the front seat passenger when the crash took place; cars at that time seldom had seat belts. She died instantly after being ejected from the car, which was believed to be traveling at 100 m.p.h.

"I was only eight at the time, and for months I just couldn't believe my grown-up friend, my sitter, Ellen, had died. I spent a lot of time mourning for her. Now, you have to understand that folks in our family have the ability to see into the other world," he said, looking at his mother, who nodded in agreement.

"Yes," Catteen said, "my mother had some of the same ability to know things, to be sensitive to the presence of spirits or ghosts, or whatever you want to say. It's like we can understand what these people without bodies *want*. We can think at them and get responses to our queries."

Charlie resumed, "Since 1968, whenever I'd pass that death site, I could see Ellen still standing there, maybe in shock or denial that she had died. Sometimes, if I was quiet, I could hear the screech of brakes and the horrible impact of the car. It was unnerving, and, at first, I didn't accept that I could do something about it.

"Fast forward to 2005—that was the night I decided I had to bring Ellen home. Mom dropped me off on what was a dark and deserted curve in the road near the overpass. I saw the accident take place all over again, and I heard screams. It took a minute to spot Ellen and begin communicating with her. I told her she didn't belong there, and she was mystified, as she saw me as an eight-year-old. 'Come on, it's time to go home,' I said, and started walking over toward Route 9, to make the left turn onto the Lake Shore Road, which was the route to Ellen's home. After some prodding she came to me and began walking with me. I could see Mom's car up ahead, parked on the shoulder, waiting to be our escort along the 5.5 mile walk.

"It was dawn by the time we reached Ellen's old house in Chazy. Her family had moved on, but I saw her pause for a minute before she entered the house. She looked at me and said, 'Charlie, it's awfully chilly out here. I'll always watch over you the rest of your life.' She walked to the front door, entered, and that's the last I saw of her that day. Whenever I drive past the old accident scene, she is no longer there.

"She comes to me at times, and here is how she usually looks," he said, taking out an old high school yearbook. He pointed to Ellen's seventh grade class photo inside. Charlie indicated a thin, bright-eyed and attractive child about twelve years old. When I asked whether Ellen's death had left any lasting impact on him, Charlie said, "I didn't go to my own high school prom. There was a pretty girl who dropped hints so I would ask her, but I kept ducking her. I had the sense that *I, too, would die* on my prom night if I went. To this day, I'm sure that girl has no knowledge of what was taking place inside me."

It was a fascinating experience talking to mother and son in their old house at 9653 Route 9. "We have them here too," Catteen said. "You see, this is an old building. Back in the 1880s, this was the post office and the postmaster, Henry Hinman, and his wife lived upstairs with Henry's spinster sister, whom we always referred to as 'Miss Hinman.' Well, one day, it seems Miss Hinman, who was in her sixties, got depressed and went into the second floor bathroom in the back. She stood on the toilet, wrapped a scarf around her neck, and jumped, hanging herself in that room. Apparently she had some second thoughts on her way out, as there were many bloody scratches on the wall when her body was found. But, you know, she's *still here*. We still hear her slam the oven door and rattle her pots and pans up there, even though the room is no longer a kitchen."

"Yes, she spent this morning looking over my shoulder," Charlie said, "while I was repairing the floor downstairs. She isn't the least bit scary. When I see her, it's never a sharp image, but more of a hazy picture. She's just there, looking, and probably wondering what I'm doing. But, also, from time to time, she sends encouragement, like 'Do a good job now. Take your time.' She is really interested in everything that goes on here. We don't know if she sees the house as it was when *she* lived here, or as it is now.

"When we first came to this house in 1973, she was here, and treated us to some discordant energy. Maybe she was suspicious of us and didn't understand that our family had bought the house. Two years later, my mother, Katie, was in bad shape and needed care. She had briefly been put in a nursing home over in Vermont, but we chose to bring her back here, to our home in Chazy, though it wasn't *her* old house. Not too long afterward, my mother died. Now, *she* is here too. Katie chose not to go on yet, and seems to continue in the confusion that she began at finding herself over in Vermont. She really wants to find her old home again, but usually stays here in the kitchen, near a photo of the house she grew up in. Maybe that's second best. In life, Katie was very interested in *everything*, and that seems to be the way she still is today."

Charlie added, "Yes, just the other day I saw her inspecting my roses that I grow indoors under artificial light. She seems to like those. In life, she was famous around the village as a flower gardener, so it seems natural she'd watch over our gardening.

"Here's another benefit of having a ghost or two living in the house. Before Dad died, he bought some soft coal to burn in our old converted wood stove. Everyone knows you have to burn anthracite, or hard coal, but Dad got a 'deal' on the soft coal. So he lit the stove, and we all went to bed. In the middle of the night, I was awakened," Charlie said, "and saw Miss Hinman standing over my bed, urging me to get up. What was wrong? In the hallway, I met Mom, who said that Katie had just awakened *her*. We went downstairs and found that the air inside the house was slowly being poisoned by the coal fumes. We threw the windows open and shut down the fire. That was a close one, but our two ghost watchers seemed proud of themselves."

"Tell me," Catteen said, "are there animal ghosts, too?" I responded that there were, and that I had written up a chapter on those in my book *Ghosts of the Northeast*. "I *knew* it!" she said. "I once had a little Chihuahua named Princess. She got sick from the flea powder we used to control her fleas and lost most of her hair. The vet couldn't save her, and she died. But I still hear her walking around the floor beside my bed at night. Once, when I was very sick, she walked and walked all night long, very agitated, until I got better."

We chatted for a long time. As a collector of ghost stories, I was fascinated at the prospect of having two sensitives in one house, plus two kindly old ladies and a dog. It all seemed like a big happy family, and it was hard to tell where one world left off and another began.

Still Hanging Around

What causes a spirit to hang around on the earth plane when the body has died and been buried? Many times, there is the desire to right a wrong. At other times there is the desire to complete a job begun in the body that is unfinished because of an untimely death. At other times, there is a craving or addiction for an earthly gratification which just will not dissipate without spiritual help. This story, set in Blue Mountain Lake, NY, in the late 1800s, and is likely a combination of all three.

Life was difficult for young William Wheelock. His father, Henry, was a bruiser and a domineering influence. Young William, who didn't have his father's muscles or aggression, nevertheless did his best to live up to parental values and demands. A timber cutter and occasional sawmill employee as well as a stonemason, Henry Wheelock was continually busy in this Adirondack village, cutting, milling, or building foundations and decorative walls on the big estates. He expected young William to have both the dedication and brawn of his elder.

William, on the other hand, was more laid-back, having a love for nature's beauty, and especially for the comeliness of young ladies. He enjoyed watching patterns in the clouds and scanning the mountain valleys when they changed color every spring and autumn. When he left off his formal education at age sixteen, he developed an admiration for horses and did some part-time farm work. Horses could escape the confines of rural life, perhaps galloping off through the clouds to magic cities or European castles, or across oceans—in his imagination these animals represented freedom.

One way of satisfying his wanderlust was as a porter at Mr. Holland's Blue Mountain Lake House hotel. In season, William unloaded the stage coach baggage from North Creek Station when it arrived at the inn, hauled guests' luggage to their rooms, hoped for tips, worked in menial handyman jobs at the resort, and did general grounds-keeping chores both at the start and end of the vacation season. He especially liked harnessing the horses and feeding them because the animals were a symbol for his restless soul—*they* could go where *he* could only dream. Occasionally, he was hired to shovel heavy snows from sections of the hotel outbuildings roofs so they didn't collapse. In his own mind he was "paying his way."

However, when he returned home he was continually subjected to his father's verbal abuse. He wasn't strong enough, he wasn't wise enough, and old Henry suggested William wasn't masculine. The lad spent all his time admiring the pretty city girls who vacationed in the area, young ladies who would *never* give him a second glance on the streets of Albany, Philadelphia, or New York

City. He was a damned dreamer and needed to be punched around to gain some manliness, old Henry decided.

Life at home was hell for young William, and the sensitive lad eventually reached a point of no return. At age nineteen, hoping for something more satisfying in The Great Beyond, he slipped a noose around his neck while standing on a chair in the upstairs of his Durant Road home and kicked the chair from beneath his feet. A month later, his mother, Louisa, who had been unable to protect William in life, died of a broken heart.

Thus, William's soul prepared to pass into eternity. But his troubled consciousness couldn't make the break. Anger at his father's bullying and attraction to the natural beauty of the Adirondack wilderness held him fast. Perhaps he was also angry at himself, feeling that he had quit on life's struggles and thus, as his father had said, he wasn't a "real man." William drifted through the only house he had known in his brief life. He was free to sit by the woodstove, to roam the various rooms, and to watch the new inhabitants of the house eating and sleeping—activities that he could no longer physically enjoy.

Later, Wheelock relatives named Potter owned the house, which was eventually sold to the Ross family in the early 1900s. William and Ellen Ross owned the house and farmland until they sold it to David and Orpha Curry in 1954. After raising four children there, David died in 1989, leaving Orpha alone in the house until daughter Kate returned to care for her in the 1990s. Orpha, Kate, her sister Ellen, and brother David Sean have all encountered William Wheelock. All three women are sensitives, but it still came as a shock to find a visible and transparent young man sitting down on their beds as they prepared for sleep many nights. William always impulsively just "appeared."

When the women worked in Herkimer, NY, a caretaker would check their house, and one winter evening he had a shock. The man unlocked the back door and entered to check on the heat, electricity, and water pipes and heard a discarnate and angry voice call out from the darkness, "What the hell are *you* doing here? Get out! You're not wanted here." The caretaker didn't need a second invitation and scrammed, though he later reported the incident to the Currys. More of the same, they matter-of-factly surmised, wishing they'd warned their caretaker that William was often afoot in the old place.

In the early summer of 2005, I visited the Curry home and heard Kate cautioning someone or something as she led me to the living room, "Get away!" The dog? I had been supposed to bring a pretty, intuitive woman with me, but at the last minute she was unable to accompany me, so I'd come alone. "It's just William," Kate explained to me. "He wanted to meet the young lady." Kate ordered him back upstairs and most of my interview was peaceful and not interrupted. We toured the house, and, combining our intuitive feelings, we centered on a location in the upper hallway where William likely had spent his last moments of life.

We agreed, after the interview, that William was just too much of an aesthete, and a curious one at that, to simply depart. Orpha told me that they speak aloud to him each day, urging him to go into the Everlasting Light, but William seems content to stay there, catered to by three lovely women. His father must have passed to some other dimension of Eternity, so a solitary William appears to believe he has found heaven.

In time, apparently, souls come to recognize that no change has taken place in their dimension, and even a low-level of heaven has become stale. Then there comes a reaching out for "what's next?" And *then* the spirit guides or angels become visible. At that point, many believe, the soul is set free from its imprisonment and can seek Something Higher. But right now, William Wheelock is enjoying himself, and, except for a caution from the Currys from time to time, he has free run of the old building. And this summer's vacationing girls are just super...have you *seen* them?

CHAPTER 8

CHURCHES

A Last Sermon

In 1805, three small Protestant congregations in the Rensselaer County hills east of Albany combined their resources to build a meeting house or church. Each denomination would have use of the building in proportion to the size of its membership. In time, The Second Evangelical Lutheran Church was led by Rev. VanAlstyne, and the Baptist congregation was shepherded by Rev. Abel Brown. The Presbyterian Church was the third and largest of the sects.

By the 1830s, there was a strong Abolitionist movement in the towns of Sand Lake and West Sand Lake and the combined congregations took an active part in the Underground Railroad. Families who agreed to take part in helping fugitive southern slaves reach freedom in Canada made themselves known to the ministers. Each of those families would then be given a code name and could be identified by a specific Psalm. At Sunday services, if the pastor read a certain psalm, the family members knew that a group of slaves would be coming to their house under the cover of darkness that week. In this way, only those opposed to slavery knew what was taking place in the movement.

By 1839, the Presbyterians assumed possession of the building, as the Baptists and Lutherans were now numerous enough to have their own houses of worship. After another century, as families moved or left the area, and as American lifestyles changed, the Presbyterians could no longer support the services of a pastor and they combined with the Baptists to form The Covenant Church of Averill Park in the early 1970s.

The Town of Sand Lake bought the old church building and began the work of converting it into a Town Hall. During the transition period in 1972, Town Historian Judy Rowe sat one day with another woman, Madeline

211

Carpenter, in an upstairs rear room reading through old documents to see which would be preserved and which discarded. As the pair was preoccupied with their work, they heard the church's front doors open loudly, and then footsteps were heard walking rapidly down the aisle and toward the rear of the sanctuary, where they stopped in what Judy judges was the area of the lectern or pulpit on the altar. Then, there was silence. Maybe we imagined the sound, Judy thought, and the two resumed their work of reading. A half hour later, however, footsteps were again heard, departing from the pulpit and walking rapidly up the aisle, followed by the slamming of the church doors.

Madeline went downstairs to see who or what had been there. The old pews and pulpit were still in place, where they had been for one hundred and forty years, though church services were no longer being held there. The large old brass key for the locked front doors still hung on its hook inside the door, which she found locked. Neither the large key or the doors were moving. All the church furnishings were slated for removal, though the workmen had not yet converted the interior to work space for the town's clerks and secretaries. Madeline returned to the room without a word, only a shrug of her shoulders, and sat down to continue work.

Not much later, the phenomenon was repeated. Again came the opening of the front doors, the rapid footsteps on the aisle, then a silent pause. Then, came the retreat up the aisle and the slamming of the front doors. Judy looked at Madeline and asked, "Who do you think it was—kids? Are you going to go down and see who it is, Madeline?" Somewhat flustered, Madeline blushed, now knowing that Judy had *also* heard the previous sounds of activity. After her downstairs inspection, Madeline had nothing to report. "No, I don't think so—there's *nobody* there!" came her reply. And that settled it. They returned to their reading and sorting work.

No one ever heard the sounds again, especially after the work crew arrived and removed all the religious trappings. The pews and pulpit were disposed of and the sanctuary was converted to work space. In 2003, the Town of Sand Lake abandoned the old church for newer facilities in a new and modern Town Hall, and the old church has become the town's Arts Center.

The ghost or ghosts seem to have left, as no one hears them anymore. Who might it have been—a former church trustee? My money is on a former pastor who, in spirit, could just not *permit* the old holy place with its history of liberating enslaved humanity to pass into secular hands without just one last sermon to any and all spirits still remaining in the building. One half hour of time was adequate to say what needed saying, and perhaps the man recited one more psalm, too, for old time's sake. Then, perhaps, he laid down his own burden and liberated himself into The Light.

Got a Light?

"The old Congregational Church, built in 1822, had been vacant for almost thirty years when I bought it in 1986," John told me. "Along New York State's Southern Tier, there are many old churches, such as this one, that slowly lost membership and were then sold or abandoned. It has become fashionable since the 1960s to convert such pieces of architecture into unique homes, and that was my aim.

"My wife and I began cleaning and then installing the first partitions in order to make the church our home. In the back of the sanctuary, under the balcony, we framed out an area for our daughter's bedroom. Within just a few days, out of the corners of our eyes, we caught movements in that area, especially at night. Many times my wife and I sat watching television only to have one or the other of us observe movement back in that space."

On another occasion, when their daughter was three, she sat at the dinner table with the old altar behind her. "Daddy, who's that?" the child asked, pointing in mid-air directly behind John. He turned and observed "an accumulation of what seemed to be smoke in mid-air. It was three-dimensional and about six feet tall, and it reminded me of the wizard in the film *The Wizard of Oz*. Within the smoke or ectoplasm, if you will, I could clearly see a man's face with mustache and a goatee. As we stared, several other faces passed swiftly over the area above his shoulders—several were children, then there was an Indian, several old men, and a woman in a long dress. The apparition remained for some time, and I grabbed for my camera to record the scene, but it malfunctioned.

"I was stunned, but more curious than scared. I had never imagined such a thing; I had never *seen* such a thing!" John said. Suddenly, the phenomenon vanished.

"Then, a year later, when my daughter was about four, she came to breakfast and told us that a man had been in her room the previous night." John and his wife became worried. Was the old building vulnerable to intruders? A check of the doors and windows suggested not, but if the figure wasn't a man, what could it be? The child described the man wearing a brown suit and a brown derby hat. Who would dress like that in a *church*? "Though we had never seen one before, we began to suspect a ghost. I went at the analysis methodically: where was he moving from and to? It was always in the same spot near our daughter's bedroom, next to an old stovepipe hole in a wall. We deduced that a coal stove had once stood at that location, likely to warm the congregation during worship services.

"We didn't know much about ghosts at the time, but it seemed plausible that this guy's spirit was tending the stove over and over, even though there was no longer a congregation to keep comfortable. It never bothered us once we had a rationale for who it was and what he was doing, and the man never troubled our daughter. It was like enjoying some of the building's history that kept replaying itself."

In time John and his wife divorced, and she found a new home. Some time later, John met a new woman, became engaged, and began to plan for a future in which he'd sell his old church/house.

One night when Lori, his fiancée, visited his home, the pair ventured into the church balcony to look over the large space of the sanctuary below them. Today, she remembers that John's woodstove was quite hot that night, and, especially with the heat rising to the balcony level and ceiling, the building was quite warm. Lori stood to John's left, leaning on the balcony railing, and suddenly felt absolutely frozen as a cold energy passed right through her.

She turned to John, who immediately got a strange look on his face as the cold force swept through him, too. "Did you feel *that*?" they said to one another. Then they noticed that the cold moved along the same plane as Mr. Brown Derby's line of movement. Was he "working" that night?

Later that year, as the couple prepared to move to a new home, Lori worked to remove items from the old balcony and was startled to see their large suspended light swinging. She called John to come to the balcony, and together they viewed the light on its long chain moving in a clockwise circle over the downstairs. No wind, open doors, or other building vibrations could account for the movement. Was

The Old Church

this Mr. Brown Derby's doings, and, if so, how did he do it and what did it mean? After their amazement waned, the couple removed the fixture and chain, and the light was later sold to an antiques dealer.

Today the couple lives in a house that isn't haunted. Nevertheless, "We wonder whether the new folks in that old church ever experience the ghost, resolutely moving on his nightly rounds of fire stoking. Maybe he left along with us, but I haven't been back to see," John concluded.

214

The Rectory

St. Paul's Rectory in Greenwich

"Father William Harris and his family became good friends of mine," said Paul Fung, retired cartoonist and illustrator. "Our family used to attend St. Paul's Episcopal Church in Greenwich, NY, and we became close. My daughter used to play with their daughter. But what I experienced in that old rectory is something I'll never forget!"

Paul, nationally famous for his illustrations in the *Blondie, Mutt and Jeff, Hong Kong Phooey, Bullwinkle and Rocky,* and *George of the Jungle* comic books, is a bright and sensitive man. Perhaps it is that sensitivity that first caused him to spot the figure that had been a mere rumor in the village for years.

Before Fr. Harris came to town, Paul's daughter, Lori, had first befriended the children of the parish priest, Fr. Lowry. "When we were little girls, Monique Lowry and I were playing in the rectory one day while her mom (Anita) folded clothing across the hall in their laundry room. One rule of thumb when I played with Monique was 'No running in the house!'" said Lori, "and Anita was very stern about that. On that particular afternoon, we heard someone running up the stairs to the second floor. Anita blew her stack, 'I told you girls not to run on those stairs!' she bellowed, emerging from the laundry room. She then blushed and bit her lip when she saw the girls playing peacefully right in front of her. Mrs. Lowry wouldn't talk about the phenomenon, and I'm sure she was scared to be sharing the house with someone invisible." The Lowrys resided in the old house on Main Street between 1953 and 1968, when Fr. Harris was assigned the post. "The Harrises had two daughters, Julie and Page, though I played mostly with Page," said Lori.

Paul then spoke to me of his experiences with the entity after noting carefully that at that time, he gave no credence to ghosts or spirits. It was a hot and muggy afternoon that Fourth of July in 1972, and the two families had just returned from a circus at the Washington County Fairgrounds. In the house, Paul went upstairs to use the bathroom and get a drink of water. In the hallway, he felt a very

Paul Fung's sketch of the ghost

cool draft but attributed it to the house's air conditioning. All at once, out of the corner of his eye, he noticed a movement along the far side of the center-hallway railing. A strange figure, similar to the apparition that Fr. Harris talked about, had just crossed the landing at the top of the stairs and leaned over the railing to peer at him. "Suddenly it was as if I were in a freezer—bitter cold. At first, the image looked like a living person, except that it had no color and was all greys, blacks and whites," said the illustrator.

Fung, an artist whose life work involved observing and noting detail, saw the figure in a gown or caftan, though there were no feet visible. He descended to the ground floor then, puzzling over what he'd just seen, went back upstairs. Instantly, he was struck by the icy cold that increased with each upward step. Near the top, he looked at the ghost and the figure looked back, their faces perhaps two feet apart. "The look was hostile," Paul told reporter Marty Hughes of the *Greenwich Journal and Salem Press,* "and then again, not hostile. I wasn't particularly frightened because I don't tend to believe in such things." He did return downstairs quickly, though. A short time later, Fr. Harris reminded Paul that the air conditioner wasn't working that day.

Soon afterward, the main topic of discussion became the ghost of the rectory. Paul learned that the Harris girls, eleven and thirteen at the time, had experienced the ghosts many times. They had reported to their mother, Kim, that they had seen an old man with long hair and a robe, something like the traditional Jesus, passing through the hallway. At another time, Julia observed the figure perched atop the upstairs railing, seemingly fascinated with the family's tropical fish aquarium.

"Yes, he was always fascinated by the fish," Lori remembered. Julia then observed the figure turning toward the stair top but then descending in a circular pattern down through the walls into the downstairs studio on the side of the house facing the church. They later learned that a narrow circular stairway had once been there, but had since been torn out.

At first, the two oldest Harris daughters, who didn't know about the ghost, reported strange events to their parents. Jan, who lived in New York City at the time, came down to breakfast one day complaining about the puffs of air that kept blowing at her, as if someone stood over her bed strenuously fanning her during the night. Later the oldest Harris girl, Jody, came to visit after her baby was born. She told of seeing a filmy figure bending over her baby's carriage, looking intently at the child. She told Marty Hughes, "I got the feeling that my presence was unwelcome, that I wasn't supposed to see what I saw."

As all four children had some experience with the spirit, Fr. Harris now began to add up the vague sensations that had sometimes troubled him during the night. Several times each week, he and Kim would awaken in the night, feeling a chill and sensing that some gigantic cat was kneading the foot of the bed's mattress, actually lifting the lower corners. Then, a pressure moved with the cold toward the sleepers, perhaps upward to the level of their knees or thighs. If they moved, it would suddenly leave. Once the pressure began, they had no difficulty in finding the inspiration to leap up and turn on the bedroom lights, only to find no one else there.

On another occasion, one of the daughters was ill in an upstairs bedroom and Kim had taken the child a tray with soup and crackers. Later, with the empty tray, she descended to the ground floor and headed for the kitchen. All at once, invisible hands seemed to grasp the tray, attempting to wrest it from Kim's hands. She clamped her hands around the tray's edges and firmly resisted the seizure. At that point, the pressure of the entity departed.

Another unsuspecting family member who encountered the ghost was Fr. Harris's mother, who was house-sitting when the parents were away. Seated at the dining room table, enjoying a cup of coffee, the elder Mrs. Harris suddenly spotted a strange figure scurrying from the living room, across the foyer and into the studio room on the eastern side of the house. At first, she suspected an intruder, maybe a well-meaning member of the parish, but the figure was strangely dressed in a bonnet and full skirt. Mrs. Harris hurried into the studio to greet the visitor, but no one was there. After this initial experience, she heard family stories that gave her a chill.

On one occasion, Fr. Harris was sleeping alone in his bed when the familiar sensations began anew. He told others that, this time, he would lie quietly and not react, so that he could study the full effect of the haunting. This time, however, the pressure that he felt on his legs, then his knees, and then his thighs seemed to weigh not pounds but tons! Finally, the weight was imposed upon his chest, neck and head. He felt trapped, and his respiration became more labored. Prior to this intimate experience, the priest had never considered demonic possession as a reality, feeling it was more a form of hysteria. Suddenly, he saw a ghostly face about a foot from his head. He described it to Marty Hughes as, "fiercely hatred-hot, piercing, penetrating and burning, zapping, laser-like eyes that were tortured, demonic, bullying, other-worldly and focused."

As the priest's sensations became more frightening, he knew he had to throw off the entity's control, and somehow extricated one arm from its spell. He thrust the arm outward and through the entity's body while yelling, "Get the hell out of here! You're not scaring me! Go! In the name of Jesus Christ, go!" And that did the trick.

Later, Fr. Harris compared notes with Paul Fung, inspiring the latter to make a careful sketch of what he had seen. After seeing the sketch, Fr. Harris immediately identified his tormentor. Harris said the figure had "a long, sharp aquiline nose, severe cheekbones, a small thin mouth, pointed features ending in a pointed chin. Wisps of a grayish beard came from the lower face and chin and hung like Spanish moss." This is the very visage that Fung captured. Soon afterward, Fr. Harris stood at the lectern at Sunday Mass and spoke. "I don't like to use the word 'ghost,' but there is some manner of non-human being inhabiting the rectory. Every member of my family has either seen or sensed this presence, and Paul Fung, a well-respected member of the community, had three experiences with the being this past summer." I bet that was a first in American sermons!

Who is it? And why is this individual hanging around a building dedicated to God's service? Joseph Boies, a prominent Greenwich lawyer, built the house in 1816. Later, records show, his son, David Artemas Boies, likewise an attorney, occupied the house. At some point in the 1890s, the congregation of St. Paul's Episcopal Church bought the house as a dwelling for the rector. Since that time, when the priest served Episcopal parishes in Salem or Schuylerville, the parish rented the building to tenants, none of whom recorded being frightened by the ghost.

Metaphysicians say that where great light is present, great darkness is also attracted. Perhaps a troubled soul from the building's past chose to confront the light of a Christian family, to drive away the positive energies which it shunned in life. There is also a story of a local man, a banker at one of Greenwich's five former banks, who was apprehended in embezzling bank funds. At this point, the story becomes unclear. Most records agree that he hanged himself. One unlikely tale says that unhappy citizens buried him underneath the recotry's front porch, accounting for the west to east direction of many of the ghost movements inside. One wonders how or why such a suicide would not be interred in the nearby village cemetery. There may have been a prohibition against giving a suicide a Christian burial there. Much remains to be uncovered about this story.

The most likely version of the banker story identifies the man as an esteemed member of St. Paul's Parish, a man of great reputation and charm, who invited most of the well-to-do families of Greenwich to invest in the bank and other schemes which were fraudulent. When his deceit was discovered, it is said, the man hanged himself in the barn behind his house on Academy Street. It is possible, that he was then buried in St. Paul's cemetery. Sometimes, old tragedies become embellished. I can't believe the village government would have permitted a burial under a porch, especially as St. Paul's rectory has none. But, the banker caused the downfall of many family fortunes in town, and it is entirely possible that he cannot yet face the iniquity of his deeds.

At present, the building does not house the parish priest, but instead is rented. A sad postscript to the story is that after finishing his pastorate at St. Paul's, Fr. Harris moved with his family to North Carolina, where he left the priesthood and tried to work as an exorcist. But, a few years later, he is said to have committed suicide, himself.

Ice Cold

Railroad tycoon Dr. Thomas Clark Durant and his son, William West Durant, played a major role in the development of the Adirondacks in the second half of the nineteenth century. The mountains held a seemingly unlimited supply of timber and minerals, and the Adirondack Railway (later the Delaware & Hudson) was extended from Saratoga to North Creek, and then later to the mines. The clean mountain air lured America's wealthy families (the Huntingtons, Morgans, Vanderbilts and Whitneys) into the bosom of nature, where Durant built the "great camps" (Pine Knot, Uncas, and Sagamore, among others) to accommodate them. To attract the middle class vacationer, Durant built both an Episcopal chapel (Mission of the Good Shepherd on St. Hubert's Isle in 1880) and one for the Roman Catholics (St. William's Church on Long Point in 1890), which he presented to the village.

By 1900, the railroad had advanced as far as Raquette Lake, though the depot was across the lake from the small hamlet. The Durants then built a new post office and a general store across the water near the terminal, and grad-

St. William's Church on Long Point

ually the hamlet centered there. The Roman Catholic Franciscan fathers established a mission and camp around the old store and church, with the parish church becoming the summer camp's chapel, and the old post office/store became the rectory and main retreat house. Energetic Fr. Henry Themlin lived year round at the camp but said mass in the village church, requiring a commute of several miles across the lake's waters in three seasons and on the ice in winter.

One winter night in 1928, Fr. Henry drove home to the rectory after finishing a meeting in the village. With only the moonlight for illumination, he could not see that a large hole had been cut in the ice during the day. It was the custom in those days to harvest winter lake ice to fill sawdust packed ice houses, allowing summer visitors to enjoy perishable foods all season long before the arrival of electric refrigerators. Henry's car plunged into the gap; it was morning before searchers discovered the mishap. Even in daylight, they could see the automobile headlights shining upward from the lake's bottom. Henry's body was retrieved and, according to legend, thawed out on a board in front of a roaring fire in the rectory fireplace before the wake. Afterward, he had a well-attended funeral, and that should have been the end of it. But someone or something remains at the camp. There are a few who believe the spirit entity is William West Durant, but many others keep in mind that the rectory is oftentimes used as a Catholic retreat, and are certain that Fr. Henry Themlin has stayed on to fulfill his responsibilities.

Friends living nearby tell of ghostly footsteps echoing through the old rectory after the priest's death. The walking pattern, apparently, consisted of ghostly steps ascending the stairs, pausing at the landing, then continuing on. At some point in the 1940s, these friends say, workmen who had to repair the wall alongside the stair landing discovered a wall safe there that had been sealed since Fr. Henry's time. Inside the safe they found mass cards for still-unsaid masses and a stash of currency. All was removed: the masses were said, the money was donated to the church, the wall was resealed, and my friends believed that the spectral footsteps had ceased. Maybe.

However, during recent years, young people and clergy alike, visiting the camp during summers, have told of strange sounds and objects that seemed to move by themselves. On an August evening in 1978, Fr. Kevin Kenny and his friend, Brother Steven Merrigan, were the last two staff members remaining at the camp after a busy summer season. The final group of visiting friars had gone by boat to visit friends in Raquette Lake Village and to say their goodbyes to townsfolk. Only Kevin and Steven remained in the house, conversing quietly while rocking in front of the fireplace. There were many good memories from that summer season; soon the old house would revert to its quiet season.

"All of a sudden," Fr. Kevin told me, "we heard this tremendous pounding above our heads. It started at one end of the ceiling and moved across the length of the large room overhead. I looked at Brother Steve and asked, 'Do you hear what I hear?'"

Astounded, a wide-eyed Brother Steve responded, "I sure do!"

"Well, if that's Fr. Henry, I want to meet him," said Fr. Kevin, racing to the stairs and then upward, expecting to see a ghost in the dormitory space overhead. "Reaching the top of the stairs, however, I was met with an icy cold blast of air and momentarily stopped, getting a little apprehensive. Not being

St. William's Rectory

put off though, I continued to the entrance to the dormitory where the noise had come from. I looked into the room but could see nobody. Coming back downstairs, I said to Brother Stephen, 'There's nobody up there! Besides, how could anyone walk across the room so quickly like that, when it's filled with five beds?'" Neither one could think of a logical answer.

On the following weekend, Fr. Kevin, still in residence at St. William's Camp, was scheduled to say mass in Blue Mountain Lake and had been invited to breakfast with the Curry family there. Orpha Curry, an intuitive parish member, coyly asked Fr. Kevin how things were going at the camp. Then she dropped a bombshell with a smile, "See any *ghosts* lately?"

Fr. Kevin, not anxious that the camp's secret be revealed, responded in the negative (after all, Orpha had asked him about *seeing* a ghost), telling her that he didn't believe any stories about ghosts at Camp St. William. But Mrs. Curry, not to be rebuffed, countered with, "Did you hear any *footsteps* there, then?" Finally, Fr. Kevin told her the entire story. Orpha Curry dabbed at the corner of her mouth with a napkin, settled back in her chair, and smiled. "I *thought* you may have heard those footsteps. You're not the first, you know."

Throughout that winter, Fr. Kevin pondered his experience. Brother Stephen had also heard those heavy steps. And Orpha Curry already knew about them. Only one issue remained: who was the ghost walker? Two summers later, the camp hosted a teen group, and without a radio or television to entertain the youngsters, Fr. Kevin did what Adirondackers have done for over two centuries—he told stories around the old fireplace.

The embers in the fireplace cast a flickering orange glow, and the youths were mesmerized as the tale of the phantom footsteps was related. It's hard to disbelieve such a tale when it's emanating from a *priest*. From time to time, one of the teens would look upward at the ceiling, half expecting the heavy footfalls to be repeated. As Fr. Kevin's story concluded, there was a quiet buzz of conversation. Suddenly, the door burst open, and Willy, one of the campers that hadn't been present for the storytelling, charged into the room. "I've just been standing out there at the end of the dock, looking at the lake. Suddenly, way down in the water, I saw two bright lights shining up at me, almost like a car's headlights...."

All Fr. Kevin had to do then was give a grinning stare at his charges, as if to ask, "Well?" Everyone screamed, as another phenomenon was added to the curious saga of Fr. Henry.

Service

"I feel that a black-suited man wearing a black bowler hat just entered the house with us and walked quickly into this small parlor on the right," said Susan. We had just been welcomed to the United Methodist Church parsonage in Northville, NY, by Rev. Michael Terrell. As pastor, he was anxious to see whether two "ghost hunters" could obtain some information about the old house and its past, a building in which members of his family and congregation had experienced unnerving events.

As usual, Susan, my intuitive friend, spent some time in meditation the day before our trip, before she knew where we'd be going on the next day. She also had some insights and images that she hoped to verify, though she didn't disclose them to me at first. It was strange to drive up in front of the parsonage and see her quickly craning her neck to the side and rear of the car. "Where's the cemetery?" she asked. Then, she spotted the burial ground directly across the street from the church. "I thought so," she said. "Wait until I tell you what I got yesterday—I'll tell you about it later."

It wasn't surprising, the house being a parsonage, that she spotted a black-suited man entering the building; after all, it was a minister's house, and certainly every man who had pastored the church would have entered that front door and then, likely, walked into the small parlor (as it is configured today), which was likely his office or counseling room.

As is her wish, Sue first walked through the house alone, seeking subjective impressions, and, as usual, she was quite successful. Returning to the kitchen, where I sat and talked with Michael and a member of the congregation named Jane, she said, "Okay, David, let's go." We returned to the foyer and parlor, and Sue resumed her comments on the black-suited man. "He walks very briskly and business-like. I don't feel he's an especially warm man." I, of course, sensed nothing of this presence, and wondered aloud if the figure might have been more of a "house memory" than an active ghost. I did, however, sense a long-gone wood stove in the front corner of the room, though Michael was not able to verify its former presence when we debriefed at the day's end.

Sue and I walked toward the kitchen, and passing through the bright dining room, she spotted a woman in long-ago style dress, standing beside the sunny window. "She might just be an energy imprint from the past, as she doesn't move, but I feel she is a benign presence." Finishing the kitchen area without encountering much sensation, we walked up the back stairs. Sue balked a bit, then moved upward, telling me that she felt a very heavy presence, perhaps someone with physical burdens to carry or great worries.

At the top of the stairs, we looked into an unused bedroom, then turned away. For a minute, I wondered why Sue had no comment, then I interjected. "Sue, there's a young girl here, maybe eight, and she just stands beneath that corn-husk doll wall decoration." It wasn't a clear apparition, but rather a mental image superimposed over today's furnishings. Sue returned to the room and said, "Sure enough. Now I see her." Our descriptions matched: a shy child with clothing from perhaps the 1920s, who had jet black hair. I visualized a maroon dress on the child and got the name Trista or Krista. Did such a child ever live and/or die here?

Directly across the hall was a small room presently used for storage. Sue heard a rustling or rattling going on inside before we pushed the door open, but, of course, all was quiet once we were inside. I sensed that an extensive shelf structure had once been there on the left and supposed it might have been a linen-storage space. Sue was quite certain of the noise from the past inside the room. Then on to the upstairs bathroom, which we both felt was not the original bathroom, though no presence was sensed there.

Back in the hall once more, we turned into a large bedroom on the right. It was nicely decorated with old-fashioned framed pictures of angels and thus became "the angel room" in our discussions later. Sue had the distinct impression that if a person were inside the room with the door even partially open, they would see a man's shadow passing in the hall outside. We wondered how Michael could verify that for us later.

In the front bedroom nearest the church, Michael and Jennifer's cat sprawled on the freshly-made bed. "Boy, this kitty sure sees stuff," Susan said with a grin. "I get the image of a man continually walking to the window to check on the church next door." Then, we entered the front bedroom, a child's room, and Susan said, "Whoever sleeps in this bedroom now must surely see a light traveling through the hallway from back to front, then down the front stairs." Could we verify this later?

We crossed to the opposite room above the downstairs foyer. It was used for storage of items that I didn't at first recognize, just objects piled or standing against the wall. What caught my attention immediately was a bright gold light more sensed than seen in the front corner of the room. The light said, "Hallelujah!" to me. Sue didn't notice this phenomenon, so, as usual, I was reluctant to mention it at first. Then, we looked in detail at the objects in the room and saw they were music amplifiers and mike stands, and on the wall were pictures of Michael and Jennifer performing with bands. So, they surely were musicians, and if their musical offerings were religious in nature (what else?), then clearly, the audiences would very likely have responded in the praise that I had just sensed.

We walked slowly down the front stairs and each of us had different sensations. To Sue, there was a feeling of losing balance or walking precariously, as if the stairway were too narrow—just the sensation, no images. I, on the other hand, felt myself as a thin, middle aged woman in a violet dress. I had just gone through some papers or records or perhaps a change purse in the upstairs. Now, I had to descend to the foyer and hand over whatever I'd just gotten to a large man who waited impatiently below. I was deeply concerned over how I'd managed certain finances, and as I took the first two or three steps downward, I was filled with apprehension. Then, it was all gone. No gentleman waited below. Sue and I retraced our step upward, again comparing notes.

Using the back stairs, we returned to the kitchen where Michael and Jane sat. Sue and I sat at the table with them and began our debriefing. "Before we begin, I want to share with you all what I picked up during meditation yesterday," Sue began. "I didn't know where I was in that reverie, but there was a long line of mourners in black filing along slowly. One man in the line caught my attention and I asked who he was. He doffed his top hat and sneered at me, saying 'I'm fighting my demons.'" She later felt that the man was the minister she had seen upon entering the house, and that he was still working through some of his earthly difficulties before passing into eternity. Also, I had the experience of being in or seeing a cemetery,' she said, "and wondered if today's trip might involve such a place. I was really troubled when we got here today, as I thought we were going *to* a cemetery; David never tells me where we're going. So I had to look and look, then I relaxed when I saw the old gravestones across the street—even though we'd come to a house."

"What did you get *here*?" Jane asked. "I mean right in this dining room area?" Sue smiled and said, "Oh, the lady?" and proceeded to tell of her first trip through the house, and of seeing the woman enjoying the view out the window. Jane Watkins shot an "I told you so" look at Michael. She revealed that several times she has visited the house in her role as a lay leader and Sunday School teacher, and felt an energy just as she entered the kitchen. The sensation focused as heavy footsteps to her, and she felt sadness, though no other person was apparent, causing her to doubt her senses. Jane remembered that the cat had, at first, run down the back stairs, hair standing on end. The footsteps overhead caused Jane to ask the ghost aloud if she could assist him. At that point, the poor cat shot back up the stairs, as if the ghost had come downstairs when spoken to by Jane.

Michael then noted that at a seminary training class he had done historical research on what is now the First United Methodist Church. He found that there had been a minister named McMilton in the 1880s. A servant named Emma Groff was employed, likely as the housekeeper. Also, there were records of a baby surnamed Heath dying in the house. Rev. McMilton is known to have had a daughter. After our visit, I learned from an historian that the present manse or rectory is not the first on the site. Around 1910, the original building was sold and moved a bit down South Main Street, and the present building was constructed. This fact is important when one tries to connect the spirits we encountered with the present house, or are these individuals now in spirit from the previous building?

Michael noted that his mother, when she visited, had spotted two ghost girls upstairs in the hallway outside the "angel room." "At night, several family members sense people in the bathroom when we're all in bed, and sometimes we find the shower running at 3 a.m. Strangely, though the hallway is carpeted, we hear footsteps on wooden floors, and once in a while, the light in our bedroom goes on. We also hear heavy footsteps, like those of a large man, coming from the back hallway toward the front or top of the front stairs."

That sounded to Sue and me like a pretty "busy" house, though few of the present residents expressed fear. The pastor noted that he had a teenage niece who experienced a dark man standing over her bed at night. I told him of a relative who had a similar experience, though the woman was told by a psychic that it was only an ancestor, assuring her that she was being watched over. So, barring any physical touching, the niece might be at ease.

Michael smiled and said, "Jennifer once bought me a little music box that opens up. A little bear jumps up and spreads its arms, saying, 'I love you *this* much!' Someone or something sets it off at 3 a.m. from time to time. I like the message, but I also like my sleep," he laughed. "You didn't go to the cellar or attic. Do you want to see those?" Of course we did.

In the otherwise-empty cellar, I got the image of a man sawing firewood at a no-longer-existent saw-buck. Sue, however, simply took one look at the relatively modern wiring. "I really think the Terrell's have experienced their lights going on and off. That doesn't seem possible with this new wiring, does it?" But when we returned upstairs, Michael vouched for the interruptions. They have had the wiring examined several times, but nothing seems out of order.

Sue also noted that she sensed something foreboding in the dark area to the left at the bottom of the cellar stairs, though examination showed nobody or nothing physical there. She thought that, in a time gone by, some secretive activity may have taken place in the cellar, though she couldn't determine what that was. Michael also agreed to that, saying that it was his sensation too. Sue and he agreed that maybe it was simply the darkness that puts one on edge.

The attic was likewise almost bare. Only an old bed frame and mattress were visible. I absent-mindedly touched the mattress and was startled to get a pulsating vibration. Taking hold of the iron frame, I found the vibration even stronger. I called Sue over and asked her to touch the two items and see what she got.

It was as if the two objects were hot. She touched and immediately withdrew her hand. "If they don't need these, I suggest they get rid of them," she said. When we returned downstairs, we asked Rev. Terrell about the bed. He told us that two different men had died on that bed, which was there when he assumed the pastorate. He and his wife had simply stored the items in the attic, but after our comments, they decided to give them away.

Finally, the four of us sat in the kitchen again. Michael smiled, relating that Jennifer, before going to work that morning, had worried that Sue and I would have come to Northville for nothing, that we'd sense nothing and think their family suffered from delusions. We all laughed. Jane may have been the happiest among us. As a congregant and respected member of the church, she chose to investigate *her* perceptions, even though they might have appeared groundless. Now, she *knew* what she had experienced, and, as we left, she began to sense a kinship with the former homemaker, perhaps a minister's wife.

Michael, though he could have hewn to a dogma or doctrine, wanted to know the truth about his house. In John 8:32, it is recorded, "*You shall know the truth and the truth shall set you free.*" And St. Paul told his readers to "*test the spirits.*" The Christian message, as I see it, is one of loving investigation, a search conducted in the confidence that all things in the world are held in the hand of a Supreme Being. In choosing this approach of fearless inquiry, I believe he is both the consummate pastor and role model for those he shepherds.

Before we left, Susan and I thanked Jane and Michael for their time and honesty and suggested that prayers be offered for those whose memories or energies are still too closely tied to the beautifully-restored house on South Main Street.

On the way home, I asked Susan what she thought was the big picture of our activities. "The message, as I see it," she said, "is honesty in all we do." I agreed. Uncovering the truth of *anything* is a great service, bound to set all beings free.

Still in Control

A woman named Celia met me at a storytelling event and said it's too bad that I hadn't gone to Manhattan to seek out ghost stories. I assured her that I *had*, but she wasn't deterred. "Why didn't you ever get to St. Mark's Episcopal Church in the Bowery?" she asked. I admitted that I hadn't heard of a ghost there, but on my next foray in search of good stories of history and mystery, I beat a path to 131 E. 10th Street in New York, a wonderful old section of the city.

Near a quiet intersection just north of Chinatown sits an old church, built in 1799, the historic marker says. It replaced a one hundred fifty-year-old chapel built by the last Dutch Director-General of New Netherlands, Peter Stuyvesant (1612-1672). Many Americans remember him as the peg-legged leader who surrendered New Amsterdam to the English, who then renamed the settlement New York in 1664. For all his loyalty to the Dutch West India Company, the business organization that ran the colony, Stuyvesant seems to have been bitter at his ouster, a negative attitude that he may have carried into death.

St. Mark's Episcopal Church in the Bowery

Stuyvesant's crypt from the old chapel was incorporated into the cellar wall of the new church. Old histories of the city cite his ghostly appearances in the Governor's Mansion almost immediately following his death. Such stories continued for over three hundred years more until, in July of 1978, a raging fire consumed much of the landmark chapel's superstructure. Briefly, congregational leaders considered razing the historic building, but a group known as "Citizens to save St. Mark's" was formed and a reconstruction project was begun. At the church's reopening in 1982, Queen Beatrix of the Netherlands attended and placed a floral offering at Stuyvesant's crypt.

"I couldn't get to St. Mark's for the ceremony and only arrived there late the next day, just before the church closed for the night," Celia told me. "At least I got to see the Queen's flowers, but I had a disturbing experience, too. As I stood in the foyer, which was lit only by the setting sun, I looked at Stuyvesant's marker and at the plaque for his wife, Catherine. Then, as I turned to leave, I heard a very heavy thump on the floor. A slightly-stooped man stood in the shadows to the left, just within the inner doors. He leaned on a heavy stick of wood with which I think he had just struck the floor," she said. I asked her if it was more of a cane and she replied, "No, it was a thick piece of wood with a polished top where he held it. He was very serious, and I assumed he was the sexton, trying to hurry me out so he could lock up.

**The Stuyvesant Window
in St. Mark's**

"He seemed to wear a skull cap, and I wondered for a split second if he was Jewish. He wore a cape or cloak thrown across his shoulders and just stared at me with what I imagined were hot eyes. Figuring I displeased him, whoever he was, and as I had seen the Queen's flowers, I went down the steps, then turned to look back. No one was there. So that was my experience. It wasn't until almost ten years later that I told a friend, who announced that I'd seen Governor Stuyvesant's ghost. She got out an encyclopedia, and there, in an engraving, was his face, long nose and all. My first ghost!"

So on my journey, I was also prepared to meet old Peter, but he apparently wasn't there that day—probably out surveying The Bowery Road. But I did get to meet the current sexton, James, a friendly man. "Have *you* met Stuyvesant's ghost?" I asked.

James gave a broad smile and said he'd never met old Peg-Leg Pete, but he *had* heard unexplained noises, as have many who have worked alone in the church late in the evening. "He is most often heard in the steeple," he told me.

"Why up there?" I asked.

"I'm not sure he likes the new steeple, or maybe it's the roof," he responded. "Many people hear walking when there is nobody up there to walk. Others report the clanking of chains up in the old organ loft. The original organ, you see, was huge and took up most of the loft. It's gone now, and maybe Stuyvesant prowls up there, trying to figure how to remedy the devotional music situation." James seemed unafraid and totally dedicated to his job, which was to ready the church for a conference that night. I thanked him and walked out, only to encounter a large bronze bust of Peter Stuyvesant on the south side of the church.

He sure looked serious, so probably four hundred years hasn't tamed his fiery spirit one bit. My guess is that he's still plotting a way to get his bones up and moving again. Then, he'll have to do *something* about the English!

The Church

Palatine Church

The old grey stone building has stood in the Mohawk Valley for over two hundred thirty years now. It was there in 1777 when Gen. Nicholas Herkimer's troops returned bloodied from the Battle of Oriskany. It stood on the hillside, overseeing the digging of the Erie Canal just a short distance to the south in the 1820s. And, again, as New York State constructed a modern Route 5 along the old trail through Neliston in the early 1900s, the staunch Lutheran congregation met there and sang their praises to God.

Times, population centers, and religious persuasions change, however, and the day came in the middle 1900s when the congregation was just too small to sustain the services of a pastor and regular Sunday services. The building was shut up and reopened only on the anniversaries of important historic observances. Apparently, the building has not been quiet since then, however.

Water dowsers of the Hudson-Mohawk Chapter of the American Society of Dowsers have learned to locate more than sources of water, and a number of them specialize in both the detection and release of spirits. Several chapter members from the area, perhaps prompted by rumors, went one day in the late 1990s to dowse the grounds of the old church. Their findings led them to return with a sensitive named Karl, a local man who "sees" the spirits of those who have gone before us, entities that still revisit or remain in the places important during their lifetimes.

"It was a local history day, and the church was open for inspection by visitors," Karl told me. "It was such a nice old Protestant church and, for just a moment, it seemed vacant. Having an interest in musical instruments, Karl walked to the front of the church to sit on the organ bench. Aware that old buildings usually retain spirits, Karl expanded his awareness and realized that he had just sat down beside a spirit organist. Immediately, he heard, "This is my organ and you must respect it." A mature woman, in her late fifties, he judged, demanded to know why he was there. "Mentally, I replied, 'I'm visiting the church and I'm also interested in music.'

"She relaxed, realizing that I didn't intend to remove her from her organist position but had only come to look at the instrument and speak to her telepathically. She seemed proud of her title of organist and choir director and was happy that I appreciated her dedication.

"'We are going to have a rehearsal soon, so you shouldn't interrupt us,' the woman continued. I looked upward into the balcony and saw quite a number of spirit people had assembled," Karl told me. "Then I spotted others standing among the pews downstairs. Vague human voices emanated from the area near the pulpit, though I could see no living person there."

Then, suddenly, he was all alone on the organ bench. The sun shone warmly upon the wooden floor inside the quiet old building, and no one else was present. Had he just stepped back a moment in time? Or had he been visited by the spirit of a long-ago organist who long ago became possessive of her musical instrument and the status it gave her in this once frontier community?

One of the dowsing community, a man named Tick Gaudreau, also visited the church on one of its public holidays and became aware of an earthbound spirit in the nave. His dowsing technique allows him to greet spirits telepathically, and he did so. The spirit was a male located near an old pot-belly stove that once warmed the congregation during cold Mohawk Valley winters, and an old wood pile remained beneath the nearby stairs to the choir loft. The old man sported a threadbare black suit and informed Tick that he had been charged with keeping the stove filled and lighted and continued to do so.

Gaudreau questioned the man as to the present year and the gentleman replied, "1846." The dowser then asked the spirit if he found Tick's dress to be unusual for 1846 and the man replied, "No."

"Well, do you recognize these instruments?" he asked, pointing to his cameras.

"Yes," the spirit replied laconically. Tick was now puzzled. Such digital cameras didn't exist in 1846, if that was the spirit's reality. The dowser concluded that this man had been conscious of the passage of time and the changing styles and technology. Yet, the ghost seemed unperturbed and Gaudreau pondered how to inform the man that he had died and was now in spirit. First, he demonstrated his 35 mm. camera and the spirit was unfazed. But Tick then explained the digital infrared camera, which was quite new at the time. "I *am* dead, aren't I?" the spirit man asked.

"Yes, your physical body has ceased to exist, but as you can tell, you are still alive. You can see me, but I can't see you with my eyes. I know you're here because I feel you with my body and can hear you with my mind. It's now 2003, and this building is no longer used as a church; it's only a public monument now," Tick replied.

"I asked him if he knew of The Light," the investigator said. "He responded, matter-of-factly, 'Oh, yes.' So I then asked him whether or not he needed help going into The Light, and he answered, 'No,' and, turning on his heel and wiping his hands together, as if to say, 'Well, that's finished,' the spirit walked away from me, through the church wall, and toward The Light on what turned into a grassy meadow, gently sloping upward away from me. The man took his time, seeming to understand the route, and didn't need me to intercede with the guardians who came to help him." Tick concluded this was one of the most beautiful exits from the earth that he has witnessed.

On a later visit to the church, Gaudreau encountered a woman spirit who was not pleased to see him. In one of the "box seats" in the choir loft, he discovered a stout and well-dressed woman, who wore a light blue dress. Obviously, she had been one of the stalwarts in the former congregation. She telepathically informed the dowser that her well-to-do husband, a local businessman, had died. She knew the year was 2003 and that she was dead, but preferred to stay in her place of status with its feelings of *belonging* to The Lord, where she could pray and sing. Upon hearing the woman's family name, Tick recalled seeing it engraved on a large gravestone in the cemetery outside.

The ghost woman refused to contemplate exiting into The Light, and a psychic in the dowsing group informed Tick that the spirit could become troublesome and was best left alone. When she was ready to depart, her guides or angels would make the offer. Gaudreau resolved to visit the church again in a few years, to see if she had had enough worship in her imagined heaven and was now ready to experience the real thing.

I am indebted to Tick and his co-author, David Darrow, for the second part of this story. Readers seeking more information on dowsing for spirits and the release of entrapped souls can find answers in a fascinating new book entitled, *Spirit Rescue: A Dowser's Ghostly Encounters.*

Where Next?

A bit northwest of Schenectady is the small community of West Glenville. The road intersection there has been graced by many old homes for almost three hundred years, but the landmark, the Dutch Reformed Church,

Former Dutch Reformed Church Rectory

is much newer. It replaced the original, early 1800s building that burned in the 1960s, though the fire left the 1904 parsonage next door unscathed. And it is the pastor's residence that is the subject of this short story.

"My husband was pastor there for a few years in the 1970s," said Carol Troost. "I was an English teacher at the nearby Galway Central School, and one night I sat on the living room floor with essays arrayed before me on the carpet. Our big old St. Bernard, Garfunkel, lay beside me with his head on my leg. Suddenly, I felt him raise his head and stare intently toward the hallway.

"In the doorway, I spotted a man standing and staring at the two of us. There was nothing malevolent or scary about him—he was just a man, an observer, and he seemed curious about us. I wasn't afraid, and, not knowing quite what to say or do, I returned to grading the essays, somewhat doubting the reality of what I'd seen. When I looked up again, he was gone.

"When my husband returned home, I told him about the incident. He didn't disbelieve me, but as a rational man, he didn't believe me either. He tended to dismiss such paranormal visions, and we let the matter drop," she told me.

Finally, her husband's tenure at the church reached an end, and the Troosts built a house and moved from the parsonage. Before a new pastor came, the congregation chose to rent the old house, and did so to several tenants. The last of these were Rob and Kathy Biers, who were Carol's close friends. When a new pastor came, the congregation found other quarters for his family. A year later, Carol visited Rob and Kathy and, unable to resist the urge, asked Kathy if the building was quiet, and whether they had any strange occurrences there.

"Kathy looked me in the eye, then got a big smile on her face and said, 'Then we're *not* crazy, are we?' She told me that there were occasional ghost sightings near the top of the stairs on the second floor or in the downstairs foyer beneath it. When seen, it was always a man. On top of that, our cat refused to enter the upper hall at night, and when it had to do so during daylight hours, it raced through there without stopping!" Finally, Carol had a verification of her own experience.

She told Kathy what she had learned from Mrs. Poff, a prior pastor's wife: *her* father had come to live with her and her minister husband some years before. As he was disabled, the elder had sat during most of the day in his rocking chair at the top of the stairs, where he could look out at the West Glenville Corners. The old gentleman had kept track of the neighborhood people's comings and goings. The woman told Carol that, one day, she had gone to summon her father and found him dead, still seated in his favorite spot. Apparently, he had dozed and died in his sleep, so it was a peaceful end, but it was likely that the old man didn't realize that he had died. When there is a lack of certainty on the deceased's part, there can often be a period of ghosthood, until the realization comes and is accepted.

"I told Mrs. Poff what I'd seen in the hallway that day as I marked papers, and she confirmed my description as her father. When I visited her shortly after that, Mrs. Poff showed me a photo of her father, and we agreed on the ghost's identity. So, I shared all my knowledge and experience with Kathy, the old parsonage's new tenant, and she was so glad," Carol told me. When the next pastor came, the old parsonage sat uninhabited pending the church elders' decision as to its fate.

At the time I visited the old building, there was a big sign out front. New construction was coming, and the congregation had voted to raze the house. Bob, a neighbor who lives nearby, walked and talked with me near the old building that afternoon and told me it was coming down soon.

I shared all this with Carol, who was concerned: where does a ghost *go* when his residence vanishes? Does he continue to inhabit *the ghost of a building*? Or don't buildings have ghosts when they "die?" I told her several stories about such instances. One involved a house in Saratoga Springs, where the ghost woman took up residence in the new building that was constructed on the site, continuing to make mischief. The other tale involved the ghost acknowledging to a psychic that he couldn't continue to exist in mid-air, which led him to an acceptance that his body probably *had* died. And as soon as he accepted his physical death, he became aware of his option to enter the afterworld. And he took it.

I'm going to keep an eye on that intersection and closely follow what happens when the old parsonage is history.

CHAPTER 9

BUSINESSES AND PUBLIC BUILDINGS

Just Checking

The Stockade Inn

Schenectady (from the Iroquois Schau-naugh-ta-da) means "over the pine plains." Earliest Dutch explorers, working under the eye of Dutch agent Arendt Van Corlaer found the flats on the north side of the lower Mohawk River already a busy place with a Mohawk nation "castle" there on the traditional riverside trade route. Van Corlaer bought the tract of land from the Indians in 1661 and began legal trade with them in 1672. As he apportioned the land grant among the first settlers, Van Corlaer chose for himself the property at the junction of present-day Union and Church Streets. All the Dutch property was enclosed within a large stockade, and that ancient section of Schenectady still bears the name, "The Stockade." It was French-led Indians who invaded the snowbound, palisaded city in February of 1690, massacring many of the Dutch settlers and burning almost the entire community. Some observers believe that there are still earthbound spirits from those horrors in the old Stockade.

By 1814, having been rebuilt and having survived the French and Indian and Revolutionary Wars, Schenectady was a bustling hub of land and water trade. One of the city's first banks, The Mohawk Bank, was constructed at the corner of Union and Church Streets. Four years later, a massive vault was fashioned, and a much larger building added to the original bank building. Though commerce took place downstairs, the bank's chief teller resided on the bank building's second floor. In 1853, the entire structure became a private residence. And that residence was sold to a founder of the New York Temperance Society, Edward Delavan, in 1868.

In 1872, the building became the Union School, Schenectady's first free public high school. Then, in 1904, with many great industries in the city, Schenectady was ready for its first private men's club: the Lower Mohawk Club. Many business deals were negotiated there by agents of the American Locomotive Company, Westinghouse, General Electric, and other employers. Continual entertainment and rich banquets abounded. This is quite a bit of history, just in order to get to our mystery, but *somebody* stayed on. And the variety of ownership and usage offers much room for speculation as to the ghost's identity.

"I came to work at the Mohawk Club as a dishwasher in the 1940s," Irene Mareno told me. "Before I left, thirty years later, I was the Mohawk

Club's manager. I don't want you to think that the building was some kind of Hollywood chamber of horrors; it wasn't. Nevertheless, we had *somebody* there who kept showing up on the second floor near the billiard room. I recall that one night in the 1950s, I was working with another employee, John, in the kitchen and a nearby private dining room. As I moved past the long hallway opposite to the billiard room, I saw a man standing in the corridor. I turned to John and saw that he didn't recognize the individual either. The stranger wasn't one of the party dining there nor was he an employee, and before we could note his details of appearance or clothing, he just vanished. John suggested that we'd seen a ghost!

"I remember a time when a business group was entering for a dinner meeting and John and I stood aside, waiting for cocktails to start. Bang! There was the sound of what resembled an explosion coming from the kitchen. We hurried to the kitchen to see what happened. Nothing seemed out of the ordinary, but just then, the lazy-susan flew out of a cupboard and broke on the floor. Where did that force come from? John and I looked at one another and decided, 'Cocktails!' And off we went to our work.

"We were always hustling to attend to business and seldom had time for a ghost hunt, so after that, when moving between the private dining rooms and the kitchen, when we'd see the spirit watching us, we'd just wave and move on," she laughed. "A few years later, John found another job, but I was never afraid. Our ghost was just a leftover, like some of the uneaten food remaining after a dinner party. He was just *there* and became part of the scenery."

After John left his employment at the club, Irene said she never saw the man again. Many times she had to change fuses in the attic alone or retrieve liquor from the cellar, and nobody ever jumped out at her or made her afraid. But *some* people got scared. "We had both dining rooms and lodging rooms in the upstairs," Irene told me, "and sometimes we'd find lodgers from the third floor all dressed and leaving during the night. None of them ever said what frightened them, but those few folks were scared. One rapidly-departing guest mumbled something about seeing the Captain from the *Mrs. Muir* movie upstairs. But, of course, we know he was fictional, right?" Irene grinned again. "From time to time, our elevator would suddenly appear on one of the upper floors, but no one was inside. It wasn't one of those automatic elevators, but one that had to be started up by hand, so we never could figure out how that was done, or by whom. In any case, I had my career there and never felt that a ghost interfered with my management."

In June 2003, the McDonald family from Schenectady purchased the building without displacing the Mohawk Club members, who continue to meet for serious discussions and to enjoy the great meals provided by the new ownership. There has been a name change, however, and the old club has become The Stockade Inn. It is still a place of quiet elegance from days gone by. A large restaurant and three banquet rooms are found on the downstairs level. The second floor today, sans ghost (?), houses three private dining rooms, an antique billiards room and management offices, along with five renovated rooms for overnight guests. The third floor has been completely renovated and houses nine guest rooms with private baths. Nothing has changed—quiet luxury is still the theme. Well, sure…now! But what happened to the new owners when *they* took over?

Jeff McDonald told me that they chose to make the physical changes to the building in stages. While they were still closed during the ownership transition period, workmen spruced up the foyer, lobby and first floor. During that time, furtive movements, strange noises and misplaced objects were the rule for the second and third floors. Then, the first floor was finished and the work crews moved to the second floor. Work there went smoothly, but the eerie events continued on the third floor. When the meeting and dining rooms were updated on the second floor, the work crews went to the third floor and all was normal up there as those facilities were renovated.

Then came the big day, the old Mohawk Club opened as The Stockade Inn. Staff members were ready and waiting for the customers. Though there were no bookings for the guest rooms upstairs, and no scheduled banquets or business lunches scheduled for the second floor, they *were* ready. Suddenly, the switchboard lit up. Calls and more calls. From new clients? No, from *upstairs*. All day long, calls were coming down to the desk from *empty rooms*! While they were trying to understand how non-guests were placing calls, the old phone in the lobby phone booth (since removed) began to ring.

But that booth wasn't hooked into either the house or the Verizon lines—it wasn't connected to *anything*! The phone company repairman came and looked it all over, but just stood and scratched his head. How to figure it all? It seems to me that the spirits of countless happy customers assembled for the grand opening and were eager to get *going*. Soon, however, banquets were booked and overnight guests arrived, and today, the building is sedate once more. Are they ghosts of the new century just laying low?

And, who was checking in during the late 1900s? My bet is that it was either a spirit from old Schenectady, perhaps from the days of the Massacre, or else the Chief Teller from the bank days. Chief Tellers are fussy people, and maybe he had to stay around for a while to convince himself that Irene was really up to managing the Club. In his day, women weren't given such responsibilities!

Leo Sullivan

In 1984, Bruce and Sadie Kilburn bought an old drugstore on Canada Street in Lake George, NY. The place was a landmark of sorts, with its large blue and orange sign denoting "Sullivan's Rexall" store. Old Mr. Sullivan, the pharmacist, had passed away, and though they would no longer be able to fill prescriptions there, the Kilburns delighted in keeping the old store alive by offering just about every notion and knickknack that a summer tourist could desire. They had a small apartment and office upstairs, and in time, they bought the neighboring building and made it a gift shop annex alongside the store. It wasn't long, however, before they realized they'd purchased "a little something extra."

After closing one evening in the summer of 1984, Bruce sat in the upstairs kitchen, when suddenly his attention was caught by the apartment door slowly opening. Willie, their dog, leaped to his feet and stood guard, glaring at the hallway outside. After a minute, with a whimper, he lay down again. So began an ongoing series of phenomena that the Kilburns believe is Leo Sullivan's way of greeting them.

"There are times when just about anything here that *can* make noise *does*," Sadie said. "So many times we hear the wind chimes in the gift shop all tinkling at once, though the doors aren't open to let a breeze in. Then there is the smell of tobacco. At first, we thought it might blow in from the street during summers, so we didn't think too much about it. But in the autumn, when the street door was closed, we began to smell it often, and we have 'No Smoking' signs everywhere. In June of 2003, as I worked in the apartment and then the upstairs office, I smelled it there, too. It didn't occur to me at first that we had a ghost, but too many different people have smelled it. Randy, our clerk, asked me one day, 'Who's smoking in here?' We never could catch anyone doing so. Ron, another worker, has smelled it, too. So we did some checking and discovered that Leo Sullivan smoked a pipe, and from what we can gather, his tobacco had the same distinctive cherry aroma we get. A friend who visited and came walking toward the stairs in the back suddenly heard footsteps climbing the stairs but could clearly see nobody was there.

"Up until recently, we didn't know that much about Leo Sullivan, but asking questions got us a lot of fascinating information. Leo was famous for his great sense of humor and his pranks. He and his cronies, The Spit and Whittle Club, used to hold forth here, especially during the slow winter times. And we learned of his legendary St. Patrick's Day observances. Well, he *was* an Irishman, and some of his 'observances' of the day are hilarious. Enough said. We do wonder if that sense of fun remained in the building when he left."

Behind the store is an old rooming house owned by Mrs. Sullivan. When she returned from a trip one day, she asked the Kilburns if everything was okay, if the doors were all locked and the building secure. Sadie responded that she'd check to be doubly sure. Bruce went down to the old building and found the glass door ajar and unlocked. "That's impossible," he told me, "there is no key. It locks with a sliding bolt on the inside. We told Mrs. Sullivan about it, and she scowled, telling him that before she had gone on her trip, she had checked the building and found the door open, so *she* had closed the bolt and further secured the door firmly with a concrete block."

"The issue of locks keeps us jumping," Sadie said. "The store's back door looks out on a small rear yard that faces that back building. I'm particular about security each night when we close and often check the locks several times before we go upstairs. The sliding bolt lock on that door is difficult to move, and I have to put some real muscle behind it when I push it in. Pete, one of our workers, used to check the locks at closing time, and one night I checked them just five minutes after he did, so I'm certain all was secure. Yet, the next morning, when Ron came to open the store, he found that back door unlocked and open!"

Georgina and Bruce Nelson once had a deli and restaurant in that back building, and Sadie said, "They did a lot of work in there to bring the interior up to State Health Department requirements. There's a pass-through window into the kitchen and one day Marge, the waitress, came to the window and asked the cook who the other man in the kitchen was. The cook replied that he was alone, but Marge countered that she had just seen a stranger there peeling potatoes at the sink. Needless to say, the stranger was never found or identified. They thought to themselves, Leo? Naw, couldn't be!

"Be sure to tell him about the cobwebs," Bruce said. Sadie smiled and told me about the small hallway that leads to the back stairs. "Several times I've opened the door into that hallway and walked right into some invisible cobwebs. I've never seen them, but I sure could feel them. Now, it's impossible for cobwebs to form in that area, as somebody is passing through there every ten minutes. To make matters worse, on occasion we'll feel a bitter cold spot there." Readers likely know that both the very cold spots and cobwebs are indicators of having just walked through a spirit's space.

Bruce told me, "One morning, I opened the gift shop and saw a strange white haze in the rear of the store, where Leo used to have his stockroom. An old timer told Sadie that in the early 1930s, that section was added on for a small lunch counter. We have taken to calling the unseen visitor 'Leo;' that's who we suspect is still here. He so loved his work and the wonderful friends he'd made in Lake George that he just couldn't drop it all. He died just six weeks after we bought the store, and he likely wasn't ready to let it go in his mind and memory. He didn't like the idea of the gift shop as part of the store; he was one of those old fashioned pharmacists."

Sadie added that Leo wasn't the first owner of the building. Around 1900, it was Tripp's Hardware store. "In 2001, at the end of the summer season, we closed and began clearing the interior so carpet installation could start throughout the store. We moved the floor racks into the smallest area possible so the rug could be put down." She showed me a small space, perhaps four by four feet, and told of placing the floor display racks in there. "One of those racks was filled with wind chimes. So the carpet was installed and we just left things the way they were until we re-opened in the spring. When we got ready to open, we went in and found the wind chime rack completely upended, but still in the midst of all the other racks, where we had left it. And that reminds me of a curious dream that I had once," she said. "In 2002, I dreamed of being in the upstairs apartment bathroom putting on makeup. Suddenly I saw hands emerging from the wall, then a man walked into the bathroom with me. I was astounded and asked him who he was. 'Thatcher,' was his reply. I asked why he was there and where he was from, and he answered jokingly, 'Me mudder!'" When I awoke, I wondered if that might have been Leo's spirit in disguise. There may be someone else here, too. Nancy, another of our employees, went up to the apartment bathroom in the spring of 2002 and saw a woman in white who suddenly vanished."

Michael Hayes, who served as a pharmacist when Leo owned the store, smiled when I told him of the Kilburns' experiences. "It's a funny thing, you know. When business got slow in the afternoons, and Leo knew I could handle things, he'd go up into that room upstairs and take a nap. That was his respite."

Perhaps Leo Sullivan is resting upstairs in the place he loved best, taking his time in progressing to the next world. Probably he can already hear the heavenly choirs singing, urging him to return home. On the other hand, St. Patrick's Day isn't far off.

The Traveler

Leonor Loree, President of the Delaware & Hudson Railroad, was at the top of his game, both in business and in his weekly poker playing. His cronies included Marcus T. Reynolds, the architect, and William Barnes, the Republican Party boss in the City of Albany, NY. Sometimes, ideas turned as quickly as the cards at the game table, and the prosperous Loree one day envi-

The D&H Building c. 1920

sioned a grand D&H Company headquarters to replace the rotten wharves and shacks along the western shore of the Hudson River. Reynolds proposed demolishing the old hotels, shops, and rooming houses and widening Broadway from its original twenty-three feet, then rearranging the D& H tracks. Downtown Albany, with its many century-old wooden buildings, was a sorry sight, and the sewage oozing from ancient drains and sewers on State Street Hill often flowed downhill into the river during rainstorms, causing smelly floods along the Hudson's banks in springtime.

Loree chose Reynolds as architect and plans were made for a Gothic D&H office building resembling European guildhalls or palaces, and construction began in 1914. Within just a few years, however, the number of corporate offices was too great for the new building's limited space, so the structure was extended, with its southern end housing offices of a major city newspaper, *The Albany Evening Journal*. Half a century later, the D&H went out of business, long after the *Journal* had ceased publication. Then, the State University purchased the palatial building, which dominates the river skyline. Today, the old D&H Building is the State University of New York Headquarters.

"I often worked my security job there on weekends during the 1990s," Stephan told me. "That big old place sure has a history! One day I noticed an elderly man poking around the outside of the building, and I questioned him as to his business. He was friendly and told me that, years before, he had been a D & H Railroad building security officer and was just reminiscing. The old man said that during a transition period between owners, the building had no tenants and only security people like himself were inside. Then, he told of having spotted a woman in old-fashioned clothing one night, walking toward his security desk from the direction of the south door. Her clothing was from another era, and as the woman approached his desk, she suddenly disappeared. He was curious whether or not *I* had seen the ghost woman."

Stephan continued, "*I* never saw her, but there sure seemed to be someone or something strange going on there during my employment. The technical people in the northern, Broadway end of the building (the earliest D&H building, dating from 1914) sometimes reported an indistinct figure moving among the upstairs computer banks. Most of them believed it to be a female figure, though she vanished before they could spot any detail. Others told of a black man suddenly appearing in a work area, and just as quickly disappearing. Computer operators in those offices sometimes told of strange shadows passing across their video display terminals, too.

"At night, when I patrolled the hallways of the building, I sometimes noticed that phones would ring in the office I was approaching. Now, who would call a State University office at 2 or 3 a.m.? In any case, I'd enter the office and answer the call, but nobody was ever on the line. I'd hang up, re-lock the office, and proceed down the hall, then hear a phone in the next office ring; it was the same story when I went in and picked up *that* phone. It was almost as if some invisible force or personality were accompanying me on my rounds, giving me just enough excitement to know I wasn't alone." Stephan left the security service in 2001 when he took a new job.

Then I met Bernadette, a night cleaner at SUNY Headquarters, who was known to the security men and who had also sighted the lady ghost—up close. "It all started slowly," she told me, "and at first I'd only see a light in the downstairs hallway. At first, I wrote it off as a reflection from traffic headlights out on Broadway, but after a while I figured *that* was impossible." Most of her sightings occurred in the hallway south of the building's tower.

"The first time I *knew* something strange was going on was on a winter night in 2001, when I came downstairs from cleaning in the tower. I entered the first floor lobby, and looked toward the south end of the hallway. (That area was once the arcade and office space of the *Albany Evening Journal* and where the old security guard's desk had been).

"This time, there was clearly a ball of fluorescent light in mid-air, and I thought someone outside had a spotlight. But no, the light was slowly growing and moving directly toward me! I stared at it and began to note details within the light. First, I saw the woman, and then the old-fashioned carpetbag that she held in her right hand. Then, I noticed the parasol in her other hand. As details became clearer and she continued to move toward me, I noticed her small hat and high lacy collar and that her skirt went all the way to the floor. Her boots were pointed and had little buttons on them. She had a very elegant walk but made no noise; it was as if she were gliding across the floor.

Everything in the vision was white.

"Oh my God, I thought, I'm seeing a ghost! I *knew* what she was instantly but thought it strange that I didn't feel a chill. Suddenly, the ghost lady vanished, and I realized that I hadn't noticed any details of her face. All I could remember is that she looked a bit like Mary Poppins." Bernadette later told a security officer about the sighting, and since *he* had also seen the ghost lady, they agreed to separately write what they had seen. When the two compared their observations, they discovered them to be identical, except that the officer hadn't observed a parasol. Also, comparing notes, they discovered that the ghost lady doesn't seem to appear in the summer.

"I have pretty much been sensitive throughout my life," Bernadette told me, "and often smell roses before a family member dies. But this is the first ghost I've ever *seen*. I wonder where she is traveling to, and I wonder why she's never gotten there."

Virginia Bowers, Albany's Historian, helped me find an historical hint for the answer to Bernadette's question. "Look at the 1895 City Directory and you can find buildings that were demolished after 1914 to erect the extension of the D&H Building in which the *Albany Journal* was housed. From the old Sanborn maps, you can see that the building's tower was constructed over the former site of the old Mansion House, a hotel for both river and rail travelers."

I think she is right. Our "Poppins lady" seems to be in a hurry to get from someplace to somewhere else and walks rapidly along a route that must have traversed the old Mansion House Hotel's lobby. Now, if we were only privy to her thoughts and their traumatic nature....

An Extra Hand

How does a school acquire a ghost? Seldom does a person die in a school building, so does that mean that a disembodied spirit from outside the school district can just move in? Or might it suggest that one who worked or taught in the building, not likely a former student, remains attached to the work and simply hasn't left? Here is a curious story from Schoharie County in the Catskills.

In 1929, the hamlets of Gilboa, Conesville, Prattsville, and Grand Gorge combined their small schoolhouses into a new central school system called The Gilboa-Conesville Central School. The first building, a high school, was constructed on the hillside along Wyckoff Road. From that slope, students can see the waters of the Schoharie Reservoir, which serves as part of the New York City water supply. Many old houses in the valley were razed in 1926 when

Gilboa-Conesville School

the Gilboa Dam was constructed on the prone-to-flooding Schoharie Creek. On a hillside, reminiscent of the biblical Mt. Gilboa, the school underwent several expansions. It is the age of the school's various sections that may help us to explain why and where a ghost roams in the building.

"I went to school in the original section," Fred Wickert told me, "and there was a large combination auditorium/gymnasium at the center of the structure. Folded wooden seats stacked on long carriers were stored underneath the stage and brought out for assemblies or plays. Today that old space has been converted into a library and guidance offices, as a newer gymnasium and cafeteria were created in a later addition."

One of the school's custodians recently enumerated for Fred the strange phenomena that are irksome in his nightly duties. The man noted that most of the phenomena occur in the original building and consist of unexplained noises and subtle interference with his crew's cleaning. "After we clean certain sections and rooms, we lock a door and move on. Shortly afterward, we hear a door slam and recognize that sound as the door we just locked! When we go to check the doors, the lights inside are off and the doors are locked, and there is no one else in the hallways or building. How is it possible for a door that is locked, and thus unable to open, to slam?" he asked. "Another event that puzzles us is that after cleaning the lower (old) building and progressing up to the higher and newer buildings, we occasionally catch sight of a light burning in the old part. Someone forgot to turn it out, we figure, though all of us make sure to extinguish lights when we finish cleaning an area. We hurry back to the supposed lighted area, only to find everything dark when we get there! Even if we suspect it is a ghost light, we still are responsible for lights not turned off, so we have to go and *see*," he said with exasperation.

The man also related another puzzling phenomenon, the cool breeze that often strikes him in the hallway of the older building. "We know there can't be a breeze in that hallway unless a window or door is open; and on the evening shift that just doesn't happen. The man admitted he had heard that ghosts signal their presences with cold drafts, but he really didn't want to spend much time considering that he had a phantom custodian working alongside him!

Fred told me of another man, whose responsibility is the inter-building telephone system which is vital to school communications. "One night that man was working alone in the building, installing new wires and phones after the janitorial staff had locked up and left. He was the only person in the building, and he knew it, so he was very surprised to hear voices and slamming doors. He finished his task, rapidly departed, and vowed never to work again at night after the custodians have left. He later discovered that other school personnel who have worked late at night have heard the same spectral sounds: voices of people that are no longer there and doors slammed when there is no living hand to push them.

"One custodian's wife brought him a snack one evening when the man was cleaning in an uphill building, the one built in the 1950s," Fred learned. "She was startled at first, then chilled, to hear the ghostly sounds emanating from near the cafeteria. And then the lights in that section turned themselves on and off several times. Are the ghosts learning to move around?"

The custodians discuss such matters privately and have found no evidence for a death on the property since the first building was constructed in 1929. There is the possibility, of course, that there was an Indian death and burial there years before the white men arrived. But it is also possible that an alumnus of "The Best School by a Dam Site," as the school calls itself, has returned to restructure his or her memories of the days when gaining an education wasn't as easy as today.

Many times, individuals reach their graves with their school years remembered as the highpoint of self-discovery. Though there are further realms of learning in the Afterlife, some are timid about moving on and prefer the safety of the old high school. Perhaps, like the janitors at Gilboa-Conesville, they are "cleaning up" some details of their ended life first.

Elias

At 5:30 a.m. on October 27, 1923, a milkman making his rounds spotted flames bursting from the cupola atop Saratoga Springs City High School. He called in the alarm, and fire crews sped to the conflagration on Lake Avenue. The old school was heavily engulfed in flames and, with water pressure low, in the end, the fire department could save only the school's walls. A total loss, the ruins stood for a few more years and eventually were demolished. Fortunately, the city had a new high school already under construction a block away.

Chief Elias Shadwick c.1915

Elias Shadwick, who had been fire chief for years, was frustrated at his department's inability to knock down the flames in the old wooden building that morning. For years he had harangued the city fathers to lay larger water mains for firefighting in the downtown, and he must have done a lot of talking to himself when he returned to the city's old firehouse on Broadway. One wonders if he knew that, within six years, the city would have a new firehouse *at the scene of that school fire*. And one wonders if he also had any presentiment that he would be dead before setting foot in the new and modern Lake Avenue Station.

Through the years that I taught school and lived in the Saratoga Springs area, I heard tales of a quiet ghost in the Lake Avenue Firehouse, Station #1. I met Firefighter Frank Spensieri, who told me that, as a young fireman on the night shift in Bunk Area #1, he was awakened in the night by a shadow moving slowly past his bunk. It seemed to pause over him, as if inspecting him, and then it disappeared. "You see, each firefighter has his own bunk that no one else sleeps in, but that night I was helping out, and Joe told me to take his bunk. After my surprise (I jumped up and swung at the guy, but he wasn't there), I pondered whether it was Shadwick, just trying to figure who was in Joe's bunk!" Is Shadwick still on duty, keeping track of all the new personnel since 1929?

The firemen I interviewed were unanimous in their assertion that, if indeed there was a ghost in the building it *had* to be old Chief Shadwick. Frank told me that most of the present fire company has heard stories of such incidents or knew individuals who had such experiences in the almost eighty-year-old building, but not all were believers.

"When a man joins the Fire Department, he hears the legend of the Chief—some believe it and some don't. I don't really believe in ghosts, though I have to tell you I *know* that I saw that dark figure scrutinizing me."

Old Firehouse, Shadwick in white hat

Before 1910, when Saratoga Springs was just a village, fires were fought by volunteer companies using hand pumpers and bucket brigades. Young Elias Shadwick, a Ballston Spa native, was one of those volunteers before he was twenty, working first for the Livingston Hose Co. and then the Hathorn Hose Co. in 1884. Later promoted to Chief, his tenure included lobbying city government to get paid firefighters, creating a city fire alarm system, and establishing a pension fund for retirees. He also introduced the first motorized fire trucks to the city department.

During those years, he was severely injured at least three times on his way to fires, once having a pumper truck overturn on him. He commanded firemen at all the great hotel and commercial fires in the young city's history. Death came in 1929 from complications resulting from a final collision in his fire chief's sedan. How, I asked myself, could such a tough and "hands-on" officer just surrender life and march off into the Afterlife?

When I visited the firehouse, I was shown the upstairs #1 bunk room, with its interior and exterior windows painted black. It's hard to imagine there would be enough nighttime illumination in that room to cast the shadow that Frank reported seeing. Most of the firefighters sleep lightly on the night shift, as if expecting an alarm. Therefore, it is likely that Spensieri would not have been so deeply asleep as to dream the figure, yet he saw no details of the man's garb.

Chief Robert Cogan escorted me through the bunk area, noting that, as a fireman, he had spent twelve years of night service in that room. "I never saw a ghost," he told me. "Yes, there are many mysterious noises, such as that ventilator overhead," he pointed. "It's one of those old globe-shaped roof ventilators that long ago stopped working. I recall hearing the sound of whispering when I was a fireman and laying awake at night puzzling as to its source. As near as I can figure, the wind outside must create the sound. Strangely, even though the bearings that allow the fan to turn are rusted and worn out, once in a while it begins to turn and draw air out of this room. It's in such poor shape that I often wonder how it can operate."

I also spoke with Firefighter Tom Knight, who seems to have had the most vivid experiences. "When I became a firefighter, I just assumed the stories of Shadwick were a scare tactic the older guys used on the newbies. As time went on, and as I heard of this man or that one seeing shadowy or opaque figures at night, I came to suspect that each new fireman had to 'make peace with Shadwick.'" To Knight, it was logical, if improbable in this rational society, that each guy had to establish himself in the old Chief's esteem, passing muster for dedication to his work before old Elias would fully accept him.

Chief Elias Shadwick seems germane to this story of current phenomena because firefighters in that building are at a loss to explain who else might be roaming Fire Station #1 in the quiet hours of the night. True, a fair number of Saratoga's firefighters since 1929 have died on the job, so one must also consider these individuals, memorialized in photos on a wall just outside Bunk Area #1. If, indeed, the meandering ghost is the old chief, we immediately have to conjecture why. First, he was the longest-serving fire chief in the city's history—forty-six years. Many spirits are the conscious energy remains of dedicated individuals who cannot lay down their job when they forsake the physical body.

Secondly, why Shadwick? He never served in the new firehouse. It is common among ghosts to travel with belongings or physical objects to locations never visited in life. When the new fire station was inaugurated in 1929, most of the fire trucks and firefighting apparatus were familiar to the Chief who had died months before. Likely he had been responsible for purchasing most of it and probably had touched (and perhaps treasured) every piece of equipment. With the exception of the big Arcade Fire on Broadway in June 1902, the old 1833 school building was likely the largest building to burn during Shadwick's tenure. Such a losing battle may well have remained in his consciousness as he moved across to The Other Side. Perhaps one relives his or her major frustrations in life before departing from the earth plane in peace. Many times, ghosts represent that last bit of individual consciousness which cannot forgive itself for deeds not done or not done well.

The second photo in this story shows Shadwick and his company drawn up in front of the former fire station on Broadway (Chief Shadwick in the white officer's hat), a building that has undergone many changes, having served several times since as a restaurant. The Old Firehouse Restaurant employed many of Saratoga Springs's young people over the years as waiters, waitresses and bartenders. Several have told me of a range of experiences in the old firehouse's upstairs, formerly the bunk area or kitchen for those on duty until 1929. Sudden cold spots, objects repeatedly moved from their accustomed locations, electrical malfunctions, and "strange noises" have all been reported by former employees. Is it possible that old Chief Shadwick still patrols his old firehouse, too?

Superintendent's House

The USMA Superintendent's House

The Hudson Valley narrows as the river flows southward through the Hudson Highlands, and Gen. George Washington was quick to notice the strategic position of a plateau on the river's west bank at West Point. Garrisoned by the Continental Army during the Revolution, it is the longest-fortified military post in America today.

In 1802, President Jefferson signed a law creating the United States Military Academy there and, in 1817, Col. Sylvanus Thayer was appointed the institution's sixth Superintendent. Recognizing that the U.S. too often had to rely on foreign engineers in wartime, Thayer made engineering primary in the USMA's curriculum. Soon after Col. Thayer assumed his post, a suitable Superintendent's House was constructed, and there, the commandant held staff meetings and curriculum planning, and grudgingly entertained visiting politicians and Academy guests. In the fifty-sixth year of America's independence (1833), Col. Thayer resigned the Superintendency and subsequently held many national defense positions, including the modernization of Boston's harbor defenses. Receiving the brevet of Brigadier General, he retired from active service on June 1, 1863.

Never married, and still dedicated to education, he took part in many scientific associations and donated $300,000 to the Academy, $32,000 to build a library in his birthplace, Braintree, MA, and $70,000 to create a new school of civil engineering and architecture at Dartmouth College in New Hampshire. His body was buried at West Point in November 1877, and a memorial statue naming him, "Father of the United States Military Academy" was unveiled six years later. So, his body rests at The Point. Where is his spirit?

For many years there have been rumors of "incidents" in the Superintendent's House (designated by the

Superintendent Col. Sylvanus Thayer c. 1828

USMA as Quarters 100). Some are perhaps just oversights on the part of the participants, but other episodes have defied rational explanation. In October 1972, mid-way in his period of command at West Point, Superintendent Lt. Gen. William A. Knowlton gave permission for the ghost-hunting team of Ed and Lorraine Warren to visit his home while he was occupied in New York City for the weekend.

Traveling from their home in Connecticut, the Warrens visited Quarters 100 several times in twenty-four hours, and also lectured to cadets who were interested in spirit manifestations. Afterward, in a memo, the husband and wife team summarized their findings for Gen. Knowlton to ponder. A well-educated and open-minded man, Knowlton sought as much historical verification as was available in the USMA Archives, either substantiating or refuting the Warren's conclusions. Here is a sample of the information turned up.

In the late 1960s, when his father was the Superintendent, young Sam Koster reported that, awakening in the night, he discovered a lady in a flowing white dress standing in his room. Roused to consciousness, and demanding to know her identity, Koster saw the wraith exit by the bedroom door. This second floor bedroom was one of Lorraine's first targets, and she was not surprised to sense "...a lady in this room. She is not old, is very domineering, athletically inclined, and really not quite a lady. I get a feeling of no man [present]; and if she had a husband, he was dominated while at home." On a second visit to the room, Lorraine Warren found the woman's spirit much less cooperative.

Staff members, when Gen. Knowlton asked them to assign these qualities to a former Superintendent's wife, were torn between Supt. Thayer's Irish cook, Molly, and Benedict Arnold's sister-in-law. Traditionally, Molly gets credit for rumpling the bed covers in the bedrooms, and years ago was spotted kneading bread dough in the kitchen.

Across the second floor hallway is a bedroom often used by The Superintendent's visitors. Once, in the early 1970s, the Coast Guard Academy Superintendent, Adm. John Thompson, was lodged there with his wife. In the middle of the night, Mrs. Thompson felt a curious movement between her sleeping husband and herself. Reaching down, she discovered her wallet had somehow been lifted from her purse and placed on the bed. Lorraine Warren explained that event as an attention-getting act by a spirit, though Lorraine found no spirit present at the time of her visit.

On the house's south side, in the front, Lorraine found the former master bedroom that is now usually used by visiting VIPs, contained the spirit energies of both a man and a woman. She felt the pair were married to one another and operated as a cooperative team in collecting objects. Gen. Knowlton, on reading this memo, clearly remembered Supt. William Connor and his wife who served at West Point in the 1930s. The Connors left much personal antique furniture that they had collected in those quarters, so their conscious energies may remain, attached to the furniture.

In the building's basement, in quarters formerly used by Thayer, Lorraine encountered the spirit of a man she described as "very decided, who had no particular interest in women, and who disliked entertaining if he wasn't required to do so." That description seemed a spot-on reference to Thayer. Mrs. Warren also claimed to encounter a younger, mischievous male in an adjoining room which, unknown to her, had been used by Thayer's orderly. This second room is one where bed coverings are often found messed up, and in years gone by, it has been assumed the general's orderly is responsible, just trying to get attention. Curiously, Mrs. Warren felt the spirit man (orderly) was a black man named Greer, and visualized him dressed in a grey uniform with no collar.

Gen. Knowlton queried the Library archivists as to this Greer's identity. Though they could not be certain, because a number of men named Greer had served at The Point as Regular Army detachment, the best bet was a Private James Greer from the USMA Detachment of Cavalry in the 1870s. What intrigued Gen. Knowlton most in that response was that, hanging on the wall of his office, was a framed photo of Superintendent Gen. Pitcher and his wife, seated on the house's front porch in 1871. On one side of the picture, near those same basement rooms, stands a black orderly. Is that "Greer," and if so, why does he continue to hang around?

It is not surprising that these old buildings contain the energies and active memory patterns of those who served our country so many years ago. Defending the nation and training those who must do that safeguarding job is serious business, and many times, careers were made or broken by events at this post.

My next search at West Point will be a visit to the Fire Chief's Administrative building, which formerly housed officers until 2000. What makes this old Victorian house a delightful building in which to work is that (allegedly) the Post Band Master, sometime in the 1920s, hanged himself in the washroom. Today, papers are sometimes found scattered, doors and cupboards are discovered open or mysteriously closed, and unexplained noises occur for those unfortunate enough to be working after hours.

I have already written about a room in the 47th Division barracks (in my book, *Ghosts of the Northeast*) that the Academy no longer uses for cadet housing. That is because the barracks stands on the former location of a cavalry instructor's house which burned in the late 1800s, with the officer inside. With icy cold energies, the man continues to announce his presence, often popping out of walls in an old-style uniform. Not wanting cadet life to be a series of phenomena, the Superintendent has simply closed the room.

Nancy

Those who collect and read ghost stories are well aware that death often comes as a surprise to individuals who expected a life of at least threescore years and ten. At times, it's darned inconvenient, too. Work can be left uncompleted, careers may be cut short, goals might remain forever unreached, or justice can seem denied. Those who die in a coma or from a sudden or violent death are usually the prime candidates for ghosthood. Too many such individuals don't understand that they have passed. Here is such a story, with a blessing thrown in.

Jennifer Edens is a nurse at the Jones Hill Building of the WCA Hospital in Jamestown, NY. It is not a new building, though the structure's age probably has little to do with the components of this tale. "I had a friend, a fellow nurse named Nancy," Jennifer told me, "and she suddenly took sick and died. We missed her cheery smile and kind ways and could only hope that The Creator had a special place for her in Paradise. She and I had worked together on the rehabilitation floor, and her friends and I were always busy after Nancy's funeral, but not too busy to miss her.

"There is what we call 'the third hallway,' and it's not used much for patients. And though there are rooms all along that hall, we tend to use just the

WCA Hospital

ones on the near end. One night we got a male patient that was *very* sick, and the charge nurse made the decision to put him farther down the hall in a seldom-used room. We didn't know if we were going to lose him, but when the nurse entered his room early the next morning, the man was sitting up and cheery—what a change! He was talkative, so the nurse listened closely to his words as she was taking his vital signs and straightening him up.

"He expressed surprise that a single nurse had been stationed with him all night. Whenever he awoke in the darkness, there she was, smoothing his hair, rubbing his shoulders, and most importantly, holding his hand while the man slept. He expressed much gratitude and got steadily better during the next few days. Of course, we know that there isn't enough staff to sit with a single patient throughout the night, unless he can afford a private duty nurse. We asked him to describe the night nurse, and he gave a vivid description of Nancy."

In a way, such a story shouldn't seem extraordinary. Many caregivers enter their professions powerfully dedicated to healing others. Even though her body died, it seems that Nancy's dedication and compassion could not be curtailed by something as insignificant as her body's death. Apparently we take our ideals and deepest drives into the next world, and many mystics say that whatever principles and values we live are the ones that we face when we pass on. That seems a great motivation to clean up my own act; how about you?

Reporting In

The off-season storm had lashed the eastern end of Long Island all night long that day in 1987; by the next morning, much of the power along the southern shore was out, especially in the part of Southampton called "the estates." Over the past century and a half, many wealthy magnates and entertainers had built magnificent mansions along the shore, beautiful estates carefully landscaped and shaped—places of esthetic harmony. Now, there was chaos for public safety personnel, and with electrical service interrupted, house alarms were flashing all across the board. The Southampton Police Chief assigned rookie patrolman Eric Fromm to investigate one particular place.

"The caretaker met me outside," Eric told me, "and he was nervous. 'Someone's *in* there,' he said. I asked how he knew that and the man said he'd seen an inside light suddenly flare and then fade out. All the squad cars were out on other calls, and I had no backup, so I decided to take the shotgun from the car as *my* backup. I also brought my big, heavy five-cell flashlight. 'You stay out here,' I said to the watchman, 'just give me the key.' He complied happily.

"I entered very much on edge, listening carefully and walking softly. I checked every corner of the first floor. Nothing seemed out of place, and it was all neat. Nervously, I walked up the stairs. Each bedroom seemed undisturbed, and, finally, I was down to just a single room remaining. If someone was inside, *this* had to be the room. Immediately, I was on guard when I pushed the bedroom door open and saw the bed all messed up. It didn't help that the room, with the drapes partly pulled, was gloomy. I scanned the room—nothing. That was good. The closet? I pried the door open but nothing out of the ordinary was inside. Now where could an intruder *be*? Just then I noticed an unusual bulge in the drapes, exactly in the shape of a human body standing out of sight. I approached and swatted at the protrusion with my flashlight. There was no resistance, and the fabric just pushed aside!

So where? The only unsearched place left was under the bed. Now, I was nervous because I'd be off my feet. I placed the shotgun on the floor first, just a bit farther out from the bed than someone could grasp from underneath. If they did grope at it, I'd rearrange his arm bones with my flashlight, I thought. Nothing. So, then I placed the flashlight alongside the shotgun. Nothing yet. Slowly, I stretched out full-length on the floor until I could see under the bed. There was nobody *there* either! As I lay puzzled on the rug, I heard a woman yawn, as if she were just waking up. Must be she's in the chair, I figured, and slowly looked up over the bed. Nobody was in the chair, either. I had to conclude the room was empty, but there *was* a voice there. Nevertheless, I couldn't arrest a voice, so I slowly returned downstairs.

256

"Outside, I encountered the cringing watchman. 'The bed in such and such a room is all messed up, so I believe there *was* an intruder,' I said, ' but I can't find him.' The man looked down at his feet, and then said, 'No, *I'm* the one who messed up the bed. When the power went out last night, I came over to the house and slept in that room just to be here. But I won't ever do *that* again—that place is haunted!'"

Eric told me that story a few years after it happened, just before I began writing ghost stories. Years later, I reconnected with him and found that Sgt. Eric Fromm has had many other adventures with the unseen.

"Our old station was on the second floor of an old building in Southampton," he said. "In the late 80s, I often worked at the desk on the night shift, which meant I was always working alone. My Sergeant, Teddy, who had been a good friend and mentor to me as a rookie, had just died at age forty-three, and I missed him. But there was work to do every night, so I didn't have much time to grieve. One morning upon returning home, I was beat and hit the sack. Suddenly, I wasn't alone; my inner alarm went off, and I awoke to an opaque or shadowy figure over six feet tall standing alongside my bed. I didn't move and neither did he, but all at once I got a mental message: 'I'm here to say goodbye and am just checking in on you.' All at once, the figure vanished. Now totally awake, I asked myself whether or not it was real. And then I knew—it was Teddy, my friend, just checking in before he left this world. Rather than being scared, I was peaceful."

Since I last chatted with Eric, he'd gotten engaged and married Leslie, and had a family. He lives now in Sag Harbor in a brand *new* house. "So how do you figure—*it* has a ghost?" he asked. We talked about it for a while and I reminded him of a fact that he already knew. "Do you have antiques there?" I asked. He responded that he and his wife have a number of old pieces of furniture, including a few from a former haunted apartment on Madison Street in Southampton.

"I remember that apartment was in a very old house that had several additions" he told me. "In one of our bedrooms, there was a bookcase built to cover a window in a corner, so no light came through. One time I heard '30s music in the room and we had no radio or stereo on. When I checked it out, I discovered the sound came from that corner, though there was no device or machine there to produce that music. I figured it must be coming from the old lady's apartment downstairs, so I went down 'to check on her,' but when she came to the door, there was no sound from inside her apartment. So, I added 'ghostly music' to my résumé," he said with a smile.

"Then the attic was strange, too. The only way up there was through a door in our apartment, so you can imagine the looks that Leslie and I gave to each other when we'd hear heavy footsteps in the attic. Several times I went up there, but there was never any human being there." He laughed about one time finding an opossum upstairs, "but *that* had a different sound. Possums can't make clumpy footsteps!

"At the old police station, we had some spirits, too. Many times on the night shift I'd hear footsteps coming up to the second floor, but nobody ever came through the door when I looked. Maybe it's the old pipes, I thought, but when I'd listen carefully, I knew they were footsteps. When I was concentrating on my paperwork, looking down, I'd often catch a movement in the hallway from the corner of my eye, but when I'd look directly, there was never anyone else there," he told me.

"I remember one night I saw a definite shape just entering the restroom at the end of the hall, so I got up and walked into the room, only to find nobody there! We also had a convex mirror to show us who was in the doorway to the stairs, and often, when the footsteps came up, I'd look into the mirror but there was nobody reflected. And I remember talking with a rookie one night. Obviously, I didn't intend to brief him on the ghosts, but as we sat there chatting, both doorknobs on a nearby door suddenly began to turn. It was a Dutch door, a half-door, and you usually could see whoever was turning it. But not this time! He was really upset. *I* was upset too, but not because the ghost was back. I was puzzled as to how the spirit could turn a knob that didn't normally move; it was just a pulling knob."

Sgt. Fromm is an interesting man. He's fascinated by many enigmas in the world that surrounds us. He spends time reading on mysterious issues, and he's a trained observer, not given to panic or hysteria. His stories, either from home or the job, ring true. As with many individuals in the field of law enforcement and public safety, sooner or later, there comes a recognition of invisible others, individuals that can't produce a mug shot or fingerprints, who just don't get recorded in the official reports.

The Grey Man

In 1906, Harriet Martin Williams was searching through an old trunk in the attic of her ancestral home in Salem, NY. The ancient coffer contained memorabilia of her ancestor, General John Williams, a Revolutionary War hero at the Battles of Bennington and Saratoga. Harriet was making an attempt to understand the General and his enduring legacy to the village but also to Washington County itself. For over forty years, there had been reports of a "grey man" prowling the house, and all but a few were certain it was Williams himself. Harriet sought evidence of some unfinished business that might keep her ancestor earthbound.

Likely, the evidence that she sought was not to be found in papers or record books, but in the energy with which Gen. Williams imbued his rural community. He had come to the frontier settlement of Salem in 1773 as a physician and surgeon, but he was soon caught up in the preparations for war with Great Britain. Some local farmers were Loyalists, but Williams understood the enterprising energy of his neighbors, as it was his own. It took him but a short time to declare his loyalties to the Continental Congress and to accept a military commission.

Following the war, Williams returned to Salem, but was often away after that, serving in the Provincial Congress and eventually the House of Representatives of the new nation. His money and energy were soon invested in canal and turnpike construction in New York State, though he also had time to ply his profession of surgeon. He died physically in 1859, but apparently his spirit didn't abandon the large white house on East Broadway. Family members noted a grey shadow that seemed constantly in motion in the house. Sometimes, neighbors saw him moving about the fields or lawns, and sometimes in and out of his outbuildings.

Eventually, however, the house aged and when the Washington Academy became outdated, the Salem school district purchased the old home, razed it, and dedicated a new high school on the property in 1939. Appropriately, the school's athletic teams have been known as The Generals ever since. And with good reason. Though the high school was expanded in 1998 and an elementary school was added, the legend of the Grey Man continues in and around the original high school building. Night custodians for over sixty years have told of seeing a fleeting grayish intruder when they are sweeping the hallways at night. Sometimes, the Grey Man has been reported in the gymnasium.

Recently, at the behest of A.J. Hurley, a third grader, I spoke on ghosts to his fellow class members in the Elementary School. Many of the girls advised me that Gen. Williams has expanded his command beyond the high school and into the elementary school. And several of those girls noted that the General had been seen on an inspection tour in the girls' rest room. I responded that he was now off-limits, and it was the job of every third grade girl to order him out of their room and point him to the boys' room. "He's an old soldier," I told them. "He'll follow orders." We are currently awaiting the results.

The House Manager?

The Clemens Performing Arts Center

One of the nicest cities in southern New York State is Elmira, sometimes called "The Queen City of the Southern Tier." It was founded in 1828, when three small settlements combined to create a hub for commerce between Pennsylvania and New York State. Many valleys join there along the Chemung River, making the location a natural route for the burgeoning American canal and railroad network. Entrepreneurs and businessmen were drawn to the community, and between the 1830s and 1865, many of the prosperous community leaders aided the escape of fugitive slaves from the south on their way to Canada. The Underground Railroad succeeded because of more than a few Elmirans.

In 1868, Missourian Samuel L. Clemens visited the well-to-do Langdon family, and stayed to admire their daughter Olivia, whom he married two years later. For at least twenty years, the family summered at Quarry Farm, where Clemens, now popularly known as "Mark Twain," wrote many of his most famous works, including *Life on the Mississippi*, *The Adventures of Tom Sawyer* and *Adventures of Huckleberry Finn*. Though a global traveler, lecturer, and pundit, Twain loved Elmira and, following death in 1910, his body was returned to rest alongside Olivia and their deceased children in Woodlawn Cemetery.

Clemens was likely the first figure of national fame to emerge from the city, though there would be many others, such as football superstar Ernie Davis, Hollywood producer/director Hal Roach, astronaut Col. Eileen Collins and NBC news anchor Brian Williams. Economic prosperity provided a fertile soil for growth in the arts, and it seemed natural that, in 1925, Elmira should become a pioneer in presenting "talking pictures." Within a few years, the vaudeville business was rapidly losing ground, though crowds thronged to the 2,500-seat Keeney Theater on State Street. Warner Brothers Pictures purchased the money-making operation in 1930. Then, over two decades, came a decline, when television debuted in the early 1950s, and audience numbers slackened. Warners then sold to J.P. Dipson, who changed the building's name to The Elmira Theater, and spent over a quarter of a million dollars in renovating the place, installing air conditioning, new chairs, furnishings, and completely re-flooring the theater.

Just twenty years later a great flood, part of the backside of Tropical Storm Agnes, whipped the Chemung Valley, sending the river seventeen feet above flood level and engulfing half of Elmira in a flood. Many businesses, homes and stores were ruined and President Nixon called it the "greatest natural disaster to hit America" up to that time. Even then, having sustained major damage, the theater was renovated, repaired and was back in the movie business by Christmas. It was not long, however, before the old Keeney Theater faced a new crisis.

Transportation experts decided Elmira needed an arterial highway to connect Routes 17 and 328, and only a mobilized civic outcry prevented the old theater from being fully demolished to provide the right-of-way. The main structure was preserved and completely renovated, though the arterial route claimed the original theater's front wall and four hundred seats. The Clemens Center (The Samuel L. Clemens Performing Arts and Community Center) opened in October 1977 alongside the Clemens Center Parkway. It has been a center of community pride, as one nationally-known performer or group after another has graced its stage.

Sometimes, the performances are by the not-yet-widely-knowns. There is a major dance recital by dance students in the city every May, and it was at a rehearsal for one of those in 1999 that 10 year-old Emily emerged with big eyes. "Grandma," she said to her elder, "I've got to talk to you—outside." Frances led her granddaughter outside, where the girl asked earnestly, "Can this place be *haunted*?"

"Well, maybe," Frances replied. "It is an old theater built way back in the 1920s. It was called 'The Keeney Theater' when I was a little girl. Why do you ask?"

"When I walked past the back stairs that lead up to the lights, I looked up and saw a beautiful lady in a fancy, long blue dress. I think she had her hair long, in ringlets. She just stood there a minute, smiled at me, then disappeared," Emily told her.

"I remembered that Emily had seen her dead grandfather, who had died six years before her birth, when she was three, so I thought it possible that she had seen a ghost. But whose? Hundreds and hundreds of actresses must have played on that stage," Frances remarked. "So it wasn't until after the dance recital a few weeks later that we followed it up. Emily came out of the backstage and, again, told me she had seen the same woman's face *on a wall.* It had scared her because the face suddenly faded away. We decided that we had to get to the bottom of it, and went to the box office for more information.

"A nice woman there smiled at her and then said confidentially that 'the theater *is* home for three ghosts: two women and one man. One is the spirit of a woman who worked here for many years and just didn't want to leave her work when she died. She requested and was granted a wish to have some of her ashes placed in the theater after her cremation. Tell me, Emily, can you describe the person?' My granddaughter gave a perfect description of the woman," Frances smiled. "The box office lady smiled and agreed that Emily *had* seen the woman's spirit. The employee didn't say anything about the other lady or the man, so we didn't learn who *they* might be," Frances laughed.

I have encountered many young folks who see spirits, and it pleases them when an apparition can be identified as a deceased person associated with a house or church or theater. I interviewed several people in Elmira and found an old timer who smiled at my request for information. "It is said," he told me, "that a long-time member of the theater's pit orchestra, a woman who loved the good times she had at the Clemens, requested that her ashes be deposited in the theater after her death. I don't know if that's what happened, but the gracious woman you describe just might be her."

Then I asked about the other man and woman. Again, my informant smiled. He had known many of the stage crew and box office staff over the last quarter century and had heard many tales of others. He showed me copies of old newspaper clippings from the Keeney Theater days. "Now those other two—here's what comes to mind. There was a former stage hand, a man who loved his work. He loved associating with talented people who make beauty in our world. Let's call the guy 'Mike.' On the shows that Mike worked, his wife always came and sat somewhere in the house, enjoying the productions, but also supporting her husband's career in a way, too. If you have a man and a woman hanging around, maybe it's Mike and his wife, still enjoying the current productions."

That sounded right to me, as I've interviewed many theater folks, both performers and stage crews over the years. Many theaters are said to be haunted, but not so much in a scary way. There is a great mixture of both positive and negative energy that goes into making a production successful. The little girls that I saw readying for their dance recital in late May, 2006, were just as nervous about doing things right as Ella Fitzgerald must have felt when she was the first artist to perform in the new Clemens Center on October 22, 1977. Both dark emotions and beautiful ones often tie the deceased to the earth for a while. Funny, isn't it?

The Night Man

Old Fire Station #4

In the late 1970s in Amsterdam, NY, a strange event occurred at Fire Station #4 at the corner of Bunn and Chestnut Streets. While the experience was a unique one for the firefighter, there are dozens of such stories that are told at fire stations throughout the U.S. and Canada.

It was a late fall evening, and there had been no alarms all day for the crews at Station #4. Maybe this will be a quiet night, thought fireman Joe when he came on duty for the night shift. His partner, Sam, was already there and the two greeted one another with a nod and mumbled, "Hi ya." The evening passed quietly and around 10 p.m., Joe chose to go upstairs to the bunk area and get some sleep until there was an alarm.

"I drifted off to sleep pretty quickly," he said, "and slept like a log until what I judge was about 3 a.m. Then, some noise brought me almost awake; probably Sam moving around. I heard the door downstairs open and footsteps coming slowly up the stairs. Sam sounds tired, I thought—serves him right for staying up so late. At the time, however, it didn't occur to me that I hadn't heard the buzzer. You see, we have a buzzer on that door, so we can hear when someone opens it up.

"The footsteps continued out into the kitchen area, where the man moved around quietly. What's he want to eat at *this* time of the night, I remember thinking and absent-mindedly looked over at Sam's bunk. *He lay there asleep!* While I was trying to clear my head and figure out this mystery, and while I was still looking at Sam's sleeping body, I heard the footsteps exit the kitchen and come toward our bunks. I cleared my eyes to look at the figure that now stood beside my bed.

"It was a man, I'm sure of that, but I couldn't see any details because he was like thick white smoke, shrouded in white. The guy looked down at me. I started to get up and ask him who he was and what he was doing in the station at this time of night. But a hand came out of his clothes or shroud and moved toward me, and all at once, I felt a firm but friendly pressure on my chest, and I was pinned on the bed. He looked once more directly at me, then backed up, and went out the door. I didn't hear footsteps going downstairs, and when I jumped out of bed, I found the bunk area and kitchen were empty. I had to pinch myself to make sure I wasn't sleeping and dreaming. Nobody's going to believe this, I concluded—even Sam, because he slept through the whole thing! I'd better keep this to myself."

And he did, as so many first-time ghost experiencers do. Without a witness, most people tend to dismiss such narrations. "Only years later, just before I retired," he said, "when a bunch of the guys were sitting around talking, someone told another such story, so I felt safe enough to tell mine. And, you know what? Nobody laughed or poked fun at me. It seems like every one of them was willing to believe that some long-dead fireman, a guy who had answered his last call, had returned to the station, if just for a few minutes, to check up on something and then left. We never saw the figure again."

Under the Surface

Can ghosts go underground? Sure, I believe they can go almost anywhere a living being can go, and probably even to other places where we cannot venture. How would such a question come up?

Probably the most famous underground attraction in New York State is Howe Caverns in Schoharie County. Travelers find signs advertising the site all over the state, and the prospect of venturing over one hundred feet underground to find a magical environment has been tempting to most of us. Every year 170,000 visitors take the underground tour and admire the beautiful vista from the guest lodge. In fact, curious sightseers have been coming to this spot since 1842, and this year should produce the fifteen millionth visitor.

Early cavern explorer c. 1880

The Iroquois knew of *Otsgaragee*, the Great Valley Cave, but it was farmer Lester Howe who discovered the phenomenon of cold air blowing from the ground, searched, and found the cave entrance, then publicized it all in 1842. Clearing debris from the mile and a half long chamber by lantern and gaslights, Howe commenced operation of a sightseeing attraction that became almost as famous as Niagara Falls. However, the scenic subterranean limestone formations offered not only spectacular sights, but prehistoric limestone beds that attracted commercial interests. Investors sought the ground limestone of the nearby prehistoric reef for commercial purposes, and in time, Howe had to sell out.

In 1929, a modern corporation opened a new entrance, electrified the site, installed walkways and elevators, and Howe Caverns reopened, untouched by industry, and became even more famous. Thousands of school children visit the attraction, as I did with a group in the early 1950s.

In spring 2006, I met a man named John who is associated with the enterprise. I asked if maybe old Mr. Howe still lurked in his caverns. John was quiet for a minute, then responded, "Maybe. Why don't you come down and see?" So I did, arriving on a beautiful day in May. I met staff members Rob and Mark, each with a responsibility for day-to-day operations there. I asked my question outright, "Is there a ghost or two here?" The two admitted that they didn't know, as such a disclosure wasn't part of the tour guides' narration, but each knew of odd occurrences underground.

Rob, in charge of opening the attraction and doing an inspection each morning, attested to the fact that every person in his crews who performs these daily operations and who turns on the underground lights, has had eerie sensations in the 175 foot-deep chambers. Is it the extreme quiet or the absolute blackness of the pit? Is it the atmospheric pressure? "In the early morning and in the darkness there, one can only hear the *shushing* of the underground stream that is eight feet deep in places, tumbling down to lower subterranean levels." We chatted about that sound's similarity to the "white sound" (similar to the noise in-between television or radio stations) that can have a hypnotic effect. Some individuals (not at Howe Caverns) have experimented with white sound to produce out-of-body excursions or altered states of consciousness, and some strange psychic phenomena can result. Is *that* what happens to the morning crew? Or are there spirit entities at work? "That eerie feeling, when alone way underground, is what my workers report without exception," Rob told me.

Mark, sitting thoughtfully as he listened, smiled. His experience was *definitely* more uncanny. "I was working from the back of a boat at the Lake of Venus by myself, and everything went fine until, suddenly, there was an icy chill on the back of my neck. I half-turned to see who or what it might be, and caught brief sight of a human figure dressed in a light blue coat or shirt, but it vanished

Caverns visitors today

before I could recognize who or what it might be." That was it—his one possible ghost encounter.

In ghost hunting, we first attempt to see if a spirit visitation arises from a calamity at that spot, so I asked the pair if anyone had ever died in the caverns. "Two men," Rob told me. "Back in 1930, the mining operations way beyond our area dumped a mixture of noxious gasses into the cavern, and Owen Wallace, 35, an electrician working down there, went unconscious and wasn't missed for some time. Then John Sagendorf, an officer of the corporation, discovered Wallace missing and descended via the elevator to search for him. Sagendorf, however, was also overcome by the gas, and it was almost twelve hours before a rescue team could venture underground, only to find the men dead. So that's it," Rob explained. "Only two casualties in a single accident over 75 years ago." We speculated for a while as to whether either man might still remain in spirit at those depths.

The second approach in ghost hunting, if the evidence for a local death cause is scanty, is to ask the percipients if someone in their personal family died shortly before the incident. Mark raised his eyebrows at that query, "*Yes!*" he exclaimed. "Shortly before my experience, my uncle died, and then my grandmother." I asked if Mark felt the vaporous figure behind him in the boat had been female or male, and he felt sure that it was male. "So, you think it was my uncle?" he asked. In the end, that became our working hypothesis. Loved ones *do* have ways of finding us to say goodbye, high in the sky or deep underground.

266

I have had several such experiences of close friends or relatives passing on, only to return to contact me. I'm a sensitive, so it doesn't surprise me that these deceased individuals find me "open" to their contact. As I've said countless times in this book, the newly-deceased most often want to let loved ones know that they have passed and are okay. After that notification, many then feel they can depart for the distant regions. So a person might have but one visit or notification before the loved one leaves for good.

But there is a third theory to consider here—a matter of energy. "How long have the caverns been lit?" I asked. "Since 1929, there has been electric lighting each day," Mark said. We chatted a bit about the emotions of those countless millions of people who have encountered utter darkness down below. "Do you think they are fearful?" I asked. Both men agreed that a small percentage of visitors get claustrophobic or nervous down in the caverns. "Once in a while, in the old days, if there was an electrical failure during a thunderstorm, for example," Rob suggested, "the lights might have been off for up to ten minutes before the auxiliary generator cut in." That sure would give a person quite an experience of anxiety, especially knowing that the electrically-run elevators couldn't take them back to safety above ground any time soon.

"Of course, that long-term darkness doesn't happen anymore," Mark offered. "We now have an instant switch-over of generators if ever the main power goes off, so there is maybe a six-second gap when the lights are off, but that's all." We talked for a while about the fear energy expended below over the one hundred sixty-five years of operation. It is known that fear or anger energy can build up and remain stationary, and even cohere, thus becoming very detectable by sensitive people. Psychics who travel with me often encounter such clouds of negative energy. It is also possible that such residual vibrations might be a cause for the morning crew's unease. There is always the chance that such fear or dread might continue to accumulate, to reinforce that already present in a visitor's emotions.

That pretty much exhausted the possibilities. *Did* Howe Caverns ever have a ghost? Certainly—Mark felt and observed it. Was the ghost a prior inhabitant of the Caverns? Almost certainly not, because of the proximity of Mark's family deaths to the time of his experience. But might there be something really subtle there? *Might* the spirits of the two deceased individuals from April 24th, 1930, linger? The staff and I couldn't answer that, and I didn't have a psychic with me that day.

More than likely, in the years ahead, sensitive visitors will have to discover that answer for themselves. And one has to *visit* Howe Caverns to even begin speculating. Book your trip and let me know.

CHAPTER 10

APARTMENTS AND RENTALS

Remnants

The Old Van Guilder House

"Hey, David, I know a guy that owns a house that he's afraid to go into; you oughta check it out," a friend said. It took me some time, but I did just that, arranging for my intuitive friend, Sue, to accompany me.

Craig Fountaine's family has farmed a piece of land in the Town of Hartford in Washington County, NY, for over two hundred years. An old, faded red, dilapidated house, formerly a tenant farm-helper house now posted against trespassers, sits on a hillock not far off Route 149. The Fountaines live in a more modern house about five hundred yards away to the south. Across the road from the older house is an apparently modern barn. And surrounding it, acres of corn fields. Craig smiled when I told him that I heard he feared to enter the old house.

"Well, come take a look inside the door," he said, beckoning Sue and me. He unlocked the old portal, and we peered inside. The small, dark southern wing had a floor cluttered with discarded items, old bags of fertilizer, and lots of dust. "This is the only safe floor to walk on" he said. "Look to your left." We saw that the better part of the first floor on our left had collapsed into the cellar, and, overhead, we observed some of the upstairs floor about to tumble into the old downstairs living room. It was easy to see why even a sure-footed person might fear to wander about.

As we entered the house, Craig went first, followed by Sue. From behind the pair, I spotted a hulk of a man against the back wall, or at least I *thought* I did. He had shoulder-length black hair, a sturdy figure not over five and a half feet tall. The entity just stood with no facial expression, and then he disappeared. As these things go, one is never really sure *what* one has seen, and it is easy to attribute such visions to "imagination." Yet, as we got fully inside, I could see an old door frame where the figure had stood. If he was real, the man sure stood in the right place to have just entered. Craig later showed me the stump of an old apple tree outside that door and related a tale that neighbors had told him. Van Guilder, the tenant, and his wife apparently took out their frustrations and anger on that tree, walking outside the rear door and repeatedly striking the once-living tree with sticks and other objects. Curiously, this is a therapeutic tactic offered by some modern psychotherapists.

At the same instant, Sue had the impression of Native Americans, either there along with us, or as a part of the land's history. This didn't surprise her, as she often gets "previews" of people or sounds or other incidents that she will encounter. In this case, two days earlier, she suspected Indians would be involved. Susan's perception was that "he was very protective of the land and didn't want anybody else there. He guarded the land of his ancestors." She also felt someone urging us to "Get out!", though no sounds were audible to Craig or me. Her clairaudient abilities detected heavy footsteps upstairs, someone yelling "Hey!", and a loud bang. Just junk in here, I observed, and, not hearing those sounds, I went outside to more closely inspect Craig's old house, which he noted hadn't been inhabited since the late 1950s.

Glancing at an upstairs window, I observed a woman watching me. Her hair was pulled back, and she wore a light blue dress and apron—a typical olden-times farm wife. She didn't move, so I circled left around the house. I half-heard a discussion taking place in the side and rear rooms of the house, perhaps the old kitchen. In my mind, I saw a man seated at a kitchen table, dejectedly explaining to his wife that *they* needed to plant more corn in order to have enough silage for the winter. Her response sounded to me very depressed, as if the couple were attempting to hold on to the little they had. Craig later explained that corn was the likely crop of choice for the last hundred years on this land, and that the last occupants, the Van Guilders, had barely gotten by as tenant farmers on his father's land.

Sue asked the owner about the house's history. He told of an old map that showed a house, near the present barn and a dug well, owned by the Chandler family in the 1800s. The house caught fire in the late 1800s, and Mr. Chandler lost both his wife and daughter in the blaze. "Yes," Craig explained, "when I excavated to pour footings for this barn, I found old charred wood not too far beneath the surface. It must have been very sad for Mr. Chandler."

Once more, we turned our attention to the old red house, which we were beginning to call "the Van Guilder house." "When I was a teenager, I had a recurrent dream of being chased from here and over toward where our present house is. Something fearful was pursuing me with a large hammer. Later, when my wife and I were dating, we sat in our car one night right there," Craig said, pointing to the grass-covered driveway in front of us. "All at once, we heard loud footsteps over on the deck of the new house, but we knew nobody was home over there. We got out to investigate, and then realized the sounds were coming from the *tenant house* upstairs. We didn't go in," he said with a grin. He told of later finding a bag of diatomaceous earth, which he had stored in the old Van Guilder house, ripped open; the contents spread all over the downstairs that we had just visited together. "It was covered with animal tracks, so we attributed the destruction to a raccoon or other animal, but we still wondered...," his voice trailed off.

Craig shared other experiences with us. In the early 1990s, he was often at sea for six months at a time. On one such trip, he met an English woman whose job was stressful, and she expressed a desire for a quiet "getaway." He invited her to spend some time at their farmhouse, and, before she left Hartford, he took a photo of her standing in front of the old red house. Upon returning from a voyage, he ventured to the abandoned, old dwelling and observed that the main beam supporting the second story had severely cracked. His family decided to remove any valuables from the structure in case the house collapsed, and friends and family helped in the effort.

About six months later, while visiting with Theresa, a psychometrist who feels vibrations in objects, he gave her the picture to see what the woman might get about the English friend standing near the tenant house. Theresa had never visited the farm and knew nothing of the tenant house or its history. "Okay, who's mad at you?" Theresa asked. "Someone or something in this house is *very* angry at you." He had no knowledge of who resented him or why, but it was more information about the house which made him uncomfortable.

A few months later, his face covered with a respirator, Craig swept and cleaned the southern part of the old house's floor, taking away anything that might be of value. His mother assisted him and removed many old pieces of glassware that she took to the rear deck of the new house for cleaning. He worked on alone, pushing his broom, and suddenly became aware that he wasn't alone. Right in front of him, where he had pushed the broom dozens of times, there appeared a corn cob! Obviously, someone was signaling him, but he couldn't determine the message. When he returned home, his mother complained that some of the glass pieces from the Van Guilder house were mysteriously missing from the back deck, where she had just been washing them. They never showed up again.

After relating these experiences, Craig invited Sue and me to the barn across the road. Once we entered, we could see that only the exterior siding was new. The basic structure was old post and beam framing. My attention was immediately drawn to the ladder leaning against the loft floor. My imagination (or *was* it?) saw a man dangling on a rope alongside the ladder. For the moment, I decided to refrain from speaking about it. Sue and Craig talked about various building features. Suddenly, Sue turned to me and, almost apologetically, said, "I just don't know, but there is something *very* upsetting about that loft—almost as if someone died up there." I then told them of my sighting. Craig said there was a strong suspicion that old Chandler may well have done away with himself after the tragedy that struck his home and family. So, perhaps....

Craig told us that he had barely known the Van Guilders, but he had been told that they had Native American ancestry. Sue brightened when she heard that, since she sensed a pre-European occupation of the land by the Indians, likely Mohawks. She felt that the Indian presence is still strong, perhaps constellated in the anger of old Van Guilder, unable to make a living on land that once offered nature's bounty to his ancestors.

The old red house seems filled with desperation, the three of us agreed. A sense of failure hangs over the old building. And, across the road, the image still remains of another failure, a hanging man done in by his inability to face misfortune. Each of these situations has the makings of a haunting. Many of *our* homes and places of work can also retain depressive feelings launched long ago by our forbearers, and a wise person must take action to protect him or herself from that negativity. A daily prayer of protection is easy to do.

When I was a smart-alecky young man in my twenties, fortified by my college degree and the supposition that I knew life's full meaning, I believed that prayer was only for the weak, inept, and foolish. My experiences with haunted sites, however, have taught me the necessity of prayer and "surrounding oneself with the White Light" before venturing into places of others' misery. Susan never goes into these situations without such spiritual preparation. Neither of us wants to carry away afflictions that aren't ours. After leaving the old Van Guilder house, we each said a prayer for the peace of the grieving former inhabitants.

Russell

"In 1969, I found a small apartment at 67 E. Main Street in Fredonia," Wayne Mori told me. "Today, I will tell you that I do not believe in ghosts. That said, I still can't explain the events of my next few years there." During the years of his rental, Wayne remembers living in each of the three apartments in what had been the single-family home of a city judge. The man was a politi-

Russell's House

cian whose name Wayne can no longer remember, but he recalls that the former owner had once been Fredonia's Postmaster.

"When I moved in, I took the small apartment upstairs, one of two on the second floor. An older man rented the other, larger second floor apartment. On occasion, there were unexplained noises, odd sounds at times, but the other guy would laugh them off with, 'That's just Russell.' I had no idea who Russell was, but I knew no other male lived in the house, just an old landlady downstairs. If the other tenant was suggesting we had a ghost, I wanted no part of it."

Wayne had no unexplained events in his apartment until he went home to Pennsylvania for Christmas one year. A dedicated Christian, he kept a small crucifix fastened to his wall above the kitchen table. Returning from vacation, he found the cross balanced upside down on the table. It seemed illogical that the crucifix could have tumbled from the wall, flipped one hundred eighty degrees, and come to rest on its narrow top. Wayne began to worry that, indeed, some unknown presence *did* abide there. "I had been interested in spiritism because we lived not far from the Spiritualist center at Lily Dale, and, yes, I had attempted some parlor tricks with upside down glasses, but if those efforts attracted spirits to *my* house, I wanted no part of it and swore off such attempts at holding a séance.

In time, the other upstairs lodger became ill and had to move to a nursing home, leaving the larger upstairs apartment available for Wayne, who jumped with some apprehension at the opportunity. He welcomed the additional room, but he was a bit worried because the older gentleman had often spoken of strange lights moving about in that apartment. He also had offered a remedy, however. "Just tell Russell to go away." So, with that in mind, Wayne moved down the hall and waited. He lived there for two years with no unexplained occurrences. Then, the elderly landlady also had to move to a nursing home, making the larger downstairs apartment with wonderful high ceilings available.

"And that's when the fun started," he recalls. "First, there were the sounds, almost as if another person was moving about in the same space with me—an invisible person. I'd awake in the morning to find the lamp turned up bright. I know I couldn't have gone to sleep at night with that light on, so I now knew some of the stories I'd heard had some validity, but I continued to seek a logical explanation.

"At that time, one of the upstairs apartments was rented to a young woman named, Audrey, who came downstairs to chat with me one day while I entertained an old buddy from Michigan. The three of us sat talking in the living room. All at once, we heard the heavy front door open, someone entered, and the door closed. The person stomped his feet in the foyer and footsteps then crossed the foyer to my downstairs door. We wondered who it was and noted the shadow of two legs or feet beneath the hall door. Audrey got up to see who it was, but when she opened the door, nobody was there. And we'd heard no one walk away either! That was probably the strangest event I experienced there.

"Another time when the small upstairs apartment was vacant and a man lived in the larger one, I sat reading in my downstairs living room. I heard the front door open again, then close. I then heard slow and heavy footsteps climb the stairs and shortly thereafter, walk across the floor of the rented apartment upstairs, though I knew it couldn't be the tenant, as he came home much later." And, of course, Wayne found no one in his own apartment.

"I returned from a trip at a later date, when a policeman had just rented the small upstairs room, and the larger upstairs room was vacant. The cop was quite shaken up; telling me that he'd been alone in the house one night, when he heard noises both upstairs and down. He grabbed his service pistol and explored the entire house so he could find some peace, though he found nobody and nothing out of place. When he related this experience to me when I returned, I said, 'Oh yes, I forgot to tell you about Russell.' I won't try to describe the face he made in return."

What caused Wayne to half-believe in Russell was an encounter with an elderly neighbor who told him she'd been in the Main Street house. Wayne was surprised, until she said her visit had been sometime around 1906 when she was a girl. She remembered the Judge and his crippled son, Russell, who was moved about in a wheelchair pushed by a male nurse. She didn't think the boy had lived much longer after her visit.

The elderly landlady may have been a member of the Judge's family, Wayne thinks. If true, little Russell, after encountering the Angel of Death, may have declined the invitation to move into The Light, preferring to mature and age as a fully able man in "his house," with only an occasional signal to the strange apparitions he found living there with him. Perhaps he also was drawn to the older woman.

Today, Wayne no longer lives in Fredonia and has, in fact, entered a profession where he can exercise his spiritual beliefs fully. He understands that there *is* another life, but he is still hesitant to believe that it can be lived as a *ghost*.

"See? I told you!"

Helen was born in Astoria, Queens, in the 1950s and received a traditional Catholic grade school education, but that schooling never prepared her for her own experiences with the world of spirit. "My mother died when I was quite young, but somehow, I always knew she was there for me, and I talked to her in my prayers at night. I also felt her strong presence after I married and had my first baby. The delivery room was so filled with the scent of flowers, and nobody could figure out why. *I* knew," she told me.

In the 1970s, she and her husband moved to a two-apartment house in Jackson Heights. She has blotted out many of the details of that time, including the street, but thinks their apartment was on 74th Street. "From the time we moved into that place, I was afraid to be alone. I often told my husband that I was fearful, but we had a big Doberman dog, and my husband consoled me that the dog would protect me from anything harmful.

"I wasn't sure of that. I know I'm a sensitive woman. When I was a girl, I awoke one night and saw a dark figure seeming to sit on my dresser. He vanished. Instinctively, I knew it was someone or something bad, but it wasn't until the next day that I began to understand what it might mean. A young boy was hit and killed, beaten by boys with bats, down on street level beneath my window. So I always equated these dark figures or even the 'smoke' that I often see now that I'm older, with the likelihood that something bad is going to happen."

At the house in Jackson Heights, she told me, her husband sometimes got work as a bartender on the night shift, so she had to be alone with the children. "I kept trying to convince him that there was something bad in the apartment, but he pooh-poohed it. One day, I made him a sandwich; after he'd eaten it, he put the plate on top of the TV. Well, in just a minute, the plate flipped up into the air and fell onto the floor. 'See? I told you that there's something going on here,' I told him. He kept trying to explain it away rationally. The next day, I found the kitchen cupboards open and cups kept falling out and into the sink. We needed help!

"One of the hardest things to bear there was the moaning sounds I'd hear when I was relaxing on the couch. It sounded so evil. And there was no logical explanation for its source. When that happened and my husband wasn't there, I'd always get up, turn on the lights and call a friend…just to stay connected with somebody. Believe it or not, my husband knew a woman that they called a 'witch,' even though she used her abilities to help people. I had him invite her over; I couldn't stand the goings-on much longer."

Helen told me that the woman arrived the next day, walked through the apartment, and said Helen and her husband had to get out for their own good. "'There is some very bad energy here' the lady said. She asked if I had any candles, then lit one, and put it in the afflicted room. 'Go for a walk; go somewhere for a couple of hours,' she instructed us. 'But before you go, do you have a crucifix?' I got her one, and she tied it around the neck of a huge teddy bear that I had in *that room*. She then closed the door and we all left.

"About three hours later, we returned and found the teddy bear standing in the corner of the room. On the floor, we found the crucifix—bent!" Apparently, Helen and her family had met up with one of the darker ghosts or spirits, which *do* exist, though in relatively small numbers. In such a case, the only option is to get a professional to cleanse the house and send the spirit on its way. An exorcism can be performed, though these don't always have to be done by a Catholic or Episcopal priest. Some spirits are devilish in their behavior, and the cause for this activity is very base and dark. This is an issue that the average, well-meaning person (even an untrained clergy member) is poorly equipped to handle, no matter how altruistic their motives are or how sincere their spiritual beliefs and faith are.

The next day, Helen's husband gave the landlord their notice and the pair left, finding a new and quieter home in Copiague on Long Island. "Things are much more serene here," Helen told me. There are no more moans or spirited flinging of dinnerware. "But I still see what looks like smoke or fog," she told me. "And, it's usually a notification that someone is in trouble."

Helen related other strange activities at the Jackson Heights apartment, when she would look into the bathroom mirror and see strange reflections. Were they of her? Or of a spirit entity? Because of her visionary abilities, I suggested that Helen get some training in the positive use of her psychic abilities. As she lives close to New York City, I referred her to the people at the A.R.E. Holistic Center at 241 W. 30th St. in Manhattan, which conducts classes and conferences on various elements of spiritual development. Most of their big programs are on Sunday afternoons, when Big Apple residents have time to attend and study. The phone number there is (212) 691-7690. One can expect a wholesome and spiritual approach to psychic ability in these courses and classes based in the psychic readings of Edgar Cayce, one of the great spiritual teachers to emerge in the U.S..

Helen said she'd take me up on this fresh and positive approach. In the meantime, she still talks to her mother in prayer, thanking that woman for giving birth to her and attending the birth of her first grandchild.

Staying Over?

"I searched for a new apartment closer to work and found a nice one on Ocean Avenue in Brooklyn, on the fifth floor. The apartment had a lot of nice features such as a big arch leading into a large living room. There were two bedrooms, one each for my dad and myself," Mary told me. A professional woman in her late thirties, she told me that she had first become interested in ghosts when she had taken a walking ghost tour in New Orleans a few years before. Subsequently, she had begun to read accounts of hauntings on many Internet websites, seeking locations on Long Island that might be explored.

"With this change of residence, I didn't realize at first that I was going to live with at least one such spirit, an individual that had stayed over from another time. The building seems to date from the 1930s, and when the superintendent showed me around, I immediately felt 'some leftover energy.' I asked him if someone had recently died there, and he told me that the previous tenants had a grandfather who had lived with them for a while, but that he needed a nursing home and later died there. I didn't feel as if that old man was the one remaining, however," she told me.

"When the superintendent showed me the apartment, I had a sense of not being alone. Edgy at first as I moved in, I didn't sleep there at night, as I still had some time left on my former apartment's lease. When I had first inspected the place, I noted that the closet door didn't quite close, but I figured that could be fixed. I also noted the same situation with the bathroom door, though if Dad or I were inside, we could lock it to insure privacy. It had all looked doable, so I signed the lease in May of 2005."

When the phenomena began, Mary noted the orientation of the building, which is situated on the east side of the busy thoroughfare. At certain times of day, the sun's light is fleetingly reflected by passing traffic, as the windows all face Ocean Avenue. Such reflections are possible in the morning and early afternoon, but she doesn't return from work until dinnertime, so she ruled out the sun as a possible cause for any of the strange phenomena.

"For a few months, when I heard tapping or other noises, I had to learn which came from upstairs, which from downstairs, and which came up from the street. Many times, the tapping noises seemed to emanate from inside the living room, but at first I blew them off, ignoring them. One morning at breakfast, my father reported that he'd had the strangest experience during the night. His bedroom is at the back, at the end of the hallway, and he reported that it was as if three people circled his bed in the night, inspecting him in the darkness. It was as if the intruders were thinking or saying, 'Who's *this* guy?'"

Though she and her cat had undergone some emotional trauma at a previous apartment (a fire in which several people on lower floors had died) and the two had been scared by the sirens, loud noises, and disruption, her tomcat, Whiskers, is now at peace in the new location. "At least, he *was*!" Mary continued. "I guess one would say this apartment is a 'work in progress.' Though I smudged this place with sage and did other cleansing rituals to chase off any former negativity, someone or something is still here. From time to time, Whiskers will stop, suddenly stare up into the air, hiss, and then run away. He usually ends up under the covers of my bed, where he stays for hours. With the passage of each month, I have new episodes."

Mary noted that she likes to keep the new home clean and feels that things are quiet for some time after each cleansing. One day recently, she swept the kitchen floor, cleaned the counter and did the dishes. Only a small bowl remained in the sink, and she later dropped a fork into it. Moving to the other room a few minutes later, she heard a tapping sound from the kitchen. Cautiously, she went there and discovered the cold water running slowly onto the fork, causing it to oscillate up and down, making the tapping sound. "Now, I know for sure that I had turned off both the hot and cold water before I'd left the kitchen." I related several stories for her of ghosts manipulating both water and electricity, so she understood that such phenomena are fairly normal, though there *is* a ghost involved.

"Another happening, something I've noticed since the month I moved in, is that something small and dark seems to scoot across the hardwood floors of the hallway or living room. Can't be a mouse, I'd tell myself, because Whiskers would get him. One evening, when the lights were low and I was seated in the living room, I saw the black object dart across the archway and underneath an end table. Looking over, I could make out the dark shape and two green eyes watching me. Figuring it was Whiskers, I didn't react immediately. But when I looked out in the kitchen, I could see my cat underneath the kitchen table, staring intently at the shape in the living room. Then, suddenly, I couldn't see that form any more. At work the next day, I told a friend about the event, and she surmised that I needed to do a new cleansing of the energies in the apartment."

From time to time, Mary hears walking on the floors which, as there are no carpets, reflect all sounds. She is now certain that the noises don't come from upstairs. "One day, Dad came out of the bathroom and asked me what was up. I was puzzled and asked what he meant. He replied that I had been bumping against the outside of the bathroom door while he was in the shower. Of course, I denied it. Fortunately, he had the door locked." A few weeks later, in February 2006, she returned home after midnight and went to the bathroom lavatory. She heard the door thump, as if pushed against its frame. She looked out and saw Whiskers staring at the closed door of her father's bedroom. "It sounded as if someone or something inside was thumping that door, trying to get out! And I knew Dad was not here.

"When I'm in bed with my bedroom door open, I can only see halfway down the hall because that passage is curved. Sometime soon I really believe I'm going to see someone walking toward me. I've already imagined a figure in my mind: a man from the 1800s, about six feet tall and wearing a flat-top black hat, like an old cowboy hat." The energy seems to be getting stronger, and her house phones seem filled with static throughout daylight hours, though the phone company has investigated and finds nothing wrong."

I suggested a new cleansing ceremony, perhaps with several like-minded friends joining in. A bright light, preferably a candle, should be present. She should call all souls who are in the apartment to the living room, and lovingly, but forcefully send them on into The Light. That is where we left matters, and we're now awaiting the result.

Tenants

"I guess I've seen spirits since I was two years old," Laura Tyler told me. "I grew up in a house on Berlin Street in Binghamton, between the Conrail tracks and Spring Forest Cemetery. My older sisters had a sleep-over one night when I was four, and I watched them having fun. We had an old electric organ that had a broken plug, so it didn't work any more. In the midst of the party, the organ began to play by itself. Boy, were we all scared! How can something that's not plugged in get enough electricity to make music? It didn't make sense to me even at that age." She remembers running to tell her mother about the event when, suddenly, the organ stopped playing. She returned to the room, and the music began again. That phenomenon continued for an hour before stopping.

"There was always something going on there," she said. "One day my cousin, Jim, my sister, Lisa, and I walked near a lot that we called 'the dump' on Berlin Street where neighborhood people used to dump their lawn clippings and leaves because nobody lived there. As we walked along that day we saw a transparent man. It scared us because we could see trees in the background *through* him! But what scared us the most was that he had a rope or noose around his neck. When we ran home and told Mom, she thought we were kidding her, because a man *had* hanged himself there some time before. She thought I'd read it in the newspaper and didn't believe us. 'It looks like he didn't go very far after he died,' she sighed."

With the exception of the next house she lived in, Laura had visions and other scares in each building. When they moved to a house on Oak Street, Laura's cat was hit by a car. Just a few days later, while she sat in the living room with her sister, the cat's spirit shot through the room and disappeared. "The back room of that house was always ice cold, and I know we had a ghost there too, because I saw a man with brown hair and blue eyes just standing there once—he wasn't a family member. Sometimes, in the kitchen, we'd feel watched by some unseen person. Maybe it was the same man. It wasn't all scary, though," she told me.

"One night I had a premonition that my grandmother was going to die. I heard my dead grandfather's voice telling me that he was coming to get Grandma. And he did; she had a sudden heart attack and died. My Uncle Don, who lived with Grandma (and who doesn't believe any of this ghost stuff), later confided in me that he heard her walker clumping along the hallway in their house for quite some time after her death. Poor Uncle Don. I think he has some psychic ability, too, though he has no patience with that sensitivity. He used to live in Phoenix and shared with me his strangest experience there. Uncle Don had gone into a restaurant, sat down, then watched a man who was basically a skeleton come in and sit down. Boy, he zoomed out of there without even waiting to get a menu," she laughed.

Laura told me that she lived at 48 Howard Avenue in Binghamton in the mid-1990s and found strange experiences there, too. "The first odd thing I noticed in that house," she told me, "is that my animals would never go upstairs, but my dog would often look up there and bark, though I couldn't see anything.

"In May of 2005, my Mom and I bought our present home on Baxter Avenue, which is one hundred sixteen years old. I've come to know of at least three ghosts here: two I've seen, and one I've sensed. Within two weeks of moving in, I saw a little girl with brown hair and blue eyes who seems (by her clothing) to come from modern times. I have sighted her three times in all. The first time I saw her was in the living room, where she looked at me, then exclaimed, 'You can *see* me!'

'Yep, I sure *can*!' I told her before she disappeared."

I explained to Laura the isolation of most ghosts. Apparently, they are so focused on their own problems after dying, an event that they might not even accept, that they are unaware of other spirits nearby. How lonely they must be—in eternity, alone with their traumas, and unable to contact anyone who can help. Of course, if they would but turn, they'd see The White Light and spirit guides who'd help them onward, but most can not do this without help from the living. Ghosts get used to most living people ignoring or not seeing them. And *then*, along comes a sensitive individual such as Laura who can see and react to them. Probably both individuals are surprised, but that is the perfect time for the living to inform the ghost that *it has*, indeed, died and needs to move on.

Laura makes a genuine effort to understand the ghosts in her house, as she doesn't want her two little girls to be afraid of them. She has kept a journal since her first sighting, a book filled with numerous episodes that would frighten the average person. Her kitchen cabinets have opened and closed by themselves. And, though she listens to several types of music on the radio, whenever the song is hip-hop, the ghost seems to turn the radio off. In early May 2006, she contacted me to tell that she listened to hip-hop as she worked that morning. Suddenly, her stereo turned off again. Frustrated, she told the ghost to stop doing that, and it did; she enjoyed the music of her choice the rest of the afternoon. Later, she escorted her two young daughters to their grandmother's room for a nap. "I'll just turn on the TV for you until you get sleepy," she told the girls. Obligingly, the TV turned itself on!

"My daughters have a lot of toys upstairs," she told me. "From time to time, those toys just turn on and start making noise when nobody is up there. I guess the upstairs ghost must be the man that I saw looking at me from the top of the stairs one day recently. I got up to see who it was, and he just vanished." Sounds like a normal day on Baxter Street, I mused.

For the beginner investigating stories of ghosts, this story may not seem credible because of the great number of entities. My dowser friends, David Darrow and Tick Gaudreau, who clear spirits from houses, assure me that the population of the unseen world would astound the average person who has not made much study of that plane of existence. There appears to be a great continuum between the living and Paradise. There are those recently passed, those gradually moving upward in spirit, letting go of earthly attachments as they go, and then the old timers—those whose earthly attachments to objects, places, emotions, shame, revenge, etc. are very strong and act as chains such as Jacob Marley wore—metaphors for earthly greed that *owns us* in life, and which we cannot release by ourselves at death. Many religious scriptures warn about the accumulation of things, as they serve more to imprison our eternal being than to give us endless joy.

I found Laura to be a very perceptive woman, capable of seeing into the spirit world without fear. In our conversation, I detected a potential "healer" for troubled souls and have encouraged her to get professional training, perhaps from the instructors at Lily Dale Assembly in Lily Dale, NY. Wherever one lives in New York State, there are responsible teachers whose life work has been setting free the slaves of the netherworld. I've urged Laura to consider that liberation field as part of her own gift to others.

The Barn

In the summer of 2000, Maggie Ahrens and her family rented a house in the rural Montgomery County hamlet of Glen, NY. Behind the house stood an old barn that no longer housed livestock, though her family at first did not suspect what life *was* there. Her five children and two grandchildren, with a mix of childish energies, created a daily excitement of their own, playing in and around the old building.

One day, as Maggie hung clothes on a line in the backyard, her granddaughter, Sarah, and a neighbor boy, Dominic, played outside the barn with Maggie's four-year-old twins, Karis and Jordan. All at once, the girls screamed and the group ran fearfully to Maggie's side. "We saw a 'man shadow' wearing an orange shirt in the barn," they said with alarm. "Then he went away in the air," the youngsters exclaimed. The children knew nothing about ghosts and had no deep understanding of death. And where could they have learned a concept as abstract as "shadow people?"

"I told them to stay away from that barn because it was a dangerous place to play anyway," Maggie said, "but privately, I shuddered to think how many times *I* went down there in the dark to chop wood for our wood stove. I never saw anything, but I sure *felt* something, though I'd put it aside as just my vivid imagination."

The following spring, her son, Dan, worked with friends, repairing their dirt bikes in the barn, but, after the boys finished and returned to the house, Maggie noticed they had left the barn doors open, and sent the teens back to lock up for the night. "While you're down there, be sure to go inside and shut the storage room door too," she admonished. "Well, two minutes later, the three came running back to the house out of breath. Dan had a bump and a scrape on his head. Wide-eyed, he said the boys had gone into the barn and, turning to his left, he had spotted a man standing in the gloom—barely

282

there, but he was visible. The man had something, perhaps a magazine or newspaper, in his hands and stood in front of the window as if attempting to read it in the dim light. Dan ran out the door before he'd fully opened it, hitting his head, and the other two boys were right on his heels!"

After the second ghost incident in the barn, Maggie began to ask the neighbors about the history of the old farm. "They told me that, over fifty years ago, a farmer named Frank Wells had hanged himself in the barn at the spot where the youngsters had seen the shadow man. Then, on the other side, in the storage room, where Dan and his friends had seen the ghost reading, my landlady's second husband had died of a heart attack."

Spurred by the history of deaths and subsequent ghost appearances in her barn, Maggie sought information about ghost phenomena on the Internet. Following information she gleaned there, she bought a video camera and 35-mm. camera. A few months afterward, about 10 p.m., she decided the time was ripe to visit the barn and see what she could photograph. Her two oldest daughters, Ann and Jessica, decided to accompany her. Maggie chose to take some exterior shots of the barn before the trio entered. As Maggie clicked away, Jessica suddenly burst out, "Did you see *that?*" and began sprinting toward the house. Maggie and Ann were right on her heels, answering a breathless, "Yes!" On the safe porch, the three compared notes and agreed they had seen a man's head pop up in the barn window of the storage room, where Dan had seen the man reading.

That night, with Dan away and her two oldest girls off visiting with friends, Maggie began to be frightened and attempted to resume normal life by chatting with others logged onto an on-line gourmet food chat room. Suddenly, her enjoyment was interrupted by a neighbor's Instant Message, which popped onto her screen, informing her that Dan must have left the lights on in the barn. She knew there was *no electricity* connected to the barn, and, too frightened to visit the building alone, she called a neighbor to come help her, but by the time he arrived, the barn light was out.

A few weeks later, after videotaping the little kids' school play, Maggie emerged from the Fonda-Fultonville school and noticed an old cemetery on the left. As the burial ground had an entrance off the school's parking lot, Maggie and Ann decided to walk through the grounds and take some random video pictures, but begged Jessica to first go to the far entrance of the cemetery to watch them walk through. "It was about 9:30 p.m. and that was the first time I'd used the video camera, so I wasn't sure if I was doing everything correctly. All I could see through the viewfinder was pitch black, so after a while I turned it off. When we got home, Ann said we should look at the tape anyway, to see if we got any images at all. What we saw was enough to swear me off ghost hunting for good. The tape revealed small lights (orbs in motion) zooming all around us as we walked in the darkness, leaving light trails of some sort. But, mind you, we couldn't see these while we were walking, and they were visible only on the tape.

"That was it for me. I realized I was too amateur to ghost-hunt, though I still have all the books I bought. A short time after these events, we moved into Fonda. Each time we have moved since then, I get a few friends from my church, and we pray our way through any house we move into, and so far we haven't been bothered again by ghosts."

The Rental

"My grandfather, aunt, and uncle owned a nice old house at 85 North Forest Avenue in Rockville Center on Long Island, and I loved to visit them there. When I was a kid, about age ten," Theresa told me, "I first noticed the sound of footsteps going up and down the stairs. Everyone who lived there or visited there heard the walking at sometime or another. Then, one day, I noticed that nobody was on the stairs when I heard the walking, and at that age, I just didn't know what to make of it.

"After that, I sometimes got a strange feeling upstairs between the bedrooms and attic door, and one day, I noticed a woman standing there. I didn't know who she was or where she came from, but she stood motionless until she disappeared. I mentioned it to my aunt, and she told me that she, too, saw the woman appearing and disappearing at times. Whoever the ghost lady was, she never bothered anyone. She just came, stood there for a while, and then vanished. I'm sorry now that we never looked into the house's history, because I bet there is an interesting story there. Not too long afterward, my grandfather died, and then my uncle. So the house was put up for sale, and my aunt moved out. The house is still there, but I don't know if the ghost lady is there, too."

Theresa finished school and married and moved up the Hudson River to Hyde Park, and her husband commuted to New York City to work. After a while, however, Theresa's Long Island roots began to summon her back to 'The Island.' She reasoned with her husband that he could save some commuting time if they returned downstate, and they decided to try it again. The couple rented out their Hyde Park house and found a nice old rental house near Grand Avenue in No. Baldwin, not too far from the Long Island Railroad, and they moved there in 2001.

"It was a hot summer day when we moved in, and I sat on the front steps relaxing while my husband went to the corner store to buy subs and sodas. I had the doors all open, so I wasn't really surprised to hear the front door slam behind me. Breeze, I figured, so I stood and opened it up again. Soon after that, I sat down again, but then heard a bang from the living room. I got up and looked—three boxes had tipped over on the floor. Now, they hadn't been stacked up, yet they had mysteriously just turned over! As I sat down again, I reasoned that things shift during moving van rides—probably they had gotten top-heavy and just flipped. My husband wasn't that cool about it, however. When he got home and saw the boxes, he asked why I had turned them over, as they contained fragile objects. He was also concerned that I'd lifted heavy boxes, as I was just recovering from an operation. 'But, I didn't *touch* the boxes; they did it all by themselves,' I told him."

Her husband sat with her eating their snacks and trying to remember where the bedding had been packed, as they'd need pillows and blankets for that first night. "All at once, we heard the bathroom window slam shut. He figured that it could all be explained and went in, opened it up again, and put a paint stick in the opening to hold the window up. By the time he returned to the living room, we heard the window slam again. To make a long story short, it slammed again and again, perhaps five times, and he finally decided to leave it shut.

"We went to bed that night," Theresa told me, "and when we awoke in the morning, we found the window open with the paint stick sitting on the sink, a couple of feet away! Of course, he thought I'd done it, which I denied, and I thought that he had opened the window again, which *he* denied."

Eventually the couple got into the routine of the new house, sorting belongings, placing them in the proper rooms, and turning the rental into a real home. "Then, a couple of weeks later, I awoke to find a man standing at the foot of our bed," Theresa told me. "Nothing else, just standing there, and he had on an old-style Army uniform with tall black boots, a black hat, and some kind of a vest. I quickly woke my husband, as this sure didn't seem like a ghost. I thought we had an intruder! But my husband just couldn't *see* the guy. He got up and turned on the light and *still* couldn't see the man, though *I* still could, and I *know* I hadn't been dreaming. Then, I couldn't see him anymore, and he never was visible again, though I didn't know that would be true at that time. I spent several sleepless nights watching and waiting for him to return, but he just was gone. Eventually, I was able to sleep because I realized that the ghost had done nothing to me and hadn't attempted to scare me."

Perhaps a year later, Theresa remembers, her daughter was playing in her bedroom, when the child suddenly screamed and the bedroom door slammed shut. Why would she do *that*, Theresa wondered, and went to the child's room to open the door and ask. "The door wouldn't open. It wouldn't even budge an inch. It was as if the door were sealed shut, yet there were no locks on the door. I got a screwdriver and took the knob off but the door *still* wouldn't open. My daughter started to cry, and it suddenly all hit me at once. We had a ghost, and it was being mean! I got very upset and started yelling at whoever it was, 'You stop playing *now*! Open this door!' My poor daughter feared I was blaming her, and I had to tell her that I wasn't. I worked for an hour to open the door without success, and finally, as I stood there perplexed, the door just went 'pop' and opened itself. There was no indication of what had held it shut. My poor daughter was cringing on the other side of the room and I had to give her a big hug to comfort her. But I also knew that neither one of us had been responsible for that stuck door. So, who?

"Another night, my aunt was sleeping over in my son's room. In the middle of the night, we heard her scream. My husband and I dashed in, and there sat my terrified aunt with a big flowered hat on her head—but it wasn't hers! And it wasn't ours, either! None of us had any idea, even to this day, where that hat came from. We were just glad that she wasn't a frequent visitor to our house."

Theresa told me that, on another day, she had taken her children to school and came home to enjoy a nice cup of coffee while reading the daily paper in the kitchen. Suddenly, she heard a raucous banging downstairs. It got louder and louder, and, at first, she thought it was her sister, Linda, because Theresa had allowed Linda to store some furniture in the basement, but why was she making that *racket*? She yelled down to her sister and asked what was going on—no response, so she went down the stairs. Theresa found the place empty, but all the drawers were going in and out.

"I ran upstairs very fast and out the door, where I saw the neighbors. I asked whether somebody had died in the house, and eventually I found people who could tell me. Yes, they said, three people. One was an Army man long ago, in the Civil War times. A woman had killed herself there later on, and then a child who lived there had gotten killed in an auto accident. They all died at different times, but they were all members of a single family. The idea of the house being haunted surprised them, as they said they'd never heard a prior tenant complain. 'But,' one old woman said, 'none of those families ever stayed very long either.' So we gave our notice to Harry and moved out, back upstate!"

CHAPTER 11

MORE MYSTERY

Donna and Others

A psychic once said to me, "For a ghost, it's always the moment of death." I really didn't know what to do with that piece of information then, except to understand that ghosts exist in their own time, still trying to work out the particular problem that keeps them earthbound. Sometimes the issue is guilt, sometimes it's a denial that death has occurred and, even a feeling that all hope and promise (even that of Eternity) has been cut off. Here is a story from West Hempstead on Long Island that may incorporate all these elements.

Nancie Mangels is a fifty-year-old mother and wife who lives on Belmont Avenue in West Hempstead. "We are only the second family to live in the house, which was built in 1951," she told me. "The only tragic death to be associated with the former owners (who were related to me by my former marriage) was the death of a sixteen-year-old girl named Donna in the 1970s," Nancie told me. "Years ago, she got into a terrible argument with her mother, stormed out the door, got into a car and was killed in a horrible crash. We know it's her because, in the twenty-five years that our family has lived here, we have heard cries, doors slamming, and a female voice yelling out, 'Ma!' There is also stomping up and down the stairs that almost certainly comes from a petulant teenager." What is so fascinating to relatives is that Nancie *looks like* Donna.

One would expect this woman to be sensitive to this world of death and near-death, as she has been open to spirits since her early teenage years. At age twelve she complained to her mother that someone invisible was touching her. Just a short time later, she began to see the energy outline of a boy. Her mother told her that a younger brother, Zachary, had been born and died before her birth. Then, at age eighteen, Nancie developed a malignant condition and was rushed into surgery, where she died on the operating table— briefly. When she returned from that near-miss, she recalled her out-of-body sensations and realized that bodily death isn't the end.

"For a few years, I shared my psychic intuitions with people, doing readings for them. Nevertheless, I have had pressing personal issues to deal with in recent years," she told me. "Our family has learned to live with the entity that I'm sure is Donna, and who *has* been helpful at times. When a close personal friend of mine died suddenly and I sat grieving on the couch, I felt a gentle hand touching my shoulder and running invisible fingers through my hair, and I'm certain this is the gentle side of that girl." As we talked about the teenager, it seemed that the anger that Donna carried into the crash is still present at times in the house, frightening some who visit.

"One thing that upsets me is that after Donna died, and before I married my ex-husband, her family members planted a memorial tree for Donna in our backyard. It was there when I married and moved in, but I didn't know what it stood for. Years later, when the tree was 30 feet high, my husband cut it down and built a shed there. When I later learned that this tree had been a tribute to Donna, I was horrified, and I began to wonder if she is upset."

Some ghost experiences haven't been fun for Nancie's family. For example, her daughter, Katherine, was hit in the chin by an invisible object once, a concussion that left a physical bruise. When the girl brought school friends home, some of them had their hair pulled or were touched by invisible forces. Because Belmont Avenue is so close to the turnpike, old timers in the neighborhood suspect there are ghosts of Revolutionary War soldiers around. According to legend, as the American army marched eastward from battles near Brooklyn, the wounded died and were buried right beside the road, without a funeral service. Maybe some of those casualties aren't yet reconciled to their passing, Nancie's friends suggest.

"My older daughter lives upstairs and refuses to believe in ghosts. However," Nancie said, "one afternoon, as she came home from work, she glanced up and saw a face looking down at her. Of course, there was nobody at home upstairs. Some of this was tolerable, but other events were not. When down in the cellar once, I found something new carved into a wooden cellar support: *Jimmy, Jim*. I don't know who that is or was, and I don't know how the carved words got there. I know for certain that nobody by that name has lived here since 1951. But there has been some more disturbing stuff, too," she told me.

"Sometimes vases shatter when no one is near them. We had a big entertainment center, and one day, just after Katherine and her friends finished playing a Nintendo game, the TV screen imploded or exploded. There was glass all over the place, and the door hinges flew through the air. Fortunately, nobody got hurt, but how can ghosts cause such things? Many times my daughter and I see orbs of light, especially as they move under or around doors. I sometimes hear a tapping sound in my bedroom closet, and then there is the ghost of *Mimi*, my Doxie puppy! We experience these things in waves. Sometimes we have peace and quiet for a long stretch, then it gets 'busy,'" she informed me.

I asked how bad it gets. "You don't want to be here when the roaring starts," she said grimly. "Several years ago my daughter and I were in our respective bedrooms and heard a roaring sound, faint at first, then increasing in volume. It sounded like a freight train coming, and the noise got almost deafening. The room turned ice cold, and then it seemed the air was sucked from the room for ten to fifteen seconds. This doesn't happen often." I told her that this certainly isn't Casper, and we discussed this phenomenon that Nancie has named "The Evil One."

"What have you done to send these energies out of the house?" I asked.

"We have used a lot of holy water, as I was born a Catholic," she told me. "We have followed the old tradition of placing salt in the corners of the rooms, though we find that the holy water works best, especially in calming the Evil One. My friends have brought sage and burned (or *smudged*) it to ward off negativity. That works pretty well sometimes, too."

Of course, this latter phenomenon is the type of story that Hollywood seeks to portray as the norm in haunted houses, eliciting fear from admission-paying thrill seekers. But it is *not* the norm, and it is comparatively rare. Nancie and I talked about some of the stories I've collected and also some of the hype about the notorious Amityville Horror story.

My working hypothesis about the house on Belmont Avenue is this: The sudden death of Donna created a bitterness or cell of negative energy in the house, perhaps reinforced by the insulting cutting of her memorial tree. Nobody evicted the girl's spirit, even though a spiritual cleaner *should* have been called when the level of difficulty became apparent. A professional experienced in working with the recently deceased might have helped the girl into the next world in a gentle ceremony. However, as with most serious things that are not attended to in life, they can only get worse.

Donna's sorrow, anger, and bitterness, unresolved on the near-earth plane level, festered and became a magnet to draw even darker energies or entities from the spirit world to manifest in that house. Nancie's situation now sounds like a case for a professional exorcist, whether a member of a religious organization or not. It definitely is not a task for amateurs, though Nancie and I are exploring alternatives because her church doesn't seem interested in helping her.

I urged Nancie to get the services of a professional to assist her in clearing the house. Then, as an afterthought, I requested my dowser friend, Tick Gaudreau, (author of *Spirit Rescue: A Dowser's Ghostly Experiences*) to see what he could do about clearing the worst entity from the house. From his base near Albany, Tick sensed two women (living ones) who currently live in or visit the house. The full or partial names were right on.

Knowing nothing about the phenomena that Nancie experienced, Tick "got" a dour, old fashioned woman, similar to the stereotype of the early suffragettes or prohibitionists. In addition, he felt the entity had not been a good wife in her own life. He asked for and received permission to talk with her spirit and discovered that the lady had died of a fever long ago, and she believed it was still 1914. She let Tick know that she had no religion, but she was afraid of death and Hell, though she didn't believe in Heaven. Trapped, with nowhere to go, she lived in a state of constant fear, even though it is likely that there are "light people" or spirit guides attempting to get her attention and take her into The Light, but (as this phenomenon isn't in her belief system) she won't be enticed by those helpers.

"To sustain her fear level, something like an adrenalin rush in a living body, she knocks over objects and breaks others. And, most important, I think, to sustain her terror, she *howls*," Tick said. When I read that word, I could easily see how Nancie might experience the howling as a train's whistle or roar. The ghost woman didn't know, or couldn't admit, that she had died. Nevertheless, she was very lonely and, according to Tick, had created a thought form companion to pass the time with, someone or something to help her stay in a fearful state.

It is fairly well known that the consciousness of a dead person, if they cannot or will not see The Light or do not believe in a benevolent Hereafter, will simply remain in a state of denial—if I'm not dead, I can't get sent *anywhere*! Especially, in this case, to a feared Hell.

"She took some convincing that she had passed into spirit. I saw her dying on a bed, very scared of dying. I convinced her that she *was* now in spirit, and then a maiden aunt came to visit her and help the spirit woman to the other side. A young girl, maybe a daughter, also gave her a teddy bear to calm and soothe her anxiety. A group of spirit guides and relatives then came to help her cross. It took several minutes for her to go," he wrote.

Fortunately, there are many gifted individuals today who perform this liberation of spirit entities as an act of love, the ingredient so often missing from the lives of those who remain as ghosts. What will become of Donna, if indeed she remains in the house? Only time and experience will tell.

Enough Already!

Dawn Vinson is a hairdresser living in Harpursville, NY. Hers is a world of design, beauty and order—on the job, at least. In her house on Windsor Road, which she shares with her boyfriend and another friend, there is anything *but* order. The knowledge that there are others, invisible others, there has led her to investigate the world of paranormal phenomena. In that process, she has also expanded her psychic ability and is attempting to use that talent in a responsible way. She has accumulated many recordings and photos of the menagerie that cohabits her home.

"It sounds like a hotel, sometimes," she laughed. "It's an old place, to be sure, so I did some research and discovered that the house was built in 1889. There is some evidence from neighbors that this area was a 'station' on the Underground Railroad before the Civil War. Another neighbor told me that there had been a suicide in the house years before we moved in.

"A lot of those former residents still seem to be here, as we hear footsteps almost all night long, ending only around 4:30 a.m. When I awake and listen carefully, I can make out the sound of very heavy footsteps, which I take to be a large man, moving up and down the stairs and slowly through the hallway. But there are also the scampering footsteps of a child, and I've come to believe it is a boy."

Dawn told me that, soon after she moved in, she and her boyfriend awoke to hear a woman singing somewhere in the house. Still half asleep, she could hear the lyrics, but couldn't retain them to remember the song's title in the morning. However, it was an old-fashioned song and quite beautiful.

She believes one of the ghosts fancies her, or has at least developed a strong attachment to her without controlling her. "He's consumed by guilt. I know that because I've felt it, so I think maybe he's the suicide guy, but I don't know. Many times I hear footsteps climbing the stairs. So I start up there, too, and I run into a very cold spot and *great* negativity, almost as if I'm feeling his gloom," she told me. Dawn had heard about EVP (the electronic voice phenomenon, demonstrated on some television ghost-chaser programs) and decided to try taping some of the activity around her. She went upstairs, attempting to follow her unseen tenant, put her tape recorder down, then left for a minute. When she returned, she played back the few minutes of tape that were recorded during her absence. "Goddammit!" was what she heard, almost as if the ghost felt perturbed that she had left him.

"I then asked aloud if anyone was there," she told me, "because it sure was a man's voice. Again, when I played back the tape (as I couldn't really hear any of the speech normally) I heard the name 'Sinclair.' Now, I don't know if it is his first or last name. So far, I've not been able to get the name of the guy who committed suicide, but maybe *that* is who it is."

I told Dawn that people who take their own lives are often unable or unwilling to leave the earth plane, as they usually come to understand soon after their death that things *would* have changed, if they had only gone on and faced their problems. Then comes anger at themselves and feelings of guilt. In most cases, ghosts of those who die by suicide are hard to get rid of because they need someone to break their fixation on self-condemnation and to speak to them about forgiveness. Usually, that involves a clergyman or professional spirit clearing person; someone who can't be bamboozled by a nefarious ghost's cunning.

"Another recording produced the name 'Kareem,'" Dawn told me. I suggested that such a name, whether used by a white or black person, was most likely from an entity that passed no longer ago than the 1960s, when Arabic names became trendy, especially among black Americans. Since her neighbors didn't recall any black tenants in the house before she came, they couldn't help her identify this spirit.

"One of the ghosts seems to joke around, hiding or moving things, so, I'm sure he or she is intelligent," she said. Again, I informed her that such attention-getting antics are usually a spirit's attempt to inform the living that they are there. Being a ghost is often a lonely business; the spirit no longer has vocal cords and is physically, emotionally, and often spiritually cut off from the living. Without hands or voice, they can't easily remedy their condition of living between worlds.

"I'm pretty sure I saw the boy," she told me. "Once, I saw a young boy, about five, pop out of a chair. Whether he'd been sitting in it or hiding in it, I couldn't tell. He wore shorts, but they were in an old style, maybe from the 1940s or 1950s. I asked intuitively who he was, and I got the name 'Thomas.' I'm also sure that he is the one who shakes my bed at night, waking me up.

"One night I awoke around 2 a.m. and heard voices. I was sure that someone was breaking into the house. Then the sounds stopped, almost as if the burglars thought they'd been discovered. We all woke up and quietly explored the whole house, but the doors were locked and nobody was inside. Another one of the characters here," she smiled, "is a girl wearing a sun dress. She seems to be about nineteen and has long hair pulled back. Now, *she's* a funny one; she's only around for part of the year, just the summer. In the fall she's gone, and we don't hear or see her again until late spring the next year."

Another spirit resident seems to be an old man carrying a muzzle-loading rifle, which would place him before 1900 and perhaps as much as fifty years before that. "He's only popped up once or twice, but I wonder if he could be 'Sinclair,'" she pondered.

"I tell you," she grimaced, "it's like Grand Central Station in here some days and nights. I'm glad I have my job to go to, where things are stable and under control."

This rented house at 1190 Windsor Road either holds or attracts a variety of spirits. Some may not originate on this property, and these are the hardest ones to identify. Some may be "cruising" the spirit world and may have found vibrations, either in the house or its living inhabitants, that are attractive. None of them seem anxious to quit the physical plane, and I have urged Dawn to bring in a professional cleaner. However, she has grown so used to the ghosts that none of them terrify her now. As with so many owners of haunted places, a familiarity develops, but in that relationship, neither the living nor the deceased move on. If the universe is about anything, it's about movement and development and change. Change is the dynamic force that governs all life.

In the end, I told her, The Golden Rule regulates the world of the living and that of the spirit. If the living would not like to be stranded or imprisoned, denied Eternal Rest or Glory or The Promised Land, then we must dedicate ourselves to helping the imprisoned spirits move upward and onward. It's good for them *and* good for us.

Steps in Time

"I lived in historic homes in Staten Island and Brooklyn and never heard a peep of ghost sounds. So I expected peace and calm when my husband and I bought this Cape Cod style house in Deer Park in 1999," Carol told me. "I'm in the real estate business here in Suffolk County, and I have shown many houses. In many of them, I just get a sense of 'niceness,' that it will be a *good* place to live. And my husband and I both got that sense when we bought this house on 22nd Street."

Carol told me the house dated from the late 1940s and wasn't very old, so no one would expect it to house a ghost. And, probably, it didn't when they moved in eight years ago. "Our children were four and five when we came here, and everything was calm for about six months. Then, when my son Joey was four and a half, I looked out the window and saw him swinging happily on the swing. Then, I did a double-take—he wasn't *moving* a bit on the swing, though the swing went up very high. How could he get that much momentum? Then I looked again, and I could see him talking and laughing over his shoulder. But no one else was there! After a while, he slowed, stopped, turned around, and waved goodbye to someone and then headed for the house.

"When he came inside, I asked him who he was talking to. He said, 'Pop-Pop!' referring to my father who had died about six months before.

'But Joey, Grandpa is dead, you know that,' I said.

'Yeah, I know, Mom, but he's *younger* now. And he said to tell *you* that he loves you, and to give you a big kiss.' And, as he said that, Joey planted a big kiss on my mouth!' I was stunned. Was this a childhood fantasy?

"Then, I thought about it. My father, Richard Tarangelo, had lived over in Oceanside but loved to come to this house after we bought it. He enjoyed the fishpond in the backyard, and it gave him a chance to be with Joey, who he loved. I said, 'Did anybody come with Pop-Pop?'

"Joey said, 'Yes, Mom, but I don't know who the man *is!*'

"'Well, describe him,' I responded.

"Joey gave a detailed description, and I got goose bumps on my neck when he mentioned the stranger's large hawk-like nose. Without a doubt, that was Angelo Tarangelo, my grandfather, whom Joey had never seen. We didn't even have photographs of him around the house. My grandfather! Now, what do you think about *that?*"

Apparently, that apparition of two deceased elders was the beginning of subsequent events in the house. "Joey is quite sensitive and is now thirteen," Carol told me. "He's a real straight-arrow guy, dedicated to karate, meditation, and even Zen. His outlook is so mature for a boy his age, and he seems motivated by a strong desire to help or heal others. I wonder if he's psychic," she mused. "He still sees his grandfather and great-grandfather and even has regular conversations with them. One morning last month, when the real estate market cooled and I was very doubtful about making a sale for quite some time, Joey came bouncing down to breakfast and said, 'Cheer up, Mom, you're going to sell a house today.' I dismissed him with a 'Yeah, *right!*' and put his breakfast on the table. But at suppertime, I had to apologize to him. Against all odds, I *had* made a wonderful sale that day!"

I asked Carol to tell me about the other activity, ghostly or psychic, that takes place in her home. "It's really centered on the stairs," she responded. "When a person goes up the stairs, between the seventh and ninth step, most folks feel a cold area, just there, in that place—do we have a spirit stationed on the stairs? And sometimes, against all odds, there is a little trace of smoke or vapor in the air, just *there*. Both my father and grandfather were smokers, so maybe they're sending the sight and smell to reassure us. Many times, we'll have a visitor who asks, 'Is that cigarette smoke that I smell?' It's hard to explain it to them. Usually, when I get the smoke and cold, I will ask, 'You around today?' Usually, soon afterward, one of Joey's karate medals will tinkle or a picture on the wall will move, as if to say, 'Yep!'"

Carol told me of Deer Park's proximity to Wyandanch, with its associations to ancient Indian tribes. "I have an Indian here, too," she laughed. "Long before the Europeans landed here, Long Island was Indian land, so maybe some of the tribal leaders remain here, maybe even old Chief Wyandanch, himself. Our Indian is every bit the gentleman, and I think *he* also offers protection to this house and the land it's built on. Whoever he is, he sure is heavy-footed though!

"My girlfriend Nicole stayed with me for three weeks a year ago, and she witnessed some of the events. There is a very strong sage smell in the house at times. Now, I *do* use sage to smudge the house from time to time, but the scent will suddenly appear, months after I've used the plant. (For readers who don't know, burning sage vegetation is commonly used to clear a space of its negative vibrations, and it is commonly also used as a form of Native American blessing for an enclosure). And, as you might guess, the smell is strongest in the stairway," she told me. With a big grin on her face, she then said that visitors, especially those who don't know her family that well, will enter and gasp, 'Is that *marijuana*, I smell?' 'Not in *this* house,' I tell them!

"But even without the smell of sage, I can still hear his footsteps on the stairs at night when the house is quiet. Up three steps, then down three steps, and it repeats. It's almost like he's marching on guard duty for us," she mused. "Our poor dogs just go nuts when the Chief is around; they sit at the foot of the stairs and bark and bark. But they don't go up the stairs to challenge him either," she smiled.

"And I *also* have what must be a little girl here, too; the spirit doesn't sound like a boy. There is a lot of running throughout the house and giggling. I've seen her twice, though I don't really try to. Each time, she appears in a long-waisted white dress with a blue ribbon across the chest. She is very fair with dark eyes and wears her long, waist-length dark hair in ringlets. If she is from this spot, she must be living in another century; people haven't dressed like that in years. But what do you think? Is it possible that she was just passing through and found Pop-Pop, Angelo and the Chief? Maybe she likes all that and feels safe enough to stay and play here. As far as I can determine, there has never been another structure on this spot before our house was built, so where does she come from?" I had to admit that I didn't know the answer, but I was glad to hear everyone was getting along so well.

Later, I wondered if the individuals had gathered there, impressed with Joey's sensitivity to their world. Perhaps they are there to guide his development.

Farewells

"I have lived twenty-one years in this house," Diane Kohler told me, "and ever since my husband, Gary, died in 1997, it sure has been a busy place!" Diane lives on Fairfield Avenue in Mineola, where she came as a twenty-eight-year-old new mother in 1985. Soon after his death, she felt the need to clear her bedroom of Gary's personal possessions, and, calling her two children to come upstairs, she let them choose some of his things that they wanted to keep. Two weeks later, she had a dream.

In the dream, Gary called Diane on the phone during the night, saying, "The hospital made a mistake—I'm okay, in fact, I'm much better. I didn't die! You can come and pick me up." The dream was so real that it frightened Diane. After that dream experience, she felt his presence in the house constantly. When I interviewed her, I told her that it is fairly common to have the deceased resist accepting that earth life had ended, and this state is called *denial*.

Many times the spirit has to undergo a reorientation on the other side in order to come to an understanding of the physical life's end. Until that happens, the person's family is likely to experience many visions or voices that seem, at the time, like wishful thinking on the part of the living, but many of these *are* real contacts.

"I went to a psychic who told me that I *had to* talk to Gary and tell him that it's okay, and that he can leave his family here and go," she said. So, for the next few months, though she felt a strong presence at times, she did as instructed. Nevertheless, for quite a while, Gary seemed too earthbound to accept her instructions.

"Then, a second activity started," she told me. "My daughter has a boyfriend who is attuned to the spirit world. When Ray comes to the house, he often sees spirits. One day, he described a male spirit here that exactly fit my father, Adam, who died in 1982. As a child, Adam often played and camped out on the piece of land on which my home was eventually built." Ray had never seen a picture of her father until that day, and agreed it was him. The young man was continually upset by the spirits he encountered in Diane's house."

For personal reasons, in order for Ray to finish college, Diane invited him to live in her house. Those were not comfortable years for Ray because he is the son of a psychically gifted Dominican mother, a woman who too often used her psychic ability in a negative way. Ray had become uncomfortable with the spirit world. For two years, the family experienced lights turning themselves off and on. Doors slammed spontaneously with no human nearby and no breeze blowing. After college graduation, however, when Ray left her house to live on his own, the upsets in Diane's house diminished. As noted in other stories, the addition or subtraction of even one individual from a household can change the entire domestic atmosphere.

"My mother has a ground floor apartment in the house, separated from my family quarters by only a door. Once in a while, if there is an emergency, one of my family members will pop into her apartment, use the bathroom, and then come back in here," Diane said. "One morning, my mom, Joan, came in and was fit to be tied. 'Who was it that came into my apartment at *1 a.m.?*' she demanded. I asked my kids, and it hadn't been them *or* Ray, and I told her so. 'Well, I know what I *saw*,' she shot back. 'I heard the door open, sat up in bed, and saw a man about twenty just standing in the doorway, looking at me. When I sat up, he left and slammed the door. It's just too late at night for *that*,' she fumed. 'So I jumped out of bed and ran to the door. But when I opened it up, everything inside your apartment was quiet and nobody was there!' Mom said."

Any parent of young adults knows that, even in adulthood, our offspring are still our *kids*, and, many times, as Diane visits in her mother's apartment, she fusses or complains about what this one or that one is doing. "Funny thing," she noted. "Whenever I do that, Mom's kitchen light blinks until I stop complaining. And over in *my* apartment, where the kitchen ceiling fan is controlled by a remote, the light on that fan fixture continually blinks off and on, though an electrician tells me nothing is wrong with it!

"We have had cats and dogs here over the years, and my new dog will suddenly bark and snarl in the middle of the night. Yet on the night that the ghost man opened Mom's door, she had a cat beside her on the bed, and that animal slept through the whole incident! We have certain scents or odors here, too. One of them is a perfume that appears from time to time, and I immediately recognize it as my grandmother's. My other grandmother sends a tar smell, and I immediately know who *that* is, too. Her cat, Tim, used to spend a lot of time on the tar roof outside her kitchen window, and I used to sit at the window as a child and watch him. When he wanted to come inside, we'd open the window, and I'd smell the tar roof. When each grandmother comes, I believe it's only for a quick check-in to say 'Hello' and 'I'm thinking of you,' and then the scent is gone."

Diane recently had her first sighting of an older woman in her dining room. "While watching television one night, I looked out into the dining room, which was dark. But, even so, I could see a little old woman dressed in black, just standing there, watching me. I looked back at the television for a moment, and she was gone when I looked back in the dining room. I think she may have been the previous owner's mother, who died in this house."

Diane is not unlike many Americans who experience spirits. The world of departed loved ones is never that far away. From time to time, our loved ones seem to just drop by, perhaps in thought more than in physical form, to express their love for us, and perhaps also as a promise that we *will* all meet again.

Guides

"I've seen them since I was a little kid, and they used to scare me," said Bill. "I was maybe thirteen years old before I stopped being scared and just accepted them as part of life. Because I knew others *didn't* see them, I kept the whole thing to myself." As an adult, Bill is sensitive and dedicated to his job in the health care profession in Utica, NY. The "them" he refers to seem to be the spirits of those who have passed on. "When I tune in on them at my house in Rome, I see girls in the long skirts and tight sweaters of the 50s or 60s, and it's like they are having a party all around me. However, they also have advice for me.

"After I graduated high school at Rome Free Academy in 1974, I entered the Air Force, and, after my training, I was stationed at an air base near Tucson, Arizona. It was a wonderful place where I could be alone in the desert, just thinking or meditating when I was off duty. I worked as a medic at the base, and the work often made me ponder the purpose of life—why some guys got sick and others didn't.

"My first marriage broke up down there, and I wondered if I'd ever find a true love. Alone in my room one evening, hoping that the divorce hadn't been entirely *my* fault, I spoke out to the empty room, 'Tell me I didn't blow it; tell me it wasn't all *my* fault.'" Suddenly, one of the unseen group that surrounds Bill spoke up in an archaic English dialect, "To the third son goes the seventh daughter," was all it said. Bill pondered the words—*what the heck?* Well, he decided, *he* was a third son, so maybe destiny had a girl for him after all. But how many families have seven children, much less seven *daughters* any more? He decided to be patient.

Some months later, he went on a blind date arranged by a buddy. His date was beautiful and he was immediately enamored of her. "Wow, are there any more like you back home?" he asked. She smiled and said, "Sure, lots of them. I'm the youngest of seven sisters!" Not long afterward, they became a couple and were celebrating twenty-five years of marriage when I interviewed Bill in 2005. A marriage made in Heaven?

Eventually, Bill left the Service and returned to New York State and the Mohawk Valley that he loved. He found a job in a Utica hospital and has worked there since. "We found a house near Rome, and at first, my wife was repelled by its appearance. I admit it looked like something from the old TV show, *Sanford and Son,* all overgrown and strewn with junk. There was a big shrine to the Virgin Mary in the side yard, but that also was in a bad state of repair, with parts broken off or missing. "The strange thing about it is that *I* felt absolutely at home—I loved it!" he told me, adding that he and his wife have been happy there since.

Bill's sensitivity to the other world grew stronger as time passed. During the third year they lived in their house, Bill sat on the couch in the living room, pondering work to be done. "I was staring off into space when I suddenly spotted something out of the corner of my eye—the wick on a nearby candle was glowing, not burning, just glowing. Where'd *that* come from? I wondered. We hadn't lit that candle in weeks. Suddenly it burst into full flame!" Shortly after that incident, the voices told Bill he had to write a book about his life experiences. Mentally, he replied, "Okay, yeah, when I get a chance." Inwardly, however, he knew he wasn't a writer and tried to put off the task. And that was the beginning.

Not long afterward, his brother and brother-in-law sat watching a football game with him in that room. Bill got up to get refreshments in the kitchen, but when he returned he found the candle lit. In exasperation, he asked, "Who lit the *candle?*" The other two men, engrossed in the game, at first had no idea what he was talking about. Bill pointed out the flame and asked again. Neither one seemed to know or care. He asked them if it was lit when they came in but, again, neither seemed to remember or care, and they turned back to the television. One thing Bill knew for sure, *he* hadn't lit the candle. However, the three of them were the only people in the room. Were his guides acting up?

A few weeks later, on a bright Sunday morning, Bill ventured into the backyard. "I recall thinking, What a beautiful day—I feel good enough to do *anything*! Suddenly in my head there came a flash, a bright light. For a minute, I didn't know what had hit me. When I came to, I found myself sprawled on the ground. I tried to move and found I was paralyzed from the waist down. Figuring that the voices were a part of this predicament, I mentally asked them why they were doing this. The only response I got was 'Start the book!' Panicked, I called my wife. She came running but couldn't help me stand. I crawled and she pulled, and we got into the car and headed down to Urgent Care, a local medical clinic near our house."

The clinic did an MRI image of his spine. When the pictures were finished the radiologist entered the room and remarked that the fifth lumbar vertebra (L-5) had "exploded." He told Bill that it was about the worst situation he'd ever seen, and asked how the injury happened. What could Bill say? *A light had knocked him down?* The radiologist urged him to get a good surgeon, and Bill immediately contacted Dr. Smith, a neurologist he knew from the Utica hospital where he worked. Smith also agreed it was the worst injury to a vertebra he'd ever seen. The earliest surgery date he could schedule was in three months, so he told Bill to go home and stay immobile. The doctor also gave him pain medication if he needed it.

One morning a few months later, Bill awoke on the downstairs couch where he'd fallen asleep. He awoke hearing his wife bending over him and asking in hushed tones, "Who lit the candle?" Bill's head cleared and he looked at the candle that stood alight on a nearby table. He admitted he didn't know the answer but was sure it wasn't *him—not in his condition!*

"We have an old cat, and I'm used to hearing her pad her way around the house, but one morning I heard her walking straight to the couch where I was dozing. A voice said, 'Turn over on your stomach,' and I complied. Instantly, the cat jumped up onto my back and settled in a warm ball right over L-5. I worried she might hurt me, but she didn't. Instead, the cat radiated a very pleasant warmth as she lay there purring away; I liked that and didn't chase her off. Gradually, I felt the energy in the room increase. It was if a gigantic dynamo were whirling away somewhere. I began to feel physical pressure in my head and along my spine, and tears came to my eyes.

"As all this took place, I was facing the fireplace. The candle nearby suddenly flashed and lit itself, almost like a strobe light. This was unreal—a purring, hot cat lying on my badly injured spine and a candle across the room suddenly lighting itself! After about ten minutes, our kitty jumped down. I wondered what the loss of her heat and decreased pressure did to my spine, so I moved gently. No pain. I stretched a bit, again gently. No pain. I stood up—something that *always* aggravated my spine. No pain. To make the story short, David, I've been pain free for almost three years now.

"Poor Dr. Smith didn't know what to say. He kept saying, 'You should be in a wheelchair!' He checked me out, pronounced me fit to return to work, and signed my release from his care. I still see him doing rounds at the hospital. He always smiles at me and jokingly calls me his 'special case.' I don't think either of us *really* understands what happened. Another thing, I have had an off-and-on pain in my left leg since I was four years old, but that, too, disappeared when my back was healed!"

Nevertheless, Bill heeded the voices' assignment. He has been writing about his experiences with the other world ever since. The group still surrounds him and sometimes offers advice. "The Old Englishman has only come back once since I returned from Arizona," he told me. "Maybe his work is done for now. They have showed me mental pictures of what I know to be ten years of projects ahead, and they told me to keep writing until June 2006."

There are two other spirits in the house aside from Bill's group. One is his father, and the other is a former friend from whom he bought the house. These spirits are friendly and cause him no trouble. Somewhat ruefully, Bill told me that his friends from the old days seldom come around or call any more. "And I don't think they could understand that I'm a changed guy. I'm not sure I understand it either, but I have work to do," he said, then, with a wink, he concluded, "and I don't know anybody else who has such a marvelous life."

I came away from the interview convinced that I had talked to an adventurer of the New Age. Not an explorer of mountaintops or jungles, or even of outer space. No, I think Bill is learning to explore "inner space."

Happy Returns

Two miles south of Seneca Lake and Watkins Glen lies the picturesque Schuyler County village of Montour Falls. There is nothing for the traveler to see that would encourage a belief in ghosts, yet the spirits are there, if only briefly.

"In 1990, we bought our nice old house from Mary Sullivan, a widow whose husband had recently passed. The couple had been married for over forty years, so it was a happy and sad occasion when she handed us the key at the closing," Bart Besley said. "I remember that it was just a few days after we moved in that I awoke around 6 a.m. and smelled cigarette smoke. Could someone have broken in? While I pondered that possibility, I heard the back door close, and I ran downstairs quickly to see who it was. Neither my wife, Deb, nor I had ever smoked in the house. In the kitchen, the smell of smoke was very strong. There was nobody in the house, so I went to check out back. Strangely, the back door was locked, so I first had to unlock it. I looked all over the driveway and backyard, but there was nobody in sight. I just didn't know what to conclude—did someone enter the house, smoke a cigarette, and then leave? Or didn't they?"

Bart told me that the incident in their 401 College Avenue home kept him cogitating for the next few months, though the event didn't reoccur. "From time to time, Deb and I would see Mrs. Sullivan drive past the house slowly, evidently checking to see what changes we'd made and how we were caring for her old home. Then, one day, I encountered her and she expressed interest in how we liked our new house. I had to tell her about the cigarette smoke and the back door slamming. She got a big smile on her face and exclaimed, 'Oh, *that* was just Jack, checking to see who was living in his house now, and how you were taking care of it.'"

The former owner then revealed to Bart and his wife that Jack was ill for some time before his passing and was confined to the bedroom. "In fact, he died in that room," Mary revealed. And that *is* the very room that their family now uses as a den and computer room!

"So, that's our ghost story," Bart told me. "It only happened that once, but it has thrilled and charmed our family for some years now. My daughter, Logan, in particular, gets a kick out of hearing me retell the experience. Recently, she thought maybe she and her friends would take Jack to school with them! I bet nobody would fall asleep in class *that* day," he laughed.

Steps

In the 1970s, Betty Brayton Smith lived at 54 Seminary Street in Ft. Edward, NY. It was a nice old Victorian house and she enjoyed life there. As with most parents, she experienced a running challenge from her teenagers, especially in relation to them keeping their rooms clean.

One day, she gave an ultimatum: "Get those rooms cleaned and straightened by (a certain day and time), or *I* am going to do it!" And, as is so often the case, the deadline passed with no action on the daughters' part. Though she didn't want to do all the extra work, she had to keep her word, so when the girls were in school, Betty made the decision: *Today* is the day.

First, she decided to fortify herself with a cup of coffee and sat in her living room. She had tied the family dog out in back of the house, so there'd be no interference. Suddenly, she heard the door from the dining room into the front hallway open. She knew she was alone and that the outside front door was locked. Who could it be? It couldn't be *anyone*! The hair on her neck bristled. It took a minute to gather the courage, but she jumped up and went to look. The dining room door was closed, so, maybe she hadn't really heard it. Just as she decided she had been wrong, she heard another eerie sound.

Heavy footsteps, clearly those of a man, were slogging up the stairs to the second floor. She opened the hall door and looked at the stairs, though nobody was there. Would she go up and look, to see who was there? No, she grew fainthearted and chose to get some back-up help from her neighbor across the street. The woman said, "What's wrong with you, Betty? You're so pale, you look as if you've seen a ghost! Come on in and have a cup of coffee."

Betty took her neighbor up on the offer and stayed a few hours, avoiding the upstairs search. When it came time for the girls to return from school, she crossed the street to the house. From upstairs, she heard her daughter, Debbie, calling, "Mom!"

From downstairs, Betty answered, "I'm down here, Debbie, what do you want?

Debbie came downstairs with a strange look on her face, telling Betty that she had gone upstairs to her room because she'd heard footsteps there, but found nobody in the bedrooms when she went up. The two spent the rest of the day trying to figure out this enigma. They never reached a satisfactory solution. Likely, some former resident of the old house had returned just that once, to re-live an episode from the past. The footsteps were never heard again.

Hearing footsteps on the stairs is arguably one of the most common, thus the most often dismissed, of encounters with ghosts.

Judge Brewster

In December 1988, Dan and Gayle Alexander bought a big, beautiful old house on Water Street in Elizabethtown, NY. It was close to work and spacious enough to host local meetings and parties. "We fell in love with this place when we first saw it," Gayle told me in June 2005. "We didn't realize, however, that someone else had stayed on as a houseguest."

Judge O. Byron Brewster's House

In 1900, Judge O. Byron Brewster, Justice of the NY State Court of Appeals, sought a residence that would permit an office for his legal activities, yet a place large enough to entertain the many state and national notables with whom he was acquainted. One evening as he dined with famous young artist Rockwell Kent, Brewster verbalized his ideas for the ideal house. Kent, who was extremely busy with his studies at the Columbia University School of Architecture, took out a pencil, and, using a sheet of the Judge's paper, sketched a beautiful Colonial Revival façade. "Here, O.B., this is the front. Get an architect to fill in everything behind it," he told his host with a smile.

And Brewster found the architect and contractor, and filled in the rest. In 1932, he added a rear wing that housed his law office, "a room that no family members ventured into," said Gayle with a smile. "That was *his* private space, complete with pool table, and he never permitted his five daughters to enter." My hostess told me that the judge died in the early 1960s, and "the house is pretty much as he left it, except we moved a partition upstairs and had to replace some of the original floor and paneling when we had a water leak."

We were touring the spacious rooms as she uttered the previous sentence, and we had just entered the large "back room." She indicated a section of the ceiling that had been replaced, showing me the refinished floor underneath. Then, glancing at the wall above the mantelpiece, she said wryly, "Yes, and the only things I added in here are those sconces above the fireplace. I don't think O.B. likes them because they keep going crooked. In June of 2005, I hosted a fundraiser for a hospital group and mentioned that the Judge occasionally shows his distaste for my decoration by nudging the candles to a slant. Everyone looked. The candles were straight; I'd straightened them that morning. Then, while we sat at the dining room table, one of the women suddenly gasped. 'They've gone crooked!" she exclaimed. We looked, and sure enough, all the candles were at an angle." She noted that this is the only unfriendly activity that the ghost performs. "I *know* somebody is here, and by the ghost's actions, I figure it's Judge Brewster," she told me.

"One other thing I don't understand, though, has to do with the flowers. It seems that only white flowers will grow in the back yard." She took me to a beautifully landscaped terrace and lawn. "Here, see this spot?" she asked. "Every year *white* violets come up here. I don't want them in the grass here, so I dig them up and transplant them into the garden. The next year, they come up at this spot in the lawn again, but none of the garden violet transplants ever survive. "See those trees next to the old carriage shed?" she asked. "Only trees with *white* flowers will grow there. I don't know what to make of it, but it *will* look nice when the wedding takes place here in August. The new owners decided this backyard is a delightful place to tie the knot." We then discussed whether or not the ghost might be the Judge's wife but came to no conclusion.

"Please come upstairs," she invited, "there is one more space where guests get impressions, but I won't tell you where it is. See if you can figure it out for yourself." I suddenly felt ill equipped, as my intuitive friend, Susan, hadn't come on this expedition. Gayle and I approached our last room without me sensing much that could be considered ghostly, and she said, "Well, this is our Adirondack Summer Porch. Lots of guests stay out here." We stepped down onto the floor, and I could see how the screened area must be a delightful place to sleep during summer's hot spells. I saw nothing out of the ordinary and turned, prepared to admit defeat in the psychic realm. A lean, white-haired man with small white mustache stood between Gayle and me for an instant. He had a battered old hat and fly fisherman's jacket. For a second, I observed him threading fishing line onto his oversize reel. "I'm a friend of the Judge's," I got telepathically from him. I mentally asked his name and received, "Vernon, a friend of the Judge," as he disappeared. I shared the insight with Gayle, and she admitted that *this was* the other most active area of the old house.

Going downstairs and outdoors, we strolled to the old carriage house. As we went in, I visualized a black horse in a stall to my right, but when I blinked, there was no stall there, just a modern riding lawnmower against a partition. But, as we went further into the barn, I did find a real stall behind that partition, no horse though. In a side room, I had the impression of a man seated and taking a nip of alcohol from a bottle. When I informed Gayle of that, she grinned. "You know, Judge Brewster liked his alcohol, but his wife was in the Temperance Society, so he probably *did* come back here for a snort, as she wouldn't let him drink inside." Later, she showed me some empty rum bottles that her son had found secreted inside a wall in the house's upstairs. Gayle now has them on display in the Judge's former office, so he can at least imbibe the *spirit* of the spirits if he wants to.

We returned to the dining room as Mrs. Alexander told me of Brewster's famous house guests, including not only Rockwell Kent as an older artist, but also Governor Thomas E. Dewey of NY State, who was defeated by President Roosevelt in 1944 and President Truman in 1948. The famous have come and gone. Even the Judge has physically departed, as have his wife and daughters. But who remains in spirit?

"We'll have to leave that to the new owners," my hostess told me. "We're packing and moving out by July 31st. They know about the occasional phenomenon, but it isn't likely going to bother them because they *already* love this house," she told me. I pondered the fact that different inhabitants bring different energies into the house. Perhaps the new folks won't have any experiences at all. Conversely, they may have a circus. The new owner, it seems, is a practicing lawyer. One wonders if the old Judge will now adopt a higher profile, as he'll have a fellow professional with whom to discuss the nuances of the law. I think I'll stay in touch.

Nirvana

After the American Civil War ended in 1865, many entrepreneurs scouted the Adirondacks for profitable commercial ventures. The lumber and minerals were there, to be sure, but so was the natural beauty, and the wealthy found the splendid shores of Lake George a beautiful respite from big city life. Many of American's wealthy built grand homes along the lake in a profusion that came to be known as "Millionaire's Row." One of these millionaires was John Boulton Simpson, Jr.

Owner of the Estey Piano Company in New York City, Boulton (who inserted the letter "u" in his name, surprising the rest of the Bolton family) came from a prosperous family. "Piano Johnny" they called him as he amassed even greater wealth. Home was a beautiful brownstone in Harlem, but when Simpson and his wife, Fanny, vacationed at Bolton Landing, they fell in love with "the queen of American lakes," and they were determined to build a summer residence there on Green Island. It would be a heaven and haven combined, and the name *Nirvana* seemed to sum it all up. Their island heaven was right next door to the famous Sagamore Hotel.

The Simpsons had two daughters, Frances (Fanny) and Helen, and each was given the finest of educations and social grooming. The family gave gener-

The Boulton House, Nirvana

ously of their wealth and personal effort to the Bolton Landing area charities and educational and social institutions until the late 1960s, when Helen died.

"People who visit our home often feel there are others here," wrote Valerie, the present owner. "It's not that these spirits really bother us, but they do seem to interact with our family members and guests, and I wonder if you can offer us some insights." That type of "quiet haunting" is something I enjoy investigating, though it took a bit of time to arrange a schedule that was agreeable to the owners, my friend, Susan, and me.

On a bright sunny day in late June 2005, Susan and I met the owner, who ushered us in, then left us alone to savor the house's beauty and richness. As usual, Susan did her tour of the house alone, while I interviewed Valerie about the history of her family's eight-year ownership. Susan returned, and we went through the beautiful rooms together, agreeing that even if no ghosts were present, it was a treat just to stroll through the old Simpson mansion, though they called it a "cottage."

When we first entered the house into a wonderful foyer complete with fireplace and polished wooden columns, we saw the lake through the eastern windows. I was sure that, as we entered, a tall, elderly man, mostly bald, and dressed in servant's black, rose slowly from his seat at the left of the door. I knew him to be a memory of a previous butler who greeted the Simpson's guests at formal parties. It was as if this long-departed gentleman simply stood to acknowledge our passing, then his image left my mind.

Susan stated that her strongest impression, viewed through the northern wall of the house, as these visions are often seen, was that of a twenty-something woman wearing a white dress with a blue sash, carrying a parasol, and walking in the afternoon sun on a no-longer-existent field in the direction of The Sagamore. It was clear that an addition to the rear of the hotel (probably from the 1960s) now obscures what must once have been that field. Finding little spirit presence on the first floor, we ascended the staircase.

As we reached the second floor, I had the impression of being accompanied by a woman who was clearly a servant. "This isn't the floor, you have to come to the third floor so I can show you my room," she imparted. Nevertheless, we traversed the second floor hallway and examined each of the bedrooms. In the "tan bedroom," Sue experienced a stomachache that she knew was not hers. I wondered aloud if some woman may have died in this room, but Sue felt it was more likely a chronic ailment of a previous dweller. It is clear that some interior settings have changed over the years since Helen Simpson departed, as the house has had several owners since her time.

Next, we entered what we called "the blue bedroom," for the color of the ceramic tiles on the fireplace. Sue heard "aunt," and she felt certain that the word identified the ghost woman on the lawn, and likely a former occupant of the room. We had no definite knowledge of the members of the Simpson family at that time, and we didn't know if an aunt had ever lived or visited there. Susan then saw the woman standing motionless with her closed parasol, as if to certify that our guesswork was correct. My intuitive companion felt this woman might indeed be "the walker" that Valerie said was occasionally heard by house guests.

In the "yellow bedroom," Sue received an impression of "boys' bedroom," though in retrospect, after learning a bit about the Simpsons, it isn't clear who the boys might have been. We went to the third floor and entered a pink bedroom, which I felt certain had been the servant woman's. "Lizzie's room" came into my mind, as if to identify the woman. Then, I received the comment, "the name is Elizabeth—only the family called her Lizzie." It seemed clear that the third floor had more energy than the first and second levels. Up there, Sue heard children running, and remarked that she could hear marbles hitting and rolling on the hardwood floors, as a "memory" sound from youngsters' games of long ago.

Our intuitive heard and visualized an older woman (Lizzie?) playfully snapping a towel at children's behinds, then Sue more clearly saw the servant. "She is young, and her hair is done up tightly—it's light brown. She is being playful with the child or children, and I hear her saying, 'Off with you!' to the youngster."

In an adjoining pink bedroom, Sue both saw and heard a servant woman (perhaps the head housekeeper?) tugging on the bedspread and ordering the bed's occupant to "Get up!" No more came to her on that, so Valerie led us into a large, windowless room nearby, and Sue and I paused to see what we might pick up. She felt it may have been a child's playroom, and my thought was that it had been an exercise room for men, or else a billiards room. Valerie noted that guests who slept there often experienced little annoyances, some electrical, some auditory.

When we returned to the second floor, our hostess took us to a "red bedroom," and noted that house guests often felt an energy there and are certain that it is female, but Sue and I received no impressions. Valerie then escorted us to the cellar, which passes through onto an eastern terrace in a quaint mini-tavern having pass-through windows to the outside. "My husband and I have entertained several guests who felt chills or energies in this room, too. In the 1960s, the management of The Sagamore quartered employees in the house, and several of them passed on stories of an uncomfortable energy in here."

All in all, it was a wonderful house, still alive with psychic scenes of yesteryear, but it is also a beautiful lakeside retreat for the present owners.

A few weeks after we returned to our homes, Sue called to inform me that she had been reading *The Great and the Gracious on Millionaires' Row* by Kathryn O'Brien and found a story about "John Boulton Simpson and Family." In this tale, a letter from daughter Fanny, about to graduate from Vassar College in 1902, is excerpted, and therein is a reference to "Aunt" being one of the girl's preferred guests at the ceremony. My intuitive friend was happy to have that verification and so was I. It is often easy to doubt one's impressions, and we always appreciate a vindication of the psychic side of us all when there is a "hit."

This is not a story of raging spirits or poltergeists, and I include it as a good example of the experiences that so many of you readers have had, and then dismissed, chalking up your sensations to imagination. I have stated before that we humans are energy that manifests consciously. When we die, the energy remains where we lived or fought or worked or loved until refocused elsewhere. During that time, it seems reasonable that a sensitive person can perceive the emotions, trials and tribulations of those who resided in a house. It is as if some part of our emotions or verbal energy can stick to the walls and ceilings or even to objects that retain such "memories," even if removed from their place of origin (e.g. antiques or objects from lawn sales). Much of what Sue and I experienced that day is likely of that category.

As we left that day, I noted an inscription etched into the fireplace front, a detail that we both had overlooked when we first entered: Happy House. This is perhaps the best description of Nirvana.

One After Another

Gail grew up on Hayward Avenue in Rochester, and didn't have her first contact with the world of ghosts until she was twelve. "Two weeks after my grandmother died from falling downstairs, I saw her slowly come into focus in a downstairs closet. I screamed out her name, ran out of the bedroom, and upstairs. That seems to have opened a door in my spirit life, and since then, it's been just one after another," she smiled.

"After Grandma died, my mom was cleaning in the kitchen, and sponged off the spice rack. Putting the sponge down, she turned to some other matter, but quickly turned back to her task and found the rack covered with jelly! But Mom hadn't cleaned up any jelly, and nobody had eaten any recently, so how did it get onto the sponge? From time to time we'd hear rocking sounds up in the attic, but we didn't dare go see who it was. Then, some of the jewelry that Grandma had left behind began to disappear. It didn't just get misplaced, it vanished *forever*. Maybe she decided to take it with her," Gail joked.

"For all of us kids, it was a difficult time. My brother and sister could sense someone watching them, especially when they were in the bathroom, and eventually I wouldn't take a shower in there without my sister in the room to stand guard, though nothing ever happened after that. In my bedroom, I once awoke to hear footsteps entering the room, though nobody was visible," Gail said. "The walking stopped right alongside my bed, and it was quiet for a minute, then I heard someone take a deep breath, and, finally, the steps went toward the door again, and that was the end of that. Boy! I jumped up and left the room.

"I think we all realized it was Grandma. She hadn't been an easy woman to live with when she was alive. Seems like she chose to keep to that pattern once she was dead, too. My youngest brother hadn't gone to Grandma's funeral, so he knew only that she died, but about a month later, he got a glimpse of her in our house. He told us he saw Grandma in the closet (where all her belongings had been stored after her death) and correctly described the clothes that she had been buried in, including the necklace that my grandmother wore. We considered *that* to be real proof of him seeing her."

As with so many departed souls, one can expect them to return to the home where they lived, because hospitals are no place to hang around once one is released from a sickly body. Letting go of one's old "home" is seldom an easy matter, and a ghost can linger around its former home (or bodily home at the cemetery) for years unless sent onward by family members. It is often a difficult decision to make. Families should not worry about hurting a ghost's feelings, and, talking in love, they should send them on their way to a greater experience.

"Grandma had gone through a divorce and, afterward, loudly expressed her hatred of men. We should have known what to expect when my parents hired some painters to get the house into good shape for sale. When we left the house, they were preparing to paint an area of the house where my grandmother used to do her puzzles. Later, we came home to find the painters sitting on the steps and not working. They wanted to be paid for what they'd already done, but the men refused to do any more. They were scared off when a candle holder and a flower pot flew across that room and smashed into tiny pieces. That was quite enough!"

It was quite a relief, then, when her family moved into their new home. Gail finished out her childhood in a "normal" ghost-free house. Later, she married and moved to an apartment on Averill Avenue in Rochester. "I'd had it so good at home that I never expected to encounter ghosts there, but one night the phone rang and nobody was on the other end. A crank call? Wrong number? That's what I told myself up until the night I lay in bed, waiting for my husband to return home.

"All at once, on the bedroom wall, I saw an object take shape—it looked like a gnarled human hand. It was repulsive and scared the daylights out of me. Soon afterward, my husband and I bought a new house, but that didn't save our marriage, so I left that home, too, and I moved to Five Mile Line Road in Penfield, where I've been since 1994. I hoped to establish a normal life here again, but the ghost parade has kept up. One day, as I was folding clothes in my room, my son, Nick, came home. I heard him run up the stairs and saw him and another boy walk into his bedroom at the end of the hall. I didn't know the other child, so I went to Nick's bedroom door to ask him to introduce me.

"My son was alone in there when I looked. I asked him about it—who was the other little boy? He couldn't understand what I was talking about and told me he'd come upstairs *alone*. But I *know* I saw that other boy; it was 2:00 p.m., and he wasn't at all misty or wavy, like ghosts are supposed to be. I swear that he was a *real* boy!" I often smile when people tell me they've never seen a ghost. If ghosts can appear as solid figures, as both Gail and I have experienced, then how can one tell it's *not* a ghost when we see an apparently real person? If you like *that* question, then ponder what we mean when we use the word "real."

Gail's next adventure came when she awoke to find an elegantly-dressed old woman standing beside her bed. The intruder wore her hair in a bun and was attired in a long, expensive dress from the 1800s. "I could see her as wavy energy," Gail told me, "so I knew this one *was* a ghost. She seemed to be about seventy and was fairly small, about five feet tall and maybe about one hundred pounds in weight. I couldn't comprehend who she was or how she got there, so I pulled the covers over my head. A few minutes later, I looked again, but she was still there. I just wanted her to go away, though I don't believe I was scared. I didn't say anything to Nick or my boyfriend, Jude.

"Shortly after that, however, Nick complained to me that someone invisible had touched him in his room. A short time later, he said he had felt someone breathing on him. Both he and I have felt we were accompanied up the stairs at times, but we can never see who it is, though it is obviously a ghost. A few months after the lady appeared, Jude said to me that he had seen a strange woman in the bedroom, though she vanished. I asked what the woman looked like, and he described the exact woman I'd seen. Shortly after that, I walked into the bedroom and (speaking to the emptiness) told the old woman to go. That was 1994, and she hasn't been back."

Who the ghost boy was and the identity of the old woman were still lingering questions when Gail installed some workout equipment in the basement. As she is doing physical workouts down there, she often hears footsteps overhead on the first floor, though she knows she is alone in the house. "Once I heard 'Mom!' called really loud from upstairs, so I yelled loudly to Nick, 'What do you want?' No answer. Then, two seconds later, again I heard, 'Mom!' so, thinking there was an emergency, I went upstairs. There was nobody there, and it wasn't time for Nick to be home yet, anyway."

At the time of this writing, it's not clear how much of this mysterious activity is caused by dwellers of the spirit world and how much is the result of Gail's obvious psychic sensitivity. When we talked, I told her that all people are psychic to some extent, and everyone could improve that talent somewhat if they made the effort. "Maybe that's what took place recently in my life," she told me. "I have a girlfriend whose mother was dying of cancer. I woke up one sunny morning and was struck with what a beautiful day it was. A good day to depart from the earth, I mused. I got up and had breakfast and about an hour later, the phone rang. It was my friend telling me that her mother had died!

"I have a nightlight on all night in my bedroom, and there haven't been any more ghostly visits," she told me, "but there seems to be more activity in Nick's room. The episodes are more muted—no more spectral appearances, but recently when I was vacuuming our family room, I felt someone walk by me. I looked and saw no one, but then it happened again. And that second time, I saw a dark shadow pass by. There was no detail in that shadow, so I don't know if it was a man or woman, but it almost certainly is another ghost. I'll wait and see what that individual is up to before I call the exorcist," she grinned.

One after another. *Many* sensitive people have continuing contacts with spirits throughout life. Sooner or later, the entities will all *have to* boogie on down the road to Eternity. I advised Gail to keep an eye (if possible) on The

Shadow. Maybe, if he was doing more than just passing through, he'll need a firm nudge of encouragement into the Afterworld.

Sending Al Home

The first truly odd experience that Lisa remembers was the sudden appearance of her father in the kitchen doorway a few months after he died. "We knew it was Dad because he wore the same suit that he was buried in," she told me. "I was only fifteen at the time, and had some friends that he didn't approve of, especially one boy who was visiting the house right when Dad's spirit came. Dad didn't say anything, but had that serious 'I don't approve' look on his face before he faded out. *That* was enough for me to get his message!"

Her life went on, with few other extraordinary occurrences until she married and, in 1987, she and her husband bought the house at 303 Benton Street in Rochester, NY. "One night, when I was 27, the light beside our bed suddenly turned on. Sleepily, I turned it off, but a moment later, it turned on again! At that point I wasn't even considering the possibility that we had a ghost, and ended the situation by removing the light from our bedroom.

"Shortly after that, I began to see shadows moving through the house, and couldn't *believe* what I was seeing, but soon afterward, my husband commented that he saw the shadows too. So I told him about the light turning on upstairs and that I, also, saw those strange shadows. A short time after that, my brother-in-law and sister-in-law and their children visited. Standing in the kitchen, they both commented that they felt my husband and I weren't alone in the house, and at that moment all the knobs popped off our stove. I couldn't believe it—they'd never done that before, so I put them back on. They popped off once more!

"Then, shortly after that, when I was in the bedroom, I heard footsteps coming up the stairs and entering my room, but I couldn't see anyone. Whoever it was, seemed to stand there for a while, then turned and walked back out. It seemed that somebody had entered and just scrutinized me, and somehow, I felt it had to be my husband. Still, I called after the person, 'Stop! Who *are* you?' I heard footsteps descending the stairs and followed them, and, once more, in the kitchen, I called out to the ghost to identify itself, but he just ignored me. I went downstairs where my husband was lying on the couch and told him I knew it was him, though I really couldn't believe it. 'Lisa, I've been here on the couch for a half hour,' he pleaded."

She remembers an array of events, mostly small, but, in the end, they all added up to a ghostly presence. For example, as she sat on her bed one day, the bedspread suddenly wrinkled and she felt the mattress depress, yet no one was there. Mentally, she questioned who it was, and got the name, "Al." "He seemed to like my plants, because the hanging one in the living room would swing from time to time, and when I watched TV at night, I'd see the potted plant leaves rustle occasionally, as if something light had just passed through them. Another time, I felt a gentle caress on the side of my head, though nobody was nearby. And our ghost also moved things in various parts of the house," she said.

Her brother-in-law stayed with her family for a short time, and he complained that his bedroom doorknob often jiggled, as if someone was trying to enter, though no one ever did. Then, the man was rudely awakened in the middle of the night by someone or something grabbing and pulling hard on his arm. After that, he always locked the bedroom door at night. All of these events prodded Lisa to seek a potential cause.

"I discovered that the former owner, indeed, was named Al, and that he died in a hospital bed in what is now our living room. Shortly after that, I was contacted by Al's children, who heard strange events were taking place and came to visit with some of their children. Standing in the doorway, one of them looked at me and said to the other, 'See? I *told* you she probably had blue eyes and blond hair! You *know* Grandpa liked women that looked like that.' They told us that soon after Al's death, they had all sat around their dining room table one evening, discussing the various phenomena. All at once, the globe covering the overhead light shattered. Strangely, the family dog didn't react to the calamity and remained asleep. "That globe came apart in such tiny pieces, that it was almost impossible to pick them up," they told Lisa. "The family members also told me that Al wasn't very religious, but that, on his deathbed, a priest had been called to baptize him. Apparently, the ceremony did little to quiet Al's upsets, which he carried on into the spirit world."

She also related that, early one morning, her husband came downstairs on his way to work, and a small screwdriver that he had placed on a shelf suddenly flew off and hit him. Then, not long afterward, some paint brushes that he'd rolled in aluminum foil and placed on top of a bookcase, also flew through the air and struck him. A day later, he came home and gestured for her to come outside with him. Once outdoors, her husband said he felt the exit was necessary because Al apparently listened to whatever he said inside the house. He told Lisa that he felt Al didn't like him and described the two objects striking him. Then, a short time later, at their daughter's ninth birthday party, the girl's photograph flew off the TV and hit him on the shoulder blade. It looked as if

Al resented the happy family living in the space where he died. The family's two Schnauzers were often upset at some invisible presence, and let the spirit know of their displeasure.

"Then, Al's two granddaughters visited again. They came in and asked to use what they called their 'witch board,' something like the Ouija board. Apparently, they got in touch with their grandfather and had a brief conversation with him. My sister-in-law came in unexpectedly and, seeing I had company, told me she was going next door and to come over later. I returned to watching Al's relatives and their board. Al sent the word, 'Peaches' among the other communications to the girls before they sent him on his way into The Light, informing him that he didn't belong in the house any more. Later, when I went next door, I told my sister-in-law about the session and that the strange word 'peaches' was part of it, though none of Al's family knew what it meant. My sister-in-law was shocked—Al had known her father and her, when she was a little girl nicknamed '*Peaches!*'"

Lisa told me that, like most couples, she and her husband had their occasional spats and maybe Al chose sides, preferring the blond, blue-eyed wife over the husband. "I was often chilled to the bone, and figure that must have been Al hovering over me," she smiled. "If I ever wrote a book about all that happened here, I think the title would be, 'Nine Years With Al!'"

The house on Benton Street provided quite an education for Lisa and her family. There have been other eerie events, too. "Randy, my brother-in-law died on December 4, 2003," she related. "And on the first birthday after his death, my husband's cell phone message minder showed an incoming call from Randy. But, that was impossible because Randy's old account had been cancelled and the number was inoperative," she marveled.

"A friend of mine, Jonathan, was quite a smoker, but wanted to get me a present once, so he saved up all his Pall Mall Points and traded them in for a nice dryer. He died on October 31, and a few months later, on the anniversary of his February 12th birthday, I thought about him and said quietly, 'Love you, Jonathan.' Instantly, the dryer erupted in sparks. I'd owned it for six years and never had a problem, but now, just after I spoke to him, it short-circuited and burned out."

Not many families have had as much contact with departed spirits. However, perhaps the term "departed" is inaccurate, as our loved ones, even old Al, seem to know when we're thinking of them. "Probably we should say a prayer for them, or something nice to or about them, and never, *never* argue in front of the ghost," Lisa laughed.

Spook Hollow Country

If one were to look for improbable ghosts, one would need go no further than the Mid-Hudson Valley, where Rip Van Winkle could have returned to dozing, Henry Hudson's crew might still be at play, or Washington Irving's Headless Horseman could even now be riding on dark autumn nights. But there are other fabulous creatures still not widely known in the Empire State.

"Take the case of Rover," Debbie Sackel told me. "When I was a young woman in the 1970s, I remember finding a huge boulder not far from Lane Gate Road in Cold Spring, where I lived. On the back of the huge stone, someone had engraved the name "Rover," as if the boulder were a dog's grave marker. I asked friends about the dog, and they told me he was a legendary one-eyed ghost animal whose forest running and barking could still be heard in the highlands overlooking the Hudson. Olive Adams from Nelsonville, now deceased, wrote a number of verses on this dog's story in a 1955 book." Curious, I inquired of the specialists at the Cold Spring Historical Society, but Rover was not in their folklore collection.

"I lived with my foster parents on Lane Gate Road back then," Debbie told me, "and that's where I encountered my first ghost. In the yard one day, I caught sight of a young soldier dressed in black boots, uniform trousers, and a flowing white-sleeved shirt. Across his chest, he wore a reddish sash from which was suspended a sword. Though I most often saw him in the pasture near the house, sometimes I'd see him sweeping through our house. I didn't want to scare my foster mother, but she was pretty cool, so one day I asked her about him. 'Oh, *him*! Yes, I've seen him ever since we bought this house in the 1940s,' she replied. That made me feel better; he wasn't just a figure of my imagination. I later did some research in Putnam County history and discovered a possible candidate for that soldier.

"I think it might have been John Jacob Astor IV, whose ancestors owned large tracts of land in the county, because my grandmother owned much of the old Astor lands on Lane Gate Road, just a mile from our farm house. The wealthy Astor outfitted his own company of soldiers to fight in the Spanish-American War, and I found their uniforms to be very similar to that of my dashing soldier. J.J. Astor IV, you know, died on the *Titanic*, but maybe, after death, in his mind he chose to return to a time and place when everything had been going *his* way," she smiled.

"However, you never knew where or when that soldier would appear, and once, he really surprised me. I had come home quite late at night, almost 3 a.m., and was very tired. I went down our rickety cellar stairs to the refrigerator there and got a gallon jug of milk. As I started up the stairs in the darkness, he was suddenly *right behind me* on the steps! I fumbled the milk jug, then slipped and tumbled down the steps—me going one way and the jug going the other. I landed hard on the ground in a puddle of milk. Next morning, I had to apologize to Mom, but she told me not to worry.

"Ghosts being a reality to me now, I went down to the historical society to find out about the house and property. I knew the house had been given to my foster parents by Edith Smith, and that she was a descendant of the old Sylvanus Mekeel family who came to Putnam County in the mid-1800s."

The historian at the historical society said that many Mekeels lived in the Putnam-Dutchess County area and that most of them were entrepreneurs of some type. Debbie learned that Sylvanus Mekeel had only one daughter who survived to adulthood and married a Smith. It's hard to believe the soldier ghost could have sprung from that union, as the uniform style seemed wrong.

"Well, we've had soldiers aplenty in this area," the historian told me. "During the Revolutionary War, both an army hospital and barracks were located in this vicinity. Those were hard times for the Continental Army," she reminded me. "Soldiers went for months without receiving pay, and rations were often in *very* short supply. Neighboring farms were often raided for a hen or loaf of bread, just enough to keep the pangs of hunger away."

Apparently, the privation led some of Gen. Israel Putnam's Revolutionary War soldiers to mutiny and about twenty of them deserted. Putnam sent an officer to return the men to duty, but one of the fleeing men attacked the officer, who drew a sword and stabbed the soldier. The injured private then lifted his musket, shot and mortally wounded the officer. Both dying men were carried to the barracks, where they expired. Both bodies were then interred on a hill behind the army camp. That fact got me to wondering about Debbie's swordsman. Hmmm.

Willa Skinner, the longtime Town of Fishkill historian often told the above tale at yearly Halloween recitations, indicating that the two soldiers simply joined a legion of other local Dutchess-Putnam County Line ghosts. She often said that the region was often called "Spook Hollow" because of the many real or imagined wraiths that resided there. One of these, perhaps a prototype for Washington Irving's scary character, was a colorful headless horseman.

Throughout the 1800s, Skinner said, the region around the deep ravine at Dry Bridge was haunted by a headless horseman who continually chanted, "Jug-o-rum! Jug-o-rum!" and leaped upon passing horsemen, stagecoaches, and farm wagons that traveled the old Albany Post Road (the present Route 9). According to legend, the spirit sought any alcoholic beverages that the passersby might have secreted.

And there was one more unusual specter who appeared to haunt Spook Hollow: a fabled giant pig! In all of Ghostdom, porkers get short shrift, but this one, a monstrous being, seems to have terrorized the old Albany Post Road for many years.

The legend states that vehicles moving from Cold Spring northward to Fishkill were often assaulted by a mammoth swine, whose sudden appearance frightened the horses, who then began a frenzied run to escape the creature. But no matter how fast they galloped, the horses couldn't outrun the colossal hog. One variation on the story indicates that the forequarters of the pig ran ahead of the fleeing team, while the hindquarters lingered in the rear of the runaway coach, terrorizing its passengers. Then, as the stagecoach or wagon reached the flat lands just south of Fishkill, the two parts of the hog slammed together with a thunderous roar and the animal disappeared, leaving the travelers to enter Fishkill in terror. When Route 9 was straightened and hard-surfaced in the 1920s, the spirits seem to have lost their hold on the area and departed.

Though this last tale doesn't say so, it is my belief that the creature was headed for Albany, and that (considering the great number of "member items" budgeted by the Legislature nowadays) he certainly *did* reach the State Capitol and has resided there since.

Mr. Olsen

At the beginning of the twentieth century, many New York City residents were doing well enough financially to move out from the crowded metropolis, eastward toward Long Island. There was still plenty of underdeveloped land in the Borough of Queens, and The Russell Sage Foundation designed a high-class planned development called Forest Hills Gardens, in 1909. All of the structures, including a school, a railroad station, playgrounds and homes, were to be finished in a Tudor style. Fredrick Law Olmstead, Jr., the famous American landscape architect, was hired to design the surroundings, so that it appeared much like the British "garden cities."

One of the neighborhood's early residents was Alfred W. Olsen, who purchased a home on Ingram Street in 1941. "I lived near him for years. He was a solitary man, and I don't think he had much family. Many times I saw him reading alone in the backyard," said an elderly neighbor. Thus, not much is known about the man today, though after his death in 1967, he seems to have continued living with the Renz family, the dwelling's next owners, from 1967 to 1998. "He was already there when I was born, and I don't remember a time when he wasn't around the house doing something," remembers Gina Renz Sullivan.

"One of the first experiences to mystify me as a little girl was watching the dial on the stereo move from the rock and roll music station that we all liked, down to the classical station. Whenever the dial moved, it was always toward the classical. I took my cues from my older brother, Bobby, I guess, though I was never as scared as he was. After some inquiry, we discovered that, indeed, a Mr. Olsen, the previous owner, had died alone there. That got us kids wondering, because other youngsters in the neighborhood referred to our house as 'the haunted house' almost as soon as we'd moved in. As kids, we speculated—maybe it really was haunted!"

Gina told me of so many phenomena that are familiar to those who dwell with spirits. "Always, there was the phantom knocking sound along the banister. Once, after I was older, the basement door shook powerfully after my married older sister and I had left with our children. Had we missed one of our tykes and had that child gotten stranded in the cellar? My brother-in-law hurried to open the door, but no one was there."

When she was fifteen, Gina's sister, Carla, sat one day, listening to music in her room. A loud knock came at her door and she called, "Come in!" thinking it was Grandma, whose room was across the hall. She repeated her invitation several times without a response, then jumped up to see who was there. Nobody! She crossed to her grandmother's room and asked Grandma if she had knocked, though the woman denied doing so. Carla returned to her room, closed the door, and immediately heard three sharp knocks again on the door. The girl ran to the door, opened it, again found nobody, and dashed to Grandma's room. "You had to have knocked on my door—you're the only one here," she said. But again, the elder denied doing so, and Carla noted that her grandmother was seated exactly where she had been a few minutes before.

"I even had Grandma, who was old and frail, come into my room and check the closet and under the bed. She found nothing, so I had her leave the hall light on because I was scared. I retreated to my room. A few minutes later, Grandma stood in the doorway. 'Stop kidding around, now,' she said. I had no idea what she meant, but she told of hearing knocks on her bedroom door! Apparently, Mr. Olsen got a kick from playing jokes on Grandma and me because, a few months later when I was once again in my room, clear as day, I heard a female voice call out, 'Carla?' I ran to Grandma's room, but she denied calling me; I went downstairs to check with Mom, but no one else was home. Grandma came downstairs and helped me search everywhere, but no one was around. We went back upstairs, laughing nervously to ourselves," she smiled.

"Ten minutes later, I heard Grandma call upstairs, 'Yes, Carla? Do you need something?'—she had heard a female voice hailing her, but I know it wasn't me. Another activity was the movement of the curtain in my room. Every night I'd close it, only to awaken in the morning to find it pulled back. My sister, Crista, also had a strange experience. One day, her friend came to the house to pick her up and heard knocking from inside the window. Looking up, the friend waved back. But no one came to the door. Just then, Crista pulled up out front in a car. It hadn't been her knocking, but the big mystery was that nobody was inside. Except, perhaps, Mr. Olsen?"

Gina interjected, "Mom couldn't say she didn't know we had a ghost, either. She once heard something rubbing against the wall in the upstairs hallway, and she was the only one present that day. So, 'Mr. Olsen' became the spirit's name, and he was like a pesky family member who had his own agenda. He seemed to do what he wanted and when he wanted to do it," she remembered.

"Once when Mom was very sick, Carla, sitting in Mom's bedroom, looked up and saw a grey-haired man in the hall, outside the door,' said Gina. "'Hi, Dad, come on in,' she offered. But the man didn't enter. When the figure appeared again, Carla went into the hallway to see where her father was. She found him deep asleep in his bedroom, so maybe my sister is the only family member to get a look at 'Mr. Olsen.'"

Carla interjected, "I don't think Mr. Olsen liked men sleeping on the third floor. On occasion, when Bobby returned home to visit, there would be knocking on the walls of his room. And my husband, Steve, usually awoke to find his bed covers thrown across the room when he awoke. He, Crista, and I all had the sensation of someone sitting on our beds when we were falling asleep."

"Yes, my main contacts with the ghost involved feelings of being watched," said Bobby. "I don't know if he was malevolent or just mischievous, but there sure were times I could feel him around me; a person knows when he is under scrutiny. We grew up with noises all around the house—sounds of bumping and thumping. One summer when my parents were away, my girlfriend and I were on the second floor. We distinctly heard the front door open and voices calling, 'We're home!' My girlfriend dashed into the bathroom, locked herself in, and started crying. I ran up to the third floor. But nobody had come in—certainly not my parents. There was no logical explanation for any of it; it was a solidly-built brick house, and we never heard any noise from our neighbors. All I could figure is that Mr. Olsen had a warped sense of humor.

"What ended it for me, was an event when I was nineteen," Bobby said. "I was lying in bed, wide awake, and I got that feeling of being watched again, and it was unusually strong. I was nervous and kept opening my eyes to look around the room—then something poked me very hard, right on the breast bone! My eyes popped open, and I fully expected to see someone standing over me, but nobody was there! Immediately after this painful poke, our two dogs, Blackie and Jenny, started howling mournfully. Well," he grinned, "that was it for me. I went downstairs and slept on the couch, next to the front door, and the next day I packed my bags. My mom always said she thought Mr. Olsen was a benevolent spirit, but I guess he liked her more than me. After I left, I recalled the time Dad and I first came to look at the house. We had brought Blackie, and he walked into the house, lay down and started moaning. It made the hair on the back of my neck stand up. I should have known," he laughed.

"The family dogs often snapped awake while sprawled on the floor," Gina told me. "Their heads would jerk up, and they intently watched some invisible person or thing cross the room. While the ghost roamed the entire house, probably the greatest number of episodes took place on the third floor. We had a lamp up there that could be touched to turn it on—another touch and it was brighter, and a third touch made it brightest. A fourth touch turned it off again. It freaked me out to watch the light go through the cycle without anyone being near it. The television set in the third floor bedroom often turned itself off and on," she revealed.

Gina and I talked a bit about spirits' propensity to play with electrical devices. Likely, they are curiously experimenting with objects that didn't exist in their lifetime. At other times, being energy themselves, they understand that they can manipulate the object's electricity flow and create an incident that notifies all residents that they are still there. Remember, most ghosts are thrilled to find themselves still in existence, as many readers will one day discover. Although they may have attended their own funeral and may even have seen their body cremated or buried, what a thrill it must be to experience liberation from a body that was diseased, old, or unhappy! They would certainly want to communicate that victory over extinction to sorrowing loved ones.

Unhappiness, however, is usually carried over from this world into the next, and traumas, especially, are often a cause for the ghost to linger, trying to work out a successful conclusion to its angst.

"Everyone in our family, except my dad, had at least one run-in with Mr. Olsen," Gina concluded. "My sister's husband, Steve, when he married into the family, just couldn't believe our tales about the ghost, and once taunted the spirit. 'Come on, Mr. Olsen, show yourself!' Not long afterward, he awoke in the night to find himself sleeping on top of the blankets, though he'd been under them when he went to sleep. Another time, he awoke to find the blankets stripped off and tumbled against the far bedroom wall. He didn't dare challenge the old guy again!

"In 1998, we sold the house and began to move our belongings out. Likely, old Mr. Olsen had gotten used to us and was upset that his family was going. The new owners likely didn't believe the neighborhood stories about the ghost any more than our family did," she laughed. "But they later told our neighbor across the street that they thought my Mom, who had passed away by then, was still around. They told of 'odd things' taking place there. For us, however, that was just confirmation that all that we had experienced on Ingram Street was true!'"

Stairways

Darren Bonaparte is a Mohawk who has lived in both the American and Canadian parts of the Akwesasne Reservation. When checking a story from the Hogansburg, NY, area with him in 2006, I discovered that he had a powerful ghost experience of his own to relate.

"My best friend growing up was my cousin, Mathew, who called me up back in 1987," Darren told me. "In our conversation he suggested that I join him in a task that he was doing for his father. There was an old neighbor friend of his father's who had gone to the hospital, and Mat's dad asked if he would spend the night in that house, just to keep an eye on things. Mat asked if I wanted to stay over and keep him company, so I said, 'Yes.'

"When we got inside, Mathew sprawled out on the couch and I made myself comfortable in a big easy chair. It seems that the old man who owned the house was a collector of cuckoo clocks, and they all went off at midnight, waking us up. I guess Mathew rolled over and went back to sleep but, as I turned in my chair, I spotted an old white-haired woman in a black dress standing on the landing of the stairway behind Mat's couch. She stood looking at me for just a moment, and then faded out. Wow, I'd never seen anything like that in my twenty-three years of life! A few minutes later, I woke Mat to tell him what I'd seen. 'I believe you,' he said, then yawned, rolled over, and went back to sleep. Well, to *me* it was a big deal!"

Darren then told me of the tension and violence that broke out around the Hogansburg area of the reservation in 1990. There was growing hostility between Mohawks who wanted casinos and those who were opposed to them. The violence between the two factions eventually resulted in a gun battle in which Mathew, then twenty-two, was shot and killed.

It was a great loss to Darren and he went to the wake to say goodbye to his friend. "What really shocked me is that the wake was held in the house where Mat and I had watched over the old man's belongings. Right in the same room! And Mathew's coffin was placed where I had slept in the easy chair on the night I saw the lady ghost."

Soon after that, Darren took a job that required him to work with a computer, and seated at a PC right next to him was a woman who became a new friend. "It turned out that she was a distant cousin of Mathew, too, and had attended his wake. 'Can I tell you something strange?' she asked. 'Last night I had a dream that I was in the room where Mathew's wake was held. I looked up and saw Matthew standing on the landing of the stairs!'

I was shocked and asked her if she was kidding. 'I wouldn't kid about something like *that*,' she said.

"She couldn't have known about the experience that I had two years before—seeing that old lady on that same landing. Mathew was the only one I ever told about that. The two of us used to talk about death and the afterlife and how we'd let the other know when we passed. Now, here I was, hearing a story of Mathew's spirit standing on a spot that he and I knew was special to me! It sure seemed like a message to me from my friend."

Those events, it seems, commenced an "opening" of sorts for Darren, as not long afterward, he heard a whisper in his ear. But nobody could have been standing close enough to do that because his ear was very near a wall. And, a few years later, while attending his godfather's wake, Darren was poked in the back. Turning quickly, he found no one there—only three rows of empty chairs. Then, another time, as he walked up a stairway, he paused on the landing and was suddenly chilled to the bone. He asked a friend who accompanied him if anyone had died in the house. The friend responded, "Yes, my grandfather died right where you're standing." Later, Darren asked a wise elder about the experience and was told that stairways are a symbol of the connection between the heavens and earth, so while they are real objects, they can also serve as a way for those in the spirit world to teach us.

Surprises

Today she lives in Elmira, but for a number of years Frances Osteen had fascinating contacts with the spirit world in her house in Lowman, NY.

"Our family moved to Lowman in July 1963," she told me, "and I thought it was the most beautiful place—that there was something important awaiting me there. I remember a chilly October day that year, when I'd just come inside from outdoors. As usual, I hung my jacket on a peg and then, a minute later, when I looked, it was gone! I asked the kids where it went, and they were wide-eyed with denial. *They* hadn't taken it, so who did?

"Soon afterward, something else strange began. Old Mr. Shoemaker, the previous owner, had left a big old upholstered rocking chair in the house. At first, we thought it was simply a nice gift, but very soon we came to see that it rocked by itself—not violently," she smiled, "but steadily, as if someone was really dedicated to relaxation. The kids sure didn't know what to make of that activity." I suggested that Mr. Shoemaker might have left the chair behind pre-cisely because there *was* a spirit attached to it.

"About that time, my brother wrote me a letter from Hawaii, and I put it on the dining room table," Frances told me. "When I turned around, it had simply vanished! I was beginning to get tired of things just going off into the universe, and I got upset. My husband, Paul, and the children all denied tak-ing or moving it. After a few years, however, I understood that things *could* just disappear and might never show up again. By then, I knew that there were icy cold spots on the front stairs, and for the first time, it occurred to me that we really *had* a ghost!

"A few days later, I became certain of it. I was cleaning the upstairs and finished in one room and left it, closing the door behind me. Then, I realized I had forgotten something inside and tried to reopen the door. No way—it was locked! Then I realized the ghost probably did it just to get attention, so I calm-ly explained to the empty hallway that I had to clean the house and would the spirit *please* reopen the door. It clicked open, just like that!"

As she got to know her ghost more fully, Frances said that she liked the individual, whom she thought of as a man. And sometimes, she observed, the ghost could be a help. "One of my daughter's friends lived down the road and when she came to visit one day, the girl announced that a friend of hers named Bart was coming to visit from New York City, and she wanted him to stay with us. I really didn't like Bart and wished he hadn't come, but I tried to be hospitable. He hadn't been in his bedroom for long when he came running out. 'Who's fool-ing around?' he demanded to know. I asked what he meant, and the boy said he had been stretched out on his bed, when somebody he couldn't see suddenly came into the room and sat down on his bed. He could feel it sink under the invisible person's weight. I think he was scared and all his bravado vanished.

"The pipes in the cellar rattled, and Bart went back upstairs to his bed-room but suddenly emerged again to announce that something or someone he couldn't see had just left an impression on his pillow. He said he just couldn't stay any longer in our house, but he did. I think our ghost tamed him a bit. Shortly after Bart went home, I got up early one morning and walked into the den. There on a coat hanger was my coat that disappeared two years before. Where had it been? Why did the ghost decide to return it to me after all that time? I really don't have an answer," she said.

A month after that, Paul left Frances a note about their chickens on an old envelope. As she read the note, she absent-mindedly turned the envelope over. It was the long-missing letter her brother had sent from Hawaii! Again, questions arose in her mind about the ghost; its possible motivations assailed her.

Eventually, the decision was made to sell the house, but the first buyers couldn't keep up their payments, and Paul and Frances took it back, then sold the old house a second time after sprucing it up for the next buyer. But *that* family didn't stay long either, saying they "just didn't like the house," and they sold it to an adult book store. "The old Lowman House or Shoemaker House is still there, not far off Route 17," Frances told me. "Adult books, boy, I'll bet they're drawing some *fine* customers from out of the cellar of the spirit world," she grimaced.

"I have another story to tell you, so don't go away," she said. "Paul died in 1986 at only age fifty-four. He'd been a heavy smoker, and I tried to get him to quit," she shrugged as her voice trailed off. "When he was in the hospital, I entered his room one day and am sure that I saw his three dead sisters, sitting patiently by his bed, so I knew that he wasn't going to get better. A half hour later, I left his room and when I came back a few minutes later, he had died. It was sad for us all, but a week later, as I entered the kitchen, I caught sight of him as I turned the corner.

"Then the kids would hear him walking up the stairs, and I'd smell his cigarettes. I got angry; it was smoking that killed him, so I told him out loud to stop. And for a long time afterward, there was no more smell of smoke in the house," she said. "Both my children and grandchildren would either see him or feel his presence, and they'd talk to him. And one day, my son called to say that he'd had a chair fall out from under him and thought that was his dad just saying hello.

"Now I have to tell you about Emily," she said excitedly. "*There's* a kid for you! My granddaughter was born in 1992, eight years after Paul died, so she sure had never seen him or even photos of him. A year later, another granddaughter, Jessie came to talk with me about an upcoming operation. I think she was scared about its outcome and took comfort from holding little Emily, who was just ten months old at the time, and dearly loved by Jessie. A week later, following her operation, Jessie died. Then, a week after that, little Emily said to me, 'There's a ghost.' I didn't think the child even knew what the word meant. She said it again, and I asked, 'Where?' She pointed to a spot in the room. I asked, 'Do you know the person?' She replied, 'Jessie.' For quite some time afterward, Emily said she saw Jessie, who talked to her, saying hello quite often, but that she eventually left the house."

"When Emily was three," Frances told me, "I carried her out into the backyard—it was such a nice sunny day. The child turned and pointed back toward the house. 'Who's that man in the window?' she asked me. I turned but could see nobody, so I asked her to describe the man. She mentioned a white shirt in her description. Well, that window was Paul's favorite window to look out, and I remember him always wearing a white t-shirt around the house. Could it be that he was still with us after eleven years?"

Another curious part of Emily's nature, Frances told me, was the little girl's tendency to talk about *Alabama* from the time she could first speak. "I couldn't believe a little girl who'd never been to school would know about that state," said Frances. "But I asked her about the place, and she said, 'My old grandfather lived there—*we* lived there.' The child went on to relate a story about her sister (she has none in this life) and other family members, and also remembered traveling by boat on a river. Before going to kindergarten, Emily spoke of her old grandfather being killed by a man who came to their door one night. She remembered her sister's name, though she couldn't recall her own. 'The old grandfather's shadow went up,' Emily said with assurance, 'but he will come back, though he won't be my grandfather again.' This seemed so illogical that a child not yet five could have such an imagination about people and places that she clearly had never studied," Frances said. Was the child talking about reincarnation? How could that be?

The following year, the husband of Emily's pre-kindergarten teacher, Mrs. Hall, died. The little girl wanted badly to go to the man's funeral. At the wake, the child shook hands with Mrs. Hall and expressed her sadness at his loss, but then said to her, 'Your husband's body is here, but his shadow has left. Someday, if he wants to, he can come back, so don't be sad.' What do you make of that?" Frances asked. "*Is there* such a thing as reincarnation? Can souls choose to return to the earth? Can little children sometimes remember other places and other families? And, if so, then how final can death be?"

Those are big questions that have occupied philosophers and religious teachers for generations, we agreed. Frances had many experiences with ghosts and inhabitants of the spirit world. Yet, it was stunning to have a granddaughter who seemed able to see and hear clearly into that other plane of existence. One thing, for sure, Emily will have an experienced teacher to help her sort it all out.

CHAPTER 12

EVEN MORE HAUNTS

Two Busy Houses

The Mohawks guarded the Eastern Door of the Iroquois Confederacy, occupying much of what is now New York State's eastern valleys. They had many villages along the Mohawk River, which supplied both transportation and food to them. Many of their fortified towns or "castles" occupied the heights overlooking this waterway.

"In 1970, Bob and I arranged to put a mobile home on a lot along Route 163, going toward Cherry Valley," Sherry Byrne told me. That spring was very wet, and they had an awful time maneuvering that house up through the mud. "Once it was in place, it took us quite a while before we could settle in, moving our belongings in and out. The next morning after we moved in, Bob went out and found a long flint blade on the grass. We must have passed that spot dozens of times, coming and going, and nobody ever spotted that thing before. He held it out to me and said it looked like an arrowhead. Later, Bob took it to an archaeologist, who identified it as an Algonkian flint knife," she said in amazement. The two of us laughed that the event may have been a visit from the Mohawk Welcome Wagon.

Sherri told me that it was a strange plot of land as, long ago, a previous farmhouse there had burned during a big grass fire. Her grandfather had bought the property from the unfortunate farmer. We kept trying to assess what, in light of the strange phenomena in that house, could be the origin of the spirited energy.

"When he was younger, Bob had put aside a few gold coins that he was proud of, and one day, he took them out of the safety deposit box and went to an area coin show, where he displayed them. Then he brought them home, set them down, and asked me to take them back to the bank on Monday. But when I looked for them the next day, they were gone! We searched for that little bag for a month without finding it—we literally took the house apart, but still they were gone. One day, I got up and opened the drapes near our bookcase, where I keep my mantel clock. And there, right up against that clock, was the bag of coins. We never knew who had taken them or where they'd been stored. Well, by now, we figured there was a ghost. Maybe that spirit tried to spend the money on the other side and found out you can't *do* that, so he brought them back?" she suggested with a big smile.

Sherri told me of another strange event in that house, which has now become their year-round home, though in years gone by, when the access was bad during the winter, they had stayed with her mother in Ft. Plain. "Bob had a shirt that he really liked, but it, too, turned up missing, just like the coins. We looked and looked. We have just one big closet and it sure wasn't in there!

We checked the dirty clothes hamper again and again, and also the washer and dryer. Nothing! Several weeks later, I walked into the bedroom and discovered that shirt all clean and folded neatly, sitting on Bob's pillow. "Where did you find that shirt?" I asked him.

"What shirt?" he wanted to know. I took him to the bedroom and showed it to him—he was as amazed as I. Who do you think runs a spirit laundry and folding service, and why do you think it took them so long to return it?"

With her bright and happy delivery, Sherri had me in stitches, recounting all the odd events from that house. "One day, when my son was little, he sat at the kitchen table waiting for me to heat up some tomato soup. Standing at the stove, I poured the soup into a bowl and turned to bring it over to him. All at once, I felt somebody's hand come up under the bottom of that bowl and hit my hand, which shot the bowl and soup up into the air. That sure scared me, but even worse, my son was sitting there bug-eyed, watching it all happen, and expecting that I could explain it all. I never did," she grinned.

"Another time, my son had a friend sleep over. I was up reading quite late that night, as I had been ill. As I sat in my chair, I head a boy's voice behind the chair, "What time is it?" I looked at the clock and told him, and then all was quiet. At breakfast in the morning, I asked which of them had come out to ask me, but both denied doing so. So do we also have a child ghost here, too?

Sherri and I speculated for a time as to what former resident might still be hanging out there, a down-on-his-luck farmer? An unhappy Indian warrior? A troublesome little kid? Or somebody else? "Well, those were the thoughts we had for years. Then, in 2001, Bob came in the house with a surprised look on his face. 'Sherri, I just saw something strange. All of a sudden there was a tall figure here, and he just walked over and through the curtains. I couldn't see any detail, but it was a wispy tall man, I'm sure.' That was a first for *that* spirit, and neither one could speculate who the entity might be. The cast of intruders and pranksters seemed to be growing.

"I can't finish without telling you about our other house on Mohawk Street in Ft. Plain. My grandmother and mother lived there in two apartments. Before my Uncle Clarence died, he asked my mother to take care of Aunt Ethel when he died, so after Clarence's funeral, Aunt Ethel moved in with them. She was a very strong woman, and one might suspect her of causing some of the disruptions there, but who knows?

"Aunt Ethel moved in during the early 1990s, and almost immediately, little things like noises and disappearing objects started to happen there. We figured it must be Uncle Clarence, just trying to let us know he was okay. Around that time, I stayed there and, one night while talking to my daughter on the phone, I noticed a small patch of white light up near the ceiling. At first,

I thought it was a reflected car headlight from outside, but it remained stationary. It hung in the air for quite a while, and then slowly dropped in mid-air. I described it to my daughter, and neither of us could figure it out. Suddenly, it just vanished. Was that a spirit? It might have been Clarence."

Sherri described the light as circular, and I informed her that most ghost aficionados call such phenomena *orbs* and suspect the objects are a package of ghostly energy, though there has been little research on this supposition. Many, many haunted sites provide digital photographers with these images. What was different about Sherri's sighting is that she saw it visually.

Another time in that house, Sherri says, she was awakened about midnight, hearing soft footsteps coming up the back stairs. Who could be sneaking in? She woke Bob and told him there was an intruder. He tip-toed through their bathroom to the stairs and found nobody there. Bob made a complete search of the house, including the cellar, but there were no outsiders there. Could *that* have been Clarence? It seemed that the arrival of Ethel in the household had triggered the onset of ghostly sights and sounds.

A dedicated ghost phenomena lover might envy Bob and Sherri. They sure have had plenty of experiences with the spirit world and had their choice of two houses from which to pick. Perhaps quite a few beings from the spirit world were drawn by their good nature and wanted them to pass on some message to the living. Sherri, an herbalist, told me that she preferred her plants— things she could *see*, and which wouldn't act up on her.

What's the Point?

When the spring of 1779 came, the American Continental Army expected the British forces to break out of New York City and raid up the Hudson. The Revolutionary War had become a stalemate: the Americans were unable to capture the city, and the British were unable to make a major attack to the north. Forts at Verplanck's Point on the river's eastern shore and Stony Point on the western side were reinforced, and if they held, the Americans would prevent a major British naval force from moving north of Haverstraw Bay.

But then, in May of 1779, Sir Henry Clinton moved his forces to the area and captured both forts, permitting British troops to raid Connecticut's coastal towns. Gen. Washington dispatched Gen. Anthony Wayne and his Corps of Light Infantry to make a daring midnight attack on Stony Point, and American troops swarmed the countryside. The Americans captured the position in one hour, inflicting casualties on the British, but then abandoned the fortification three days later, as they could not hold the peninsula against superior enemy forces. It was a quick battle but a strategic one. Are there still reverberations of that carnage echoing throughout the village?

"We spent a lot of time trying to figure out where the ghost came from," Julie Morano told me. We bought the 1960s era house in 2000, and other than a bit of papering here or painting there, the house remained pretty much the way we bought it until 2003. Then, we did some major landscaping work outside and major structural redesign inside. And that seems to be when the commotion started." Julie and I discussed the fact that many ghost energies erupt when homeowners begin renovating an old house, but as this house couldn't be considered "old," would that explanation pertain in this case? I asked her what else, if anything, changed in the house that year.

"My father-in-law came to live with us in 2003," she said. "There had always been a few misplaced things before that, but, as we started renovations and Dad came, that's when things got really busy," she smiled. "When so many things began to disappear then reappear, we knew we had another visitor than Dad, so we asked the neighbors if there had been a death in the house before we bought it. The answer was no.

"I remember putting on makeup before going to work one morning, and I set a lipstick pencil on the sink. I ducked out to do something in the kitchen, and, a minute later, when I returned, the pencil was gone. I searched high and low, in the sink, in the wastebasket, everywhere. It just wasn't there. Was it in the toilet or tub? No. Could the cats have come in, snatched it, and carried it away? No, they were asleep. After searching everywhere, I returned to the bathroom. There it was—right on the sink top where I'd left it! Every couple of months something disappeared. Who or what was doing it?

"Joe had to travel on business, and because he does a lot of close-up work, he wanted to be sure he had his glasses. When he reached for them one morning, to pack in his luggage, they had vanished. He searched high and low, but they were gone. And he had to make the trip and come home with a headache. Soon after he came into the house, he found the glasses on top of the mantelpiece over the fireplace. He'd *never* have put them there. Who was doing this?"

Most homeowners who have ghosts understand the predicament—what to *do*? And what if we're *imagining* it all? "Maybe we're just getting forgetful as we grow older," Julie said. "At first, when we considered the possibility of a ghost, we thought of American Revolutionary War soldiers who died in this area. After all, we're not that far from Camp Hill Road. Wherever you look around the Suffern/Pomona/Stony Point area, there are historical markers. We know that many people died in those battles. Could we have an unhappy soldier ghost here?

"We have a friend named Lisa who finally convinced us that we weren't going nuts. She came to house-sit for us when we were away. There we were in another town, and I got a panic call from Lisa on my cell phone," said Julie. "She told us of sitting on the couch with the cats and suddenly hearing her name called from behind her. Then, she said she'd heard her name called again, and, turning, she saw a man walk from the bathroom into a bedroom. It wasn't Joe's father. And there was nobody in that bedroom when she went to check!"

As he worked on the renovations inside the house, Joe took a break from sawing and sanding and dropped his safety goggles into a tool bag. When he resumed work, though he searched high and low in that bag, the goggles just had vanished. Thinking he had dropped them elsewhere, he searched the house but didn't locate them. Finally, he returned to the tool bag to begin his search from the beginning. He opened the bag, and there they were, inside. It's funny, but ghosts sure can make us doubt our own memory or common sense with their antics.

Lisa told me that the Morano cats live indoors and are never let outside, so it surprised Joe and Julie one day when they pulled into the driveway after having been away, and saw their cats scampering playfully across the lawn. "After catching the cats and bringing them inside, Joe and Julie locked all the windows. But that precaution seemed not to deter the ghost, who opened a sliding glass door a few days later, letting the cats escape once more," Lisa said.

"So time had to be spent in rounding up the cats, taking a head-count, and bringing them home. My business (Groom and Zoom) involves grooming dogs and cats, and I know the anxiety that pet owners experience when their animals get lost, so next time I went to their house, I yelled at the ghost or ghosts, 'You'd better stop letting these cats out! You're pissing me off! They are *indoor* cats and letting them out is dangerous for them—so knock it off!' I don't know if it was *what* I said or the *way* I said it, but the cats were never set free again," she laughed.

Julie told me that her son, Joey, once came to visit and couldn't find the cats. Had the ghost stolen *them*, too? Then he went into a bedroom that we were renovating. We had bi-fold doors on the closet, though we hadn't put the knobs on them yet. So to make them open or close, a person would have to lean hard against them. At the time, the doors were securely closed, so he pushed them inward, and *there* were our cats, imprisoned," she laughed.

We speculated what kind of force would have been necessary to either open the doors or close them. If this was the ghost's deed (and who *else* could have done it?), how do they muster that amount of force? Neither of us knew the answer. Additionally, Joey found all his clothing tumbled from the closet shelves inside the closed doors; even cats couldn't do that. If it was a ghost message, what was the point? "Look, someone *else* is here?" "See how much *fun* I'm having?"

Shortly after that event, Joe changed out of his work clothes one night, taking money from his work pants pockets and placing it on the dresser. In the morning, as he dressed for work, he found the money had vanished. No matter that he looked under the bed and dresser or in clothes piled on top of the dresser, it was gone. He left the room to ask Julie if she had taken it, and after she denied doing so, he returned, only to spy the money right where he'd put it the previous night. Just like the lipstick pencil—how do they *do* that? And *why*?

I told Joe and Julie that this "now you see it, now you don't" activity seems to be a typical attention-getting behavior for ghosts. I estimated that, in over 80 percent of such disappearance cases, it is a soul newly-arrived in the spirit world who wants to inform his or her loved ones that they're okay, that they have survived body death. When I've investigated such houses with a psychic, this is the most common motive that they can discern. The basic issue seems to be "appearing and disappearing, here, then gone,"—just like the person's life. So who died?

Joe said that his dad's two brothers had died in 2003, shortly before his father came to live with them in Suffern. Likely, they (or one of them) came to let Dad know that they had successfully passed over and were still in existence. Dad, who has since moved out, apparently didn't get the message. But the ghost uncle or uncles may have recognized that Joe and Julie, to say nothing about their friend Lisa, are sensitive and *will*, sooner or later, figure out the intent behind their showing off, and then, the Moranos will tell Dad, right?

However, I have another suspicion. Julie and Joe have created a beautiful new house and yard. A ghost that has worked hard all *his* life and is finally at "loose ends," so to speak, may be in no hurry to leave this property. It's attractive. Joe and Julie *will* eventually tell Dad that a ghost brother or two is still around. But, in the meantime, there are fascinating house guests, and the cats are so much fun to play with!

Walton Spirits

Ghost stories that involve the reappearance of a parent, grandparent, or an old friend's spirit are perhaps the most heart-warming of the tales I've collected. But then, there are the troubling stories, a genre that the entertainment media enjoys foisting on us, though they are the exception and not the rule in the world of ghosts. In *Haunted Saratoga County*, I dealt with this subject in a Saratoga Springs story having the double-entendre title of *Spirits*. Here is a similar tale from the Delaware County village of Walton.

"My brother, Dan, and I lived with our parents at 12 High Street," Pat Goodrich began, "and we had an older fellow named Bob Bourne who lived with us. You know how it is when you're a young man—you go out and try everything, so my brother got into alcohol pretty deeply. One night he came staggering in and poured himself a glass of booze. "You have had enough to drink, you don't *need* any more," a stern voice said. "Come on, set it down on the dresser," the unknown gentleman advised, and he helped Dan get undressed and into bed. My brother went out like a light, leaving the filled shot glass sitting there.

"In the morning, Dan got up and came to the breakfast table. Bob and I sat eating, and my brother said to Bob, 'Thanks, I probably didn't need that last drink anyway.' Bob looked him with a blank expression. 'What are you talking about, boy?' Dan told how the previous evening he'd come home drunk and someone ('it *had* to be you, Bob!') had taken away his drink and got him into bed. "The glass of booze is still sitting right on the dresser, next to the bottle,' Bob told the older man. 'Now don't tell me *you* didn't do it! Who else could it have been?' And Bob said to him, "Look Dan, I went to bed early, and I never even heard you come in!' That's a story that we talked about for years," Pat said, "and in the light of the other stuff that happened in that house, we began to think the stranger had to have been an angel or maybe a ghost," Pat told me.

He recalled for me the many nights when he heard the silverware rattling in its downstairs kitchen drawer. "The noise bothered me so much that I'd walk down there in the dark, but no one was around—the family was all asleep. Each time I got to the kitchen the noise stopped, but when I returned to bed, it would start up again." He recalled another phenomenon that troubled him deeply. In his late teens, he often heard a deep breathing, almost a wheezing sound in the upstairs at night. It troubled him and he determined to find its source, though he suspected the sound came from Bob's bedroom across the hall. "So many times, I got up and went to Bob's room, but it was silent inside. Then, when I returned to bed, I'd hear that labored breathing again. I never learned who was doing it or why," he said.

Such noises are often the remnant of a former resident's consciousness, one who died (perhaps of emphysema or bronchitis or another respiratory disease) at that spot. What appears to have happened, as it does in so many such cases, is that the deceased has not finally broken its grip on the earth plane. In his or her mind, the mind still identifies with (clings to) that illness; it is what defined their last days of life, and they are yet unable to release it. So those who experience these events are hearing an energy attachment that the soul has to its former physical existence. Until that can be broken, probably through the prayers or ceremonies of the living, the individual's consciousness remains trapped, unable to move upward to a consciousness of its soul self. For this reason, lights (such as candles) play a large part in the release of spirits. The deceased must first become conscious of The Light, which represents Eternity, before it can be aware that it has *an alternative* to remaining in the consciousness of that last vestige (though painful) of the former life.

I asked Pat why his family assumed the mysterious man was an angel, and he told me that there was a much darker side to life in that High Street house. In later years, after moving away, he talked to family members and all remembered feeling a nighttime sleep paralysis, an inability to move, though awake, and of seeing strangers moving through the house. "They seemed to travel in threes," Pat told me. "When I was still young, I'd sometimes awake at night and see them moving through the hallway—three of them. I was terrified because they were always dark and mysterious, and I could never wake enough to confront them. That feeling of vulnerability was horrible."

I asked if he'd ever been touched by the dark people, and he said "No. What I did do, though, to release their hold on me, was to utter the word 'Christ' or 'God' or to pray that they go away. And it always worked. Immediately, the paralysis stopped and the bad threesome vanished."

In this discussion, I spoke to Pat about some of the current Alien Abduction literature, in which purported abductees claimed that the only way to make the aliens (the UFO kind) leave their house (and end the paralysis that seemed part of the abduction attempt) was to *will* the spell to be broken, often by the extremely difficult movement of a single finger or even the eyelids. I still don't understand the relevance to Pat's case, but the similarity is compelling. Are all aliens ghosts? Or vice versa? Or are only some of them related to the others?

I asked Pat if he was the only one to see the terrible trio, and he told me that his mother, in later years, told him that *she* had once seen the threesome standing in the door of her bedroom, causing her to be paralyzed. She told him that she saw the strangers wearing dark, hooded cloaks and noted that they all had rotten teeth. A psychologist might work with this vision as a projected part of the patient's inner problems and unresolved difficulties and see them as an externalization of trauma that could now be healed, with the number three pointing at wholeness or healing. In any case, *both* mother and son could verify the entities' presence.

What to make of it all? Angels, I guess, take care of themselves and don't need our help. Perhaps the older being was Dan's guardian angel. If so, maybe he was also an ongoing protector of the Goodrich household, preventing the Terrible Trio from hurting family members.

But who *was* the evil-appearing triad, and in what respect were they *real*? If they represented unresolved inner emotional problems in mother and son, perhaps they were eventually vanquished. Certainly, moving away from the house stopped the phenomenon. What if they were a form of itinerant evil, cruising the spirit world and sojourning for a while on High Street? If so, what brought them there or kept them there?

As in the *Spirit* story, there is a palpable gloom in the home when a family member sinks into crime, drug addiction, or alcoholism. Gifted sensitives or psychics can see or feel it as a tangible energy. In time, if left unresolved, the darkness of the addict can attract more negative energies from outside the home, so it is well that Dan eventually ended his drinking habits and moved on to become a married and successful man today, though he no longer lives in Walton. So many of the Biblical cleansings were done by special individuals who determined not to let darkness or despair dominate their lives or the lives of others.

It is also possible that the alcoholism might have been fostered by the "stuck-ness" of the ghost energy already in the house—the heavy breather who could not let go. It is also conceivable that that person had *also* been a drinker and in some manner had partially *possessed* Dan, making it difficult for him to remain sober.

"I left there in 1980, and my family sold the house in 1984" Pat told me. "Years later, when I drove through town and stopped to gas up at a convenience store, a young woman spoke to me and asked if I wasn't one of the people who used to live at *that house*. I told her I was, and she was terribly curious about the possibility that I had heard or seen 'something' there. I never told her the full story, and am sorry that some negativity still seems to remain in the house. My family got out of it with only a bad memory."

Visitors

"When I was five years old, I awoke in the night to hear a symphony tuning up," Lana Gontzes told me. "I thought the television was on and went to see what the program was. The living room was dark and the TV was off, so I went back to bed. No sooner had I settled back into bed, than it happened again, then again. It was the strangest thing, but when I told my parents about it, they said I'd been dreaming. But I *knew* it was real." After that, she had many experiences with what many thought were imaginary events.

After she married, Lana, her husband, and daughter moved into their first home in Malvern, in 1987, and she found the energies already there, waiting for her. The vacuum cleaner turned itself off and on and most of the house lamps did the same—all in the first two months. "I had a cat sleeping beside me on the bed one night, and suddenly he did a flip up into the air and came back down, still asleep. It was almost as if an unseen hand flipped him up into a somersault. Soon after that, both Lana and her daughter told her husband that they'd heard footsteps upstairs, when no one was there. "You must be imagining it," he said confidently.

Soon after that, however, Dad awoke in the morning and called his daughter into his bedroom. "Why were you walking up and down the stairs last night? Were you hungry?" The little girl firmly denied being out of bed, saying she'd slept soundly all night. Was she a sleepwalker? They never found evidence for that before.

"I have a friend who is quite sensitive," Lana told me, "and whenever she comes over to my house, little things happen. The woman is afraid of the house because little objects seem to move by themselves when she is here. Our dog, *Pootie*, also used to sit at the bottom of the stairs, asking to be carried upstairs, but he wouldn't make the journey by himself. We figured he was afraid, but of what?"

Lana then told me a bittersweet story that likely had nothing to do with spirits in her house, but it was one of those spiritual experiences that a woman can never forget. "I had a dream of my Mom, who had died. Actually, I had two dreams, but they were both the same and mysterious. Mom was happy and bright, and the dreams were filled with light. We were at a farm, and Mom showed me a little white duckling. 'I'm going to take this one and put him in the water, but I'll leave *you* one, too,' she said to me. I didn't know what that meant. Then came a dream in which Mom was directing the addition of a new room to our house." She confided to Lana that "You'll *need* one." Lana questioned her mother about it, and the mother said "You need one *now!*" The next morning, Lana discovered that she was pregnant.

"But we had so many physical problems with that pregnancy. Then, Mom returned in a dream, wearing blue earrings. I looked at her and wept, 'But I wanted pink!' I told her. 'This is all I have,' she told me. My husband, a doctor, expressed his desire not to have a fourth child—I couldn't *believe* it! Then the baby was stillborn. I was grief-stricken." That sorrow added to the marital upset, and, not long after, Lana and her husband divorced. She wondered later if that baby was represented by the little duck taken by her mom in the dream.

Lana said that as she was regaining her health after the baby's death, a psychic friend visited her and picked up the fact that a child had recently died in the house. "But then she said, 'There is *a little girl* here, too…up in the attic.' That couldn't be true, I told her, but when we went to the attic, she pointed out an antique baby book that I'd collected. 'Open it and see the second daughter of that family,' she instructed. Inside, I found a second daughter of the family had died of typhoid a century before. At that moment I felt a small hand pushing in the small of my back."

Each time she went to the attic, Lana felt the pushing, and finally said to the ghost girl. "You have to stop. This is *my* attic and you can't push me out of it!" The pushing stopped. Beside the antique baby book, Lana had collected other old keepsakes. One of those was a French bisque-head doll in its original clothing. "The little girl who had owned it had cut the doll's blonde hair, but I treasured it," Lana told me. "I contacted a psychic, Alana Lynch, from Valley Stream. When she visited me, she said that a ghost nanny had come with the doll because, likely, the nanny had nursed the little girl who formerly owned the doll. I was astounded at that," she told me, "because one of my friends told me he had seen a uniformed woman, probably a nanny, going up to my attic. I wondered if I was getting a house full!"

She decided to see who else had lived in her house and began to search its history. Lana discovered that the wake of a previous owner, a Mr. Rider, had taken place in her living room, and she wondered if he had remained. The Rider estate had sold the house to a young doctor, who did several renovations, but then died suddenly. After that, she and her husband came to live there in 1987. "I think that doctor might still be here, too," she said. "He had done a lot of the construction here, putting on a new roof by himself. His tools had often disappeared while he worked, one of those indications that a ghost is present, right?" she asked.

"Ever since then, whenever I have to hire a contractor, I feel that young doctor is here to help or advise me. I'm sure he helped me avoid some disreputable characters who wanted to work on my house. Sometimes the workers have lost objects, such as a hammer or stapler. Whenever I hear about lost tools, I know the ghosts are active."

So the house on Hempstead Avenue has been quite a school for Lana in her almost twenty years of residence there. It seems clear that the spirits are friendlier than some of the living ones who apply to fix up her house. In the meantime, she is gaining a working knowledge of the spirit world: how ghosts become ghosts, and how and why they remain attached to possessions. It will be interesting to see what she does with all her new-found discoveries.

Up In the Air

"We could be doing a lot of things with our lives, but Maria and I have found that fixing up and selling houses is really enjoyable," Bill Heinrich told me. His wife smiled in agreement. We sat in an up-for-sale old 1840s farmhouse that the couple had just restored in the Town of Hebron, NY. Our conversation didn't center on Washington County, however, but rather on the Village of East Massapequa, at the eastern edge of Nassau County on Long Island.

The old Will Rogers House

"Just before our marriage in 1986, I bought the house at 425 Clocks Boulevard as our first fixer-upper," Bill continued. "The big old Victorian had once been a single-family home but had later been transformed into four apartments, two up and two down. We discovered it had been comedian Will Rogers' house back in the 1920s when he performed in the Ziegfeld Follies. When he began his Broadway career in the Ziegfeld Follies, Rogers used to do a lasso-twirling act accompanied by humorous patter, but in the mid-twenties he went swimming in the old canal across the street and hit his head or shoulder under water, and after that, suffered a little paralysis, so he became just a stand-up comedian, a "Cowboy Philosopher," minus the rope tricks.

"Will kept his horse in the carriage house out back, and spent a lot of time with his friend Fred Stone, a Hollywood producer who had a house across Clocks Blvd. Famous people like Annie Oakley are known to have visited there. In time, Will moved on, and we think the house was then turned into a boarding house," Bill continued. Maria added, "When we held our first lawn sale, a neighbor came by, introduced herself and we chatted. In the conversation she shared that once a year, always on the same day, she could smell a cake baking in her kitchen though she wasn't using the oven. Maybe that revelation set the stage for what we were about to experience in our house."

All the previous tenants had moved out when Bill bought the house. During that period they met and chatted with youngsters who used to live in the apartments. "A little nine-year-old girl named Jeanne Marie lived upstairs and told us that often, when she was in the bathtub, she'd see an old lady in a long black dress pass the open bathroom door. We thought that strange, as her grandmother was the only elder in the house. Then, I asked one boy, Raymond, how he liked living in the house, and he responded that it was okay, he guessed, but that there was an old lady that lived upstairs with them, though Raymond was the only family member to see her. We didn't know what to say to either story. We have both believed in the paranormal, and we were intrigued that such a character, or several, might be in the house. I guess we needed some proof," Bill laughed.

After the downstairs tenants left, they expanded the dining room and kitchen to their former large sizes and knocked down some of the more recent partitions. They converted the attic into a bedroom for the upstairs apartment. It is in that area that Raymond saw the old lady. Some time in the late 1980s, Bill and Maria noticed that their black Lab mix dog, Lestat, refused to go up the stairs: He'd look upward, whimper a bit, then walk away.

Eventually, the couple decided to sell the house, as they were drawn to live upstate, so they asked the remaining tenants to vacate. "We thought that it had always been so full of life, and that we'd like to sleep in each of the bedrooms before the sale went through," Maria said. "Then came the night when we were alone with only Lestat and our new Border Collie mix puppy, Skunk, in the house. All the furniture was gone, and we bedded down in sleeping bags in an upstairs bedroom," Bill said. Lestat had allowed himself to be escorted to the room and cuddled near his owners.

Bill resumed, "That night was the scariest one of my life." As I watched the couple, I noticed that each had a story to tell about the experience. Bill went first: "I was sleeping, I guess, but the whole thing wasn't really a dream; it had an entirely different quality to it—much more life-like. I saw and felt myself flying in circles around the bedroom. It wasn't a smooth flight, but kind of jerky. All of a sudden, it was as if my personality was squelched and I was now looking out through someone else's eyes. The memories were no longer mine, but another person's. I kept trying to scream at the horror of no longer being me and having someone else's experiences going on inside me. My continued effort to scream gradually brought me back in touch with my own body and mind. But now, I was squished up against the ceiling, in a corner of the room. I was back in my own body, and now I could hear music playing. Maybe it was big band style or classical, I couldn't remember when I finally awoke. All I could do is wonder why my neighbors were making all that music in the middle of the night. I awoke with my heart pounding and half sat up. Then I spotted Maria, obviously disturbed and fidgeting. She had just awakened, too. I told her, 'It's okay, it's just the room.'"

Then it was Maria's turn to narrate. "As I sat there awake, I remembered a dreamlike state in which I had been flying low, whirling inside the room, circling the round coffee table [which didn't exist in real life] and being chased by something I couldn't see. I felt like an antenna, absorbing all kinds of energies. It reminded me of drug parties from the 70s that I'd seen on television or in movies. I sensed that there were many others there, though I saw no one else. Then the whole room seemed to tip, and I felt scrunched into a corner of the room's ceiling. I could hear rock and roll music coming from somewhere. Then, I was awake and sitting up, and Bill was asking me if I could hear the music. I was so afraid of the experience that I said 'No,' but later admitted I *had* heard it. It was the strangest night we'd ever spent."

Bill related their experiences of the next day. The pair noted the telephone answering machine light blinking and pushed the "listen" button. "We heard a lot of static, such as we'd never heard before on that device. Just static for quite a while, then way in the background we could make out faint human voices. Unfortunately, we couldn't make out what anyone was saying. I hate myself for having erased it soon after, because I wonder if spirits of some kind had left us a message on the recorder. Maria and I surmised that this had always been a house full of human energy and maybe the spirits there, alone with us for the first time, had felt 'dammed up' and unable to function, so they used our machine to contact us."

I told the couple about what is known today as EVP (electronic voice phenomenon) in which many ghost hunters have recorded seeming voices in apparently haunted houses. The resulting sound is much as they described it to me.

At first, I thought this was a singular experience for the couple, but Bill then began to reminisce: "When you gut an old home, you get a lot of vague sensations, what I call chatter. When we bought this house and began renovations here on Chamberlin Mills Road in Washington County, we had many mild sensations, but nothing visible or clearly audible." They looked at one another, smiled, and then Bill continued, relating another of the former houses they'd fixed up and sold. "Yes, in that place, we'd be working downstairs and all of a sudden hear all the upstairs doors slamming. We didn't even bother to speculate whether it was wind or ghosts because *none of the upstairs doors were hanging on their hinges!* One of our fixer-uppers was here in the Town of Hebron, and I remember snow had fallen outside, and as I looked out the front window, I saw a middle-aged woman crossing the front yard near the creek. She wore a long, orange print dress and a kerchief and carried buckets with each hand. I was taken aback. Who *was* she, and why was she working out there? I looked away for a minute, and then, when I looked out again, she was gone and there were no footsteps in the snow.

"It dawned on me that this unusual sight was likely a long-ago farm wife still doing her chores as a ghost. In another place, I experienced a man with long, black hair in a black frock coat leaning over me. I had to order him to leave, as I had work to do." We all chuckled. It seemed that both Maria and Bill had more sensitivity to the other world than seemed apparent at the outset of the interview. In retrospect, it appears they were quite tuned in to this other side of Life, though only the aerial gyrations in the house on Clocks Boulevard had ever frightened them.

In summary, I noted how the shared experience seemed much like brief possession cases I'd studied. It was as if the ghost person wanted to show the young couple how they *felt* as disembodied spirits, then having done so, released the pair. We talked for a while about the necessity to speak out forcefully to spirit entities that become too intrusive. Most of the time they *will* back off.

I left the beautiful old yellow farmhouse with its "For Sale" sign out front. "We just bought an old nearby church," Maria called out, "you'll have to come see us when we get in *there*." We all laughed. Ghosts, unless they take you out for a spin, aren't usually *that* much trouble, so I looked forward to the Heinrich's call.

The Hillside

Today an attractive modified mobile home sits amid flowers and trees on a Curry Hill Road hillside overlooking Sloansville, NY, in the Mohawk Valley. It is quiet and beautiful on the property that Beverly Garcia and her husband bought in 1995, but it hasn't always been that way.

"When we first came here, we lived in the old house down there that my in-laws bought" she said, pointing downhill at the dilapidated ruin now overrun with vegetation. "Two hundred years ago it was a hotel and was known to be haunted even then, but it contained fourteen rooms and was spacious, though it was not a wonderful place to live. It was like boot camp for a city gal with two small children to manage the place. There were infestations of snakes, bats, moles, spiders, flies, and the attic was filled with pigeons. It had once been the property of the Kelly family, and you can find their graves in the cemetery just up the road," she said.

Though her psychic abilities hadn't fully developed in those days, Beverly immediately suspected there were "others" on the property. Her daughter kept seeing a "tall man" in her bedroom, a figure that frightened the child at night. Reluctant to go to bed too early, the girl often fell asleep on the downstairs couch and had to be carried to her upstairs bedroom each night for twelve years. Beverly's son didn't see any ghosts, but slept with his baseball bat nearby, "just in case."

343

"We even called a priest to come out and bless the house with holy water," Beverly told me. "He came with a nun, but neither of them would go upstairs. Father handed me the holy water and told me that I could sprinkle it up there as well as he. Nice guy.

"In those days I tried raising chickens for eggs and meat, like the 'country people' did. We had fifty chickens and roosters, but one day while we were out, they escaped, and our two German shepherds killed forty of them just for sport. When we tried to turn the other ten into meat, we found that killing chickens was too gruesome for us, so we ended up buying eggs and meat at the store from then on. After the snake infestation, we knew we had to get out of that old building."

The Garcias bought a new double-wide trailer and installed it on a foundation about two hundred yards farther uphill and south of the old hotel, where it sits today. "We left much of our old furniture there in the Kelly house when we moved, but I jokingly invited any of the ghosts who wanted to do so, to come up to my new house. I think some actually took me up on it," Beverly smiled.

"My grandson, Michael, who was four at the time, was the first to note the visitors. He told of seeing a red-haired boy that he called 'Puppet' and said the boy was his 'invisible playmate.' When Mike had trouble learning to swim, we told him that Puppet wasn't afraid of the water. Michael picked up the invisible Puppet and threw him in the water. He never spoke about his friend after that, but he *did* learn to swim. Even *I* began to see the shadow of a young boy moving in the hallway toward Michael's room sometimes, though there was no physical person to cast that silhouette. Finally, I went into Mike's room, knelt down to kid level and asked, 'Wouldn't you rather be with other children, with a family of your own, and with your own toys? You can't continue to play with these toys because you can't really touch them. If you go into the Light, you'll see your mother waiting for you on the other side.' After that the child ghost seemed to have left. But Mike still saw others."

He told of seeing or sensing a raggedy man like a vagrant and got the name "Richard." Beverly attempted to contact the man and telepathically heard the man say, or think, to her, "I was a drifter and died on this property, but no one knew. I just wanted other people to know I was once here." Beverly then decided to create a small memorial that Richard could see and appreciate. She found a ten-inch flat stone and painted "Richard was here" on it, then engraved a cross next to the inscription. She placed the stone behind the old hotel where it wouldn't be disturbed and planted an azalea shrub alongside it. "I prayed to God to help him move fully to the other side, and I believe that happened, as nobody has sensed Richard since then."

Farther up Curry Hill, near the cemetery, lives a woman that Bev refers to as "Kate," and Kate told her of another similarly strange episode. Kate's adopted Korean-American son, David, came to her and said he was experiencing difficulty in sleeping because he heard a girl crying in a small depression along the wall of his bedroom, and it scared him. She deduced it probably was a real experience and not a dream, but who might the little girl be? Discussing the matter, Kate and her son wondered if it might be David's sister, who was known to be living in deep poverty in Korea. After their chat, David returned to bed but couldn't sleep, as his bedroom doorknob kept turning. He called to Kate, who came to the bedroom and saw a white mist hanging in the air. She told whoever it was to leave her house because it wasn't welcome. When she turned on the light, the specter had vanished.

Kate thought David might sleep better if his bed was brought into her bedroom for a while, but the boy couldn't sleep well there either. He kept hearing someone walking in the hallway. Eventually, the pair did get to sleep that night, but David continued to feel watched by someone invisible. Kate called Bev to see if her friend knew how to banish the spirit. Beverly took oil and blessed it, then marked the boy's bedroom door with a large cross. She blessed the spirit and then ordered the little ghost to go into the Light. Adding her own experiences, Bev wrote an article and sent it to *FATE* magazine, where the incidents appeared in the June 1998 issue.

Shortly after the article appeared, a work crew from the local prison did some debris clearing work along Curry Hill Road and cut grass and brush from the old cemetery at the top of the hill. After they left, Bev visited the graveyard and noticed two newly-uncovered stones. One was the last resting place of Mary Kelly, who died at age fifteen in 1852. The other was that of her sister, Irene, who died in 1853 at age fourteen. Now, sunlight filtered through the trees and the cleared site seemed more appropriate and beautiful as a final resting place for two girls that never reached adulthood. Perhaps, if the crying girl was one of these, she no longer needs to feel abandoned or unknown.

As Michael and David have reached adolescence, their own contacts with the spirit world have become more infrequent, while Beverly's have increased. Beverly Garcia (Eia) now has established a website, www.spiritwisdom.com, from which she passes on to others both beautiful photographs and wonderful thoughts about life. Her psychic intuition has vastly increased and she offers those insights to clients at a fee, specializing in personal and grief issues.

Uncle Charlie

The Sellars House today

"When I first moved into the house in May of 1971, I found it in rough shape. It had been built about 1848 and had a wing added in 1866, and it was always an upper class dwelling," John Sincavage told me. "I bought four floors and a basement that I didn't know about at first—it sure was a house in need of repair. Nevertheless, the craftsmanship and design elements were classic, and I fell in love with the old house and determined to make it into a home."

He didn't marry until August, so he took a college student as boarder that summer. The young man commented about "something strange on the stairs," but John dismissed the remark. Then, after the wedding, Cathy and John met the ghost that they named *Uncle Charlie*, as he was just like a member of the family. "Apparently, he loved our old house at 49 W. Fifth Street in Oswego, so we let him stay. Or was it the other way around?"

John told me the first owner of the property in 1827 was John Park, whose lot extended over to 4th Street, "and he had an older 1832 house on the far part of the lot. In my research of the property, I always figured he built that for his mistress," John said with a smile. "Nevertheless, he left the main part of the land to his daughter, Sophie, who married Nathan Rowe. And that couple built the house. They always had servants and a chauffeur after automobiles were developed."

The Sincavages began to renovate the building, one room at a time. "In the wing, we found that the 'music room' had been divided into two rooms by previous owners," said Cathy, "so we removed the partition in order to have

346

one big room again and decided to repaper the walls. We felt a presence right from the start, but also decided he was benevolent, so we didn't worry until the tools began to disappear—especially the screwdrivers. There was a room in the back of the house that we seldom entered, and one day I found most of the missing screwdrivers out there—*lined up in a row* and covered with rust. Now, the odd thing was that these tools hadn't been gone long enough to be oxidized, so Charlie was always a puzzle to us."

John told me that they dubbed the spirit "Charlie" because it's easier to be haunted by someone with a name. "Nevertheless, there *was* a former owner, a Charles Bond, who was something of a drinker, so he was a possible candidate for head ghost. Old timers told us that Charles used to enter the foyer and toss his hat onto the gladiator statue that contained the gaslight. Now, if one covers up that gas light, one can create a pretty explosive situation, so maybe Charles had someone looking out for *him*, too."

"As we proceeded in renovating the music room, we came to believe that Charlie was just keeping an eye on the house, to make sure that things were restored and taken care of properly," Cathy said. She related the frustrations they had in the renovation of the music room. "We chose some beautiful wallpaper to put on the walls, but it wouldn't stick. Or if it did stick at first, we'd come back a while later to find it sagging or fallen to the floor. It was high quality paper, and we called the wallpaper company's representative to come over and look at the situation. 'Our paper just does *not* do that!' the rep exclaimed. So we tried again, with the same pitiful result."

"Then, we discovered that the plastered ceiling was peeling too much, and we'd have to remove it, and when we did, we found a beautiful painted ceiling underneath! We'd have covered that over and lost its beauty forever! So we left off trying to fix up the ceiling and then, guess what? All the paper we put on the walls then stayed on beautifully. From all that bother, we came to suspect that Uncle Charlie is a preservationist or historian of some kind," John laughed.

John and Cathy agreed that the house was always warm and wonderful for their four children. Whenever something unexpected happened, of course, the kids would say, "Charlie did it!" In October 1980, the Sincavages gave an interview to Don McCann of the *Oswego County Messenger*, and Cathy related that Charlie sometimes spoke to family members. "He speaks to my daughter and me once in a while," she admitted, "but I like to tell myself that it is imagination. However...I don't always believe myself. He called my name one night when I was alone, and I thought it was John coming home early. I could have passed it off as imagination, but our dog heard it, too. She went to the foot of the stairs and stared upward."

John added, "Yes, there was that, but at other times when Judy, our black cocker spaniel, was upstairs, she'd go to the top of the stairs, cock her head and listen…to *something*. We never knew what. That front foyer was two stories, with a beautiful turned stair rail around the upstairs opening. There were some lounge chairs and a table lamp up on that landing, with the lamp sitting just below the level of the rail. One night I heard a 'clunk!' and rushed out to find the lamp all the way downstairs. It should have broken, but it didn't even have a dent. Now, you know that for *that* to happen, some force had to *lift* the lamp *up and over* the rail for it to fall. Charlie?"

From time to time, the couple heard the glass milk bottles in the kitchen clinking together and Cathy said, "We'd say to one another, 'I didn't hear that sound, did you?' Then we'd laugh and forget it."

"But there were attic windows that were fastened with a bolt," said John, "and every so often we'd feel a very cold breeze downstairs in the wintertime, so I'd go to the attic and find one or more of the windows open. I never tried to figure it out; I just re-bolted them and went downstairs again." Cathy told McCann, "Sometimes we'd hear doors opening and shutting and a male voice would say, 'Where are you?' We had a psychic come to the house and she decided the presence is definitely male and very friendly, and enjoys having us around."

By 1984, three of the children were in college, and the couple decided that if they were ever to leave Oswego's cold winters and get to Florida, that they had better put the house up for sale and move before another generation fell in love with the house. "We concluded a sale in June 1984, and, just before the closing, I returned to the old house to pick up a few small things. I walked through the building and felt the coldest cold I've ever felt. Charlie, or any other spirits that might have been there, were literally giving us the cold shoulder, showing their displeasure that we were leaving," John told me. "The cold seemed to be pushing me out. Or maybe, Charlie was just reminding me what I was going to miss in the winter. The children, needless to say, were sad about leaving, but they all had careers to follow, so we did the closing, left for Florida, and never looked back."

In 1998, Ron Sellars and family moved into the old house. The previous owners had not mentioned any specific ghost activity since the Sincavages left for Florida, so the 1999 events came as a surprise to the Sellars family.

"Our house, because it's on a slope, has a cellar that has been transformed into living space," Ron told me. "There is a side entrance to that room, and our fourteen-year-old daughter was fast asleep on a couch down there when I walked in one morning. What caught my attention was that the door to the outside stood wide open and there was a broken plate on the floor. The girl said she'd slept soundly all night and heard nothing. There was no evidence of an intruder, but now that I've heard about Uncle Charlie, I have begun to piece events together," he laughed.

"It's not even what you'd call a presence today, but we do have times when the front door is almost impossible to open. No matter how hard we pull, it won't open. Ten minutes later, if we try again, it opens easy as pie! My other major experience came on a day when I was in the house alone," Ron smiled. "All at once, I heard water running through the pipes when I was downstairs. It almost certainly came from the lavatory on the top floor. Today, I can't understand why I didn't go up and see who it was, but I *knew* I was alone, so why go? If it is Uncle Charlie, we have no sense of fear or uneasiness. It's just a nice old century-and-a-half old house. It is just 'lived in,' and if there is a ghost and it's Charlie, we know he is watching out for us all."

Ron's story is so like many of those where people live with a ghost who, though unseen, really doesn't irritate people so much that they want to send the spirit on its way. Peaceful co-existence seems to be the best way to describe the relationship. It's like having a pen-pal, just in a different dimension.

Afterword

There are good people of all religious faiths and of no formal religious affiliation who *do* care for the sidetracked spirit travelers. These individuals spend countless hours in prayer and spirit communication, freeing souls one at a time. Many of the formal religions also have those individuals commonly known as exorcists, and these people also do the most difficult work. Few Americans understand how great this burden is for those ministers and priests. In a conversation with a diocesan exorcist a few years ago, I was told that the man's backlog of cases that needing clearing was *several years long.*

By now, my readers know that I say, "The Golden Rule does not end at the grave." If we claim membership in a religion based on unconditional love, then where can we draw the line? Can we love our departed friends and relatives any less than the ones who brighten our lives each day? Should we not want as much for the dead as the living? Of course, some faiths teach that, once the body dies, that's it—the soul has gone (home to God, we'd like to believe) and can no longer be helped or changed. My personal experience belies that simplistic approach.

I have come to know that *all* life is continuous, in the body or out. Prayers for the well-being of the dead *can* flow forever out into space and time and help release trapped souls. Old doctrines need to be refined to generate at least as much compassion for those in transit to Paradise as we have for losing sports teams, lost pets and rained-out graduation ceremonies. As a wise man once observed, however, "It's hard to love that which we cannot see." Many might ask, "What's in it for *us*? What do I get out of being nice to ghosts?" Those trapped at *that* level of comprehension aren't yet ready to hear the answer. And when they are ready, they will discover that release work is not for the idly curious or fools.

Plenty of people the world over have, nevertheless, had contact with the unseen. Old doctrines based in fear simplistically refer to those "don't wanna know, don't wanna go individuals" as demons and treat them as evil. Funny, I should think their prayer would be that *even demons* deserve compassion for being troubled and separated from the Creative Force that brought them into existence.

During a number of walking meditations this past year, I have felt an urgency in regard to Humanity's future. I have come to expect a great "dying-off" among humans in the next few decades, with the South Asian tsunami being just the opening act. I do not believe this will be the end of the world, which so many earnestly hope for (thereby escaping the fruits of their misguided actions and lives). But I do expect these will represent a higher level test of how *loving* the survivors can be. What happens when the spirit world becomes flooded by millions of simultaneous deaths? Likely, The Creator has plans for that, but I suspect that the living ones will have to take part in the therapy if we are to demonstrate our impersonal love. I believe this to be the next "put up or shut up" step in Humanity's evolution.

In the course of collecting the preceding stories, I have met many troubled, though idealistic young adults. Many of these clearly demonstrate sensitivity to the spirit world, an ideal precondition to discovering ways of helping the spirits. The great need for these young adult individuals (if their healing promise is to be fulfilled) is the development of powerful *self-discipline*, so as not to become disarrayed or dismayed by the antics of the reluctant dead. Departed spirits are often stuck between worlds because of the unhealthy attitudes that they had for life when in the flesh. And because they are dead, they don't automatically become altruistic and nice, or even truthful to the living ones who want to contact them for recreation. Many are as dark and scheming in spirit as they were during their lives. This is likely why they got stuck between worlds after death, and perhaps many of these fear a judgment or final resolution to their life. Others may just not believe in an afterlife and remain suspended, awaiting a next act.

Anyone wishing to work with spirits of the dead must be *sure* of what they are doing and why. Each must have a mature understanding of life itself, and its ultimate purposes, before he or she can aid the departed ones. Religion *can* provide that grounding, but too often, orthodoxy creates more fear and avoidance than cosmic love. Nevertheless, I sense a new, less-formal spirituality (based more in altruism than punishment) is gradually coming into being around the world. I hope it develops quickly enough to assist those who soon will rush out to meet their Maker. Surely, we first must learn to love those we *can* see, before we minister to those we cannot see. And that primary job alone, may take much more time than remains to us in the present Age.

Ghosts and spirits have been with us for longer than recorded history extends. For eons, fear has been the typical response to their appearance. And, as government and organized religion know well, fear is a wonderful tool for controlling the masses. Yet, Fear is also the direct opposite of the Love that all such groups claim to espouse. Beware of those who seek to control your life through fear-making.

Acknowledgements

I am indebted to all the following, who provided me with stories, research, photos or other materials to include in this book:

Vance Agee
Maggie Ahrens
Gayle & Dan
    Alexander
Gail Allegretti
Adrienne Alonzo
Bill Ankin
O. Barreto
Juanita H. Bass
Andrew Baurdiel
John & Wendy Becker
Diane Bednarek
Bart Besley
Logan Besley
Denise Bills
Denny Blacek
Valerie Blesser
Lisa Board
Don Boland
The Bolster Collection
Darren Bonaparte
Betty Boos
Virginia Bowers
Carol Breunig
John Bruno
Sherri & Robert Byrne
Helen Cackener
Mike Carnevale
Robin Carnevale
Carolyn Carver
Venitra Clark
Chief Robert Cogan
Al Cormier
Ellen, Kate and
    Orpha Curry
Tisha Dolton
Mike D'Aquino
Cindy Dardano
David Darrow
Dan & Sue Dayton
Basil Debelack
Lisa DiFalco
Adele Dekowski
Ellen DeLalla
John Doyle
Neil Drew
Catteen Dumar
Charles Dumar
Jennifer Edens
Bill Eichenger

Camille England
James Fekete
Andrea Ferraiolo
Helise Flickstein
Craig Fountaine‾
Amanda Star Frazer
Helen Frellick
Sgt. Eric Fromm
Paul Fung
Beverly Garcia
Victoria Garlanda
Tick Gaudreau
Catherine Gawelko
Ed Gazel
Michele Geissler
Bill Getz
Debbie Giorgio
Frank Giotto
Stella Gittle
Lana Gontzes
Stephan Gonzalez
Pat Goodrich
Mary Grisanti
Tony Grisanti
Mary Ann Guerriero
Justin Haner
Tom Hathaway
Lois Hauenstein
Michael Hayes
Christine Hearst
William & Maria
    Heinrich
Steve Helmin
Audrey Hill
Historical Society of
    Fulton, NY
Frank Hoenig
Jack Hojohn
Theresa Houghton
Robert Hughes
Ruth Huzarewicz
Vinnie Jockino
Debbie Johnsen
Anne Kassell
Michael Kenna
Fr. Kevin Kenny
John Kerbs
Bruce & Sadie Kilburn
Sharon King
Tom Knight

Diane Kohler
Carl Kolsbun
Michael Latreille
Margaret Laurie
The Liberti family
Rebekah Loveless
Juliane Lupino
Lauren Macchia
Carol Manno
Irene Mareno
Patricia McCarthy
Michelle McConville
Jeffrey McDonald
Shirley McFerson
Maria & Eric Molders
Julie Morano
Barbara Morehouse
Wayne Mori
Frank & Eva Musgrave
Janice Nessel
Vicky Nodine
Patrick O'Connor
James Olcott
Emily Osteen
Frances Osteen
Catie O'Toole
Colleen Park
Jenn Peper
Kathleen Dudley-Perry
Chet & Pearl Peters
Jay & Sherry Peters
Nancy Pluto
Jessica Politano
Joe Puglisi
Putnam County
    Historical Society
Marty Quinn
Colleen M. Ramsey
Adrienne Ratigan
Sgt. Eric Reinhardt
Rebecca Remington
Rosemarie Remington
Russell Roberts
Tom Robinson
Lt. Pat Rocco
Theresa Romero
Ken Rossi
Judy Rowe
John Sagendorf
Darriel Sanaboia

Scott Schneider
Sally Schoonmaker
Ron Sellars
Sarada Setchfield
Celia Simmons
John & Cathy
    Sincavage
Betty B. Smith
Lloyd & Diane Smith
Ron Smith
Rob Snow
Robert Snowicz
Southampton
    Historical Society
Mark Spaulding
Frank Spensieri
Erwin Splittgerber
St. Mark's Episcopal
    Church in the Bowery
Adrienne Stabler
Sarah Stancato
Gina R. Sullivan
Phil Tarbell
Rev. Michael &
    Jennifer Terrell
Lisa Thompson
Jeff Tomazewski
Clayton Townsend
Sue Trentacoste
Carol Troost
Prof. Gary Truce
David & Stacy Tucker
Laura Tyler
Gordon & Joreen
    VanLint
Dawn Vinson
Virginia Waldron
Jerry Wasciewicz
Jane Watkins
Mary Weidman
Rob Weingarten
Clara West
Fred Wickert
Bernadette Wilsey
Susan Wilson
Alex Wipf
Ron Wolfe
Gerri Yager
Tom & Louise Yots
Amy Zingler

INDEX